Social Media Marketing

A STRATEGIC APPROACH

Second Edition

Social Media Marketing

A STRATEGIC APPROACH

Second Edition

Melissa S. Barker

Donald I. Barker

Nicolas F. Bormann

Mary Lou Roberts

Debra Zahay

CENGAGE
Learning·

Australia • Brazil • Mexico • Singapore • United Kingdom • United States

CENGAGE
Learning®

Social Media Marketing: A Strategic Approach, Second Edition
Melissa S. Barker, Donald I. Barker
Nicolas F. Bormann, Mary Lou Roberts,
Debra Zahay

Vice President, General Manager, Social Science & Qualitative Business: Erin Joyner

Product Director: Jason Fremder

Senior Product Manager: Mike Roche

Product Assistant: Allie Janneck

Content Developer: Ted Knight

Marketing Director: Kristen Hurd

Marketing Manager: Jeffrey A. Tousignant

Marketing Coordinator: Casey Binder

Art and Cover Direction, Production Management, and Composition: Lumina Datamatics, Inc.

Intellectual Property:

　Analyst: Diane Garrity

　Project Manager: Betsy Hathaway

Manufacturing Planner: Ron Montgomery

Cover Image(s): iStockphoto.com/Rawpixel Ltd

For product information and technology assistance, contact us at
Cengage Learning Customer & Sales Support, 1-800-354-9706

For permission to use material from this text or product, submit all requests online at **www.cengage.com/permissions**
Further permissions questions can be emailed to
permissionrequest@cengage.com

Library of Congress Control Number: 2015960964

Student Edition
ISBN: 978-1-305-50275-8

Cengage Learning
20 Channel Center Street
Boston, MA 02210
USA

Cengage Learning is a leading provider of customized learning solutions with employees residing in nearly 40 different countries and sales in more than 125 countries around the world. Find your local representative at **www.cengage.com.**

Cengage Learning products are represented in Canada by Nelson Education, Ltd.

To learn more about Cengage Learning Solutions, visit **www.cengage.com**

Purchase any of our products at your local college store or at our preferred online store **www.cengagebrain.com**

Brief Contents

Contents

Chapter 8 | Video Marketing   141

Chapter 9 | Marketing on Photo Sharing Sites   157

Chapter 10 | Discussion, News, Social Bookmarking, and Q&A Sites   175

Chapter 11 | Content Marketing: Publishing Articles, White Papers, and E-Books   193

Appendix | XYZ Coffee Company Social Media Marketing Plan   303

Preface

Social Media Marketing: A Strategic Approach is built upon an eight-step planning cycle that helps ensure the development of a winning SMM plan. This model incorporates the conceptual foundation and practical techniques necessary for creating a comprehensive and effective SMM plan. The model also provides a framework for developing a personal brand, a subject given chapter-by-chapter coverage in the second edition.

This planning cycle begins with observing an organization's current goals, presence and competition on the social web, followed by the establishment of SMART social media objectives and effective strategies to achieve them. The next step is to define an organization's target markets and campaign-specific audiences on the social web. This process makes it possible for a company to identify the social media platforms with the highest concentrations of its target audiences and determine how they are participating on those platforms, which enables the organization to select the optimal social media platforms for reaching its target audiences.

Interaction on the social web is guided by informal rules of engagement and general principles of appropriate behavior (social media ethics). Marketers must be aware of these precepts before attempting to participate in social media or risk alienating the very market segments they hope to connect with and influence.

With these guidelines in mind, as well as the company's social media goals, strategies, target audiences, and prime social media platforms, marketers can craft actionable platform-specific marketing tactics. The execution of these tactics allows an organization to implement its social media strategies across multiple platforms and realize the company's marketing goals. The bulk of this textbook is dedicated to learning how to create and deploy specific marketing tactics using online platforms and the mobile web.

Social media tools that make the process more efficient as well as more effective are given detailed coverage. In addition, extensive consideration is given to monitoring and measuring the progress made in reaching social media objectives and demonstrating return on investment. Feedback, both qualitative and quantitative, provides the means to continuously adjust and improve the elements of an SMM plan to maximize the chances of success.

The final chapter draws upon all the preceding material in the textbook to demonstrate and explain how to develop a formal SMM plan with multiple references and illustrations from a real world sample plan (presented in its entirety in the Appendix). Hence, this textbook provides a rich and robust cumulative learning experience with deep contextual relevance that endows the reader with an enduring understanding of the process of effective SMM planning. This process provides the social media marketer with a strong foundation for dealing with the ever-changing audiences, platforms and technologies of the social web.

Melissa S. Barker

Melissa S. Barker is a digital marketing consultant and public speaker, currently working with Jive Software, Puppet Labs, and Gates NextGen Open Source Courseware Grant. She has coauthored five textbooks, including the best-selling *Internet Research Illustrated*. In 2010, she created the first accredited social media marketing certificate in Washington State. She teaches search and social media marketing, as well as other related courses at Spokane Falls Community College. Melissa holds a B.A. in public relations and advertising from Gonzaga University, and an M.B.A. from Willamette University (expected in 2016). She has held key roles in digital marketing management at Siber Systems, Own Point of Sale, Integra Telecom, Jive Software, and Oregon Public Broadcasting. Melissa has become a recognized authority on LinkedIn, and a sought-after speaker at conferences, such as InnoTech and ITEXPO. For more information, visit: www.linkedin.com/in/melissasbarker

Donald I. Barker

Donald I. Barker has authored, coauthored, and contributed to forty cutting-edge and best-selling textbooks on subjects ranging from computer operating systems and expert systems to Internet research and social media marketing. He holds an M.B.A. from Eastern Washington University. As an assistant professor of information systems at Gonzaga University, he won the Best Theoretical Paper Award at the International Business Schools Computer Users Group's Annual North American Conference. In addition, he received several Jepson Scholarship Awards for notable publications in the field of artificial intelligence. As a senior editor of *PC AI Magazine*, he wrote the popular *Secret Agent Man* column. For more information, visit: www.linkedin.com/in/donaldibarker.

Debra Zahay

Debra Zahay is professor of marketing and chair of marketing, entrepreneurship and digital media management at St. Edward's University in Austin, Texas. She holds her PhD in marketing from the University of Illinois, Urbana-Champaign, Illinois, an MBA from Northwestern University, Evanston, Illinois, a JD from Loyola University, Chicago, Illinois, and an AB from Washington University in St. Louis, Missouri. Dr. Zahay is also the president of Zahay, Inc., a digital marketing strategy and education consulting firm.

Dr. Zahay has been teaching internet marketing, search and social media marketing, data management, and related topics at the university level since 1999 and has taught full-time at Aurora University in Aurora, Illinois, Northern Illinois University in DeKalb, Illinois, North Carolina State University in Raleigh, North Carolina, and DePaul University in Chicago, Illinois.

Dr. Zahay researches how firms can use customer information to increase firm performance. Some journals in which she has published include *Journal of Interactive Marketing* (Best Paper 2014), *Journal of Product Innovation Management, Decision Sciences,* and *Industrial Marketing Management.* She co-authored the third edition of the Cengage textbook *Internet Marketing: Integrating Online and Offline Strategies* with Mary Lou Roberts, solo-authored a book with Business Expert Press, *Digital Marketing Management: A Handbook for the Current (or Future) CEO.* Active in her profession, she is a long-standing member of both the American Marketing Association and the Academy of Marketing Science, where she has served as track chair. She has served as conference co-chair for the Direct/Interactive Research Summit. She serves on the editorial board of the both the *Journal of Marketing Analytics* and *Industrial Marketing Management* and is editor-in-chief of the *Journal of Research in Interactive Marketing.*

Mary Lou Roberts

Mary Lou Roberts is professor emeritus of management and marketing at the University of Massachusetts Boston. She holds a PhD in marketing from the University of Michigan. After retiring from full-time teaching, she continued to teach Internet marketing and social media marketing at the Harvard University Extension School for a number of years.

Other books include *Internet Marketing: Integrating Online and Offline Strategies* (third edition with Debra Zahay, 2013), *Direct Marketing Management* (second edition with Paul D. Berger, 1999), and *Marketing to the Changing Household* (with Lawrence H. Wortzel, 1984). In addition, she has published over fifty papers and conference proceedings in the United States and internationally. Her research has received awards including a Robert B. Clarke Best Paper award and a Dean's Award for Distinguished Research.

She has served as a convener, chair, and reviewer for many US and international journals and conferences as well as serving on the boards of directors of professional and nonprofit organizations, including the American Marketing Association and Mass Audubon. She has consulted and provided training sessions for corporations, government agencies, and nonprofit organizations

Dr. Roberts is active on social media. In addition to the Google+ and Facebook sites that support both students and instructors in Internet marketing and social media marketing, she has several Pinterest boards and personal accounts on other sites, including Instagram. She posts professional updates on LinkedIn and SlideShare and tweets on a regular basis.

Janna M. Parker

Janna Parker is assistant professor of marketing at James Madison University where she teaches strategic Internet marketing. She holds a DBA in marketing from Louisiana Tech University. Her previous academic appointment was at Georgia College and State University where she taught integrated marketing communications, social media, and other related topics in undergraduate and graduate courses.

Dr. Parker's research interests are retailing, advertising, and social media. She has published in *Journal of Business Ethics* and *Journal of Consumer Marketing.* She is active in many professional organizations and has served as a reviewer and track chair. She is the director of social media for the Academy of Marketing Science.

Acknowledgments

We are indebted to the instructors, students, and reviewers that made the first edition of *Social Media Marketing: A Strategic Approach* a success. In addition, we are grateful to our ever-supportive editor at Cengage Learning, Mike Roche. He brought us together to create the second edition, and has been a dependable source of information and encouragement. Ted Knight, of J. L. Hahn Consulting Group, managed the production process, with skill and good humor.

Professors Barker and Barker, Zahay, Roberts, and Parker have been teaching Social Media Marketing since its early days as a marketing and communications discipline. Being in the forefront of a rapidly evolving discipline has its challenges, as well as its rewards. Our students have contributed important knowledge and insights about the working of social platforms, and the activities of social media users. Busy practitioners have given generously of their time and expertise to assist us and our students in understanding the real-world practices that make successful social media marketing a reality. For all these sources of information and inspiration, we express our profound gratitude, and our best wishes for a productive social media journey together.

Dedication

To our families for enduring the hassles of living with an author; to our students for their enthusiasm and insights; to the many practitioners who have been supportive. MSB/DIB/NFB/MLR/DZ/JP

The Role of Social Media Marketing

Social media marketing (SMM) has emerged as a vital business force offering vibrant career options. It offers important benefits to marketers but some aspects are still not widely understood. SMM has experienced dramatic growth in recent years and is poised for substantial growth and change in years to come.

Social media is growing by leaps and bounds. It is estimated that by 2016 there will be around 2.13 *billion* social media users around the world. That is up from 1.4 billion in 2012 and it represents over 63% all Internet users.[1] Marketers are working hard to reach this huge social media audience. This book is intended to help both students and businesses understand the social media landscape and the changes that are taking place and to learn and how to approach it strategically.

Many businesses struggle with social media because they lack a definite plan. They start with an end in mind instead of creating a strategy and objectives. A company might start a Twitter account or a Facebook page, but it is not likely to see results unless there is a clear understanding of its marketing objectives. Like any form of marketing, a strong strategic plan for social media is required for success. This book contains chapters on establishing strategic goals and objectives and monitoring plan achievement as well as a chapter on the SMM plan itself and a sample SMM plan.

The advent of social media has also posed a challenge to traditional marketing methodologies. Marketing budgets are increasingly focused on digital, and the jobs of marketing professionals have changed as a result.

LEARNING OBJECTIVES

After completing this chapter, students will be able to:

- Explain why social media is important to businesses around the world
- Define SMM
- Explain the seven myths of SMM
- Relate a brief history of SMM
- Explain characteristics of SMM and ways in which it differs from traditional offline marketing
- Describe typical positions that are available in SMM

(Continued)

Advertising has increasingly moved to the Internet and to the mobile web, with even long-time print magazines such as *The Atlantic* shifting to a largely digital-based revenue strategy.[2] For many firms, the focus is now online, which makes knowledge of SMM especially valuable for students and/or soon-to-be job-seekers.

This book is organized into two core sections: the first four chapters will lay the foundation for engaging in social media, including marketing strategy and objectives, targeting specific audiences, and the background rules of social media. The remainder of the book will encompass more detailed elements of SMM and how to adapt the strategy to specific platforms and international audiences. By creating a solid marketing plan and choosing the right tools, a business can expediently and successfully navigate to its marketing goals and objectives.

What Is SMM?

There are many definitions of SMM. This one from technology marketing site Mashable is straightforward and covers most of the important issues:

> *Social media marketing refers to the process of gaining website traffic or attention through social media sites.*
>
> *Social media marketing programs usually center on efforts to create content that attracts attention and encourages readers to share it with their social networks. A corporate message spreads from user to user and presumably resonates because it appears to come from a trusted, third-party source, as opposed to the brand or company itself. Hence, this form of marketing is driven by word-of-mouth, meaning it results in earned media rather than paid media.[3]*

SMM has a number of important aspects:

1. *Creating buzz or newsworthy events, videos, tweets, or blog entries that attract attention and have the potential to become viral in nature. Buzz is what makes SMM work. It replicates a message through user to user contact, rather than the traditional method of purchasing an ad or promoting a press release. It emulates word of mouth (WOM) in the physical world and consequently can have a great deal of impact.*

A classic example, one that alerted many marketers to the power of social media, is "United Breaks Guitars." It all started when musician Dave Carroll's guitar was damaged on a United Airlines flight (Figure 1.1). He spent the next 9 months trying to recover the $1,200 it cost to have the guitar repaired. As he tells the story, phoning and emailing only got him the run around. So he, with the help of musician friends, created a video at the cost of $150. On July 6, 2009, he posted it on YouTube. Within 24 hours the video had over 150,000 views; 24 days later it had over a million views and major news organizations as well as social media users had picked it up.

United contacted him agreeing to pay the repair costs and offered $1,200 in flight vouchers, which he declined. Two years later he estimated that his message had reached as many as 100 million people, courtesy of all the media mentions. All this created a storm of negative publicity for United.[4]

It is important to point out that no one can control, or even do a good job predicting, when a social media post will go viral. But marketers understand that they need to pay attention, perhaps even to improve their customer service.

Figure 1.1 Dave Carroll with His Guitar

2. *Building ways that enable fans of a brand or company to promote a message themselves in multiple online social media venues. Corporations or brands can create pages on major social platforms where they can offer followers information and promotions like coupons. They can reach huge audiences on these platforms as will be shown in the next section of this chapter. As we will discuss in Chapter 3, these huge audiences can be segmented using profile data and behavioral data from the platform to reach targeted audiences or to attract paid advertising.*

3. *It is based around online conversations. SMM is not controlled by the organization. Instead it encourages user participation and dialog. A badly designed SMM campaign can potentially backfire on the organization that created it. To be successful SMM campaigns must fully engage and respect the users. Each type of platform, as discussed in Chapter 5, has its own way of engaging followers. How to conduct SMM in ways that bring positive response instead of public backlash is the subject of Chapter 4.*

4. *Social media is part of a larger media ecosystem of owned, paid, and earned media, which represents a way for marketers to leverage their own brand efforts. These media are defined in Figure 1.2.*

As you can see, paid media describes the traditional print and broadcast media, which are now joined by paid advertising on social media platforms and blogs. Paid advertising on social platforms is not a major focus of this book, although it will be discussed briefly in Chapter 4.

The Internet gives brands the opportunity to own their own media outlets ranging from their websites to their Facebook and LinkedIn pages. It has made each brand its own publisher, responsible for content of many kinds and for its dissemination. Much of the focus of this book is on creating content and marketing campaigns on different types of social platforms. Only the marketer's owned platforms are within her direct control.

The most valuable media of all in this ecosystem is earned media. When people begin talking about a brand and its content, they spread the word with no additional effort on the part of the marketer. Even more important, this digital WOM confers much credibility on the brand, especially if recognized experts or influentials are talking on Twitter, Facebook, their blogs, and other channels. Like traditional public

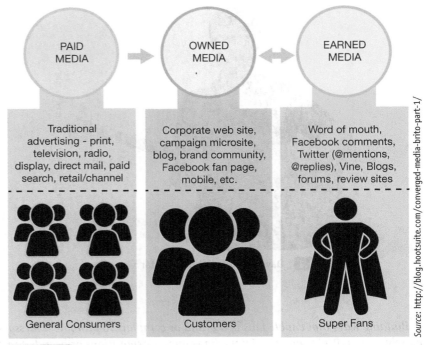

Source: http://blog.hootsuite.com/converged-media-brito-part-1/

Figure 1.2 Paid, Owned, and Earned Media

relations, the brand cannot control the nature of this conversation but positive WOM in earned media can give the brand a significant boost.[5]

The combined impact of these aspects of SMM makes it quite different from traditional marketing in the offline media. As a result a number of myths have grown up around SMM, which help to explain both misconceptions and challenges of the discipline.

The Seven Myths of SMM

SMM is one of the best ways that businesses can drive sales, build relationships, and satisfy their customers. Although social media has increased in popularity over the years as a marketing tool, there remain some common misconceptions about SMM. The following are seven of the most common myths that business professionals have regarding SMM.

SOCIAL MEDIA MYTH #1: SOCIAL MEDIA IS JUST A FAD

WRONG Social media continues to grow by virtually any measure you use. Figure 1.3 shows the number of active accounts for the world's 10 largest social media networks as of August 2015. The chart shows Facebook in the lead with almost a billion and a half active users. It also shows huge user bases for a number of messaging apps that are not widely used in the United States like the Chinese platform Tencent QQ. Twitter, Skype, and Google+ all made the top 10. Most surprising is Instagram in tenth place. Over 300 million active users is not bad for a platform founded in 2009![6]

Businesses want to invest their time and energy in marketing tools that will be useful in the long term, versus wasting limited resources on a flash-in-the-pan technology or a fad. Some business professionals question whether social media will remain a powerful marketing and communications tool or if it will eventually fall by the wayside. To resolve

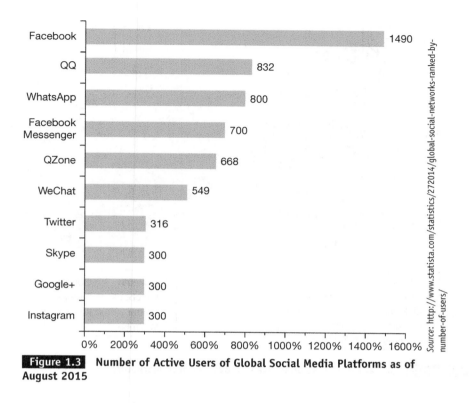

Figure 1.3 **Number of Active Users of Global Social Media Platforms as of August 2015**

this issue, it is helpful to look at the foundations of social media, which are built on age-old concepts of community, socialization, and WOM marketing.

The "social" component of social media has been part of human interactions since the dawn of time. People are inherently social creatures to some extent. What has changed is the media by which people are able to express social impulses. As technology has advanced, so have the media available for social behavior. Initially, social interactions were limited to in-person meetings, then mail and letters, then telephones, then email, and now social media, or web-based social interactions.

The underlying premise of social media—that people are social and want to connect with other people—has been stable over time. The difference is that people are now able to connect with each other in a more efficient and scalable way. Facebook allows users to see what friends from high school are up to without ever speaking to them. Photos of friends and family from across the world can be viewed on photo sharing sites. In these and many other ways, social media allows people to keep up to speed with many connections in quick and efficient ways.

Like the Internet, social media is a not a flash in the pan because of the human desire to socialize and because the media of the Internet continue to evolve at a rapid rate, providing new and attractive means for people to interact. Although social media will only expand in the foreseeable future, specific social media platforms (technologies or platforms such as Facebook and Twitter) change considerably over time and other platforms rise and fall in popularity. The social media marketer must be alert to ongoing changes in the social media environment.

In the face of all this change, marketers will focus on the platforms most used by their target audiences. Figure 1.4 shows an interesting contrast between the platforms used by B2C marketers, with Facebook in the lead, and B2B marketers, where LinkedIn holds first place. This reflects the different audiences for B2C and B2B marketing. Notice, however, that Facebook, Twitter, and LinkedIn are the top three platforms in both market spaces,[7] just in a different order.

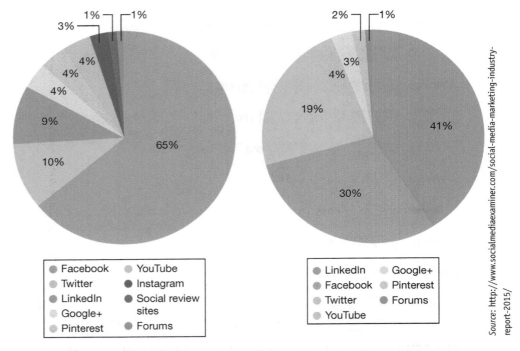

Figure 1.4 Social Media Platforms Used by B2C and B2B Marketers

SOCIAL MEDIA MYTH #2: SOCIAL MEDIA IS JUST FOR THE YOUNG

WRONG Many social media skeptics still think that social media is a tool primarily for the young: kids, teenagers, and college students. The reality is that older users are among the fastest growing demographics on most social media sites. Pew reports that in 2012 it found for the first time that over half of all adults age 65 and older were Internet users and that 46% of them used Facebook. Older adults are more likely to own a tablet or an e-book reader or both while only 13% owned a smartphone in 2014.

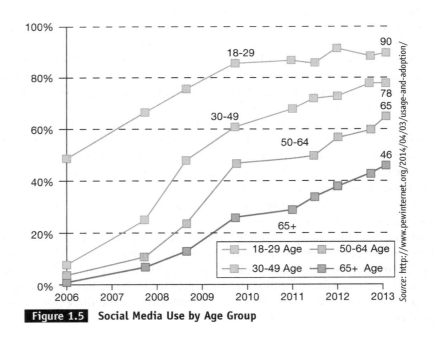

Figure 1.5 Social Media Use by Age Group

The age disparity in social media use continues to exist as shown in Figure 1.5. Young adults are still the most likely to be social media users, but use among older adults, especially those in the 50–64 age group, has grown rapidly in recent years.[8]

The growth in social media usage rates among older adults carries over into the mobile sphere according to comScore. The young are still the heaviest users of mobile social media as well as the fastest growing group of users. However, among tablet mobile social media users, adults aged 55 and over represent the fastest growing group.[9]

Social networks are increasingly being adopted by older populations and are becoming incredibly diverse, with users spanning all age and income brackets. This diversity means that most businesses, if they are willing to look, can find their target consumers on social media sites. It also means that they should not simply try to appeal to a large, heterogeneous audience. They need to hone targeting skills for their own messaging and for paid advertising.

SOCIAL MEDIA MYTH #3: THERE IS NO RETURN ON SMM

WRONG But that's not to say that measuring the return on SMM is easy. It requires careful planning, careful execution, consistent monitoring, and the discipline to analyze and gain business insights from monitoring data. This textbook has a chapter dedicated to planning and one to social media monitoring that shows how the two marketing elements work together to make it possible to measure social media return on investment (ROI).

Although ROI is a specific monetary value determined by an established method, social media return is measured in a variety of different ways and is not always as clear-cut as financial ROI. Figure 1.6 indicates that 70% of marketers surveyed in 2014 agreed or strongly agreed that SMM helps them improve sales. Those who have been using SMM the longest are most likely to support the statement with agreement becoming stronger the longer they have been social media marketers.[10] Sales are the ultimate measure of marketing achievement, so this data makes a powerful case for SMM. That being said, there are many ways of measuring success that stop short of return on monetary investment.

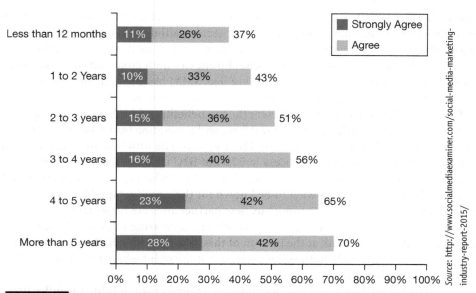

Source: http://www.socialmediaexaminer.com/social-media-marketing-industry-report-2015/

Figure 1.6 Marketers Who Agree or Strongly Agree that SMM Helped Them Improve Sales

There are a lot of lists of "best" or "favorite" social media campaigns. *CIO* magazine published its own list of the best of 2014, and just 3 examples of the 12 listed show the many ways in which social media marketers measure success. Selected examples are:

- At or near the top of everyone's list of the best of 2014 is the Ice Bucket Challenge. The challenge was started by a single victim of ALS, simply to raise awareness of this devastating disease. Celebrities took it up and the ice bucket videos quickly went viral. The ALS Association took it up as an official fund-raising activity and reported that *$220 million was raised*. Most of that money went to research and a year later researchers were identifying gains already made.[11] Another measure of success is that the challenge was repeated in the summer of 2015. Sequels are rarely as successful as originals, but the renewal of the challenge was itself newsworthy.

- Coke's Share, a Coke campaign, was started in Australia and had expanded to over 50 countries by the time it went viral in the United States in the summer of 2014. Names replaced the Coke logo on soda cans and consumers were invited to visit Shareacoke.com, personalize virtual Coke bottles, and share them with their friends on social media. The campaign reported over *125,000 posts* on various social media platforms with 96% of the consumer sentiment either positive or neutral.

- Taco Bell began its campaign for a Taco emoji during the winter of 2014. It petitioned the Unicode Consortium, which regulates emojis. A petition on Change.org gathered over 30,000 signatures. "This campaign was an attention grabber because it pulled cleverly from two culturally relevant tech trends: emojis and community activism," says Wire Stone's [senior strategist Lily] Croll. The campaign kept the chain's core *product in the social media conversation* and received mainstream press attention.[12] In June 2015, the consortium released code for a taco emoji, seemingly guaranteeing it a spot on the emoji keyboard.[13]

While there are many ways to measure marketing achievement and various metrics may be appropriate based on the objectives of a given campaign, in the end sales represent the definitive accomplishment for marketers.

SOCIAL MEDIA MYTH #4: SMM ISN'T RIGHT FOR THIS BUSINESS

WRONG Figure 1.4 has already shown that both B2C and B2B marketers use social media. The same is true of businesses in all economic sectors, although there are issues in sectors like financial services where both disclosure and security issues affect the ways in which social media can be used. Likewise, businesses both large and small use social media. Since most social media platforms are free, SMM has a special attraction for small businesses, including local retailers and services businesses.

Figure 1.7 shows that for all marketers the top benefits of SMM are increasing exposure, increasing traffic, creating loyal fans, and generating business intelligence. Each of those benefits applies equally to B2C and B2B. The fifth benefit, generating sales leads tends to be a more formal process in B2B but B2C marketers are also interested in identifying potential purchasers. Likewise, *thought leadership* is a term more commonly used in B2B but all marketers want to be known for their product quality and expertise. Improved search rankings and strong business partnerships are important to all marketers. Notice that, important as they clearly are, increasing sales and decreasing marketing expenditures rank at the bottom of this list of benefits of SMM.[14] The greatest benefits tend to occur early in the sales cycle, not at the point where purchases are being made or sales are being closed.

Given the power that social media endows consumers with, it is little wonder that users are increasingly screening out traditional advertising media and focusing their attention toward social media where they control the content. Many businesses have

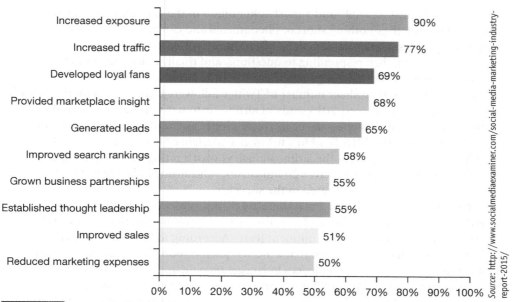

Figure 1.7 Benefits of SMM

based their success on marketing through television, radio, newspapers, yellow pages, or direct mail. However, these methods are losing their power in the marketplace. People are watching less traditional TV and are instead viewing videos and television online. Radio is being replaced by online streaming music on sites such as Pandora.com and Spotify. Newspapers are in dramatic decline, while blogs such as the Huffington Post are growing in popularity. The printed Yellow Pages are more likely to be used to hold up a computer monitor than to locate a business, with the abundance of online white page and yellow page directories. Direct mail coupons end up in the garbage because the same coupons can be found online and on mobile sites. To keep up with their changing audiences, marketers find it necessary to join the social media tsunami.

In some instances, social media can have a powerful impact in an industry or in a situation where it seems unlikely to be useful or both. In addition, it will probably take time for the full impact of SMM to be felt. Such was the case with JetBlue Airlines that operates in an industry known for being near the bottom in customer satisfaction rankings.

In February 2007, JetBlue's corporate image was dealt a serious blow when weather and "…a shoestring communications system that left pilots and flight attendants in the dark, and an undersized reservation system," caused about 1,000 flight cancelations within 5 days, stranding thousands of passengers on Valentine's Day.[15]

In an effort to reach out to customers, CEO Neeleman appeared in an unscripted YouTube video, apologizing for the airline's mistakes and announcing a "Customer Bill of Rights," which outlined steps the airline would take in response to service interruptions. The airline's apology was disseminated on traditional offline media as well as on social media, with the whole incident receiving considerable attention in the news media. The admission of complete responsibility for the incident and an acknowledgement of the pain it caused passengers, coupled with a credible promise to fix it, amounted "to the perfect business apology—in fact, it is likely to become a generally accepted standard for how business errors should be handled."[16] As a consequence, the video apology received a significant number of comments, most of which were positive because it felt authentic and genuine.[17] Recognizing the power of social media to connect with the traveling public, JetBlue set out to develop a full-fledged SMM strategy.

The centerpiece of that social media strategy has become JetBlue's Twitter account, which grew from a mere 700 followers, as of March 7, 2008, to approximately 1.1 million followers by August of 2009[18] and almost 1.96 million in the late summer of 2015.[19] This kind of growth is nothing short of phenomenal and can be directly attributed to the company's social media strategy of first using Twitter to see what people were saying about them, then responding to questions, and finally engaging in full blown conversations with their customer base.[20]

More important than sheer number of Twitter followers is the impact on the airline's corporate image. J.D. Powers 2015 study of airline customer satisfaction found that "JetBlue Airways ranks highest in the low-cost carrier segment for a 10th consecutive year."[21] In addition, the 2015 Temkin Customer Experience Survey announced that "JetBlue took the top spot [in the airline industry] with a rating of 75%, placing it 52nd overall out of 293 companies across 20 industries." The airline industry itself ranked twelfth of the 20 industries covered in the survey.[22]

The HubSpot blog explained that there are three teams who tweet from the @JetBlue account—the marketing team, the corporate communications team, and Laurie Meacham's customer commitment team. According to her, "employees don't feel pressured to hit a response goal by sending quick responses to every single tweet that comes in. We want our employees to engage *smartly,* and for the conversations to be organic and natural. We look for opportunities to add value and connect with our customers, not just respond to every single mention that comes our way." With some 2,500 mentions on Twitter each day, it behooves JetBlue to use its social media resources wisely in pursuit of their corporate goals.[23]

SOCIAL MEDIA MYTH #5: SMM IS NEW

THE TECHNOLOGY IS NEW BUT THE PRINCIPLE IS NOT SMM is not really new. Most of the marketing principles, based on social, behavioral, and economic concepts, have been around for many years, but new technology and media are changing the role those concepts play in modern marketing efforts. For example, brands are very excited about the potential to harness online conversations on blogs, Twitter, and social networks. The behavior—talking about brands and businesses—isn't new and is more generally called WOM marketing. The difference is that these conversations are now public, online, and viewable for the indefinite future.

The newest aspect of social media is the technology that enables open and transparent online conversations. Some companies don't want to "get on" social media because they are afraid of what consumers might say about them. The reality is that consumers are already on social sites, talking about businesses on their Facebook pages, blogs, and Twitter accounts, whether a business acknowledges this or not.

SOCIAL MEDIA MYTH #6: SOCIAL MEDIA IS TOO TIME-CONSUMING

SOCIAL MEDIA DOES REQUIRE A CONSISTENT TIME COMMITMENT One of the biggest business concerns about using SMM is the amount of time and resources it will take. The time and the human and technology resources required to manage SMM depends on the size of the business. Large companies that have thousands of online mentions a day will have to dedicate more resources to social media than a small business. However, large businesses can devote more technology to social media efficiency, like the Cisco listening center described in Chapter 2. The time commitment required to manage social media will also depend on the specific social media strategy and approach used.

Most of the concern about time and resources comes from small- and medium-sized businesses. After the initial setup and strategy, these businesses should be able to manage their social media programs effectively with only a few hours per week. Social media doesn't have to be time consuming when done right. The problem is that many people log on to Facebook, Twitter, or LinkedIn and become addicted to checking out what friends are up to, exchanging messages, or generally spending far more time than necessary for business promotion.

There are three key ways to limit the time investment in SMM. The first is to look for underutilized employees who can spend some of their time on SMM. For example, a receptionist may not be busy the entire day, and many retail stores and restaurants have downtimes during which human resources are not fully utilized.

The second opportunity is to leverage efficiency tools. There are a number of sites, such as Hootsuite, TweetDeck, and CoTweet, which make managing social media easier. By using these tools, social media efforts can be streamlined. We will discuss these tools in detail in Chapter 14.

Finally, using mobile devices is a key way to boost efficiency in SMM. This is especially helpful for publishing multimedia content. Smartphones (a Blackberry, an iPhone, or an Android phone) can take a picture or video and instantly post it onto Facebook, Twitter, or a blog in only a minute. This speed makes managing SMM even easier and less time consuming. The importance of mobile in SMM will be discussed in Chapter 12.

SOCIAL MEDIA MYTH #7: SOCIAL MEDIA IS FREE

WRONG Many businesses are excited about social media because the media itself is free. Nevertheless, while most sites do not have a fee for usage, social media isn't really free. First, there is the cost in terms of personnel time and technology resources, as well as the fee of using consultants or agencies involved in building and executing the social media strategy. Social media takes time, as indicated in the previous section, and that alone means it is not free.

Second, similar to other media and advertising, in addition to costs from posting content, there are also costs to producing and creating content. Imagine if it were free to run TV commercials. Companies would run lots of commercials, including more bad ones that drive fewer sales. Free access means no barrier to entry and greater competition for consumer attention. Good commercials would still have costs for creativity and production in order to produce a sequence memorable enough to be recognized and remembered. In a similar way, strong social media strategies may entail costs for top-quality creative or development efforts, depending on their scale.

Finally, many businesses engaging in social media invest in a guide or consultant to help them through the process. Consultants can help businesses get off to a quicker start and avoid common pitfalls, as well as save time and money.

Regardless of whether or not there are actual out-of-pocket expenses associated with social media, the resource and time costs should not be forgotten. As time spent on social media is not free, it must be allocated wisely in order to generate maximum results. Hopefully, this text will provide the tools necessary to get the most impact out of time spent on SMM.

The History of SMM

Currently, social media is said to have reached critical mass with 73% of adults in the United States having a profile on a social network.[24] Still, this trend emerged from humble beginnings, as illustrated by the social media timeline in Figure 1.8. Using a loose interpretation, one could say that the first social media existed as soon as the first postal service was created, which allowed people to communicate across great distances instead of just face-to-face. However, SMM in the most relevant sense for this book became viable with the development of the Internet in the late 1960s. The early Internet

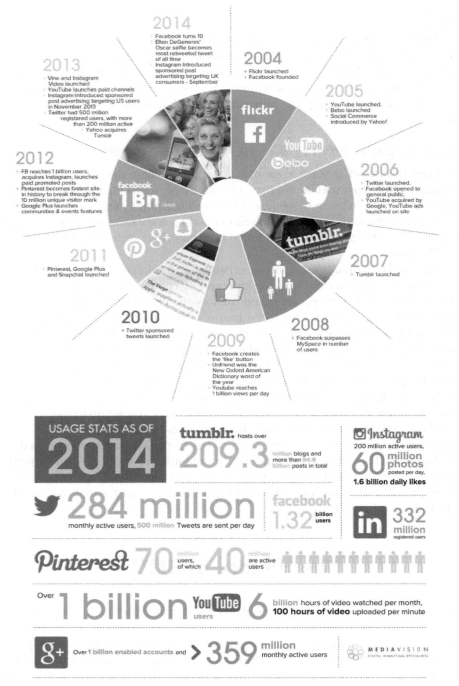

Figure 1.8 A Social Media Timeline

was created for the use of professors and researchers working for the Department of Defense. Those researchers began using the ARPANET (the Advanced Research Projects Agency Network, a core of what would become the Internet) resources for nonwork purposes, and usage quickly began to grow. Early online marketing efforts would soon follow; the first *spam* email message was sent in 1978![†]

The earliest ancestor of today's diverse social media platforms is most likely USENET, developed by Duke University graduate students Jim Ellis and Tom Truscott in 1979. Users can post articles, which are organized into *newsgroups* depending on the topic. Other users can subscribe to newsgroups they find interesting; often some post responses to an article they read, forming a *thread*. Unlike bulletin boards or online forums that have an administrator or central hub, USENET is a conglomeration of separate servers run by different organizations or Internet service providers (ISPs), which exchange articles and threads with each other. In this way, articles posted by one user can reach many others eventually, and people can comment and have their voices heard. These are the core principles of social media.

Following USENET, there was an explosion of different web-based services designed for people with common interests to share information. The WELL (Whole Earth 'Lectronic Link) was created in 1985, starting out as a dial-up bulletin board system (BBS). This quickly developed into a dial-up ISP in the early 1990s, dramatically expanding its user base. Its online forums are still hosting discussions today. Other dial-up BBS systems like CompuServe and Prodigy were fulfilling a similar function by hosting user-driven discussions about various topics.

The growth of social media paralleled the increasing development of computing and Internet transfer technology. While in the 1990s most Internet users were on dial-up connections with speeds under 56 kilobytes per second, within 10 years broadband technology such as DSL and cable Internet became available, increasing transfer speeds by thousands of times. As more data was transferred quickly, social media networks became more advanced and included elements other than just plain text. In 1999 Napster was developed, allowing users to quickly share media files such as music and video with each other. *Wikipedia* was established in 2001 and continues to be a leading source of relevant user-contributed information.

Figure 1.8 chronicles the development of major social media platforms. The years 2003 and 2004 were highly significant for social media with the creation of MySpace, Delicious, Second Life, and Facebook. The photo-sharing site Flickr was created in 2004 and YouTube for sharing videos in 2005. Twitter came along in 2006. Some of the original platforms have gone into serious decline during this brief period and do not even show in Figure 1.8. New platforms continue to arise, each seeking to draw in more online participants and develop its own market share. As a result, the history of social media platforms is still being written.

The groundbreaking texts for social media as a serious academic and marketing field were also being written during that same time period. The possibilities for brand-related online social interaction and community were being explored. Since the mid-2000s, a slew of instructional books have been published, focused on specific areas of SMM, search engine optimization, and other web-based marketing tactics. Some experts have made their careers out of this developing field; Guy Kawasaki, Chris Brogan, and

---

[†]The first mass email message was sent to 393 people out of the 2,600 ARPANET users at the time in order to advertise a new computer model created by Digital Equipment Corporation. It was sent by Gary Turk. For more information, see: NPR News (2008, May 3), "At 30, Spam Going Nowhere Soon," hosted by Andrea Seabrook (transcript online, retrieved September 8, 2011, from http://www.npr.org/templates/story/story.php?storyId=90160617); Tom Abate (2008, May 3), "A Very Unhappy Birthday to Spam, Age 30," *San Francisco Chronicle*. Retrieved September 8, 2011, from http://articles.sfgate.com/2008-05-03/business/17155925_1_spam-e-mail-world-wide-web

David Meerman Scott, to name just a few, have become household names in SMM. Obviously, this is a rapidly evolving field and it has corresponding job opportunities to be discussed in the final sections of this chapter.

Why SMM Is Different

A common misconception is that SMM just means using new online social media sites to do traditional marketing, but this is often not the case. The traditional marketing approach, emphasizing the four Ps (product, price, place, and promotion), has become second nature to many professionals. While the traditional marketing perspective still has important lessons for future marketers, in the new terrain of social media, it has to be adapted or in some areas changed completely.

Several aspects distinguish SMM from so-called traditional marketing. The first is control vs. contributions. Traditional marketing seeks to control the content seen by the audience. Old school marketers attempt to dominate the territory and try to exclude their competitors' messages. On the Internet, and in social media especially, control over content consumed is in the hands of consumers and marketers ignore that truth to their detriment.

SMM emphasizes audience contribution and relinquishes control over large parts of the content. Effective social media marketers can sometimes influence what participants say and think about their brand, but rarely can they control the conversation entirely. Indeed, the very nature of social media can make controlling the conversation seem rude and domineering. Avoiding this pitfall makes knowledge of social media important even for persons engaged in traditional marketing.

The second important distinction between traditional and SMM is trust building. Firms cannot fully control the content that users will create, so to build their image, companies must develop trusting relationships with their audience. Unlike traditional advertisements in which consumers expect some exaggeration or spin to be applied to the product's image, on social media it is important to be earnest and down- to-earth. All communication must be authentic, in tone and in context.

The importance of trust emerges from how social media messages are consumed. In traditional marketing, the signal is one-way: from the firm to potential customers. However, social media involves many-to-many communication with brands being only one participant. The audience's attention cannot be taken for granted; deliver boring, inaccurate, or irrelevant information and they will look elsewhere. Unlike an advertising campaign with a set beginning and end, social media is an ongoing conversation. Companies that bend the truth will be eventually held accountable and have to explain their actions. This pattern appears in numerous case studies throughout the book. On social media, trust is slow to earn but very easy to lose. Successful social media marketers consider building trust with the audience to be of paramount importance.

SMM is a unique combination of marketing creativity and technology. We see examples of creative use of marketing technology on an almost-daily basis. The TV commercial pictured in Figure 1.9 is only one example.

In just 30 short seconds, the TV spot shows celebrities ordering pizza using a variety of technologies.[25] Richard Sherman Tweets, Eva Longoria uses her TV remote, Sarah Hyland shows how she uses a pizza emoji to text her order, and Clark Gregg orders his with a tap on his smartwatch. Domino's calls it "AnyWare."[26] These various online technologies are being featured in a commercial on traditional TV. That is another key theme of this book. SMM does not exist in a vacuum; it is part of digital marketing, which, in turn, is part of the overall marketing effort.

Source: https://www.youtube.com/watch?v=Zdy0I7m3hwo

Figure 1.9 Richard Sherman Tweets to Order a Domino's Pizza

The Domino's pizza ordering system is only one innovative use of technology from one brand. There are new and different SMM efforts visible on an almost-daily basis. The pervasive and ever-evolving nature of social media means that SMM offers an interesting set of career options.

Careers in SMM

Throughout this chapter, we have documented the phenomenal growth of social media and the accompanying growth of SMM. From virtually nothing in 2003, social media has grown to be measured in billions—from billions of users to billions of dollars in sales influenced by social media. Clearly that growth has not occurred without growth in the number of jobs in the field. Numbers are hard to come by because many social media marketers have transitioned from other jobs in their company and because many marketers work only part time on social media, but one has only to look at the online job boards to verify that a talent hunt is ongoing.

Developing Your Personal Brand Online

"We are CEOs of our own companies: Me Inc. To be in business today, our most important job is to be head marketer for the brand called You."[1] So says famed strategy consultant Tom Peters, author of a book entitled *The Brand Called You*. In this book, published in 1997, he makes a powerful argument for personal branding and marketing. Peters continues to update his views on personal branding on his personal website. The website links to his blog, which has a category Brand You.[2]

[1] Martinuzzi, Bruna (July 9, 2014). "How to Build an Unforgettable Personal Brand." Retrieved on March 27, 2015, from https://www.americanexpress.com/us/small-business/openforum/articles/how-to-build-an-unforgettable-personal-brand/
[2] (n.d.), tompeters!. http://tompeters.com/

Any person taking this course probably already has some kind of an online presence. How widespread that presence is, how positive it is, and how helpful it will be to your ongoing career development are all important questions. We will explore the topic of personal branding in topic boxes in almost all the chapters in this book. Each will focus on the role of the chapter's content in your own personal branding process.

We will use the basic model popularized by Dan Schawbel in his books, website, and blogs and in his writing for Forbes and other business publications. Having only recently attained the age of 30, Dan has made himself into a successful business using the personal branding techniques he espouses.

His model has four stages:

Step #1 Discover. In the first step, you will learn about yourself and the distinctive characteristics that will make your brand unique. This is a journey of personal discovery and self-assessment, and it should be an honest evaluation of your strengths and weaknesses and the career-related skills you possess or need to develop. As you go through this process, you may want to develop a personal value statement that succinctly describes who you are and what you have to offer.

Step #2 Create. In the second step, you will create a personal marketing portfolio to support your brand. The portfolio should include your resume in both offline and online formats. It also includes supporting documentation like cover letters and recommendations. The portfolio must have a home, preferably one that can easily be found by hiring managers. Creating a personal website is an excellent approach. Both Wix[3] and Weebly[4] are free and easy to use and allow you to develop a site that will be a good home for the content you create in this and other classes. You may also want to create a blog or use another Internet platform to create and disseminate content that reinforces your brand image.

Step #3 Communicate. By the time you reach the third step, you have developed your personal characteristics and skills and you possess a portfolio of content that supports your brand. You have identified the audience(s) you need to reach with your brand message and where and how they consume content. Now you are ready to distribute and promote this content to the important stakeholders in your career space.

Step #4. Maintain. In the final step, you will continue to create and disseminate content that supports your brand. You will put tools in place and develop a routine for using them to monitor the development of your brand and to ensure its security on the web and in whatever offline environments it resides.

Each of these stages will be discussed from various perspectives as we move through the book.

It is important to remember that social media is not the only foundation on which your personal brand rests. This model is from *Me 2.0*. You can see that it encompasses offline tools like public relations and networking as well as online tools like search engine optimization in addition to social media.

---

[3] http://www.wix.com/
[4] http://www.weebly.com/

Dan Schawbel's Octopus Model of Relevancy

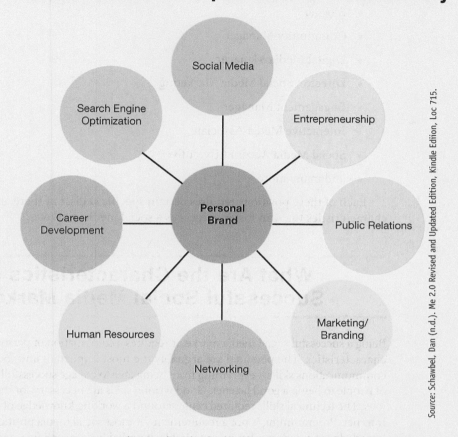

Source: Schawbel, Dan (n.d.). Me 2.0 Revised and Updated Edition, Kindle Edition, Loc 715.

There are numerous writers who deal with the topic of developing and taking advantage of a personal brand. We will reference many of them as the personal branding discussion continues. One who concentrates on personal branding and related subjects is Professor Denny McCorkle. His website is Digital Self Marketing Advantage, and you might want to follow him on one of the channels listed on the site. Another is Professor Theresa Clarke who publishes The Marketing Career Info Weekly on content curation site Paper.li. You can find the link to subscribe @TheresaBClarke.

The largest job sites give considerable reassurance that SMM is a fertile discipline for job seekers. There are many types of social media jobs, whether at the entry level[27] or more advanced positions.[28] There are many jobs available at any given time on a wide variety of general job sites like Monster.com and specialized sites like MarketingHire.com. In addition, many marketing news sites accept job postings. Early in your job search register with one or more of the recruiting sites so you can follow the types of jobs that are being listed, where they are located, and what skills they require. Make this part of your required reading list.

In this book, we place emphasis on developing your own personal brand. Most chapters have a box like the one in this chapter that give specific advice and resources for developing your personal brand. You should consider this an essential step for obtaining a position in SMM. For one thing, developing a personal brand online requires many of the skills companies are looking for when they hire people for social media positions.

There are many types of positions available in SMM. These are only a few selected job titles from a much longer list on a career site:

- Blogger
- Community Manager
- Digital Media Manager
- Director, Social Media Marketing
- Engagement Manager
- Interactive Media Associate
- Social Media Account Executive[29]
- and many more

Each of these positions requires certain specific skills, but there are some general characteristics that can foster success as a social media marketer.

What Are the Characteristics of a Successful Social Media Marketer?

Being a successful social media marketer requires a combination of personal and technical characteristics. The personal are arguably the most important and focus on good communications skills—everything from being able to engage successfully with diverse groups of people to being a good listener. Good writing skills are necessary for most social media jobs. The technical skills required center around a working knowledge of computers and the Internet. Programming is not a requirement for most social media positions. However, some knowledge of search marketing is desirable. It probably goes without saying that proficiency on at least the three leading social platforms—Facebook, Twitter, and LinkedIn—is essential.

British website WeAreSocialMedia has a set of suggestions that would benefit all job seekers. They are:

- **Stay on top of social media trends.** Subscribing to a few leading newsletters in the field will help you keep up to date.

- **Be prepared to think and act quickly.** Social media marketers must react swiftly and well to events that impact their brand. Unfortunately, this often includes nights and weekends.

- **Be comfortable with analytics.** The monitoring chapter in this book establishes a knowledge base in social media analytics that all social media marketers need.

- **Learn to write for social media.** Basic writing skills come first, but then the social media marketer must learn to engage others in 140 characters or less (Twitter), to communicate in short videos (Vine), and even to deliver brand messages in ephemeral media (Snapchat).

- **Establish and maintain your social media presence**—a portfolio or even better, a full-fledged personal brand.

- **In all you do, show yourself to be an effective user of social media.** Post relevant and engaging content and be consistent in the way you deal with social media. Avoid anything that will reflect negatively on you. Interact regularly and positively on all your social media platforms.[30,31]

This is not only good advice for people who wish to work in SMM but also for those who wish to work in some other aspect of marketing. That could be anything from search engine marketing in a digital agency to product management for a consumer products company to sales representative in a B2B services enterprise. The importance of a personal brand applies whether the field is digital or traditional, B2B or B2C, product or services. The importance of skills like good communications does not vary, nor does the desirability of at least a moderate level of technological proficiency.

All this advice may sound like common sense, and it probably is. However, many people make damaging mistakes on social media and those mistakes can come back to haunt them for a long time.

The characteristics for success as a social media marketer may not sound very rare or difficult to develop. Arguably, large parts of the population have the skills to do social media; indeed, as shown by the enormous growth of sites like Twitter, Facebook, and LinkedIn, much of the population already is "doing" social media! Platform proficiency is essential, but being an effective social media marketer requires more. *It requires being able to translate business or marketing goals and objectives into the execution of social media strategy.* Developing the skills and knowledge emphasized in this book will help a person compete against others in the growing field of SMM and to rise to the top in this dynamic area.

Understanding best practices for the various aspects of SMM will assist you on your journey. Each chapter has its own set of subject-specific best practices. Here are some general SMM best practices to get you started.

Best Practices for SMM

1. Begin with a strategy backed by a SMM plan. Random or inconsistent use of social media will not produce any benefits.

2. Be honest and transparent in all your social media efforts. Attempts to misinform or deceive will soon be "outed" to the detriment of the brand and the marketer. Building trust will be amply repaid in the long run.

3. Identify your target audience and understand its media behavior before you begin. There are many ways to engage on social media and different audience will respond to different kinds of communications.

4. Welcome participation and feedback from your audience. Remember, the audience controls the communications, not the marketer.

5. Remember that what you know today may not be valid tomorrow. SMM changes with the evolution of technologies and of audiences and the social media marketer must be vigilant and nimble to keep up with the changes.[32]

This book has knowledge and resources that will help you begin the exciting journey as a social media marketer or as a professional in a related field. Welcome to the journey and best wishes!

Notes

1. (n.d.). Statosta, "Number of Social Network Users Worldwide from 2010 to 2018 (in Billions)." Retrieved August 16, 2015, from http://www.statista.com/statistics/278414/number-of-worldwide-social-network-users/

2. Peters, Jeremy W. (December 12, 2010). "Web Focus Helps Revitalize the *Atlantic*," *New York Times*. Retrieved July 3, 2011, from http://www.nytimes.com/2010/12/13/business/media/13atlantic.html?_r=1

3. (n.d.). Mashable, "Social Media Marketing." Retrieved August 16, 2015, from http://mashable.com/category/social-media-marketing/

4. Barker, Melissa S., Donald I. Barker, Nicholas F. Bormann, Krista E. Neher (2008). *Social Media Marketing: A Strategic Approach* (Mason, OH: Cengage Learning), pp. 9–11.

5. Brito, Michael (2013). Hootsuite, "Your Content Strategy: Defining Paid, Owned and Earned Media." Retrieved August 17, 2015, from http://blog.hootsuite.com/converged-media-brito-part-1/

6. (n.d.). Statista, "Leading Social Networks Worldwide as of August 2015, Ranked by Number of Active Users (in Millions)." Retrieved August 17, 2015, from http://www.statista.com/statistics/272014/global-social-networks-ranked-by-number-of-users/

7. Stelzner, Michael A. (May 2015). Social Media Examiner, "2015 Social Media Marketing Industry Report," p. 29. Retrieved August 16, 2015, from http://www.socialmediaexaminer.com/social-media-marketing-industry-report-2015/

8. Smith, Aaron (April 3, 2014). Pew Research Center, "Usage and Adoption." Retrieved August 21, 2015, from http://www.pewinternet.org/2014/04/03/usage-and-adoption/

9. (August 19, 2015). "Charts, Mobile Social Media Consumption Grows across Age Groups." Retrieved August 20, 2015, from http://www.marketingcharts.com/online/mobile-social-media-consumption-grows-across-age-groups-58224/?utm_campaign=newsletter&utm_source=mc&utm_medium=headline

10. Stelzner, Michael A. (May 2015). Social Media Examiner, "2015 Social Media Marketing Industry Report," p. 19. Retrieved August 16, 2015, from http://www.socialmediaexaminer.com/social-media-marketing-industry-report-2015/

11. Alfaro, Lyanne (August 20, 2015). *Business Insider*, "Your $220 Million to the ALS Ice Bucket Challenge Made a Difference, Study Results Show." Retrieved August 21, 2015, from http://www.businessinsider.com/your-220-million-to-the-als-bucket-challenge-made-a-difference-2015-8

12. Martin, James A. (March 25, 2015). *CIO*, "12 Standout Social Media Success Stories." Retrieved August 21, 2015, from http://www.cio.com/article/2901047/social-media/12-standout-social-media-success-stories.html#slide11

13. Ledbetter, Carly (June 17, 2015). *Huffington Post*, "The Taco Emojo Is HERE, People," Retrieved August 21, 2015, from http://www.huffingtonpost.com/2015/06/17/taco-emoji-here-finally-sort-of_n_7604410.html

14. Stelzner, Michael A. (May 2015). Social Media Examiner, "2015 Social Media Marketing Industry Report," p. 18. Retrieved August 16, 2015, from http://www.socialmediaexaminer.com/social-media-marketing-industry-report-2015/

15. Bailey, Jeff (February 19, 2007). "JetBlue's C.E.O. Is 'Mortified' after Fliers Are Stranded," *The New York Times*. Retrieved October 31, 2011, from http://www.nytimes.com/2007/02/19/business/19jetblue.html?pagewanted=all

16. Goolpacy, Peter F. (n.d.). "The Perfect JetBlue Apology," PerfectApology.com. Retrieved October 31, 2011, from http://www.perfectapology.com/jetblue-apology.html

17. McNaughton Marissa (August 12, 2010). "JetBlue Case Study: Social Media, with Emphasis on the Social (Part 1 of 4)," The Realtime Report. Retrieved October 31, 2011, from http://therealtimereport.com/2010/08/12/social-media-with-emphasis-on-the-social-1/

18. Wasserman, Todd (June 1, 2011). "How JetBlue's Social Media Strategy Took Flight," Mashable. Retrieved October 31, 2011, from http://mashable.com/2011/06/01/jetblue-social-media-success/

19. (n.d.). https://twitter.com/JetBlue

20. Barker, Melissa S., Donald I. Barker, Nicholas F. Bormann, Krista E. Neher (2008). *Social Media Marketing: A Strategic Approach* (Mason, OH: Cengage Learning), pp. 18–20.

21. (May 13, 2015). J.D. Power, "Airlines: A Transportation or Hospitality Business?" Retrieved August 26, 2015, from http://www.jdpower.com/press-releases/2015-north-america-airline-satisfaction-study

22. (March 19, 2015). "JetBlue and Southwest Lead Airlines in Customer Experience." Retrieved August 26, 2015, from https://experiencematters.wordpress.com/2015/03/19/jetblue-and-southwest-lead-airlines-in-customer-experience/

23. Kolowich, Lindsay (July 28, 2014). HubSpot, "Delighting People in 140 Characters: An Inside Look at JetBlue's Customer Service Success." Retrieved August 26, 2015, from http://blog.hubspot.com/marketing/jetblue-customer-service-twitter

24. (n.d.). Statista, "Percentage of U.S. Population with a Social Network Profile 2008 to 2015." Retrieved August 26, 2015, from http://www.statista.com/statistics/273476/percentage-of-us-population-with-a-social-network-profile/

25. (August 14, 2015). YouTube, "Domino's TV Commercial 2015—Domino's AnyWare Party." Retrieved August 26, 2015, from https://www.youtube.com/watch?v=ZdyOI7m3hwo

26. Wohl, Jessica (August 14, 2015). *Advertising Age*, "Celebs Click, Text, Tweet and Tap to Order Domino's." Retrieved August 26, 2015, from http://adage.com/article/cmo-strategy/celebs-click-text-tweet-tap-order-domino-s/299965/

27. White, Sarah (January 6, 2015). Monster, "Top 6 Entry-Level Social Tech Jobs." Retrieved August 24, 2015, from http://www.monster.com/technology/a/Entry-Level-Social-Media-Jobs

28. Life, Brazen (January 13, 2014). AOL Jobs, "6 Social Media Jobs That Will Be Big in 2014." Retrieved August 24, 2015, from http://jobs.aol.com/articles/2014/01/13/6-social-media-jobs-that-will-be-big-in-2014/

29. Doyle, Alison (n.d.). About Careers, "Social Media Job Titles." Retrieved August 26, 2015, from http://jobsearch.about.com/od/job-title-samples/a/social-media-job-titles.htm

30. (February 17, 2015). DigitalGurus, "How To Get a Job in Social Media." Retrieved August 26, 2015, from http://wersm.com/how-to-get-a-job-in-social-media/

31. Boyd, Carla (October 23, 2013). DigitalGurus, "Dos and Don'ts—A Guide to Using Social Media While Job Hunting." Retrieved August 26, 2015, from http://www.digitalgurus.co.uk/blog/dos-and-donts-guide-using-social-media-while-job-hunting

32. Odden, Lee (July 2009). TopRank Blog, "Best and Worst Practices Social Media Marketing." Retrieved August 23, 2015, from http://www.toprankblog.com/2009/02/best-worst-practices-social-media-marketing/

Goals and Strategies

The single most important action a social media marketer can take to increase SMM success is to create a well-thought out SMM plan with carefully crafted objectives. A major reason for the failure of SMM programs is lack of a good plan.

After completing this chapter, students will be able to:

- Define a social media plan
- Explain the SMM planning cycle
- Describe each step in the SMM planning cycle
- Identify ways to listen and observe the social web
- Describe the Valid Metrics Framework and its role in setting SMM objectives
- Explain how to create social media strategies

(Continued)

Beginning with this chapter, the remainder of the book will focus on the steps necessary to create an effective SMM plan. Two of the most important steps in this planning process are goal setting and strategy determination. Before moving forward with SMM activities, an organization should first determine what it wants to accomplish and then how best to do it. Without goals, it will be unclear in which direction to go or how to ultimately measure success. With a well-defined destination in mind, appropriate strategies can be designed to achieve these goals. As such, the process of setting goals and determining strategies is crucial for success in the field of SMM.

What Is a SMM Plan?

A SMM plan details an organization's social media goals and the actions necessary to achieve them. Key among these actions is the understanding of corporate and marketing strategies and the creation of promotional strategies. Without integrated strategies and solid SMM plans there is little chance of successfully executing SMM.

- Detail how to link social media goals to actions
- Explain the importance of word of mouth as advocacy in SMM
- Identify best practices in developing social media strategies

SMM Planning Cycle

Creating a social media plan is a continuous process, as illustrated by the SMM Planning Cycle in Figure 2.1. Skilled social media marketers constantly monitor the progress of the plan's action elements, modify them to improve results, and test alternative approaches. It is important to methodically carry out all of the steps in Figure 2.1 when constructing a social media plan (Chapter 15 will demonstrate how to use these steps to build a SMM plan).

Figure 2.1 Social Media Planning Cycle

THE SMM PLANNING CYCLE

- **Listening** to what people are saying about a company or brand enables the organization to determine its current social media presence, which in turn guides the setting of social media goals and strategies to achieve them. Another important reason to listen to the social web is for competitive intelligence (i.e., information about what people are saying about competitors and what the competitors are saying about themselves). Listening also reveals the way in which people talk about products and brands, including specific words that are used. It is critical to find out what people are already talking about before becoming part of the conversation.

- **Setting goals** involves conducting an analysis to determine an organization's strengths and weaknesses and the opportunities and threats in the competitive environment (SWOT). Often a competitive analysis is performed of the strengths and weaknesses of key competitors. By performing these appraisals, marketers can then choose the social media goals that satisfy unmet needs of consumers, capitalize on the strengths of the company and seize opportunities, while minimizing organizational weaknesses and external threats. Threats come not only from competitors but also from advances in technology, industry trends, and general economic conditions.

- **Defining strategies** must be done on a case-by-case basis, using all available pertinent information. The "8 Cs of Strategy Development" (covered later in this chapter) provide guidelines to help an organization reach its marketing goals. These suggestions are intended as broad guidance for marketers and must be adjusted to each organization's unique strengths, weaknesses, opportunities, and threats.

- **Identifying the target audience (market)** is done by pinpointing the location, behavior, tastes, and needs of the target audience. Choosing the appropriate target audience requires an understanding of the market segments served. In most cases the SMM plan will target one or more of the available segments, not all. Careful choice of target audience for a SMM campaign enables a company to organize its marketing strategies to efficiently reach those most receptive and likely to become customers and even brand advocates.

- **Selecting tools** Social media marketing has spawned a plethora of tools to assist with virtually every other activity in the planning cycle. There are tools to schedule posts on various social networks, tools to track brand mentions or hashtag usage, tools to help prepare images for posting, tools to assist with search engine optimization (SEO), tools to shorten links—and so on. Some are single purpose tools—shortening links, for example. Others incorporate multiple activities as when a tool to shorten links is incorporated into a tool for posting on multiple networks. Tools have become essential to navigate the complex world of SMM and Chapter 14 is devoted to a discussion of tools and their uses.

- **Selecting platforms and channels** identifies the paths on the web by which content will be transmitted to the target audience. Social media platforms are generally understood to be the websites on which social media communications take place. Social networks like Facebook and Twitter and blog publishing sites like Blogger and WordPress are only a few of the many examples. Channels are broader entities, composed of multiple platforms and other technologies. For example, mobile is generally considered to be a channel made up of various elements like mobile websites, apps, and telecommunications services.

- **Implementing** is the process whereby the goals, strategies, target market, and platforms are taken into consideration in creating actionable social media platform-specific marketing tactics. Executing well-defined tactics makes it possible for an organization to implement its general social media strategies across multiple social media platforms and realize the company's marketing goals.

- **Monitoring** is the process of tracking, measuring, and evaluating an organization's SMM initiatives. Monitoring the enormous number of communications—daily, hourly, and minute-by-minute—is a formidable task. Monitoring is the subject of Chapter 13 and tools are the subject of Chapter 14.

- **Tuning** is the constant and continuous process of adjusting and improving the elements of the plan and its implementation to maximize the chances of success.

The book is structured around this social media planning model. Listening, setting goals, and defining strategies are explained in detail later in this chapter. Chapter 3 covers identifying the target audience. Chapters 5 through 12 discuss platforms and implementation, providing guidance regarding the execution of strategies and social media platform-specific marketing tactics. However, it is first necessary to lay a foundation for learning how to successfully execute these platform-specific marketing tactics, which is why Chapter 4 presents the Rules of Engagement for participating on the social web.[1] Chapter 14 discusses the importance of social media tools and gives examples of currently-popular ones. Monitoring the progress of SMM is explored in Chapter 13. Finally, Chapter 15 puts it all together, by presenting an example of a SMM plan, with special emphasis on the constant and continuous need to tune, adjust, and improve the plan and its implementation.

Listen and Observe: Five Stages

Before jumping into SMM, it is important to observe the surroundings, and consider the target audience as well as the social landscape in general. During the listening and observing stage, marketers should follow conversations about a particular brand and company, its competitors, and the relevant industry on as many social media platforms as possible. This procedure will not only gauge the overall tone of the communities, but more important, it will identify where the organization's target audience hangs out and what they are doing there.

STAGE #1: LISTEN TO CONVERSATIONS ABOUT A BRAND OR COMPANY

The first stage is listening to and observing conversations about a particular company. As advised by Brian Solis in a post for the Harvard Business Review blog, "[l]isten to the conversations that are already taking place" and "[p]ay attention to the nuances of these conversations."[2] What are people saying about this brand? What good and bad comments have been made? How do people feel about the company? Listen to the conversations taking place on blogs, Twitter, discussion forums, website, LinkedIn, Facebook, and so on, to understand how the company is perceived. Both positive and negative remarks can show where opportunities may lie. In addition, knowing what consumers are already saying will help in preparing responses for common questions or problems. Anticipating areas to address, and understanding the way consumers talk about them, will provide an advantage when entering into SMM.

STAGE #2: LISTEN TO WHAT PEOPLE SAY ABOUT THE COMPETITORS

Next, listen to what people say about a company's competitors, and what those competitors are saying about themselves. How do people perceive the pros and cons of the competitors in the social space? How do these comments influence business opportunities? In addition to listening to how people feel about competitors, it is helpful to identify the most *competitive areas* of the social media landscape. What are the competitors doing on social media? Who are they targeting? What seems to work? Assessing the competitive landscape on social media sites will show how buyers are meeting sellers on social media and may provide insights that can be leveraged when later building a strategy. Learning from others' social media approaches will help build a powerful strategy quickly while refining it to suit different needs.

STAGE #3: LISTENING TO WHAT PEOPLE SAY ABOUT THE INDUSTRY OR CATEGORY

After observing the competition, begin listening on a broader scale: the overall industry. What are consumers (or potential consumers or members of the target audience) saying about the industry? Is the sentiment strongly positive or negative surrounding certain issues? What conversations occur between firms in the industry? Does this create opportunities? Understanding the conversations taking place around a certain industry will help gauge what people are interested in and frequently talk about. We will discuss content in Chapters 7 and 11, but it is important to remember that social media content must connect with consumers on an issue they are passionate about (which typically is not a particular brand). Listening at the category or industry level will help one understand what the consumers in that industry are really interested in talking about.

Blake Chandlee, Vice President of Global Partnerships at Facebook calls this "chatter data" to distinguish it from quantitative data. In an interview with the *Sloan Management Review* he says, "Chatter data is what people are talking about when they're watching television or when they're watching a sporting event," he continued. "What kind of reaction are they having? Are brand mentions included? How are brands representing themselves in that kind of chatter? What kind of, say, hair color? That might affect a hair care company." The data can be used to help brands like Procter & Gamble and Unilever better understand their hair care customers. However, he warns that "privacy will always be the primary underlying consideration, which everybody has to consider because the consumer backlash if they find you using their data inappropriately is significant and quick."[3]

STAGE #4: LISTENING FOR THE TONE OF THE COMMUNITY

The next stage is to observe the tone of the community. Essentially, this means observing how your consumers naturally interact with each other on social sites. What technical jargon, acronyms, or slang do they use? How do they interact with each other? What words are most often used to describe specific brands, competitors, or industries? How are brands participating, and who is getting the most attention? What are the unwritten rules of participation? How do they talk, and what are they interested in? When engaging in social media, it is good to fit in and sound like other consumers. To accomplish this, it is essential to first know how relevant social media users communicate with each other and the etiquette of communicating on different social sites. This knowledge will facilitate integration and participation in the community.

STAGE #5: LISTENING TO DIFFERENT SOCIAL MEDIA PLATFORMS AND CHANNELS

Finally, when listening to social media, be sure to access multiple social media channels to identify where target audiences hang out and what they do there. The participants on Facebook may be dramatically different from those on Twitter, LinkedIn, or blogs. Each social media channel has a distinctive audience (target market) with unique interests, behaviors, and characteristics (Chapter 3 explores this topic in depth). For example, according to the Pew Foundation in 2014 more than half of all online users 65 and over used Facebook while half of young adult Internet users (18–29) used Instagram. Pinterest was dominated by women and half of all users of LinkedIn had college educations.[4] Since the users on each site and the social networking structure are different, it is important to listen to conversations across a variety of social media channels.

Listening and observing is the key first step in the social media planning stage. Time spent observing will pay off when planning the rest of the social media strategy and will help avoid an embarrassing faux pas along the way. Like all the rest of SMM listening has become a complex task and an organizational entity called either a listening center or a command post is often used to manage the complexity.

Listening as Part of Personal Branding Strategy

Personal branding experts agree that, just as listening is the first step in developing a corporate brand, it is equally important as you go about developing your personal brand. It is especially important to listen to relevant conversations, to understand the tone of the community, and to understand which social media platforms and channels are being used.

This comparison, though, begs an important question. How do you know what is relevant, how do you identify the appropriate community?

The answer is that your brand is YOU! It is up to you to decide how you want to be perceived as your career develops. Put another way, you have to define the outcome before you create the process of getting there. That outcome is your personal branding statement.[1]

Consultant Megan Marrs shows the way to develop what she calls an outcome statement to guide your personal branding efforts.

Lesson #1. Be honest about the nature of your appeal to others. How does your personality impact the experience others have with you? What sort of emotional reactions do you arouse in others?

Lesson #2. You must condense your offering into a sentence or a phrase that captures its essence. That is hard to do; even harder to do well. You may be surprised at these personal mission statements published by Fast Company:

- Denise Morrison, CEO of Campbell Soup Company

  "To serve as a leader, live a balanced life, and apply ethical principles to make a significant difference."

- Sir Richard Branson, founder of The Virgin Group

  "To have fun in [my] journey through life and learn from [my] mistakes."

- Oprah Winfrey, founder of OWN, the Oprah Winfrey Network

  "To be a teacher. And to be known for inspiring my students to be more than they thought they could be."[2]

Lesson #3. Be clear about your personal goals in the industry or in your chosen profession. Do you intend to be the CEO of a financial services company? Do you aspire to be a recognized leader in SMM who has several respected publishing channels? What is it that you really want to be or do?

Lesson #4. Make this all come together into a personal mantra. Oprah Winfrey might say, for example, "to inspire people to be more than they thought they could be."

Lesson #5. Your personal brand cannot describe some mythical creature. It must be authentically you. It must be capable of inspiring trust and credibility. If your personal brand is not authentic, nothing else you do matters.

---

[1]Schawbel, Dan (September 23, 2014), "Why You Need to Start With the End in Mind." Retrieved on January 22, 2015 from http://danschawbel.com/blog/why-you-need-to-start-with-the-end-in-mind/

[2](February 25, 2014), "Why You Should Write a Personal Mission Statement and 5 CEOs Who Did." Retrieved on May 9, 2015 from http://www.fastcompany.com/3026791/dialed/personal-mission-statements-of-5-famous-ceos-and-why-you-should-write-one-too#1

PR guru Chris Penn puts the issue more succinctly. He says that you must "distill your essential quality," the quality that makes you and your work unique.[3]

However you develop it, your personal branding statement tells you where to begin listening. What subjects would you identify as keywords for the "inspiring others" example? If you want to become a CEO in financial services, what keywords would you pick? In either case, how would you identify a few people to follow, say on Twitter? In fact, how would you determine the best social platforms on which to follow your role models? How would you understand the tone of the conversations you are following?

In personal branding, as in all other aspects of SMM, thoughtful listening is the first step!

[3]Penn, Cristopher S. (n.d.), "The Reason Why Your Personal Brand Sucks." Retrieved on January 22, 2015 from http://www.christopherspenn.com/2010/02/the-reason-why-your-personal-brand-sucks/

Listen and Observe: Listening Centers

Facebook and Twitter are generally one and two on the list of social media networks most used by marketers. In late 2014 Facebook had 1.35 *billion* active accounts.[5] Those Facebook users shared almost 2.5 million pieces of content per *minute*. During that same minute Twitter users tweeted almost 300,000 times.[6] Obviously these are only two networks so the total number of communications per minute, hour, day, and so on simply boggles the mind.

How does a marketer even find the relevant messages, much less identify the important ones and respond if necessary? Many tools have been developed just to aid in the gargantuan task of listening and responding. The tools themselves are the subject of Chapter 14. While we are on the subject of strategic listening, however, we should introduce the concept of listening centers. Dell established one of the first permanent social media command posts in 2010. Since then many other corporations have done the same. Social media listening centers have also become an important part of major events.

THE NATIONAL FOOTBALL LEAGUE LISTENS TO SUPER BOWL CONVERSATIONS

The National Football League (NFL) established an early social media listening center for Super Bowl XLVI in 2012. The contenders in that game were the New York Giants with 1.5 million Facebook fans and the New England Patriots with almost 3 million. That insured a high volume of social media activity, which was monitored by a team of over 20 "strategists, analysts and techies", according to Mashable. The team began monitoring fan conversations on the Monday before the game and served the 150,000 attendees by tweeting everything from parking directions to information about Indianapolis' attractions.[7] Host committee communications manager Taulbee Jackson declared the activity an "enormous success." He says, "It had a direct reach of about 49,000 people in the Indianapolis area over Facebook, Twitter, Foursquare and YouTube. Overall, the command center delivered some 1.8 million online impressions each day for the Indianapolis host committee."[8,9]

Fast forward to February 2015 and a bigger-than-ever social media presence for Super Bowl XLIX. The NFL again had a social media command center and many brands had their own. In fact, Budweiser, a perennial Super Bowl ad favorite, had four listening centers spread across the country. Nissan, who was returning after a long Super Bowl hiatus, had two.[10] The listening centers must have been busy, because it was the most social Super Bowl thus far and the traffic was huge.[11]

Super Bowl XLIX was the most-watched game ever with 114.4 million viewers. As many as 1.3 million viewers were streaming the game during crucial moments. It was also the most-tweeted game ever, with 28.4 million game-related tweets sent during the telecast.[12]

In fact, one blog declared mobile the big winner in the game. That verdict was partly based on the fact that the three game apps that bought TV ads experienced a huge increase in download activity after their ad was broadcast. It also reflects the traditional skepticism of digital marketers, who have measures of engagement, about traditional broadcast advertising. Traditional advertising finds it hard to demonstrate advertising return on investment (ROI) or even the type of audience engagement documented in Figure 2.2. Traditional advertising also lacks a mechanism for listening.

Facebook offered advertisers a targeted Super Bowl audience based on listening data. According to Ad Age, "People who post something Super Bowl-related will be added to an audience pool—and the aggregated data will be anonymized—alongside the more than 50 million people who interacted with Super Bowl-related content on Facebook last year. Advertisers will be able to buy ads against Facebook's Super Bowl audience leading up to and during the Super Bowl." The targeting data was expected to be updated in almost real time during the game.[13]

The performance of the targeted ads was not disclosed. However, Facebook reported that over 65 million worldwide "joined the conversation," posting, commenting, and

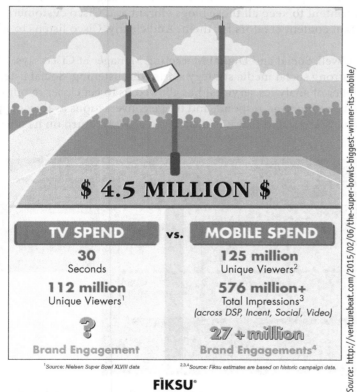

Source: http://venturebeat.com/2015/02/06/the-super-bowls-biggest-winner-its-mobile/

Figure 2.2 Traditional versus Social Media in the 2015 Super Bowl

liking game-related content while it was going on. They posted an animated timeline that showed activity by state at some key moments and revealed that the top three audience categories for game-related content were all women![14]

CISCO DEMONSTRATES THE IMPORTANCE OF SOCIAL MEDIA LISTENING IN B2B MARKETING

Corporate listening centers are permanent installations that can have an important impact on the corporate brand or brands. The center introduced by B2B marketer Cisco in 2012 was described as state of the art and used Cisco's own technology plus an outside supplier for analytics services. The heart of the center is 6 touch screens as shown in Figure 2.3. According to the Cisco Digital and Social Blog they are listening to:

- "Social Media Customer Engagement. Highlighting CiscoLive conversations and engagement

- Twitter-based global heat map. Where? Real-time global tweets are displayed

- Social Media Influencers. Who? What influencers are tweeting about Cisco

- Product Family Landscape. What conversations are happening around both Collaboration and the Data Center and Virtualization architectures

- Social Media Word Cloud Highlighting current trending topics"[15]

Blogs are an important part of the conversation for many marketers. An examination of the Cisco site in 2014 shows around 50 blogs arranged by subjects including technology, industries, and countries and regions. The U.S. blogs feature the Cisco Social Rewards box shown in Figure 2.3. Viewers are invited to become guest bloggers in areas of their expertise and to earn a variety of badges for their participation. It takes a lot of content to keep all those blogs vibrant and Cisco customers and partners are important content creators for them. And clearly, Cisco listens to what the bloggers say.

Charlie Treadwell, Social and Digital Marketing Manager at Cisco says, "The foundation of a strong social media strategy starts with listening. Social listening with Radian6 [a supplier of analytics services] has allowed us to get closer to our customers and focus on how we monitor, respond, and triage conversations as they happen across our organization." Cisco stated that it had achieved a 281% return on its investment

Source: http://blogs.cisco.com/

Figure 2.3   **Touch Screens in Cisco Listening Center and the Social Rewards Invitation**

in social media listening in four key business areas: more creative use of services to achieve industry thought leadership, increased productivity for employees who are able to access relevant content wherever they are, reduced expenditure on marketing research, and increased profit by uncovering sales opportunities that might have otherwise been missed.[16]

Setting Goals and Objectives

The Cisco example shows that listening to a wide range of social media sites and observing the location, behavior, tastes, and needs of the target audience is key to successful SMM. It helps marketers set optimal goals and determine the most suitable strategies to achieve them.

It is important to keep in mind that goals must be flexible in the light of new developments while engaging in social media. Sometimes, unintended benefits from social media engagement are discovered. For example, after Vistaprint, an online printing company, got started on social media, they noticed that many people were seeking customer support through Twitter. In reaction the company engaged its customer service department, connecting that department to questions from Twitter so that service professionals could respond directly to the tweets. This recognition of customer needs allowed faster service for customers needing assistance and also resulted in cost savings to the firm through reduced phone time spent on customer support.

Customer service is one of a handful of key objectives that marketers often adopt. According to a Forrester survey, the most popular business objectives for social media include brand awareness, building brand preference, acquisition of new customer leads or sales, loyalty programs to retain current customers, and providing customer service (Figure 2.4).[17] Social Media Examiner's 2014 industry survey adds that marketers find that their social media activities also resulted in increased market insight, improved search rankings, better business partnerships, and lower marketing costs.[18]

Accomplishments like increased market insight, improving business partnerships, and even lower marketing costs may seem to be reasonable outcomes of SMM. You may, however, question what search ranking is doing in that list and wonder if there are other potential benefits that are not listed.

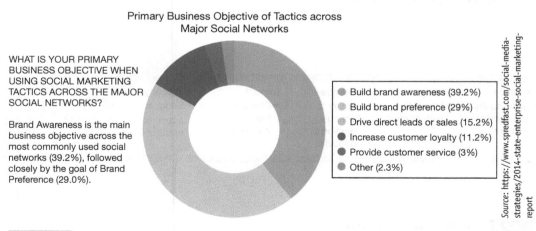

Primary Business Objective of Tactics across Major Social Networks

WHAT IS YOUR PRIMARY BUSINESS OBJECTIVE WHEN USING SOCIAL MARKETING TACTICS ACROSS THE MAJOR SOCIAL NETWORKS?

Brand Awareness is the main business objective across the most commonly used social networks (39.2%), followed closely by the goal of Brand Preference (29.0%).

- Build brand awareness (39.2%)
- Build brand preference (29%)
- Drive direct leads or sales (15.2%)
- Increase customer loyalty (11.2%)
- Provide customer service (3%)
- Other (2.3%)

Figure 2.4 Why Marketers Use Social Media Marketing

Search ranking has changed significantly since the early days of the Internet. Gone are the days when a few well-chosen keywords and a large number of inbound links would guarantee a high ranking on search engine results pages (SERPs). What has caused the change? Social media!

The myriad details of SEO are beyond the scope of this discussion, but the oft-repeated slogan that "content is king" sums it up. The 2014 SearchMetrics study found that two new content-related ranking factors, relevant terms (first) and proof terms (twelfth) were high on their list of the factors most highly correlated with a high search rank. Links remain important in terms of quantity and especially in terms of quality. Of the ten most important ranking factors *seven* were social signals. They ranged from Google +1s (second) to Tweets (tenth).[19]

In addition to the primary SMM objectives shown in Figure 2.4 there are other objectives that can be secondary in SMM campaigns. Some that are frequently alluded to include:

- Achieving a desired brand positioning

- Producing new product ideas

- Being prepared to handle reputation management in a crisis

- Supporting public relations and advertising campaigns.

This discussion suggests that there are more "benefits" from SMM than just the primary objectives would suggest. If there are many objectives that are possible in SMM campaigns, how does the marketer go about choosing a relatively small set for a specific SMM campaign? The answer, of course, is to think about what the business needs to accomplish. While true, that still does not provide specific guidance for developing campaign objectives.

WHERE DO ACTUAL OBJECTIVES COME FROM?

Setting Social Media Marketing Objectives. There is beginning to be some agreement about the types of objectives that are appropriate for SMM although many marketers still have their own favorite variant of the ones shown in Figure 2.5. This concept was developed by AMEC, an international communications association, after a review of the many conceptual frameworks currently found in SMM.[20] It represents a strong framework for understanding SMM objectives and the metrics associated with them, which will be discussed in Chapter 13.

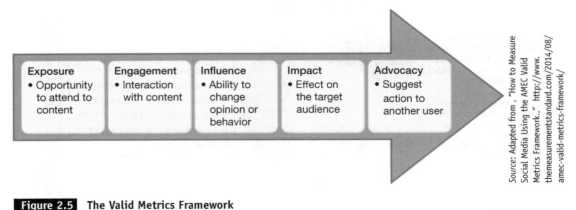

Figure 2.5 The Valid Metrics Framework

Some of the generic terms are familiar in advertising or other communications disciplines. Some have gained prominence as we attempt to understand the workings of SMM. The generic concepts are:

- Exposure is the opportunity to see and/or hear a piece of content in any channel. This is the broad definition of exposure. It does not mean that a viewer has paid any attention to or has comprehended any part of the content. It simply means he had the opportunity to do so. Exposure is a term long used in advertising.

- Engagement is a term popularized by social media marketers and its exact definition is hotly debated. It is most often measured as some variant of time spent on the piece of content. However, definitions vary widely so you are advised to look for the definition any time you use an engagement statistic.

- Influence is a reasonably intuitive term that describes the ability to affect attitudes and behavior. The topic influence in social media is so important that special tools have been developed to measure it. Klout is one well-known tool, but there are others that also have their adherents.

- Impact is also used in a reasonably common manner: how does a SMM activity affect business results? Specifically, how does it affect the attainment of goals? The impact marketers would most like to measure is the Return on Promotional Investment (ROPI). That is difficult to do, as we will discuss in Chapter 14.

- Advocacy is a term long used in traditional promotion, especially in the attempt to understand the effect of word of mouth (WOM). Communications studies have long demonstrated that various topics have identifiable opinion leaders and that these opinion leaders do have an influence on followers. The topic of advocacy has become especially important in SMM where marketers can make specific attempts to locate or to create advocates and can measure the extent of their success.

This is a progression that may parallel the purchase journey itself. A person must first be exposed to a communication before she can become in any way involved with it or be affected by it. If the communication has an effect, it may result in a behavior. If a person engages in a behavior and the results are satisfactory, the person may choose to share it with others. That describes the chain of events that social media marketers are trying to stimulate.

The terms that make up the Valid Metrics Framework, however, are not necessarily used in the objectives themselves. The framework represents a useful way of thinking about the type of objectives that are appropriate for a given stage in SMM efforts, but marketers must dig deeper to come up with the specific objectives for a campaign.

Campaign-Specific and Platform-Specific Social Media Marketing Objectives. It helps to understand objectives as a cascade (Figure 2.6). Overall business goals are the basis for objective setting at any level of the organization. Corporate business goals, however, are broad—driven by the vision and mission of the business. After the vision and mission statements have been created, actual objectives are generally financial in nature. They cover at least a year; in some instances longer time frames are used. Corporate goals allow all business functions, including marketing, to understand what they need to accomplish in order to fulfill their role in achieving the business objectives.

In a similar fashion marketing objectives, usually stated in terms of sales or market share, point the way for all marketing functions including SMM. Marketing objectives are generally part of an annual marketing plan and consequently have a time frame of 1 year.

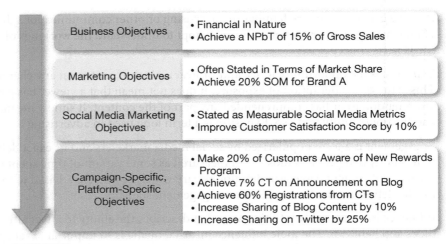

Figure 2.6 The Objectives Cascade for Social Media Marketing Objectives

Social media marketing objectives can be stated as goals to be achieved over a similar planning period of perhaps a year. Often, however, they are stated for a specific campaign, for example, one to introduce a new loyalty program or another to increase sharing of content on one of the business' platforms. Within a campaign more than one platform is often used and there should be specific communications objectives for each platform. For example, a campaign to increase sharing of blog posts might want to encourage sharing posts via Twitter and have an objective of increasing retweets of blog material by 25%.

Notice that none of the objectives have any information about how they are to be accomplished. They are goals only. The "how to" is the topic of the Action Plan section which follows in the formal marketing plan.

There is something missing, however—the issue of time frame that should be explicitly stated as part of the objective. A brand may choose to run a new customer acquisition program during one time frame or on a particular platform and a customer loyalty and retention campaign during another time frame or on another platform. The two campaigns need to be planned and evaluated separately. That is one reason why it is wise to choose a limited number of goals for a single campaign. For example, it is hard to see how customer acquisition and customer loyalty goals could receive equal attention in a single campaign. Regardless of how many objectives are chosen for a specific campaign, having a clear idea of the goal is critical to the success of a social media campaign.

There is a standard for judging the quality of goals and objectives at any level. It is the SMART acronym, popular in many aspects of the quality management discipline. All objectives should be judged by the following criteria:

S pecific
M easurable
A chieveable
R ealistic
T ime delimited

Social media marketing campaigns vary in duration, so it is especially important to specify the time frame for each objective.

This discussion shows that SMM has very specific objectives that are part of the marketing, and hence of the business, goals of the organization. The implication is that strategy is a vague term when used in the context of promotion, including SMM. It does not imply the creation of economic value like it does when discussing corporate strategy. Marketing campaigns, however, can be said to have strategies that give them direction.

Determining Strategies

There are some key considerations when setting SMM strategies.

WHAT ARE THE OVERALL GOALS?

Look at the mission and general marketing goals of the organization when creating SMM strategies. Social media marketing should not be an isolated part of the marketing strategy; rather, it should link into a broader marketing plan. The building of SMM strategies that support the overall strategic goals of a company will also make it easier for the strategies to win support within the company.

WHAT WAS LEARNED FROM LISTENING?

The listening stage should have unearthed information about the company, its target audience, competitors, and the industry as a whole. Marketers should be able to answer the following questions:

- How do people feel about a company, product, service, person, or issue?

- How are competitors using social media platforms?

- Which media platforms appear to be the most viable in order to achieve SMM goals?

- Where does a company's target audience hang out, and what do they do there?

- How can this information be used to identify strategic opportunities?

WHAT BEST PRACTICES CAN BE APPLIED?

This book offers a variety of best practices and case studies showing how to apply SMM for the building and expanding of an organization's presence. Best-in-class examples of SMM can inspire future SMM plans. Look to best-in-class examples, even from firms outside the specific industry you are interested in, to help shape marketing goals and strategies.

GOALS MAY CHANGE . . . BE FLEXIBLE

The social media planning model is a fluid circle; it is flexible and adaptive. After gaining experience in social media, measuring the results may lead to a change in goals or strategies. For example, customers may primarily want to use Twitter for customer service, or perhaps most existing customers are only active on Facebook. Be open to adaptation, as social media may work in unanticipated ways.

Whatever the specific platforms and tactics used, social media strategy can best be described as a broad statement of what marketers want to achieve for the brand in social media. When SMM is described as strategic it implies that all actions are taken with a goal in mind. They are not simply random tweets or use of a platform because it is currently popular.

THE EIGHT C'S OF STRATEGY DEVELOPMENT

1. Categorize social media platforms by target market relevancy.

2. Comprehend the rules of the road on the platform by listening and learning how to behave, successfully spark conversation, and engage the participants.

3. Converse by acknowledging and responding to other users of the platform, always remembering to be a contributor, not a promoter.

4. Collaborate with platform members as a means of establishing a mutually beneficial relationship with the platform participants.

5. Contribute content to build reputation and become a valued member, helping to improve the community.

6. Connect with the influencers so that you can enlist them to help shape opinions about your product or service.

7. Community participation (and creation) can elicit valuable consumer suggestions for improving products and services.

8. Convert relationships built in social media to the behaviors specified in the objectives.

Linking Goals with a Call to Action

Once clear marketing goals are established, it is important to link those goals to a call to action. This process will help design and measure social media campaigns more effectively. In order to measure success, you need to clearly define what someone's desired action would be—your "call to action." With a clear and measurable call to action, it's possible to measure actual conversions due to a SMM campaign.

A call to action is simply the behavior you want the potential customer to exhibit at each stage of your marketing campaign. There may be different calls to action for each aspect of an Internet marketing or social media strategy. For example, the goal may be to get blog readers subscribed to an email newsletter or webinar, so the call to action for webinar listeners may be for them to sign up. Following this, there may be a series of calls to action that increase the engagement level with the consumer, earning the right to ask for more information and eventually to close a sale.

Your call to action should flow naturally from your marketing goals. Table 2.1 shows some examples of calls to action based on different marketing strategies.

Marketing goal	Call to action
Lead generation	Sign up for webinar
	Call for consultation
	Complete form for consultation
Brand building	Watch video
	Click on links
	Read content
	Fan/friend/follow brand
	Sign up for newsletter

Table 2.1 Marketing Goals and Lead Generation

Getting to the sale is the final step in a chain of actions. For example, one chain of actions leading to a sale may be:

- Click on blog post from Twitter or Facebook

- Sign up for email newsletter

- Sign up for webinar (collect lead scoring and contact information)

- Have salesperson call

- Purchase

- Convert the customer to a brand advocate

In each instance, the goal is to increase the level of interaction and engagement through small, incremental steps. Although the ultimate desired action is probably to generate a sale, the best way to get there involves intermediate steps that *end* in selling the product. It is also important that the call to action be integrated firmly with the actual content being provided. A call to action that seems artificial, forced, or overly aggressive is less likely to be successful. As author and CEO Sunita Biddu notes, "[b]eginning and nonprofessional writers often think that throwing in a few standard selling phrases will accomplish the call to action. The truth is that the call to action must be an extension and continuation of the entire marketing piece. If you have not convinced the potential buyer of the value of your product or service before they get to the call to action, it will not work."[21]

At every stage, the call to action must implicitly answer the consumer's question, "what's in it for me?"

Why should someone click on a link, give an email address, or sign up for a consultation? Having an effective call to action at every stage means answering these questions in advance. As one online entrepreneur claims, "[t]he whole point of using this very specific marketing design is to make sure that wherever on your site your visitor is, you are getting them closer to do what you want them to do."[22] Effective social media marketers should already have some idea what their audience's goals, motivations, and communication preferences are (through the listening process). A strong call to action will put that knowledge to work, by designing a compelling message that keeps consumers engaged and coming back for more.

Self-Promotion vs. Building an Army of Advocates

A final strategy point to consider when building a social media plan is the value of building an "army" of passionate brand defenders, advocates, and enthusiasts. Creating advocates is the final element in the Valid Metrics Framework. Advocacy goes beyond focusing social media efforts around brands themselves and simply publishing content about the brand. It is a more complex concept than simply measuring social media "success" based on the number of followers or mentions.

While social media can be a platform for businesses to share their content, it can become even more valuable by building the number of people who are passionate about a business and requesting them to create content or to share it. These brand advocates will talk to their friends—not because of a contest or prize—but because they are truly passionate about a business and want to tell the world. The customers and business partners Cisco recruits to be guest bloggers fall into that category.

Building and cultivating these relationships can deliver direct value for a firm. First, this is basic word-of-mouth marketing that we previously discussed. Building

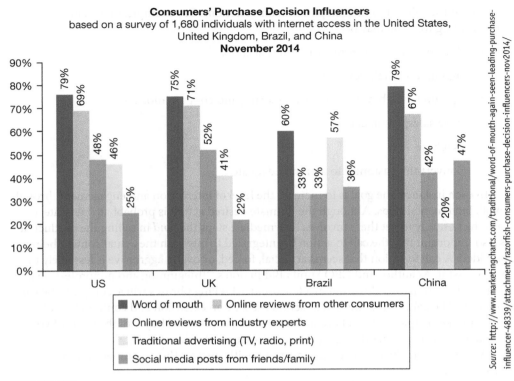

Consumers' Purchase Decision Influencers
based on a survey of 1,680 individuals with internet access in the United States,
United Kingdom, Brazil, and China
November 2014

Legend:
- Word of mouth
- Online reviews from other consumers
- Online reviews from industry experts
- Traditional advertising (TV, radio, print)
- Social media posts from friends/family

US: 79%, 69%, 48%, 46%, 25%
UK: 75%, 71%, 52%, 41%, 22%
Brazil: 60%, 33%, 33%, 57%, 36%
China: 79%, 67%, 42%, 20%, 47%

Source: http://www.marketingcharts.com/traditional/word-of-mouth-again-seen-leading-purchase-influencer-48339/attachment/razorfish-consumers-purchase-decision-influencers-nov2014/

Figure 2.7 Factors That Influence Purchase Decisions

relationships and rewarding or giving attention to your fans are key drivers of WOM. Word of mouth, in turn, is key to consumer purchasing behavior.

Figure 2.7 shows WOM to be the leading purchase influence in four different countries. Word of mouth far surpasses the influence of traditional advertising in all except Brazil where the difference is small. Perhaps even more surprising is the fact that consumer online reviews and expert online reviews are consistently second and third as purchase influencers. The importance of posts from friends and family varies across the four nations and the different cultures they represent.[23]

In addition to influencing purchasing behavior, customer advocates are the people most likely to come to the brand's defense if needed. As a result of circumstance or human error, eventually a business will offend or upset someone. Having honest, regular people who are not employed by the company defend the brand can turn an entire conversation around. These unpaid advocates can be one of the greatest assets to a social media campaign. In the next chapter, we discuss targeting and market segmentation to aid in finding these valuable brand advocates.

Some very passionate brand advocates can start off as disgruntled customers or skeptical purchasers. Many customers are flattered when businesses take time to respond personally to problems. If a company responds quickly to negative comments and resolves the situation professionally, it can change an initial bad impression into a lasting positive one. An angry customer may initially be hostile, but after the situation is resolved, this person feels relief and gratitude. People whose input has been taken seriously or who have been assisted in resolving a difficult problem know that the company respects them and values their time. In return, these people will be more likely to speak positively about the brand.

Building these positive relationships can result in natural positive recommendations from people who never need to be compensated; these relationships also pay dividends of goodwill and increased sales well into the future.

Best Practices for Developing a Social Media Strategy

There are many important aspects of developing a good social media strategy as we have discussed in this chapter. Most experts would agree that these best practices are essential in the strategy development process.

1. Start with a road map. That is your SMM plan. At a minimum it should specify:

    a. Who your target audience is and the audience characteristics

    b. How you plan to interact with the audience

    c. How you will measure the success or failure of your activities

    d. How you will adjust to stay on track to meet your objectives.

2. Listen before you start interacting. Just as you would not walk up to a group of people at a party and start talking (even worse, start talking about yourself), you must listen strategically before you engage with your audience. Then offer respect, empathy, and content of value before you ask anything of them.

3. Welcome audience participation, feedback and collaboration, and use these conversations to locate and nurture brand advocates.

4. A successful social media strategy or execution is not built overnight. Give it an adequate amount of time and, not incidentally, resources to become successful.

5. Be flexible. Social media itself is constantly evolving. Audience tastes and behaviors also evolve over time. Competitors adopt and change strategies. A social media strategy cannot be cast in stone. It must have the capacity to adjust to change in a way that furthers the achievement of business and marketing goals.

Notes

1. Uhrmacher, Aaron (2008, July 10), "How to Develop a Social Media Plan for Your Business in 5 Steps," Mashable. Retrieved August 5, 2011 from http://mashable.com/2008/07/10/how-to-develop-a-social-media-plan/
2. Solis, Brian (2010, July 19), The Conversation, *Harvard Business Review Blogs*. Retrieved January 13, 2011, from http://blogs.hbr.org/cs/2010/07/social_medias_critical_path_re.html
3. Brokaw, Keslie (2014, October 27), "Online 'Chatter Data' is Big Data Gold," *MIT Sloan Management Review Blog*, November 7, 2014 from http://sloanreview.mit.edu/article/online-chatter-data-is-big-data-gold/
4. Duggan, Maeve et. al (January 8, 2015), "Social Media Site Usage by Year," *Pew Research Center Internet Science & Tech Blog*. Retrieved March 12, 2015.
5. Statista, "Number of monthly active Facebook users worldwide as of 4th quarter 2014 (in millions)." Retrieved March 12, 2015 from http://www.statista.com/statistics/264810/number-of-monthly-active-facebook-users-worldwide/
6. Gunelius, Susan (July 12, 2014), "The Data Explosion in 2014 Minute by Minute – Infographic," ACI Blog. Retrieved March 12, 2015 from http://aci.info/2014/07/12/the-data-explosion-in-2014-minute-by-minute-infographic/
7. Laird, Sam (January 21, 2012), "Super Bowl XLVI Gets a Social Media Command Center." Retrieved March 11, 2015 from http://mashable.com/2012/01/21/super-bowl-xlvi-social-media/

8. Laird, Sam (February 7, 2013), "Super Bowl's First Social Media Command Center an 'Enormous Success'", *Mashable*. Retrieved March 11, 2015 from http://mashable .com/2012/02/07/super-bowl-social-media-command-center/

9. Staff (January 20, 2015), "NFL Network Live On-Location From Arizona for Super Bowl XLIX," *NFL Communications*. Retrieved February 21, 2015 from http://nflcommunications .com/2015/01/20/nfl-network-live-on-location-from-arizona-for-super-bowl-xlix/

10. Johnson, Lauren (January 6, 2015), "What Does It Take to Win the Super Bowl on Social Media?" Retrieved February 21, 2015 from http://www.adweek.com/news/advertising-branding/what-does-it-take-win-super-bowl-social-media-162121

11. Marketing Charts Staff (February 12, 2015), "Super Bowl 2015 Data (Updated)." Retrieved February 21, 2015 from http://www.marketingcharts.com/television/super-bowl-2015-advertising-viewer-attitudes-and-spending-trends-50857/

12. Pallota, Frank (ND), "Super Bowl XLIX posts the largest audience in TV history." Retrieved February 21, 2015 from http://money.cnn.com/2015/02/02/media/super-bowl-ratings/

13. Peterson, Tim (January 21, 2015), "Facebook Packages Own Super Bowl Audience for Ad Dollars." Retrieved February 21, 2015 from http://adage.com/article/special-report-super-bowl/facebook-lets-brands-target-people-discussing-super-bowl/296678/?utm_source=digital_email&utm_medium=newsletter&utm_campaign=adage&ttl=1422460201

14. Walker, Alex, and Robert D'Onofrio (February 1, 2015), "Super Bowl XLIX on Facebook." Retrieved February 21, 2015 from http://media.fb.com/2015/02/02/super-bowl-xlix-on-facebook/

15. Rivas, Nancy (October 23, 2012), "Cisco Unveils Social Media Listening Center Showcasing Latest Technology #CiscoListens." Retrieved November 11, 2014 from http://blogs.cisco.com /socialmedia/cisco-unveils-social-media-listening-center-showcasing-latest-technology-in-the-executive-briefing-center-ciscolistens

16. Ciarallo, Joe (April 14, 2013), "How Cisco Achieved 281% ROI with Social Listening and Salesforce Radian6." Retrieved November 11, 2014 from http://blogs.salesforce.com /company/2013/08/cisco-social-listening.html

17. (ND) "2014 State of Enterprise Social Media." Retrieved October 30 2014 from https://www .spredfast.com/social-media-strategies/2014-state-enterprise-social-marketing-report

18. Selzner, Michael A. (May 2014), "2014 Social Media Marketing Industry Report," Retrieved October 30, 2014 from http://www.socialmediaexaminer.com /SocialMediaMarketingIndustryReport2014.pdf

19. September 9, 2014, "The 2014 Rank Correlation Analysis and SEO Ranking Factors for Google U.S.," Retrieved October 30, 2014 from http://blog.searchmetrics.com/us/2014/09/07 /the-2014-rank-correlation-analysis-and-seo-ranking-factors-for-google-u-s/

20. August 25, 2014, "How to Measure Social Media Using the AMEC Valid Metrics Framework." Retrieved December 4, 2014 from http://www.themeasurementstandard.com/2014/08/amec-valid-metrics-framework/

21. Biddu, Sunita (2009, March 27), "Writing the Call to Action in Marketing Copy," *Ezine Articles*. Retrieved July 1, 2011, from http://ezinearticles.com/?Writing-the-Call-to-Action-in-Marketing-Copy&id=2150600

22. Gislason, Jeremy A. (March 5, 2010), "Marketing Call to Action—Strategies to Convert More Visitors into Sales and Leads," *Ezine Articles*. Retrieved January 7, 2011, from http:// ezinearticles.com/?Marketing-Call-to-Action---Strategies-to-Convert-More-Visitors-Into-Sales-and-Leads&id=3879072

23. Marketing Charts staff (November 13, 2014), "Word-of-Mouth Again Said Leading Purchase Influencer." Retrieved December 5, 2014 from http://www.marketingcharts.com/traditional /word-of-mouth-again-seen-leading-purchase-influencer-48339/attachment/razorfish-consumers-purchase-decision-influencers-nov2014/

Identifying Target Audiences

Precise targeting of audiences of all kinds has always been a hallmark of data-driven marketing. That is especially true of digital marketing. SMM has added not only huge quantities of behavioral data but also types of targeting not imagined in other marketing channels.

The Importance of Targeting in SMM

Marketers have long recognized the importance of identifying the target market for their product or service. Digital marketing in general and SMM in particular has added measurably to their toolkit for targeting.

WHAT IS TARGETING IN SMM?

If your answer to that question is "getting the right message to the right person" you are partially correct. However, that is a traditional media answer, not a digital one. The Content Marketing Institute identifies the challenge for digital marketers as being:

> The right **person** to get
>
> The right **content**
>
> At the right **place**
>
> At the right **time**

- Discuss uses of keywords, hashtags, and emojis in targeting branded posts
- Identify best practices for targeting branded posts

In the right **format**

In the right **language**

On the right **device**[1]

That is a formidable challenge! Data and tools associated with social media are available to help marketers meet it.

The Targeting Process in SMM

The most common characteristics marketers use to identify and profile target markets are demographics, geographics, and lifestyles or psychographics. Behavioral data, what people are doing (or what they tell marketing researchers they are doing), has always been part of the process but has become more valuable as a result of the actual (not reported) behaviors provided by digital marketing. Digital marketing has added a wealth of data from the online clickstream to the basic "what did they buy, which promotion did they buy it from" data of the offline direct marketer. Social media has added some interesting additional features. We will, for instance, discuss targeting by emoji later in this chapter.

Identifying and segmenting the target market is a key marketing activity. However, it is not the last step before a promotional campaign is launched. Rarely does the marketer want to reach the entire target market—all the market segments—with one campaign or one message. Usually the campaign is designed for a single market segment. In digital marketing, it is possible to fine-tune targeting beyond the entire market segment to a small target audience, often behaviorally defined, that will be especially receptive to a particular promotional message. For example, in Chapter 2, we discussed the 2015 Super Bowl as an example of the growing importance of mobile engagement while attending or watching sporting events (Figure 2.2). To somewhat over simplify, one audience is attending the game and using their mobile device during the game while another audience is watching from home on traditional TV. Actually sports fans who are not attending may watch on traditional TV, with or without using a mobile device while they are watching, or they can watch on desktop computers or mobile devices. And those are only the major audience groupings. Think of what all goes on before, during, and after a Super Bowl game, and you will quickly realize that a huge audience (not all of whom are actually sports fans) is watching the event in various contexts that can affect their attention to marketing messages and their inclination to act on them. That complexity is the essence of targeting in SMM. Figure 3.1 shows identifying the target audience and audience segments as the first step in SMM audience targeting.

Once the target audience for a campaign has been identified all the teams working on the campaign—and there are often several—must be fully briefed on the nature of the target audience. There are many ways to do this, but using personas has become a popular option among digital marketers of all kinds. Personas bring life to the bare bones of audience statistics and they are useful for everyone from web designers to copywriters to graphic artists. Marketers have increasingly recognized that personas are worth the time and effort it takes to develop them.

With the characteristics of the target audience firmly in mind, the rest of the campaign can be developed and executed. Figure 3.1 shows essential activities in developing a media plan to reach the selected target audience(s). The first step is messaging objectives. Is the marketer introducing a new social media channel, say adding Instagram to its social media platforms? Is the pizza marketer introducing a new pie, or perhaps a new way to order as in the Domino's ad in Chapter 1?

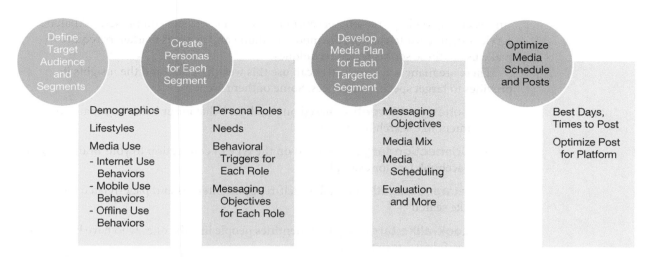

Figure 3.1 Steps in Targeting SMM Campaigns

The media mix includes the social platforms that will be used in the campaign. It also includes other online media like email or online advertising as well as traditional offline media. Other digital media and offline media may play important roles in SMM campaigns, but in this chapter we will concentrate on the planning of the social media component. Each medium must have a specific schedule, and campaign effectiveness must be monitored and evaluated.

Returning to the specifics of social media, the final step in the media plan is to optimize the postings on each social channel so they will be best attended to by the target audience. Each channel has its own best days and times of day to post. Posts themselves need to be configured to meet the criteria of the specific platform in order to achieve prominence on it. In some cases, there is also a need to optimize posts for search engine visibility.

Good SMM requires that platforms be carefully chosen to reach the right target audiences. Once that is done each major platform will offer assistance in targeting specific platform audiences. Each platform has its own programs to encourage marketers to use it, and we will provide examples from several of the largest platforms. First, however, let's look at how digital data is improving marketers' ability to target specific audiences.

"BIG DATA" EXPANDS OPTIONS FOR IDENTIFYING AND TARGETING AUDIENCES

You have probably heard the term big data. How do you interpret it? If you said the massive amount of data that is available from the digital clickstream, you would be correct. Today the definition has broadened to include data from audio and video files. How the data is collected and stored is beyond the scope of this book and is not a major concern of most marketers. However, marketers do need to understand the basic ways of analyzing big data and the new options it makes available in disciplines from supply chain management to audience targeting. They also need to understand that the volume of data will explode once again when the Internet of Things becomes widespread and even your scotch bottle is able to send and receive messages.[2]

The amount of data that comes from all this activity defies traditional marketing analytics—regression-based predictive models, for example. Big data provides too many data points for a regression model. Consequently, other technologies like pattern recognition, data visualization, community recognition and link prediction within social networks, social influence analysis, and machine-learning techniques like neural networking are needed. In addition, much of the data processing takes place "in the cloud," on large remote servers operated by IT services companies.[3,4] Analytics services firms exist to support the model-building and analysis marketers require to make use of these sophisticated techniques.

There are many ways marketers can use this wealth of data and the insights it provides to target specific audiences. Some of them are:

- **Behavioral targeting** based on purchase behavior or behaviors that convey intent like search behaviors

- **Connection targeting** based on the type of connection to your brand page, a Facebook fan, for example

- **Interest targeting** based on self-reported interests and page-related behaviors like search

- **Look-alike targeting** that identifies people like the ones who have been successful targets in the past

- **Custom targeting** that allows the marketer to upload his own data, an email list, for example

- **Location targeting** based on the location provided in the user's profile or by geo-targeting data, which determines the user's current location. This type of targeting will be discussed in more detail in Chapter 12, Mobile Marketing on Social Networks. Uses include:
  - Send offers to customers while they are in the vicinity of a retail store
  - Send personalized coupons to customers while they are in stores
  - Help customers find the location of items in the store[5,6]

When looking at these types of targeting, there are two important warnings, however. First is that not all platforms offer all the types of targeting listed and some offer their own special targeting options in addition to the ones listed. It depends on the type of data they obtain from their users. Second is that advertisers usually receive new targeting options first, with brand pages receiving them at a later date. The social media marketer must carefully examine the targeting options for each platform.

Marketers, however, need to take the possibilities into account when planning their campaigns and targeting audiences for them. Target audience descriptions then become much richer than the ones for traditional media. Some hypothetical examples include:

- Facebook users over 55 years of age who use Facebook at least once a week and belong to one or more travel interest groups (fall and winter tour packages)

- LinkedIn users in the states of Illinois, Ohio, Indiana, Michigan, Wisconsin, and Minnesota who list SMM among their skills (SMM conference in Chicago)

- Instagram users who post from Los Angeles beaches over the Labor Day weekend (a local restaurant)

- Brand page fans who visit one of the brand's retail stores (special limited time in-store coupon offer)

- and others too numerous to list

These are simple examples limited to a single platform. Long-term, multi-platform targeting is possible and adds to the plethora of opportunities available to marketer. The marketing opportunities are limited only by the creativity of the marketers themselves.

THE PERSONA DEVELOPMENT CYCLE AS PART OF THE TARGETING PROCESS

Many experienced marketers use personas, but the dilemma for a person new in the field is how to develop personas from scratch. There are many possible ways to create user personas, including intuition, trial and error, and costly market research, but only a few that have been modeled and studied academically. One such approach is the Three-Step Persona Development Cycle, which was created by Michelle Golden and which contains the following steps:

- **Identify Persona Roles**, listing all relevant personas by role.

- **List Needs and Situational Triggers** from personas' perspectives, defining concerns, symptoms, and problems.

- **Create Messaging Objectives** suited to each persona's needs that you have the expertise to address (and note those that you don't).[7]

These steps can be broken down in more detail. First, think of a few well-known companies or consumer groups that are relevant to a specific industry or business. Then, consider the roles those people within these organizations take in their interactions with others. In particular, focus on buyer roles or buyer personas: those who make decisions about which products or services to spend money on. For a firm this could be the chief financial officer or general counsel, while in a household it would be the person who spends the majority of that household's income. Also, consider external stakeholders who are indirectly influenced by the buyer's decision; these may be taxpayers, donors, employees, or regulatory agencies. During this stage it is important to be specific and think of as many potential buyer roles as possible, although you may not ultimately develop a persona for some of the roles deemed less important or low-value market segments.

In Chapter 1 we discussed the success JetBlue has experienced with SMM. The basic persona they use to guide their SMM efforts is the low budget traveler who wants comfort at an affordable price. One tweet to this target audience urged them to "Fly like a BOSS, pay like an intern" and gave a special link to a page with $49 one-way fare offers. The persona describes their customer as younger than the typical airline traveler, reachable by social media and with high expectations for quick response on social media.[8]

Second, consider the needs and situational triggers for the personas identified earlier. Figure 3.2 shows a typical segmentation of airline travelers with 4 segments—business, leisure, family, and special needs travelers. It also shows 5 stages in the flight, concentrating on the in-flight issues. The research identified 26 in-flight issues—things like food service, entertainment, and Internet access. Business travelers identified 13 of the issues as important, the special needs only 3, while the Family and Leisure segments identified 5 and 6 important issues respectively. Are the most important issues the same for each segment—say business travelers and families traveling with children?

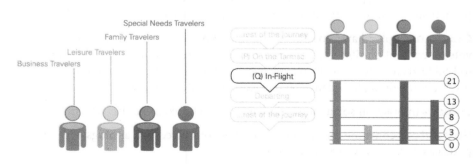
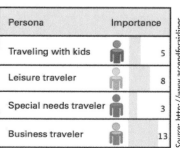

Figure 3.2 | Generic Air Traveler Personas

Persona		Importance
Traveling with kids		5
Leisure traveler		8
Special needs traveler		3
Business traveler		13

Source: http://www.ascendforairlines.com/2014-issue-no-1/customer-journey-mapping-walk-customers-shoes.

Almost assuredly they are not. Knowing which issues are important to each segment represented by a persona not only tells the marketer how to market to the segment but also gives other operations groups like flight services information that helps to keep customers satisfied.

The third and final step is to create messaging objectives, which are "purpose-oriented goals for your communications" with each of the personas defined earlier.[9] In order to be effective, a social media marketer must tailor her or his message toward each group being addressed. Which of the identified issues will be most effective in persuading business travelers to fly JetBlue? What do families who are considering a flight on JetBlue need to know? JetBlue has a "Families in Flight" page on its website that describes special services for families, gives travel tips, gives tips for getting through security, and provides a page with downloads that include a video and various activities and games to print out and bring along on the flight. Some of this content is easily converted to other platforms. For instance, if a family traveling with children provides a mobile number in the reservations process, a link to the children's activity page can be Tweeted.

In other words, once a social media marketer knows what information a buyer will need before making a purchase, it is possible to design a social media strategy that provides a buyer with the relevant information, making the individual more likely to buy the product. Later, as feedback arrives, it will be possible to adjust these messaging objectives based on new information about the personas. Thus, like the social media planning cycle, persona development is also a fluid process that should be constantly evolving.

THE FORRESTER SOCIAL TECHNOGRAPHICS LADDER

Some social media researchers have done pioneering work in developing personas, which can be of use to social media marketers who are developing their own brand personas. The most influential of these is the Social Technographics Profile, pioneered at Forrester Research in 2012 and updated with new research data each year since. The Social Technographics Profile uses demographics such as age, location, and gender to group social media users into personas based on their social media activities. Technographics is the methodology by which Forrester surveys consumers, similar to demographics and psychographics but restricted to technology behaviors. These personas are represented by rungs on the Social Technographics ladder shown in Figure 3.3.

The Social Technographics Profile consists of the following personas:

- **Creators** develop blogs, articles, videos, music, images, and art, and then upload them to social media platforms and are at the top of ladder.
- **Conversationalists** participate in group discussions, engage in conversations on Twitter, and update their statuses on Facebook and LinkedIn.
- **Critics** evaluate and comment on content produced by creators and conversationalists, post product ratings or reviews, comment on blogs, and participate in community's discussion forums, as well as correct wiki articles.
- **Collectors** upload and save favorites on bookmarking sites such as Delicious, vote on content on sites such as Digg, tag photos on sites such as Flickr, subscribe to RSS feeds to automatically receive new blog posts, and perform the valuable function of helping to organize and categorize content on the social web.
- **Joiners** interact on social networks such as Facebook, LinkedIn, and Eon.
- **Spectators** consume the content that others produce, such as blogs, videos, podcasts, forums, reviews, and so on.
- **Inactives** are Internet consumers who are not involved in social media.

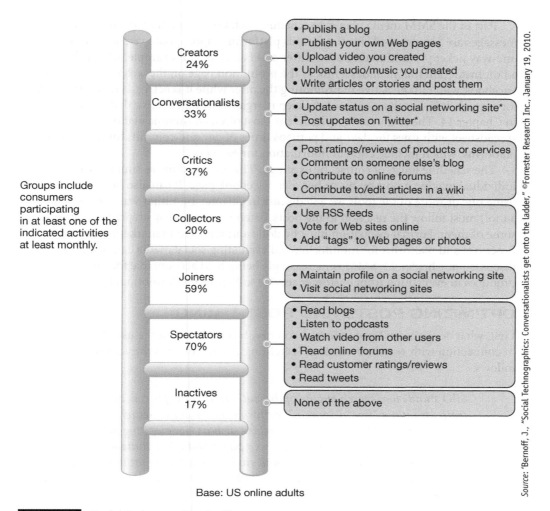

Groups include consumers participating in at least one of the indicated activities at least monthly.

Creators 24%
- Publish a blog
- Publish your own Web pages
- Upload video you created
- Upload audio/music you created
- Write articles or stories and post them

Conversationalists 33%
- Update status on a social networking site*
- Post updates on Twitter*

Critics 37%
- Post ratings/reviews of products or services
- Comment on someone else's blog
- Contribute to online forums
- Contribute to/edit articles in a wiki

Collectors 20%
- Use RSS feeds
- Vote for Web sites online
- Add "tags" to Web pages or photos

Joiners 59%
- Maintain profile on a social networking site
- Visit social networking sites

Spectators 70%
- Read blogs
- Listen to podcasts
- Watch video from other users
- Read online forums
- Read customer ratings/reviews
- Read tweets

Inactives 17%
- None of the above

Base: US online adults

Source: "Bernoff, J., "Social Technographics: Conversationalists get onto the ladder," "©Forrester Research Inc., January 19, 2010.

Figure 3.3   Social Technographics Ladder

The Social Technographics ladder not only reveals *what* people are doing on the social web but, perhaps just as important, *where* they are doing it (i.e., which social media platforms they are using). To reach their optimal target market, social media marketers must know where to aim and the Social Technographics ladder provides a helpful set of persona profiles to assist in understanding the target audience. Forrester offers a free Social Technographics Profile Tool to help brands understand where their target audience falls on the Technographics ladder.

COMPLETING THE MEDIA PLAN FOR EACH AUDIENCE SEGMENT

Once the personas and associated messaging objectives are complete, the social media marketer is ready to compete the other elements of the media plan. Next comes the media mix. JetBlue, for example, not only uses Twitter, but it also has an active Facebook page and an Instagram page. Facebook provides another platform for customers to surface issues and JetBlue to reply. Instagram seems to primarily feature pictures of JetBlue destinations and associated events, but it includes a link for customer to submit issues. JetBlue has a planned approach to both Twitter and Facebook, but much of what happens on any given day depends on what customers post on one platform or the other. It is also important to remind ourselves that social media is only one part of JetBlue's integrated media plan.[10]

Part of the SMM media plan is to schedule each post on each platform. Some of the messages are "repurposed" for the various platforms—appropriate versions of the $49 one-way ticket promotion on both Twitter and Facebook, for example, with a shot of the ad on Instagram that includes a link to the promotion page on the website. Twitter and Facebook will both be active in promoting the offer while it is active. If that sounds like a lot of work, it is, but there are tools to keep it organized and effective that we will discuss in Chapter 14. The social media schedule is most often communicated in an Excel spreadsheet with rows for days and perhaps times of day and columns for individual platforms, which include content information for each post.

The schedule must, of course, be executed. That can be done as simply as an individual making a post on his or her own Facebook page. It can also be automated, using one or more of the tools we will discuss in Chapter 14. Either way, someone (or a tool) must follow the reaction to the posts, listening and perhaps replying to at least some of them. Formal evaluation must be done and reported to marketing executives. Processes and platforms for monitoring and evaluating social media campaigns will be discussed in Chapter 13. SMM is increasingly being held accountable for the results it produces in everything from customer service to Return on Promotional Investment.

OPTIMIZING POSTS AND POST TIMING

First, what do we mean by *optimizing*? You may be familiar with the use of the term in connection with search marketing. SearchEngineLand defines the acronym SEO as follows:

> SEO stands for "search engine optimization." It is the process of getting traffic from the "free," "organic," "editorial" or "natural" search results on search engines. All major search engines such as Google, Bing and Yahoo have primary search results, where web pages and other content such as videos or local listings are shown and ranked based on what the search engine considers most relevant to users. Payment isn't involved, as it is with paid search.[11]

You often hear this referred to as "search engine visibility." While the process is different in SMM, the goal is the same—to make everything from a user's profiles to her blog posts to her Pinterest pins as visible as possible to everyone on the platform and sometimes also in search engine rankings.

Second, how do we optimize social content? Unfortunately, there is not a one-size-fits-all answer to that question. The bad news is that every platform is different when it comes to optimization. The good news is that there are many publishers on the web who provide information on the subject. However, since each platform is different, it is a large subject and we will give only a few examples.

Facebook, as the largest platform, provides the first example with recommendations shown in Figure 3.4. It shows that most brand posts are made on weekdays with the best days being Thursday and Friday. "Best" is measured by Facebook engagement—the number of viewers who liked, shared, clicked, or commented.[12] The best time is between 1 p.m. and 3 p.m. (assume Eastern Standard Time in these recommendations and adjust if necessary for your audience). The infographic quotes Buddy Media as inferring that "the less people want to be at work, the more they are on Facebook!"[13]

Figure 3.5 paints a very different picture for Tweets, however. Weekends are best—Saturday and Sunday. The reason appears to be a difference between business audiences, who are most engaged during the week and consumer audiences who are most engaged with Tweets on weekends. The best time is between 5 and 6 p.m.[14] Is that because people are engaging with their Tweetstream while commuting home from work?

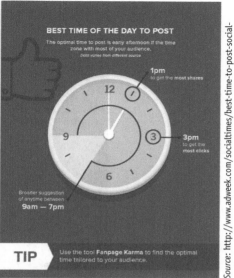

Figure 3.4 Best Days and Times to Post on Facebook

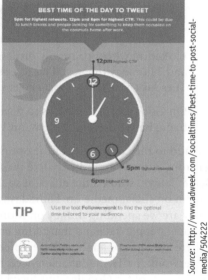

Figure 3.5 Best Days and Times to Post on Twitter

One of the leading visual platforms, Pinterest, shows still another pattern. Figure 3.6 shows Saturday as the best day and the best time as evening between 8 and 11 p.m., with activity being the greatest at 9 p.m. However, if you are in the fashion industry, the optimal time to post is Friday at 3 p.m.[15] Does the overall optimal time being in the evening have to do with the entertainment value of the visual platform? Is it reasonable to surmise that fashion at 3 p.m. on Friday is correlated with weekend shopping plans?

According to the same infographic:

- The other leading visual platform, Instagram, does not exhibit a best day to post but does find that off-work hours produce a higher level of engagement with brand posts than do working hours.

Figure 3.6 **Best Days and Times to Pin**

- LinkedIn, with a primarily professional audience, finds Tuesday, Wednesday, and Thursday the best days to post while posts made between 10 and 11 a.m. on Tuesdays garner the most clicks and shares.

- On Google+ the best days to post are Monday through Friday with the best time being between 9 and 11 a.m. on Wednesday.[16]

To add to the complexity of the optimization issue, optimal days and times may differ from industry to industry like the fashion industry on Pinterest. Unilever, owner of Ben & Jerry's, studied the effect of social media and found that people talked about ice cream on social media on Thursdays and Fridays and bought ice cream on Saturdays. "So why are we spending money on Mondays and Tuesdays?" Mr. [Shawn] O'Neal [VP-global people data and marketing analytics] asked.[17]

There are tools to analyze these differences with Fanpage Karma for Facebook and Followerwonk for Twitter as referenced in Figures 3.3 and 3.4. Both of these are paid tools. A free tool for Google+ produced the analysis of Prof. Roberts's Google+ account that is shown in Figure 3.7.

Her results resemble the overall for the platform, with posts made on Monday achieving highest ranking although the optimal time, presumably for engagement, is between 11 and 12 noon on Saturday. Are professors working on their classes for next week on Saturday morning? Of special interest is the top posts listing, which helps the owner know what content works best for her on this platform. This illustrates that the optimal data reported for the selected platforms, all obtained by sampling large number of users of the platform, are useful. However, brands need to investigate what is best for their industry and monitor results for their product to be assured of doing the best possible job of reaching their own target audience.

With that in mind we turn to an examination of the ways in which some of these same platforms assist users in reaching their selected audiences.

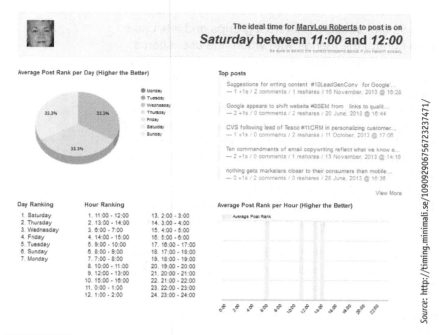

Figure 3.7 Best Days and Times to Post for a Google+ User

Targeting Ads and Posts on Social Platforms

There is an important caveat as you read this section—in this chapter we are attempting to keep the focus on targeting brand posts, not targeting advertising. Why is this an important issue? First, there is the practical issue—brand posts are owned media with no advertising costs. Ads on social media platforms are paid media, usually pay-per-click (PPC) advertising or sponsored posts; either way there is a cost. Second there is the technology issue. Since advertisers are paying for their media space, they usually get the targeting options first, often long before they are available to brand pages. The result is that brand pages generally have a more limited set of targeting options than do ads. In general, personal pages on any platform have a limited set of targeting options like "everyone" or "your circles." The targeting options for personal profiles are primarily based on the way people set up and manage their pages, not on the big data options that are available to brand pages and advertisers.

Identifying Audiences for Personal Branding Efforts

As part of your personal branding effort you will become a participant in various communities. Those communities form the basis of the target audience for your brand. Social media platforms have a variety of ways to help you identify specific audiences for it. In Chapter 6, we will discuss how to use Twitter for developing a personal brand. Google+ allows you to create circles that categorize members of your community—for instance, your classmates who will be resources throughout your career or people who work for companies that you might like to include in your job search. Facebook allows the creation of interest groups and lets users create lists that can be used to control the friends with whom the user shares. Many of the platforms allow direct messaging of personalized content. All you learn in this chapter can be put into practice as you build a community around your brand and categorize members into meaningful audiences.

LinkedIn, however, has become established as the indispensable platform for business professionals and we will concentrate most of this discussion on it. In Chapter 5, we will discuss creating a personal profile on LinkedIn. That is an essential step, but profile creation can be more effective if the user understands the audience he wishes to reach with the profile. Having created a vibrant profile, the user is advised to join LinkedIn groups and to participate actively in them. It is also important to connect with people on the platform. You are building your target audience so be sure the people you connect with are relevant to your career plans.

The rest sounds straightforward. Having identified your audience on LinkedIn, you simply share your profile and your career aspirations with them, right? Actually, that would be a huge mistake!

Lesson #1. LinkedIn groups expressly forbid self-promotion. The platform describes self-promotion as follows:

> While the specific details of what's considered self-promotion depends on the group, topics such as webinars, books, blogs, motivational speaking events, software sales, and real estate can be considered self-promotion. Try to avoid words like *buy*, *sell*, or *attend*.[1]

However, what is considered potentially unacceptable behavior on the platform goes further: It includes these kinds of group behaviors:

- Sharing a link in multiple groups at the same time. The content may not be relevant to all groups.
- The content of a discussion that promotes the user's website or blog or other specific sites.
- A post using inappropriate words or content that was not professionally oriented.

If a group member violates any of these rules, the group manager has the option of requiring that posts be moderated before they are posted online. If the post is deemed inappropriate in any way, it will not be accepted.

LinkedIn offers assistance to the individual user by offering possible connections that make sense based on his profile and other contacts and by offering a Relationship tab that helps organize and manage those contacts.

Lesson #2. The LinkedIn Relationship tab provides information about how you are connected to another user, allows you to see the messages you have exchanged, and lets you make notes on the relationship and how you plan to further it. An especially useful feature is ability to set a one-time or recurring reminder to follow up with the connection. You find the Relationship tab near the top of the profile

---

[1] "Self Promotion in Groups," LinkedIn. Retrieved September 14, 2015, from https://help.linkedin.com/app/answers/detail/a_id/49409/ft/eng

of each of your connections. The Relationship tab is not available on the LinkedIn mobile app at this time.[2]

Lesson #3. Use the Tag feature on the Relationship tab to assign tags to connections. This allows you to assign your connections to categories provided by LinkedIn or to create your own tags. You can see a list of all the contacts you have grouped under a tag you create. There is, however, people from seeing your posts on LinkedIn.[3]

Lesson #4. You can categorize your contacts on LinkedIn but you cannot build a list that allows you to message all contacts in a category at the same time.

There are two main take-aways from the discussion of LinkedIn. First, you can make contacts, learn a great deal about them by studying their profiles and interacting with them in groups, and assign them to categories on LinkedIn. The platform, however, is very alert to spam and job seekers want to avoid being seen as spammers at all costs.

Second, you should use the direct messaging feature for LinkedIn contacts with great care. Contacts can easily block you if they object to the nature of your message.

If this sounds a bit discouraging, remember that LinkedIn works hard to create an environment where professionals can interact without opening themselves to spam. They have also created an environment where professionals feel comfortable posting jobs and looking for potential candidates for positions. Learn to use the Jobs tab on the platform, keep your profile complete and up-to-date, and make connections offline and online. And, very important, don't post content or try to take targeting shortcuts that will damage your branding efforts.[4]

Lesson #4. Consider using a tool to uncover profiles of relevant LinkedIn members. LinkedIn's toolbar includes Jobs Insider, which offers useful support for your job search.[5] Other tools have a cost associated after a trial period, but they may prove to be valuable. LinkedIn's own Social Selling service for individuals is one.[6] A widely-used tool called Diver is another.[7] There are other tools that include extracting source contact data as one of their services

Lesson #5. LinkedIn may be the repository of much of your personal branding content, but you can develop communities on a variety of platforms and reach them with targeted content that will enhance your brand.

Develop your audiences carefully and use them with respect. If you do, they will be a huge asset to your personal brand.

---

[2] Herman, Jenn (April 28, 2015), SocialMediaExaminer, "How to Use the LinkedIn Relationship Tab to Improve Your Networking." Retrieved September 14, 2015, from http://www.socialmediaexaminer.com/use-the-linkedin-relationship-tab-to-improve-your-networking/

[3] Clark, Karen (n.d.), "How to Sort, Tag or Categorize Your LinkedIn Contacts," MyBusinessPresence.com. Retrieved September 14, 2015, from http://www.mybusinesspresence.com/how-to-sort-tag-or-categorize-your-linkedin-contacts/

[4] McCorkle, Denny (April 20, 2014), Business2Community, "Do's & Don'ts When Using LinkedIn for Personal Branding & Job Search." Retrieved September 14, 2014, from http://www.business2community.com/linkedin/dos-donts-using-linkedin-personal-branding-job-search-0857814

[5] (n.d.). "How to Use the LinkedIn Jobs Insider." Retrieved September 20, 2015, from http://www.dummies.com/how-to/content/how-to-use-the-linkedin-jobsinsider.html

[6] (n.d.). LinkedIn, "The Social Selling Era Starts with LinkedIn Sales Navigator." Retrieved September 20, 2015, from https://business.linkedin.com/sales-solutions?u=0

[7] (n.d.). "Search Better," Broadlook Technologies. Retrieved September 20, 2015, from http://www.broadlook.com/products/diver/

AD TARGETING ON SELECTED PLATFORMS

Because the targeting options for posts follow the targeting options for ads it is useful to understand a bit about ad targeting works on social media platforms.

Facebook is one of the few platforms that make ad targeting options visible on personal profile pages, and they are worth exploring. On your Home page, scroll down to the bottom of the right column and find several links including Privacy where you can make choices regarding your personal data, Ad Choices where there are options for preventing Facebook advertisers from collecting data about you, and Advertising, the page on which advertising campaigns are set up. It is possible to set up an ad and investigate targeting options without ever submitting a credit card and actually executing an advertising campaign. This is a useful exercise to help understand the targeting options for paid advertising, which form the basis for the more limited set of options available to the brand page.

As of late 2015 Facebook is the only major platform that offers data based targeting options to brand pages. Virtually all, however, offer targeting to advertisers. Twitter, for example, offers advertisers a number of targeting options, a few of which are:

- Follower targeting with a number of choices including followers of competitors and audiences whose characteristics are similar to the brand's own audience

- Behavior targeting that uses data from Twitter business partners about online and offline product-related behaviors

- Keywords that are used either in Twitter searches or in Tweets[18]

- Event targeting in which Twitter furnishes a global event calendar, provides audience data from last year's event, and enables targeting of the audience for the current year's event[19]

Pinterest is relatively new to advertising and only began to offer targeting in 2015. Pinterest advertising is primarily in the form of "promoted Pins." Targeting by product category, for instance makeup or home décor, is one option and by interest categories like travel or DIY is another.[20] Pinterest believes that much pinning activity infers future purchase intent and is working on ways to use that in targeting.[21]

TARGETING AVAILABLE TO BRAND POSTS

Google+ has a built-in targeting mechanism with its circles. The platform also makes available targeting by age and location to brand pages. Until November 2015 the platform allowed hashtag searches of pages. Google+ has eliminated the search option for individual pages and has added Collections. The page owner can use Collections to organize his posts by subject matter. This may be useful to individuals but it was widely seen as unfriendly to brand pages.[22]

In spite of Google's actions, search by hashtag has become a key feature on other platforms. Hashtags themselves have become an important source of analytics data as well as ideas for everyone from journalists to content marketers. In 2015 it became possible to access the trends in real time.[23] It could be argued that hashtags are especially important in helping marketers to form communities of interest on visual platforms like Instagram[24] and video platforms like short-video site Vine.[25] Since Instagram is owned by Facebook and Vine by Twitter, it seems that hashtags have the potential to become another source of big data to be used for targeting purposes.

Perhaps the most intriguing discovery and potential targeting item to come along recently has been the emoji. Emojis surfaced in the late 1990s in Japan where the

DoCoMo mobile phone was the rage among Japanese teenagers and texting exploded. NPR sums up their appeal perfectly with a headline, "Why 140 Characters, When One Will Do?"[26] The phenomenon quickly became global, managed by the Unicode Consortium, which decides which emojis will be added to the lexicon and therefore to keyboards like iPhone's and Gmail's. On the visual platform Instagram, users have been adding emojis to their posts for quite some time. In April 2015 Instagram started allowing users to include emojis in hashtags. That makes it possible for a brand to search for hashtags on Instagram and use trending hashtags in brand posts. That makes them searchable and therefore able to reach targeted audiences.[27]

In addition, brands are developing their own emoji keyboards. The Baltimore Ravens announced that they had 53,000 downloads of their emoji keyboard, shown in Figure 3.8a, during the first weekend after it was introduced.[28] These icons offer an infinite variety of ways in which the football team can track, listen to, and engage with their fans. Brands of all kinds are using them. Twitter added its first branded emoji when it gave Coke its own crossed bottles symbol—and, of course, announced it on Twitter (Figure 3.8b).[29]

While new developments like emojis are trending in terms of targeting, it is also important to look at a final example of platform support for targeting brand posts. As it has done in so many social media developments, Facebook is leading the way—a way that is likely to be followed by other platforms in the months and years to come.

AUDIENCE TARGETING ON FACEBOOK

Facebook has gone through a number of iterations in which brands first found it necessary to develop profiles, then fan pages, then were given the option of creating brand pages that had more features than personal pages. This was followed by several

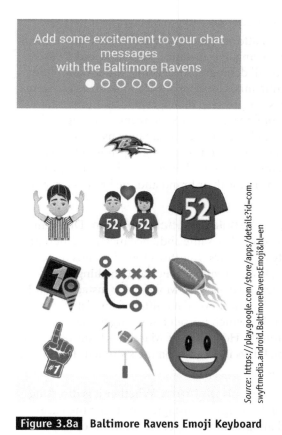

Source: https://play.google.com/store/apps/details?id=com.swyftmedia.android.BaltimoreRavensEmoji&hl=en

Ready for some fun? Tweet #ShareaCoke 🍾 to help set a new @RecordSetter record for the world's largest cheers. *clink!*

#ShareaCoke

RETWEETS 452   FAVORITES 625

Source: https://twitter.com/twitter/status/644541644939882500/photo/1?ref_src=twsrc^tfw

Figure 3.8a Baltimore Ravens Emoji Keyboard

Figure 3.8b Twitter Announcement of Coke Emoji

upgrades of features, including targeting options, available to brands.[30] Initial targeting options for brand pages were demographics, specifically:

- Gender
- Relationship Status
- Educational Status
- Age
- Location
- Language[31]

Later Facebook introduced targeting by interests that are supplied by the brand as they develop the post. As a social media marketer types in the interests, the tool makes suggestions that guide the marketer toward interests that are common in the Facebook community. For all types of targeting only the targeted users see the targeted posts in their newsfeed, although the posts can be seen by all on the brand's timeline.[32]

Targeting options do differ somewhat from one platform to another, and the careful social media marketer understands best practices on the platforms she uses. However, there is a set of best practices that apply across platforms.

Best Practices for Targeting Branded Posts

In order to obtain the most precision in targeting of social media audiences marketers should:

- **Understand what platforms are used by the target audience and how they are used.** Social media platforms, the way visitors make use of them, and user behaviors are constantly evolving. For instance, Facebook and Twitter have become major news sources for all demographics, with Twitter dominating the Breaking News category and Millennials looking at Facebook for news more than any other site.[33] Men are the fastest-growing demographic on Pinterest, which was originally 70 to 80 percent female.[34] Over 90 percent of teenage cell phone owners text on their phones, and over one-third are now using messaging apps. African American teens are most likely to use messaging apps, followed closely by Hispanic teens.[35] Brands must monitor changes like these and give careful consideration to what they mean for their brand and the brand's activity on social media.

- **Optimize content and posting schedule for each platform.** Different audiences tend to use different platforms. The same audience may use different platforms in different ways. A study from MarketingProfs found brands most likely to post on Instagram, Facebook, and Twitter on Friday (finishing up before the weekend?), but the most effective days were Monday for Instagram and Sunday for Facebook and Twitter.[36] The Facebook data differs from data from a different source presented in Figure 3.3, which is itself a warning to marketers to follow SMM data widely and carefully. However, the MarketingProfs data that shows brands posting on nonoptimal days in all five channels studied should be a huge warning to all SMM managers.

- **Use the targeting capabilities of each platform.** Whether it is directing posts by hashtag on Twitter or emoji hashtags on Instagram or using the Facebook options to target to specific demographics or specific locations or a specific demographic in a specific location, the targeting possibilities offered by platforms are rich and getting richer. That alone is enough to warrant consistent and thoughtful use, but the targeting options for branded posts are free just like the platforms. Targeting options offered by big data marketing services firms may be even richer and more precise. They are, however, not free.

- **Monitor results on each platform and continue to improve content engagement and overall marketing effectiveness.** SMM is best seen as a process of continuous improvement. Each social media campaign produces data that can be used to improve the next campaign. The broad data about social media platforms and users presented in this chapter and throughout the book is informative and provides a useful starting point for strategy development. However, as illustrated in this chapter, platform data may differ from one industry to another. Data from one firm to another in the same industry can, and often does, differ. The brand's own data provides the best foundation for future campaigns, although it may need to be supplemented by outside data.

The emphasis in SMM often seems to be "more is better," more followers, more likes, more posts, more platforms. While having a large pool of potential customers is desirable, messages are only useful if they reach the right people. This chapter has emphasized that successful SMM targeting is more than just the right content to the right person. The message must also be received at the right place, at the right time, in the appropriate format, in the correct language, and on the right device. Careful targeting, using all the techniques and tools at the marketer's disposal, is the key to meeting that challenge.

Notes

1. Lau, Michelle (September 7, 2015), "How to Get the Right Content to the Right People at the Right Time: A Look at *This American Life*," Content Marketing Institute, Retrieved September 7, 2015, from http://contentmarketinginstitute.com/2015/09/right-content-right-time/?utm_medium=email&utm_source=Act-On+Software&utm_content=email&utm_campaign=How%20to%20Get%20the%20Right%20Content%20to%20the%20Right%20People%20at%20the%20Right%20Time%3A%20A%20Look%20at%20This%20American%20Life&utm_term=READ%20THIS%20ARTICLE

2. Martin, Chuck (September 9, 2015), "Brands Enter the World of the Internet of Things," MediaPost. Retrieved September 9, 2015, from http://www.mediapost.com/publications/article/257931/brands-enter-the-world-of-the-internet-of-things.html?utm_source=newsletter&utm_medium=email&utm_content=headline&utm_campaign=85928

3. Mitchell, Robert (October 23, 2014), "8 Big Trends in Big Data Analytics," ComputerWorld. Retrieved September 7, 2015, from http://www.computerworld.com/article/2690856/big-data/8-big-trends-in-big-data-analytics.html

4. Gandomi, Amir and Murtaza Haider (April 2015), "Beyond the Hype: Big Data Concepts, Methods, and Analytics," *International Journal of Information Management*. Retrieved September 7, 2015, from http://www.sciencedirect.com/science/article/pii/S0268401214001066

5. Ganguly, Sonny (March 17, 2015), "Why Social Media Advertising Is Set to Explode in the Next 3 Years," Marketing Land. Retrieved September 7, 2015, from http://marketingland.com/social-media-advertising-set-explode-next-3-years-121691

6. "Marketing ROI and Location Data," IAB (February 2015). Retrieved September 7, 2015, from http://www.iab.net/media/file/IAB_Marketing_ROI_%26_Location_Data_WhitePaper.pdf

7. Golden, Michelle (2011), *Social Media Strategies for Professionals and Their Firms* (Hoboken, NJ: John Wiley), pp. 84–89.

8. Sprung, Rachel (October 25, 2012), "7 Companies That Totally 'Get' Their Buyer Personas," HubSpot. Retrieved September 8, 2015, from http://blog.hubspot.com/blog/tabid/6307/bid/33749/7-Companies-That-Totally-Get-Their-Buyer-Personas.aspx

9. Dent, Julie (2014), "Customer Journey Mapping: A Walk in Customers' Shoes," Ascend. Retrieved September 8, 2015, from http://www.ascendforairlines.com/2014-issue-no-1/customer-journey-mapping-walk-customers-shoes

10. Chereskin, Kerry *et al.*(October 19, 2011), "JetBlue Media Plan." Retrieved August 27, 2015, from http://www.slideshare.net/tomburr2/jetblue-media-plan

11. "What Is SEO?" SearchEngineLand. Retrieved September 9, 2015, from http://searchengineland.com/guide/what-is-seo

12. "How Is Engagement Rate Defined?" Facebook. Retrieved September 11, 2015, from https://www.facebook.com/help/178043462360087

13. Bennett, Shea (January 6, 2015), *AdWeek*, "What Are the Best Times to Post on #Facebook, #Twitter and #Instagram?" Retrieved September 11, 2015, from http://www.adweek.com/socialtimes/best-time-to-post-social-media/504222

14. *Ibid.*

15. *Ibid.*

16. *Ibid.*

17. Neff, Jack (September 18, 2015), *Advertising Age*, "Unilever Finds Social-Media Buzz Really Does Drive Sales." Retrieved September 18, 2015, from http://adage.com/article/digital/unilever-social-media-buzz-drive-sales/300426/?utm_source=daily_email&utm_medium=newsletter&utm_campaign=adage&ttl=1443132217

18. "How to Target Your Twitter Ads," Twitter. Retrieved September 13, 2015, from https://business.twitter.com/target-your-ads?location=na&lang=en

19. Dinkar, Jain (July 23, 2015), Twitter, "Introducing Event Targeting." Retrieved September 13, 2015, from https://blog.twitter.com/2015/introducing-event-targeting

20. Bennett, Anna (January 21, 2015), Business2Community, "Pinterest 101 for Business: Focus on Your Target Audience's Interests." Retrieved September 13, 2015, from http://www.business2community.com/pinterest/pinterest-101-business-focus-target-audiences-interests-01132148

21. Sluis, Sarah (May 19, 2015), AdExchanger, "Pinterest Adds Audience Targeting, CPA Model to Promoted Pins." Retrieved September 13, 2015, from http://adexchanger.com/platforms/pinterest-adds-audience-targeting-cpa-model-to-promoted-pins/

22. Hines, Krishi (December 8, 2015). "Google+ Changes: What Marketers Need to Know," Social Media Examiner, Retrieved December 15, 2015 from http://www.socialmediaexaminer.com/google-plus-changes-what-marketers-need-to-know/

23. Barrett, Brian (June 18, 2015), *Wired*, "Google Trends Now Shows the Web's Obsessions in Real Time." Retrieved September 13, 2015, from http://www.wired.com/2015/06/google-trends-real-time/

24. Sonorso, Eric (August 19, 2014), "How to Use Instagram Hashtags to Expand Your Reach," Social Media Examiner. Retrieved September 13, 2015, from http://www.socialmediaexaminer.com/instagram-hashtags/

25. Long, Mary C. (August 5, 2013), *AdWeek*, "Vine Announces Trending Hashtags, Further Antagonizing Haters." Retrieved September 13, 2015, from http://www.adweek.com/socialtimes/vine-trending-hashtags/480848

26. NPR, "Why 140 Characters, When One Will Do? Tracing the Emoji Evolution" (June 30, 2014). Retrieved September 14, 2015, from http://www.npr.org/2014/06/30/326937998/why-140-characters-when-one-will-do-tracing-the-emoji-evolution

27. Tyler, Kevin (March 15, 2015), MediaPost, "Connecting with Emoji on Instagram." Retrieved September 14, 2015, from http://www.mediapost.com/publications/article/250052/connecting-with-emoji-on-instagram.html

28. Tode, Chantal (July 30, 2015), Mobile Marketer, "Baltimore Ravens' Emoji Keyboard Sees 53K Downloads in First Weekend." Retrieved September 14, 2015, from http://www.mobilemarketer.com/cms/news/messaging/20983.html?utm_source=feedburner&utm_medium=feed&utm_campaign=Feed%3A+homepage-news+%28Mobile+Marketer++Homepage+Feed%29

29. Twitter, "#ShareaCoke." Retrieved September 18, 2015, from https://twitter.com/twitter/status/644541644939882500/photo/1?ref_src=twsrc^tfw

30. Weaver, Jason (March 30, 2012), Mashable, "The Evolution of Facebook for Brands." Retrieved September 16, 2015, from http://mashable.com/2012/03/30/facebook-for-brands/#pIfABGoT9gkb

31. Loomer, Jon (December 10, 2014), JohLoomer.com, "How Brands Can Maximize Facebook Organic Post Targeting by Interest." Retrieved September 16, 2015, from http://www.jonloomer.com/2014/12/10/facebook-organic-post-targeting-interest/

32. Vahl, Andrea (March 23, 2015), SocialMediaExaminer, "How to Use Facebook Organic Post Targeting." Retrieved September 16, 2015, from http://www.socialmediaexaminer.com/facebook-organic-post-targeting/

33. Barthel, Michael *et.al.* (July 14, 2015), Pew Research Center, "The Evolving Role of News on Twitter and Facebook." Retrieved September 17, 2015, from http://www.journalism.org/2015/07/14/the-evolving-role-of-news-on-twitter-and-facebook/

34. Perez, Sarah (November 14, 2014), TechCrunch, "Men Are Now Pinterest's Fastest-Growing Demographic." Retrieved September 17, 2015, from http://techcrunch.com/2014/11/13/men-are-now-pinterests-fastest-growing-demographic/

35. Lenhart, Amanda (April 9, 2015), "Mobile Access Shifts Social Media Use and Other Online Activities," Pew Research Center. Retrieved September 17, 2015, from http://www.pewinternet.org/2015/04/09/mobile-access-shifts-social-media-use-and-other-online-activities/

36. Nanji, Ayaz (January 29, 2015), MarketingProfs, "The Best Days and Times to Post Content [Infographic]." Retrieved September 13, 2015, from http://www.marketingprofs.com/charts/2015/26922/the-best-days-and-times-to-post-content-infographic#ixzz3mUob2VJN

Rules of Engagement for SMM

Marketers can find social media difficult to navigate because there are many unwritten practices and bits of etiquette that social media participants are expected to abide by. Slip up, and the unwary social media marketer could incur bloggers' wrath or be labeled a spammer. Hence, the rules of engagement in social media are as important as those in everyday life, but not always as familiar. A social media marketer must have a firm grasp of these rules and the norms that govern interactions on the social web.

LEARNING OBJECTIVES

After completing this chapter students will be able to:

- Define the rules of engagement for SMM
- Explain the difference between permission vs. interruption marketing
- Describe the initial entry strategy of passive vs. active
- Detail the principles for success in social media engagement

(Continued)

Being a successful social media marketer requires more than marketing and technical skills. It requires a knowledge of the rules of the road in social media and understanding of the appropriate way to communicate on social platforms.

This chapter will provide the general rules of engagement for success in SMM as well as guidance on how to avoid costly mistakes by behaving properly on the social web. Something to keep in mind is that social media involves discussions between real people about issues or products that they care about. Typically, these conversations are not about the particular brand a social media marketer is hoping to promote. Therefore, one must *earn* people's attention, and that means playing by generally accepted standards.

This chapter contributed by Janna Parker

Treat a person's social media properties, whether a blog, Twitter stream, or Facebook page, as though they were the individual's online homes. Depending on the circumstances, the social media marketer may be an invited guest (the person requested to follow or receive updates) or may be dropping in unannounced (by following someone and hoping to gain that person's attention or interest). It is polite, both in real life and online, to build some rapport before making requests of someone's time and attention. A first interaction should never be requesting a favor, especially when dropping by without an invitation!

- Describe the rules of effective social media interaction
- Define SMM ethics
- Explain how to make ethical social media decisions
- Describe the global perspective of SMM

Permission vs. Interruption Marketing: Developing the Social Contract

Seth Godin coined the distinction between permission marketing and interruption marketing.[1] Traditional marketing relies heavily on interruption marketing. When using interruption marketing, companies purchase the right to interrupt people and demand their attention. TV advertising, magazine ads, billboards, pop-ups, radio ads, and so on are all created to interrupt a viewer at what he or she is doing (trying to watch a show or listen to the radio, for instance) and make that person view or listen to a marketing message. Marketers in the interruption field don't have to worry about whether or not a consumer *wants* to see their ads, as firms paid for the right to display them regardless. Viewers or listeners realize that seeing ads is part of the cost they pay in order to consume some media content (TV shows, radio, magazines, etc.).

The content of interruption ads is focused around selling a product or service that provides value to the target market. The goal of the ad is to showcase the product, highlight its benefits, reduce information search costs, and create a persuasive case for someone to make a purchase. Effective placement of the advertising must occur in order for the advertisement to be effective. Media scheduling includes comparing the demographics of the audience to the target market of the product or service being advertised.

Thinking in this way helps explain why advertisements can create value for consumers. By reducing the time spent gathering information about a product, ads make the real cost of purchasing lower, increasing both company revenue and customer satisfaction. Ads also serve a signaling function, because it is most profitable to advertise a high-quality product. In *Exchange and Production: Competition, Coordination and Control*, noted economists Armen Alchian and William Allen explain that "A seller's long-term survival rests on continued consumer acceptance—at least for products that continue under the same brand name. We therefore expect a positive correlation between a seller's *continued* advertising and quality of product and profitability: Good products make advertising more profitable."[2]

Reducing information cost to consumers and the reputation effect are two justifications for traditional advertising. In spite of its downsides, interruption marketing in the form of mass TV and radio broadcasts and print publications does have its uses today and it often helps consumers more than firms! More informed customers will drive a harder bargain, increasing competition between sellers and pushing down prices.

The problem for modern advertisers is that people are already bombarded by ads although the estimates of just how many vary widely. One often quoted study puts the number of ads and brand exposures per day to 5,000 or more and conventional ads at over 350.[3] Ads can be seen on urinal cakes, the backs of restroom stalls, napkins, airline peanuts, and even on sheep![4] Consumers are becoming increasingly talented at tuning out much of this advertising. People will record shows in order to fast-forward the commercials or change the station when an ad comes on the radio. There is also a growing trend toward "banner blindness": consumers know where to expect ads on a web page, and their eyes do not focus on those areas.[5] Internet viewers mentally block out the ads because their peripheral vision allows ads to be briefly seen and then ignored.

How is it possible to gain attention and build a brand in this sea of marketing? Unless a company has millions of dollars to spend, traditional broadcast advertising is not an option since the cost of one ad placed in a prime time television show can cost hundreds of thousands of dollars. In 2014, the average cost for a one spot in the popular show "The Big Bang Theory" was $344,827 making it the most expensive program on broadcast channels.[6] Even less expensive traditional media is frequently too expensive for smaller companies. The more economical answer is social media and permission-based marketing. In a permission-based marketing model, the budget is less important than a solid strategy combined with passion and compelling personalities. Permission marketing evens the playing field and allows new talent to compete more effectively against large, entrenched brands.

Permission-based marketing, on the other hand, relies on attention being earned from the audience. Permission marketing is when consumers consent to being marketed. This form of marketing may add value to consumers' lives, causing them to welcome and request certain marketing messages. Opting into an email newsletter, following an account on Twitter, or signing up for text message alerts are examples of permission marketing. Permission marketing is an important element of SMM. Another term for permission SMM is *organic social media*. Permission marketing has been used successfully in launching new brands. In a product category dominated by Gillette and Schick, a small company named Dollar Shave Club started selling razor blade cartridges online on March 1, 2012. As the name of the company suggests, people join and are sent a monthly supply of razor blades for as little as a dollar a month plus a minimal shipping charge. The blades are not available in stores and when Dollar Shave Club entered the market, their promotional mix consisted solely of permission marketing via social media. Founder and CEO, Michael Dubin explained the purpose of the club and its products in a wildly popular YouTube video (Figure 4.1).[7]

Source: https://www.youtube.com/watch?v=ZUG9qYTJMsI

Figure 4.1 Dollar Shave Club's First YouTube Video

By September 2015, Dollar Shave Club had over 68,000 followers on Twitter[8] and a vibrant Facebook page that showcases a continuing series of entertaining videos. It had surpassed Schick as the Number 2 seller of razor blade cartridges.[9]

The basic rule of permission marketing is both a blessing and a curse: money is not enough to buy the way in. Effective permission marketers *earn* the attention of their audience. This need is part of what makes SMM difficult to navigate; it requires earning attention from people who *have a choice* about whether or not to engage with the marketing campaign. There are many strategies available, but people tend to choose engagement with brands that are authentic, are transparent, show care and empathy, respect consumers' time and opinions, and have a human presence online. In the early days of SMM, strategies were developed using only a permission-based or earned approach to marketing. Relying on this approach alone no longer works because there is also an interruption component of SMM in the form of sponsored and paid posts. Facebook, Twitter, and most of the other social media sites and networks have started selling advertising. On November 11, 2014, Facebook made an announcement that a new policy would go into effect on January 1, 2015,[10] and that the policy was based on consumer research. In their newsfeeds, users will now see less of the organic promotional posts from the businesses that they have chosen to follow on Facebook and they will see more paid sponsored posts. This new policy of Facebook means that companies cannot rely solely on permission marketing when developing their social media strategies since many organic posts will not be shown on the newsfeeds of the Facebook fans. An effective social media strategy must include elements of both permission (organic social) and interruption (social adverting).

Social Media Examiner's 2015 Social Media Industry report asked marketers how many of them were using paid social advertising. As shown in Figure 4.2, over 80% of them use Facebook ads with Google ads rather far behind at 41%. LinkedIn, Twitter, and YouTube also have a significant amount of paid adverting. Marketers expected to increase their ad spending on all platforms except Twitter during the next year. Sponsored posts, Twitter cards, and all the other forms of social advertising are a form of interruption marketing.

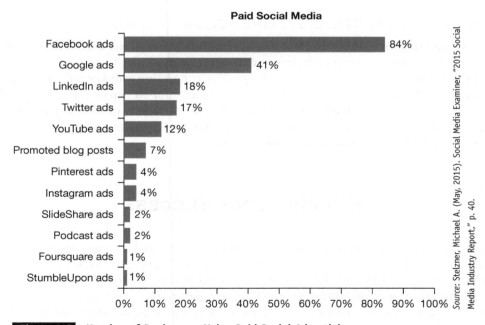

Figure 4.2 Number of Businesses Using Paid Social Advertising

Social media marketers need to determine which mix of interruption and permission marketing fits best within the overall marketing strategy. Even companies such as Dollar Shave Club have moved toward mixing the two types. Dollar Shave Club not only utilizes sponsored posts as interruption marketing, but in November 2014, they also began to use television advertising and spent $64.5 million to Gillette's $43.4 million.[11]

Although individuals generally feel that marketers don't have the *right* to be on their Twitter stream, Facebook page, or blog, most people have accepted that advertising is necessary for the platforms to exist. Advertising is the only way that these networks can generate revenues.

Initial Entry Strategy: Passive vs. Active

When engaging in social media, there are two types of engagement: passive and active. For either big brands that may face risks from participation or businesses that are just getting started with social media, it can be helpful to begin with a passive strategy that then evolves into a more active one. In other words, test the water first and then jump in.

THE PASSIVE STRATEGY: SEARCH, LISTEN, AND RESPOND

If one is new to social media, beginning with a more passive approach is a good way to get started. This approach links back to the first step of the SMM cycle: listening.

To implement a passive approach, start by searching out mentions of your business, its competitors, and the category or industry. Spend some time listening to what people are saying. After achieving familiarity with the conversations, responses can begin.

Responses can be relatively simple: "Thanks for including our product in your blog post. We really appreciate it. Please give me a call if you have any feedback or additional comments." Simply saying thank you and answering questions is a great first step. Again, resist the urge to directly sell or market; rather, begin by responding to people who mention your company or who provide a clear opening to start a conversation.

THE ACTIVE STRATEGY: CREATE AND ENGAGE

The second stage of SMM is an active strategy in which the marketer creates content and engages in conversations through different social media channels. This stage involves actively creating and building social media profiles, connecting with key influencers, and starting or participating in conversations. Many brands jump to step two right away, and start creating content without really understanding their audience or without gaining some experience on how their audience wants to interact. Consider starting slow with a passive strategy before jumping into content creation.

Principles for Success

To be successful in SMM requires giving the community (the audience) something of value. In his book *The Next Evolution of Marketing: Connect with Your Customers by Marketing with Meaning*, Bob Gilbreath discusses the importance of value-contributing marketing content as a way of earning attention from the target audience.[12] People spend time online for three basic reasons: to connect with people, to get information, or to be entertained. A successful social media strategy has to associate itself with at least one of these three reasons.

Successful social media strategies typically meet one (or more) of the PARC principles for success. PARC stands for the initial letters of *p*articipatory, *a*uthentic, *r*esourceful, and *c*redible.

PARTICIPATORY

Brands that are successful on social media are participatory. They interact with the community, answer questions, and thank those who respond. Participating in the community and existing groups or events is important. Big brands often want to run their own show and create their own community, groups, and events. If there is a genuine need, starting fresh is always an option. However, in most cases, there are existing communities whose trust can be earned by showing interest and by participating in those communities. It is faster, simpler, and almost certainly cheaper to work with an existing social media community rather than trying to start a new one. Play on the terms of the community and support its events through positive posts or comments. Participating in dialog will eventually bring results.

Be ready to respond and be conversational. In social media, there is an expectation of two-way communication. Many users will assume that businesses who are active on social media will respond to blog comments, tweets, or Facebook posts that mention the brand. Be open to conversations and participate actively in the community. Taco Bell has been recognized within the advertising industry as a leader in the use of social media. Taco Bell is known for engaging in conversations with both followers and other brands on Facebook and Twitter. One high school swim team member received a custom made Speedo from Taco Bell after posting on Facebook that he would like a "customized Speedo that says think outside the buns on the back." Taco Bell's response was to ask for his size and address so that one could be made and mailed to him.[13] The result is shown in Figure 4.3. The lively discussion on Facebook garnered 2,705 likes and caused Mashable to declare it another "epic social media win."[14]

AUTHENTIC

Being authentic is vital to the success of any SMM campaign. The Internet spreads information faster than any other means of human communication. A signal can travel around the globe in seconds and reach billions of potential receivers. This rapid spread of information makes deception functionally impossible as a long-term strategy for any company. Sources can come from inside or outside a business, from employees, neighbors, friends, or just from a passerby who hears something. Any single person can quickly broadcast an incriminating secret and reach a larger audience than ever before.

Source: http://www.adweek.com/adfreak/taco-bell-agrees-send-facebook-fan-custom-think-outside-buns-speedo-146345

Figure 4.3 The Taco Bell Speedo

Information is spreading more quickly, so strategies that are deceptive or lack authenticity run a serious risk of being outed (i.e., discovered and broadcast). In the age of information, a lack of authenticity is a surefire way to lose credibility and public respect for a brand.

But authenticity is more than telling the truth; it also implies conversing without forced attitudes or a false demeanor. Being authentic is hard to pin down, but it is easy to tell when someone is trying too hard to sound either serious or cheerful. Social media interactions should be professional, but they should also be personable at the same time. Sharing some harmless personal information or anecdotes can do a lot to make an online interaction more interesting and memorable. Putting a human face to the brand helps build connections. Providing honest and sincere responses will earn goodwill, trust, and ultimately business.

Keep in mind that people do business with others they know, like, and trust. By being authentic, a business can build a positive brand reputation that pays future dividends in sales and customer loyalty.

One of the reasons for the success of Dollar Shave Club is their use of videos that feature the CEO, Mike Dubin and his employee, Alejandra in the shipping department of the company. Mike's rumpled appearance and engaging conversation with both the camera and Alejandra who calls the boss by his first name, Mike, contribute to this authenticity.

RESOURCEFUL

When doing permission marketing, businesses have to present useful and relevant content. One of the best ways to do this is to be resourceful: that is, provide the audience with helpful information. Giving the audience a genuinely useful resource is a powerful method for earning trust and gaining attention through social media. There are many potential ways that a company can become a resource online. Social media can be used to solve customer service questions or deal with complaints. For example, in Chapter 1, we discussed the success JetBlue has experienced with customer service on Twitter. Simply tweet the message @jetblue and a customer service rep will answer the question or resolve the problem. Some social media tools make this even easier for firms. For example, a service called Get Satisfaction allows visitors to a site to share feedback and ask questions, and users can vote up or down others' suggestions.[15] The company can also share responses to suggestions or questions posed by users.

Being a resource for customers is so important in B2B marketing that you find frequent lists of the "top thought leaders" in various aspects of marketing and SMM. One who almost always makes the SMM lists is Jeff Bullas. Here's what Webbiquity blogger Tom Pick says about him:

> Jeff Bullas — does *anyone* know more about blogging than Jeff? He's one of those guys who seems to defy the laws of time and space by being able to consistently churn out bookmark-worthy blog posts, speak at events all over the planet, write ebooks, and still engage actively and prolifically on social media.

And here's what he has to say about the team of Cheryl and Mark Burgess:

> Cheryl Burgess would unquestionably be on the list. In addition to being an expert on enterprise b2b marketing, she's the co-author (with Mark Burgess) of The Social Employee, and *the* authority on how to inspire employee social media advocacy inside large organizations.[16]

These marketers work hard and consistently to maintain their thought leader status. The discussions through the book on building a personal brand provide the basics on how to establish yourself as a resource. The rest is about intelligent application of the rules of engagement and plain old hard work.

CREDIBLE

Social media is a powerful way for an organization to earn its audience's trust by being credible. There are two sides to credibility. The first is building a reputation for knowledge and expertise in the field, and the second is building a brand's trustworthiness. Knowledge-based credibility is often referred to as demonstrating thought leadership; by showcasing original thoughts and ideas related to the product or the industry in general, "[t]his form of content brands a company, a consultant, or a nonprofit as an expert and as a trusted resource."[17] Having strong credibility in the form of knowledge or thought leadership is especially useful in B2B markets or for those trying to build a personal brand.

To build trust-based credibility, businesses have to be ready to share information and explain the rationale behind decisions to customers or potential customers. When problems emerge, businesses can gain credibility by admitting their mistakes, by asking the community for understanding or support, and by taking action to remedy the situation. Communicating openly can build credibility and make relationships with the audience stronger. This was illustrated by JetBlue's SMM success. The trials and tribulations endured by Walmart over the course of developing a viable SMM strategy provide another example,

The saga begins with the *Wal-Marting across America* blog, started in September 2006. The subject was a couple traveling in their RV, using Walmart parking lots as rest areas. They would blog about how much all of the employees they encountered liked their jobs and other PR-friendly messages for Walmart. However, when the significant financial relationship between Walmart and the bloggers was revealed, many people were displeased and felt the company had been dishonest. Even though the bloggers involved were real fans, Walmart's secretive approach drew negative media coverage and hurt the company's credibility.[18] Still, the company knew that social media was important and persevered.

To break into more platforms, Walmart set up a promoted Facebook account in 2007. Its page gained fans at a very slow rate; even after several months, membership in various anti-Walmart groups was still larger than Walmart's promoted account![19] The page had a feature tailored to college students, where roommates could input information and get fashion advice for their dorm room. Other forms of participation on the page were severely restricted. Users felt their comments were ignored and discussion was being quashed, and these feelings spawned even more negative remarks. Walmart's initial Facebook campaign was largely regarded as a failure for the company.[20] In spite of all these issues, Walmart now has a robust Facebook presence that generates a considerable amount of user feedback. Given the occasional controversies that beset the firm, not all of the feedback is positive but the Facebook page shows Walmart responding to both customer problems and compliments.

Over the years, Walmart has experimented with many other platforms and types of social engagement. Sometimes the results have been controversial as with their ElevenMoms blog, founded in 2008. About a year later, this community-building effort was embroiled in a broader controversy in which bloggers were found to be accepting money and gifts from businesses in return for positive blog posts. The ElevenMoms pleaded "not guilty" at the time.[21] Walmart once again persevered. There is now a Walmart Moms page on the website in which a group of moms "like you" provide "an everyday guide to living well."[22]

By 2014, Walmart had established a significant social media presence with a clear social media strategy. Their targeted presence includes Facebook, Twitter, and Pinterest. Walmart also uses market segmentation strategies. Each Walmart store now has its own Facebook page that contains information specific to the store's geographic location. On Twitter, the company uses @WalmartToday (Figure 4.4) as a hub for several accounts, @WalmartNewsroom, @WalmartAction, and @WalmartGiving. It is also linked to the Walmart Today blog.

Source: https://twitter.com/WalmartToday

Figure 4.4 The Walmart Today Twitter Hub

This sizeable number of social media accounts paints a picture of a complex business, but even more of a business that has used social media effectively to establish and sometimes to reestablish credibility. On all the social platforms, there is emphasis on the stories of real people—employees, customers, and suppliers—going about their daily lives with the support of Walmart. For the social media marketer, Walmart's journey of discovery provides a useful model of learning and tenacity in the challenging world of SMM.

SMM Ethics

What does it mean to be ethical while using SMM professionally? Generally speaking, the same code of ethics that applies to traditional marketing can be applied. However, due to its highly interactive as well as long-distance nature, social media brings its own set of challenges and complications to marketing ethics. Here are some principles to keep in mind when making those difficult decisions.

HONESTY

SMM is based largely on personal interactions. Unlike traditional advertising, where it is often expected that some spin will be applied to the message, people use social media channels to communicate with friends so that honesty is highly valued. Social media messages are exposed to public view, so expect a high degree of scrutiny: facts will be checked, and promises will be expected to be kept. Building a reputation for honesty is a valuable asset in SMM. Honest and transparent communications should be a priority for both ethical and practical reasons.

PRIVACY

Do not collect or distribute personal information without consent. When implementing a social media campaign, it is helpful to have as much information about your target audience as possible, but obtaining that data should be balanced against protecting user privacy. More aggressive information-gathering software can be interpreted as malware, a computer virus, or just an annoyance to users. Violations of user privacy can quickly destroy a site's reputation and severely damage a company. When collecting user data, it is best to employ passive approaches that allow people to input information voluntarily. Do not collect any more information than is necessary about users, and be very careful that it does not leak to outside parties.

RESPECT

Showing respect for people means treating them as equals, as reasonable individuals with goals and lives of their own. While online interactions can be highly impersonal, there is always another person somewhere in front of a screen. Do not present manipulative messages, create false identities for testimonials, or hijack user profiles for promotional purposes. Using these questionable tactics hurts the quality of information online and inconveniences everyone. Show respect for online participants rather than attempting to herd them with deceptive claims.

RESPONSIBILITY

Mistakes or errors will inevitably occur during a SMM campaign. When a customer has a valid complaint, a technical problem arises, or some other crisis looms, there are three steps to take:

- **Acknowledge**: Find out what the problem is, and take responsibility for the situation.

- **Apologize**: If someone is angry, first attempt to calm her or him down. Apologize, and determine what would give the individual resolution.

- **Act**: Implement promised changes or make other restitution. Inform the complainant(s) that the problem is being addressed.

To responsibly handle a situation, all three of these steps must be undertaken. Still, it is important to avoid promising *too much* while apologizing because then it may be impossible to act! If the problem is beyond the realm of social media (i.e., a technical problem or corporate policy), then a SMM specialist can only do so much. Taking responsibility must be done in realistic ways; an empty gesture is worse than a modest promise.

Observing Social Media Etiquette Helps Achieve Your Personal Branding Goals

This chapter prepares you with the rules of engagement needed to be an effective social media marketer. All these rules apply to your personal branding effort. In addition, there are rules of etiquette that apply to individuals that everyone would be advised to follow in both their personal and their professional social media activities.

Lesson #1. Use different accounts or profiles for your professional and personal communications. This is another place where business and pleasure don't mix. In the early days of social media, many of us made the mistake of posting both personal and professional content on a single account, likely to be a Facebook page at that time. We found that the page became such a mishmash that it appealed to no identifiable group of our followers and the result was often abandonment of the page. So keep the business separate from the personal. And be careful how you define *personal*. It should mean personal updates and communications that you are happy for most of the people you know to see. It does not mean your most intimate secrets that will embarrass you if seen by your favorite aunt—or by a potential employer!

Lesson #2. Don't post pictures and videos of people without their permission. If it's all happening in real time, just be sure they know you are doing it. If they are not present, ask their permission before you post. By the same token, don't tag a picture of someone caught at an unflattering moment.

Lesson #3. Don't play the game of the Internet trolls. In case you haven't met a troll yet, they are the commenters on various platforms who invariably have something nasty to say. In most cases they should simply be ignored. If given attention, their level of misbehavior is likely to increase in ferocity or frequency or both. Moderating blog posts is a good idea. On many platforms, you may be able to delete the comments or block the commenters altogether. There are two exceptions to this rule. In a personal situation, if the behavior becomes threatening, you need to carefully consider bringing it to the attention of the relevant authority. In a business situation, if you see a flood of comments, civil or not, about a particular issue, it needs to be investigated.[1]

Lesson #4. Don't react too quickly. This is virtually a corollary of #3. Take time to think and to respond in a kind manner, supporting your answer with any relevant facts. Do your research and consider your response; don't let yourself get caught up in the moment.

Lesson #5. At all costs, avoid the drunken post. Actually, also make a habit of not posting when you are really tired, jet lagged, or angry. Once sent, a message can never really be recalled. You may delete it from your page, but it will still reside on many other pages.

Perhaps this final lesson sums it up all in one simple rule.

Lesson #6. Don't post anything anywhere on the Internet that you would not want a potential employer, your boss, a current customer, or a potential client to read. A post may be seen at once or it may be discovered months or even years later, by design or by accident. Either way a careless statement can come back to do significant damage. Remember that you cannot take it back. You must observe etiquette and the rules of engagement in such a way that you do not create content that does permanent damage to your personal brand.[2,3,4]

Hootsuite University has a video that provides good recommendations and a nice summary at https://www.youtube.com/watch?v=ootxiibcOWc

[1] Brandon, John (June 15, 2015), "5 Ways to Handle Comment Trolls on Social Media," *CIO*. Retrieved October 1, 2015, from http://www.cio.com/article/2935933/online-reputation-management/5-ways-to-handle-comment-trolls-on-social-media.html

[2] Kievman, Nate (n.d.), "Social Media Etiquette: 10 Commonly Overlooked Best Practices in Social Media," Linked Strategies. Retrieved October 2, 2015, from http://www.linkedstrategies.com/social-media-etiquette-10-commonly-overlooked-best-practices-in-social-media/

[3] Ramsay, Lydia (2010), "Top 12 Rules of Social Media Etiquette," Business Know-How. Retrieved October 2, 2015, from http://www.businessknowhow.com/internet/socialmediaetiquette.htm

[4] (n.d.). "20 Social Media Etiquette Tips," Alltop. Retrieved October 2, 2015, from http://holykaw.alltop.com/20-social-media-etiquette-tips

Making Ethical Decisions

This set of ethical principles for SMM should be read as a starting point rather than the final word. As technology and involvement in social media continue to evolve, new ethical situations will arise. Software tools to mine for user data are becoming ever more sophisticated but so are antiviral, ad-blocking, and anti-cookie programs to combat them. Deciding which practices to employ will be complex and will be based on both the tools available and the ethical limits and norms of the online community.

In a situation in which ethical standards could possibly be breached, it is best to err on the side of caution and avoid a potentially unethical action. The Internet has a long memory, and past actions can linger indefinitely. Gaining a reputation for unscrupulous tactics can seriously tarnish a SMM career and make finding employment more difficult. Even if questionable decisions seem like the only option, it is better to spend time doing more research and use creativity to solve the problem instead. It is better to learn through trial and experience rather than cut a career short by using unethical practices.

Global Perspective

Social media is an international phenomenon. As Internet access becomes more widely available, the number of people in online networks is certain to grow. As a result, communicating across national boundaries is an essential skill for any social media marketer.

CULTURAL DIFFERENCES

Adapting the message to fit the expected audience was discussed in Chapters 2 and 3, but this lesson is especially important when part of the community has an international background. Do some research beforehand to determine which regions or nationalities are active on each social media network. Then tailor communications on each platform to reference likely areas of interest or commonality.

Depending on their culture as well as personal preferences, different people have varying standards of contact and familiarity with others met through social media. Some will be more eager to participate in social media efforts than others. To avoid misunderstandings, be friendly but not invasive when seeking contacts.

HOW TO AVOID CONFUSING YOUR GLOBAL AUDIENCE

Expressions, proverbs, or folksy sayings that are clichés to a domestic audience may be unfamiliar to an international one. Some may be translated strangely or sound very odd to a foreign audience. Similarly, remarks intended as sarcasm or metaphor may not be interpreted as such if there is a language barrier. Avoid making jokes or references overly dependent on popular culture, puns, domestic sporting events, etc. A nonnative speaker is less likely to find these remarks interesting and may even find the reference irrelevant or confusing. This does *not* mean to dumb down material for international audiences but rather adapt to different cultural contexts. Making jokes that are only funny to native speakers or are easily lost in translation may leave international users feeling excluded.

To avoid confusion, it is best to make messages polite, concise, and direct. Before posting, mentally ask whether there is any part of a message that could easily be misinterpreted or cause your overall idea to be misunderstood. This is good practice when crafting messages to any audience, but especially when different languages and cultural backgrounds are involved.

GOOGLE TRANSLATE

Often, people who communicate globally through social media turn toward online translation services in order to bridge languages. Google offers one of several popular translation engines. Becoming familiar with Google Translate (or an equivalent website)

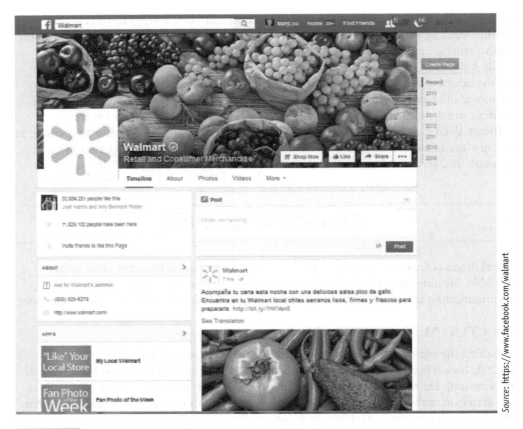

Source: https://www.facebook.com/walmart

Figure 4.5 Walmart Facebook Page

is a valuable skill for SMM. Translation services can help gather what international audiences are saying about different brands.

Be careful when using online translations to create new content because sometimes the results can be rough or can lack important context. One good way to determine whether a message is likely to be misinterpreted is to translate that message into several other languages and then back into English. Is the content still recognizable? If not, revisions might be necessary. On Walmart's Facebook page shown in Figure 4.5, the company recognizes the importance of its Hispanic customers with a post in Spanish. A translate button is available for non-Spanish-speaking visitors.

Achieving familiarity with online translation will broaden the audience with whom a social media marketer can interact. These expanded contacts can be essential to the success of a marketing campaign. Learning to communicate and interact persuasively with an international audience requires skill and finesse, but the growing availability of online translations makes that task somewhat easier.

Best Practices: Following the Rules of Engagement for SMM

Social media involves *earning permission* to join in *personal conversations* with *real people* who don't usually want to be the target of advertising. Most people use social media to build personal relationships, and they are generally not looking for new products. Being aware of the following nine rules of engagement will help a new marketer avoid common mistakes entering the field of social media.

RULE #1: USE SOCIAL MEDIA CHANNELS AS INTENDED

Use all social media channels and their different communication methods as intended. Be aware of how the community is using channels and stay within the existing norms of communication. Look to how the general community is using each social media channel, then use some common sense about the channel's intended use, and keep usage within these standards.

For example, on Twitter, users can either send a *tweet*, which is a general public message to all followers, or a *direct message*, which is private and sent to a specific individual. Some people unfamiliar with this channel send direct messages promoting their blog/business/product to all of their Twitter followers. An untargeted message for all followers should be sent as a tweet, not as a direct message. On LinkedIn, you should not send out generic invitations to people that you do not know. If you want to make a new connection, first look to see if you have a common connection and ask for an introduction. Failing to follow site-specific conventions is one of the quickest ways to get unfollowed or called out on social media sites. Misusing social media channels in this way is a mistake made by people new to Twitter and self-styled social media experts alike.

RULE #2: DON'T BE A DIRTY SPAMMER

Don't send people in a network unwanted messages without their permission. Just because someone follows a page or group does not mean that they want promotional or sales messages.

For example, one LinkedIn member downloaded his entire list of LinkedIn contacts and sent an email promoting new products. There are two problems with his marketing approach. First, some people will feel that it is a form of unwanted spam. Connecting on LinkedIn does not constitute permission to be included on mass emails. Second, he violated rule #1 by using a channel (email) in a way not intended. Only a person requesting to be included or one who has opted in would expect emails. Taking email addresses from LinkedIn to do direct marketing is a violation of trust.

Many new marketers assume that average people *want* to receive their marketing pitches, but that is rarely the case. Give the audience the chance to opt out and don't mass-message people without their permission. People's general aversion to spam means sending unsolicited mass messages is a quick way to lose trust and annoy the audience. Don't send mass communications unless it is an urgently important issue or a person has opted in to receive group messages.

RULE #3: ASSUME PEOPLE DON'T CARE ABOUT THE PRODUCT

Related to the previous rule on spamming, it is helpful to assume that most people on social media sites do not care at all about the product being marketed. Sure, a few might, but most people are not interested. They care about saving money or solving a specific problem.

Just because someone follows or friends a company page does not mean they want to endlessly hear about that business. Consider: what is in it for them? Why would they care?

Some business owners think that they are doing a service by directing marketing at people. One small business owner thought he was doing people a favor by messaging them about his product. He would search on Twitter for people in his city with a keyword related to his product, follow them, and if they followed him back, he would send them a direct message with a sales offer. The reality is that this approach is still seen as marketing aggressively in a social space. Be aware of this attitude. If the approach is too forward, others will perceive it as a sales pitch, and it may taint their perception of the information provided. Be cautious of directly marketing to people, especially when it might not be expected or invited.

RULE #4: HAVE A PERSONALITY

Some people are hesitant to be personal on public social media sites. They want to keep their content strictly professional and business related. The reality is that people connect with other people on a deeper level than they can connect with a brand.

Figure 4.6 The Mars Curiosity Rover Celebrates Its Finding of Possible Water on Mars

Sharing some personality helps build common ground and trust. A bureaucratic or forced tone is not a very appealing call to interact. Instead, building a feeling of trust and common interest makes it more likely that people will find the social media campaign to be engaging and worth participating in.

There is a professional line to be drawn, of course; it is a bad idea to get excessively personal or share intimate details. However, talking about music tastes, coffee brands, or other harmless character traits builds common ground and human connections. Always try to inject some personality into SMM and keep a sense of humor about the process.

The NASA SMM team has done a great job of creating a personality for the Mars Curiosity Rover, which has been exploring Mars since 2011.[23] In Figure 4.6 from the rover's Twitter stream, the reader can see that the robot is very excited about having located possible signs of water on Mars.

RULE #5: PROVIDE CONTEXT WHEN SEEKING CONNECTIONS

Many social networks are intended for connecting with people already known. Facebook and LinkedIn are both sites where the network should ideally be centered on people one has met face to face. However, for SMM, it is necessary to expand that circle to people who may help provide business now or down the road. Therefore, having a tactful way to add new connections that may rarely or never be seen in person is extremely important.

When sending a request to connect with someone—whether it is on Twitter, Facebook, LinkedIn, or even via email—it is helpful to provide context for the connection. What is the reason for connecting with that person? Providing context is simple and just requires a quick note: "Hi, John, I saw that we are both members of group X, and you have posted some really smart discussion topics. I would like to add you to my network," or "Hi, Sally, we met last week at a networking event, and I wanted to follow up and say hi. You mentioned you were interested in social media marketing, so I went ahead and added you to my newsletter distribution. If you are not interested, you can opt out at any time." Adding a brief note for context will lead to higher acceptance rates on connection requests.

RULE #6: BE TRANSPARENT

Social media has changed the way information flows. Information is now available quickly, and it travels across the world in an instant. This means that businesses have to be more transparent in their interactions. Consumers can talk to each other and read about each other's experiences. They can research a company and its employees fairly easily.

This access to information means that companies have to be upfront with their information. Consumer reviews will inevitably highlight issues or problems. Be prepared to address them in an open and honest manner. Keeping secrets from customers is no longer a viable business strategy.

RULE #7: TALK ABOUT THE TOPIC

Businesses will often find discussion threads, Twitter conversations, groups, or blog posts that are related to their business line. Often their first instinct is to jump into the conversation with a marketing message. This is a mistake.

It is a good idea for the company to join the discussion, but it needs to make sure to focus on what the conversation is about, not just do self-promotion. A business that interrupts conversation threads to talk about its product is perceived like a loud braggart at a cocktail party. Pretty soon, no one wants to converse with the firm. Being overly self-centered is a quick way to be ignored at social gatherings, both in real life and online.

To avoid being shunned, talk about the conversation topic that is being addressed, not about the product or service being marketed. Don't hijack conversations and try to shift them to other purposes. People see through this easily, causing a loss of trust and in extreme cases getting the marketer kicked out of the group or off that social media site.

RULE #8: SOCIAL MEDIA PROFILES ARE NOT BILLBOARDS

Keep in mind that people do *not* create social media profiles for marketers to use. Marketers may think they are doing favors by leaving product messages on relevant blogs or discussions. However, most people are not excited to see posts from random businesses on their personal sites. What is intended as a useful product suggestion may be perceived as unwanted graffiti on someone's beloved blog and may generate a strong negative response.

Don't use other people's social media profiles or websites as a way to promote a message. It is best to engage in discussions without doing overt marketing unless it is directly on-topic. Generate original content and use that to get the message out instead of posting unwanted messages on others' sites.

RULE #9: BE NICE

Being pleasant and nice is very simple, but some businesses have a hard time grasping this principle. Politeness costs nothing, but it can make a huge difference in the responses that a SMM campaign receives.

An easy "please" and "thank you" can go a long way. Look for opportunities to publicly or privately thank people who help out or make positive comments about the product. On the other hand, when asking someone for a favor, be sure to ask nicely and not demand too much.

Look for opportunities to give back to other people in the same social community. Promote their events, blog posts, or products. Providing a link, positive recommendation, or other traffic-building measure for someone else can help a lot in earning his or her gratitude. In the long run, the return from these small favors adds up.

In the face of a social media landscape that seems to change on an almost-daily basis it is pleasant to realize that there are some principles that resist change. They make up the rules of engagement of SMM. The principles include honesty, responsibility, and respect for other social media users and for their privacy. Social media marketers who participate with authenticity and who keep these principles in mind have a much better change of creating the trusted brand that is their goal.

Notes

1. Godin, Seth (1999), *Permission Marketing: Turning Strangers into Friends, and Friends into Customers* (New York: Simon & Schuster).
2. Alchian, Armen, and William R. Allen (1983). *Exchange and Production: Competition, Coordination and Control,* 3rd ed. (Belmont, CA: Wadsworth), p. 278.

3. Johnson, Sheree (September 29, 2014), "New Research Sheds Light on Daily Ad Exposures," SJ Insights. Retrieved September 30, 2015, from http://sjinsights.net/2014/09/29/new-research-sheds-light-on-daily-ad-exposures/

4. Carvajal, Doreen (April 24, 2006), "Advertiser Counts on Sheep to Pull Eyes over the Wool," *International Herald Tribune*. Retrieved January 11, 2011, from http://www.nytimes.com/2006/04/24/world/europe/24sheep.html

5. Benway, J. P., and D. M. Lane (December 1988), "Banner Blindness: Web Searchers Often Miss 'Obvious' Links," *Internetworking*, vol. 1.3. Retrieved January 11, 2011, from http://www.internettg.org/newsletter/dec98/banner_blindness.html

6. Poggi, Jeanine (September 25, 2014), "Football and 'Big Bang' Are Broadcast TV's Most Expensive Ad Buys," *Advertising Age*. Retrieved September 20, 2015, from http://adage.com/article/media/football-big-bang-tv-s-expensive-ad-buys/295130/

7. "DollarShaveClub.com — Our Blades Are F***ing Great," YouTube (March 6, 2012). Retrieved September 30, 2015, from https://www.youtube.com/watch?v=ZUG9qYTJMsI

8. (n.d.). Twitter. Retrieved September 30, 2015, from https://twitter.com/DollarShaveClub

9. Neff, Jack (September 8, 2015), "Dollar Shave Club Claims to Top Schick as No. 2 Razor Cartridge," *Advertising Age*. Retrieved September 27, 2015, from http://adage.com/article/cmo-strategy/dollar-shave-club-claims-top-schick-2-men-s-razor/300247/

10. Facebook for Business (November 14, 2014), "Update to News Feed: What it Means for Businesses." Retrieved September 27, 2015, from https://www.facebook.com/business/news/update-to-facebook-news-feed

11. Wolff-Mann, Ethan (September 8, 2015), "Dollar Shave Club Claims It Passed Schick to Be No. 2 in Razor Cartridge," CNNMoney. Retrieved September 27, 2015, from http://time.com/money/4024897/dollar-shave-club-passes-schick/

12. Gilbreath, Bob (2009), *The Next Evolution of Marketing: Connect with Your Customers by Marketing with Meaning* (New York: McGraw-Hill).

13. Stampler, Laura (January 7, 2013), "Taco Bell Is Sending a High Schooler A Custom Speedo Because of a Facebook Post," *Business Insider*. Retrieved September 27, 2015, from http://www.businessinsider.com/taco-bell-sends-high-schooler-custom-made-speedo-2013-1

14. Laird, Sam (January 3, 2013), "Taco Bell Comes up with Another Epic Social Media Win," Mashable. Retrieved October 2, 2015, from http://mashable.com/2013/01/03/taco-bell-epic-social-media-win/#qg3JeYUE9Pqz

15. (n.d.). Customer Community Software—Love Your Customers, Get Satisfaction. Retrieved December 30, 2010, from http://getsatisfaction.com/

16. "10 Top Marketing Thought Leaders in Social Media," Webbiquity (May 21, 2015). Retrieved October 2, 2015, from http://webbiquity.com/social-media-marketing/10-top-marketing-thought-leaders-in-social-media/

17. Scott, David Meerman (2009), *The New Rules of Marketing & PR* (Hoboken, NJ: John Wiley), p. 133.

18. Gogoi, Pallavi (October 9, 2006), "Walmart's Jim and Laura: The Real Story," *Bloomberg Businessweek*. Retrieved May 23, 2011, from http://www.businessweek.com/bwdaily/dnflash/content/oct2006/db20061009_579137.htm

19. Kwan, Ming (November 7, 2007), "Poor Walmart: A Social Networking Nightmare Scenario," *Wikinomics*. Retrieved May 23, 2011, from http://www.wikinomics.com/blog/index.php/2007/11/07/poor-Walmart/

20. Wilson, David (October 11, 2007), "A Failed Facebook Marketing Campaign," *Social Media Optimization*. Retrieved May 23, 2011, from http://social-media-optimization.com/2007/10/a-failed-facebook-marketing-campaign/

21. Christine (August 17, 2009), "The Truth about the Walmart ElevenMoms," From Dates to Diapers. Retrieved October 1, 2015, from http://fromdatestodiapers.com/the-truth-about-walmarts-elevenmoms/

22. (n.d.). "Walmart Moms," Walmart. Retrieved October 1, 2015, from http://wm5.walmart.com/Tips-Ideas/LP/Walmart_Moms/19240/

23. (n.d.). "Launch," NASA Jet Propulsion Laboratory. Retrieved October 2, 2015, from http://mars.nasa.gov/msl/mission/timeline/launch/

5

Social Media Platforms and Social Networking Sites

Web sites that facilitate social networking are called social media platforms. These platforms can be categorized in to the popular social networking sites and those sites used for microblogging, collaboration, photo sharing, etc. Each of these platforms plays an important role in social media management and will be discussed in detail in the chapters that follow. This chapter outlines the history of social media platforms and discusses the primary marketing uses of the major social networking sites.

List of Social Media Platforms

While social networking is as old as humanity and word-of-mouth marketing, the practice has moved online much more recently. Social networking is based on network theory, which can be used to show how telecommunications networks, networks of friends, and even nodes on the Internet can be connected. Networking theory explains how traditional word-of-mouth (WOM) marketing, became eWOM marketing and therefore allowed for information to be transmitted rapidly on the Internet. Because people are connected, information travels along their connections. Because people are now connected electronically, information spreads even more rapidly. The idea of the central node of the network means that some people are more influential than others online because they are central to groups sharing information. Companies seeking to market their products via social media, often align with influential bloggers or key users whose opinion is respected. That way, companies know that they are getting their information

LEARNING OBJECTIVES

After completing this chapter, students will be able to:

- Describe types of social media platforms with emphasis on social networking
- Recount a brief history of social networks indicating how they have grown in the United States and globally
- Identify the benefits of marketing with social networks

(Continued)

- Explain some ways in which both B2C and B2B marketers use social networks
- Define a white label social network and understand how it is used in marketing and customer engagement
- Summarize some predictions about the future of social networks
- Identify best practices for marketing with social media platforms
- Create their powerful LinkedIn profile

out quickly from those who are well-respected in the field. An example is the Keurig coffee maker, which uses influential bloggers to launch new products.

There are many ways to be active socially. Broadly speaking, these types of social interactions facilitated by the Internet are termed social media platforms. Under this category there are multiple sub-categories, with the best known probably being social networking sites like Facebook, LinkedIn, and Google+. These sites are often what we think of when we think of social networking. Decidedly Social lists 13 types of social media platforms.[1]

1. **Social networking sites** *Facebook, LinkedIn, Google+, CafeMom, Gather, Fitsugar*

2. **Microblogging sites** *Twitter, Tumblr, Posterous*

3. **Publishing tools** *WordPress, Blogger, Squarespace*

4. **Collaboration tools** *Wikipedia, WikiTravel, WikiBooks*

5. **Rating/Review sites** *Amazon ratings, Angie's List*

6. **Photo sharing sites** *Flikr, Instagram, Pinterest*

7. **Video sharing sites** *YouTube, Vimeo, Viddler*

8. **Personal broadcasting tools** *Blog Talk radio, Ustream, Livestream*

9. **Virtual worlds** *Second Life, World of Warcraft, Farmville*

10. **Location-based services** *Check-ins, Facebook Places, Foursquare, Yelp*

11. **Widgets** *Profile badges, Like buttons*

12. **Social bookmarking and news aggregation** *Digg, Delicious*

13. **Group buying** *Groupon, Living Social, Crowdsavings*

These social networking platforms have been assigned to various chapters following this one:

Chapter 6: Microblogging
Chapter 7: Content Creation and Sharing: Blogging, Streaming Video, Podcasts, and Webinars.
Chapter 8: Video Marketing
Chapter 9: Marketing on Photo Sharing Sites
Chapter 10: Social Bookmarking and News Aggregation, Collaboration
Chapter 11: Content Marketing: Publishing Articles, White Papers, and E-books.

Although microblogging can be considered its own chapter, the microblogging sites are also considered to be social networks under most classifications. Therefore, eBizMBA states the top social networks are Facebook, Twitter, LinkedIn, Pinterest, and Google+. Twitter will be covered in the microblogging chapter and Pinterest in the Photo Sharing chapter, but we will discuss the uses of the other top three networks for both business to consumer and business to business marketing.

The 2000s saw the explosive growth of social networks, with names like Facebook, LinkedIn, and the now out-of-favor MySpace becoming part of the common vernacular.[2] More interactions could take place online, lessening the need for face-to-face or phone conversation. Not only personal information, but product information was shared online. In order to be profitable, social networks must either rely on the advertising (Facebook) or subscription (LinkedIn). These networks, although often perceived as providing a service to the users, must make money somehow.

Importantly, social media users are fickle. The top social networking sites have changed in recent years driven by the tastes of the new generations. The Millennial Generation (especially those born in the 1990s) grew up using social network sites to interact in ways that closely paralleled the culture of cliques and exclusivity commonly found on both high school and university campuses. For example, Facebook's invitation and approval process for entrance into an individual's sphere of friends and acquaintances ensures exclusivity, which is largely credited with making the social network an immediate hit among millennials.[3] Now the tide has turned again and Instagram is the second largest social network in the United States. With the ability to share visual images easily, Instagram appeals to Millennials and the next generation after them (let's call them Generation Z). Although social networks' initial appeal was to the younger generation, eventually social networks were introduced that appealed to other demographic groups, such as business professionals (LinkedIn) and women (Pinterest).

Today, social networks are among the most popular sites on the social web.[4] A social network site is an online service on which members can establish relationships based on friendship, kinship, shared interests, business advantage, or other reasons. A social network site facilitates these interactions by letting members build a public or private profile, specify who can connect with them, and share their connections with others. Social network services simplify the process of sharing information, such as interests, events, status, and pictures, within individual networks.

Social network sites are the latest development of a prior Internet phenomenon, discussion boards (discussed in Chapter 10). Instead of just sharing thoughts and information, users began to develop communal relationships. A virtual community, a term first coined by Howard Rheingold in his 1993 book by the same name, focuses on building relationships using discussion boards to converse about topics of shared interest.[5] Technology's ability to aggregate personal characteristics makes it easier than ever to connect to others with similar background or interests.[6]

Online communities were the forerunners of social networks. While other virtual communities are driven by thoughts and ideas, social networks are primarily organized around people, not interests.[7] People join to connect with existing contacts and to keep in touch with old friends, not primarily to engage in discussion. Understanding the background and general expectations that members have of social networks is essential when developing a marketing presence on these platforms.

Social networks online have encouraged the development of brand communities. The brand community concept is not new: the Harley Davidson HOG club, the Saturn car community, and other examples pre-date the Internet. Brand communities can now be developed online and may be the brainchild of the brand itself or a group of loyal fans.

A Brief History of Social Networks

One of the first social network sites was SixDegrees.com, launched in 1997 by Andrew Weinreich, a well-known entrepreneur and Internet executive.[8] Weinreich drew his inspiration for the site from the "six degrees of separation" theory, which claims that "anyone on the planet can be connected to any other person on the planet through a chain of acquaintances that has no more than five intermediaries."[9] SixDegrees.com let users build profiles, display a list of their friends, and traverse these lists. Although each of these functions had already been implemented by dating services and virtual communities, SixDegrees.com was the first to combine them. Despite attracting millions of users, the site could not attract sufficient funding or advertising to sustain its business model and closed in 2000. Nonetheless, "it paved the way for the likes of Facebook, LinkedIn and many more [social networks]."[10]

In 2001 Ryze.com was launched by Adrian Scott to help people make connections and grow their personal networks.[11] Scott introduced Ryze.com to his close friends in San Francisco, many of whom went on to become the entrepreneurs and investors behind such social network sites as Friendster, Tribe.net, and LinkedIn. This tight-knit group believed that its respective social networks could coexist without competition.[12]

However, Ryze.com never achieved critical mass, while Friendster enjoyed a meteoric rise and suffered an equally precipitous fall, with *Inc.* magazine calling it "one of the biggest disappointments in Internet history".[13] At the heart of Friendster's catastrophic failure was the alienation of its early adopters, which (in large part) came about because of continued intermittent service problems and the routine practice of deleting user accounts that appeared suspicious. On the upside, Tribe.net eventually carved out a loyal niche audience, while LinkedIn grew to become the second-most popular social network.

In August 2003 MySpace was launched by a group of eUniverse employees with Friendster accounts who were inspired by its potential, and decided to mimic the social network's more popular features.[14] The founders of MySpace "wanted to attract [the] estranged Friendster users," according to cofounder Tom Anderson.[15] However, it was the 2004 mass influx of teenagers into MySpace that accounted for its swift rise in popularity. By May 2005 MySpace had become the fifth-ranked web domain in terms of page views, according to ComScore's Media Metrix.[16] The notoriety of MySpace attracted the attention of News Corporation, which purchased the social network site for $580 million in July 2005.[17] On August 9, 2006, MySpace reached its 100 millionth account.[18] By 2007 MySpace was considered the leading social networking site in the U.S., valued at $12 billion.[19]

However, all that was to change. On February 4, 2004, Mark Zuckerberg, an undergraduate at Harvard University, launched "Thefacebook," originally located at thefacebook.com.[20] Unlike previous social network sites, membership was initially limited to only people with a harvard.edu email address, a restriction that created the perception of an intimate, exclusive community. Within twenty-four hours of launch, 1,200 Harvard students became members. A month later, over half of the undergraduate population of Harvard had created a profile.[21] The social network quickly spread to other Boston-area universities, then to other Ivy League universities, and gradually to most of the colleges and universities in the U.S.[22]

The name of Zuckerberg's social network was officially changed to Facebook.com in August 2005, after the domain name was purchased for $200,000.[23] On September 2, 2005, U.S. high school students were allowed to join Facebook, substantially increasing its target market.[24] Then, the social network spread to educational institutions in other countries, beginning with schools in the United Kingdom.

In September 2006 Facebook expanded its registration policy to anyone older than thirteen with a valid email address.[25] This expanded access foreshadowed a boom in Facebook's popularity. On April 19, 2008, Facebook overtook MySpace in traffic.[26] MySpace continued to experience a steady decline in membership, attributed to such factors as "the failure to execute product development," a failure to innovate, sticking with a "portal strategy," and too many ads.[27] However, membership in Facebook skyrocketed, reaching 100 million by August 2008, 350 million by December 2009, 500 million by July 2010, and 750 million active monthly users in June of 2011.[28]

As of this writing, Facebook is the most popular social network, as shown in Table 5.1. Facebook has raised more than $1.3 billion in funding, with the *New York Times* estimating the value of the privately held company at a whopping $200 billion in 2011. Facebook went public in 2012 in one of the largest initial public offerings in history. In 2015, its market valuation did reach $230 billion, making its market capitalization the tenth largest in the S&P 500. In fact, Facebook generates 81% of the content shared to social networks, being particularly strong in the health category.[29]

Social Network	Estimated Unique Monthly Visitors (millions)*	Quantcast Rank**	Alexa Global Traffic Rank***	Launch Date
Facebook	900	3	2	2004
Twitter	310	8	8	2006
LinkedIn	255	19	9	2003
Pinterest	250	13	26	2010
Google+	110	28	NA	2011
Instagram	100	145	36	2010
Tumblr	80.5	139	91	2007
Flickr	65	139	91	2004
Vine	42	335	1172	2013
Meetup	40	701	296	2001
Tagged	38	615	408	2004
Ask.fm	37	113	179	2010
MeetMe (formerly Yearbook)	15.5	635	2328	2013
Classmates	15	285	4022	1995

Table 5.1 Top 15 Social Networking Sites Worldwide Updated April 1, 2015

Estimated unique monthly visitors according to eBiz\MBA Inc.
**Quantcase ranks "websites based on the number of people in the United States who visit each site within a month. It includes sites with estimated traffic as well as sites with traffic that Quantcast has independently verified. Quantcast directly measures site traffic through the implementation of the Quantcast asynchronous tag on each website."*
***Alexa Global Traffic Rank estimates a site's popularity, with traffic data from Alexa Toolbar users and other diverse traffic sources, using an ascending scale where 1 represents the highest traffic rank.*

Of course, this success has spawned many competitors, as can also be seen in the table. However, about 30 million businesses now have a Facebook fan page and are paying 122% more for advertising than a year ago.[30]

A GLOBAL PERSPECTIVE

With a plethora of social networks launching, as illustrated in Figure 5.1, most of the attention has gone to the U.S. superstars, such as Facebook and LinkedIn. However, in other countries, different social network sites have risen to prominence, even ones built by major corporations. As an example, Google launched Orkut on January 22, 2004, and although the social network never gained significant U.S. market share, it became popular in both India and Brazil.[31] Despite recent trends showing Facebook making strong inroads in India and Brazil, Orkut, Google's previous attempt at a social network, remained a well-known brand in these countries before it was closed in September of 2014.[32] China has five powerful social platforms which include social networking capabilities as outlined in Table 5.2, with three of them, QQ, Qzone, and WeChat being owned by Tencet (Table 5.2). Renren was the leader but has made some missteps in recent years. The leading social network in China, QQ, has more than 800 million users.[33] Vkontakte (VK) dominates in Russia, with over 100 million members and an Alexa traffic rank of 34.[34] As well as using major social networks, the Brazilians

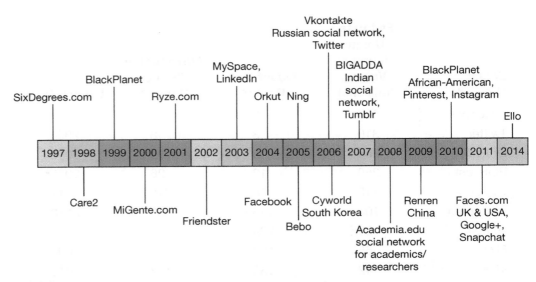

Figure 5.1 Timeline of the Launch Dates of Major Social Network Sites

Platform	Description	Monthly Active Users in Millions (2014)
QQ (Tencent)	Messaging platform includes text messages, video, and voice chat	829
QZone (Tencent)	Social networking and blogging, fan pages	644
WeChat (Tencent)	Voice and video chat plus e-commerce	438
Weibo	Microblogging capabilities including video and live broadcasts	167
Renren	30.3	214

Source: eMarketer, January 2015[35]

Table 5.2 Chinese Social Media Platforms (millions; %change; %population)

also use the Chinese network Baidu. As a consequence, marketers who want to reach a global audience should take into consideration these other social networks.

Benefits of Marketing with Social Networks

One consequence of online social networks has been to blur the line between business and personal life. With contacts overlapping between business, family, school, and so on, keeping private life out of the public eye is increasingly difficult. While previously only celebrities and politicians could expect public scrutiny of their actions, much personal information (especially contributed by young people) can now be found on the Internet.[36] While some are concerned about the implications of widespread information sharing, it can also be argued that this "transparency is in sum a good thing for individuals and society." In any case, online sharing of popular interests is highly valuable to a social media marketer. For example, Twitter is the place to share sports and news information, whereas Pinterest users share more content on beauty and fitness and shopping than other platforms.[37]

Marketing with social networks has several advantages for firms, allowing them to "find talent, build brand awareness, find new customers, and help conduct brand intelligence and market research."[38] Job search portals and professional networking platforms (such as LinkedIn) have become a popular way to match job seekers with employers. Further, with the large population segment participating on social networks, such networks have become an excellent way to seek out clients or customers. The term brand intelligence refers to information that businesses can collect about their customers, from basic demographics to topics of discussion to detailed feedback. Instead of costly market research, monitoring social networks can gather general sentiments, opinions, and customer needs with great efficiency.

The best marketing with social networks comes not from the company but from the customer or fan base. For example, the Facebook page for Coca-Cola started out with two fans. When the company saw how successful the page was, instead of trying to squash it, they bought the page and were able to use it to propel the brand forward.

These days, Coca-Cola is a top brand around the world with its successful "open happiness" campaign as well as on Facebook and uses a sophisticated content marketing strategy using content that is both "liquid," which is shareable, and "linked" which reinforces its brand image.[39]

The brand stories shared online talk very little about the product and more about how Coca-Cola can help people, like making it possible for migrant workers to phone home or for customers to send a Coke across the world to a friend. Today, the Facebook page is the top brand page with 89,805,855 fans, almost twice as many as McDonald's. Facebook gave Coke's customers a place to voice their brand enthusiasm. Many stars and celebrities top the Facebook "Leaderboard" and have more followers than some corporate brands. (See Table 5.3)

When considering which social media network to use we should consider the characteristics of the target audience as noted in Chapter 3. The following is just a sample of characteristics of the audience that should be considered when selecting a social media platform. The characteristics are noted and an example is included.

- Is the target consumers or professionals? LinkedIn would be a good choice for business professionals, other social networks for consumers.
  - Is the target male or female? Some networks appeal more to females, like Pinterest.

- Where do they hang out? Fish where the fish are. If your customer base likes Instagram, market there.

- Is my product visual? Instagram, Pinterest, and YouTube make sense for a visual product.

- Are my consumers content oriented? If sharing and posting is important, consider Facebook or another interactive network. If blogging is important to your customers, consider LinkedIn or Google+.

- Do they like to collaborate? Wikis and other sharing sites might be important.

- Are product demonstrations needed? YouTube provides wonderful product demonstrations for visual products like home repair equipment.

The capabilities of the network should also be considered. Table 5.4 shows the capabilities of each of the networks to create groups, communities, or lists and provide blogging capabilities. Due to their information-sharing capacity, social networks can also be used as a new distribution channel for marketing messages. Marketers must be aware that people participate on social networks primarily to connect with friends, not

	Sorted by Fans		
Name	# of Fans	Twitter Followers	Total
1. Facebook for Every Phone	523,804,524		523,804,524
2. Facebook	161,672,513	13,910,716	175,583,229
3. Facebook Sales Germany	161,672,513		161,672,513
4. Christiano Ronaldo	102,423,960	35,101,572	137,525,532
5. Shakira	100,254,055	30,497,967	130,752,022
6. Eminem	91,856,145	19,309,193	111,165,338
7. Vin Diesel	90,936,177		90,936,177
8. FC Barcelona	81,619,589	4,760,823	96,380,412
9. Rihanna	81,597,602	44,200,649	125,798,251
10. Real Madrid CF	80,801,655	15,609,429	96,411,084
11. YouTube	80,628,812	50,329,306	321,209
12. Lionel Messi (Leo Messi)	75,577,410		130,958,118
13. Michael Jackson	75,219,554	1,813,172	75,577,410
14. Bob Marley	73,033,926	1,289,218	77,032,726
15. Will Smith	72,958,357		72,958,357
16. Justin Bieber	72,336,188	62,926,195	135,262,383
17. Katy Perry	71,953,133	68,707,147	140,660,280
18. Harry Potter and the Deathly Hallows	71,782,600		71,782,600
19. Taylor Swift	70,696,977	56,492,999	127,189,976
20. The Simpsons	69,507,607	2,195,363	71,702,970

Table 5.3 Facebook Page Leaderboard

Source: http://fanpagelist.com/category/top_users/ April 21, 2015

Source: https://www.Facebook.com/

to search out new products. However, an advantage of networks such as Facebook is that they encourage users to have many conversations with different people or brands, all occurring at once.[40] If marketing messages are engaging and valuable to social network users, they may be welcomed by users. Social networks allow a brand to engage its target audience in ongoing conversation, which can both draw in new business and increase customer loyalty, as illustrated by the Coca-Cola example.

	Facebook	LinkedIn	GP	YouTube	Twitter	Pinterest/Instagram/Snapchat
Personal Page	✓	✓	✓	✓	✓	✓
Company Page	✓	✓	✓	✓	✓	✓
Groups	✓	✓	Communities			Group Boards to which others may pin
Lists	✓	Create prospect list and send direct message if part of same group	Circles		✓	
Blogging		✓	Blogger	Video Channel for Video Logs (Vlogs)		

Table 5.4 Marketing Applications Available for the Major Social Networks

Some business executives worry that participating on social networks might make their company appear unprofessional or invite negative commentary. To some extent these fears are justified; if there is negative sentiment about a company, some of it will show up in comments on the firm's social networking profiles. Negative comments, however, are not the disaster that many predict them to be. Instead of searching the Internet for negative reviews, false information, or bad press to refute, a social network profile can become the lightning rod for criticism, concentrating it in one location for easy response. Instead of controlling what people say, build their trust with earnest communications.[41] As a space to respond to criticism and receive feedback, participating on a social network has many benefits to a firm.

Marketing with Social Networks

Many businesses are motivated to interact on social networks, but large numbers of these companies do not have much payoff from their efforts. On a social network, it is especially important to enter with a strong understanding of the strategies and objectives (discussed in Chapter 2). The first step is to decide on goals and objectives that should be achieved.[42] Otherwise, due to its informal nature, social networking can easily become a distraction rather than an aid for firms. To avoid this problem, develop a solid plan before marketing on a social network.

The next decision involves the target market. Different social networks attract extremely different clientele, so knowing who the audience is and where to find them is essential. For online marketing, most campaigns will fall into one of two categories: business-to-consumer (B2C) and business-to-business (B2B) marketing. Facebook and LinkedIn are two networks frequently used for these respective purposes. These two will be used as instructional examples for B2C and B2B marketing, but similar tactics may likely apply on other social networks with equal results.

BUSINESS-TO-CONSUMER MARKETING

For businesses specializing in consumer products or services, social networks can be a great way to locate and market to potential customers. Most social networks make it easy for members to like, share, or become fans of a brand. Therefore, the emphasis needs to be on content, more specifically, creating content that is "share-worthy" in the eyes of the consumer. The end goal is to share content that makes the audience want to discuss it further with friends. This can function as word-of-mouth advertising as consumers share their likes with each other.[43] Social networks can also advance a brand's position in relation to competitors by making a company seem more memorable or personable. However, accomplishing these lofty goals demands "persistence, consistency, and genuine intentions."[44]

To have maximal reach to consumers, focus on the places where most consumers are spending time. At the present time, Facebook is the giant of casual social networking, so establishing a presence there is crucial for B2C marketing.[45] While Facebook is the "most marketer-friendly" of the major social networks, it still requires finesse in order to market on its social network effectively.[46] There are a huge number of professionals and brands operating on Facebook, so the competition can be fierce. Few companies can afford to ignore Facebook, as it is the largest social network in the United States (see Table 5.5). However, Instagram represents the trend toward photo and image sharing and is growing rapidly (see Table 5.6). This topic of photo sharing will be covered in more detail in Chapter 9.

To begin marketing a brand on Facebook, start an account. Do not create a profile; those are intended for private users and are not as helpful for marketing. Instead, create a page that will represent the business.[47] Pages allow users to follow or become fans of a company without giving access to their personal information as would occur from friending a profile. This feature makes pages more functional and engaging for marketing to consumers.[48] A page is Facebook's recommended approach for creating an officially branded business presence.[49] Customize the page to reflect the company's style and values, but provide some content distinct from the firm's primary website.[50]

Once a page has been created, it must be updated frequently with new content. How often? Too-frequent updating can overwhelm a fan's newsfeed and become an annoyance. Do not update more than three times per day. Quality is much more important than quantity because boring or repetitive content can be easily hidden on Facebook.[51] Focus on content that is relevant and engaging for Facebook users.[52] Generally, Facebook content should be light, funny, and informative, or it should give a special deal or value. Give useful tips, or ask open-ended questions that will interest the audience.[53] Not every content item must be original: sharing links to interesting items can also be valuable.[54]

One avenue for Facebook content to go viral is through "likes." When a Facebook user likes a page, comment, or other material, it is displayed to her or his friends, who have an opportunity to like the item as well. In this way an appealing post or idea can spread rapidly through Facebook friend networks. However, users are often picky about which items they will like. To get an idea of what sort of content to post, look at others' Facebook pages—particularly those of businesses offering a product or service similar to the one being marketed—and see which statuses or comments are being liked the

Social Site	Users Millions	% of Population
Facebook	157.1	48.9
Instagram	77.6	24.2
Twitter	53.1	16.5
Pinterest	47.1	14.6
Tumblr	20.0	6.2

Table 5.5 U.S. Social Network Users and Penetration 2015

Source: eMarketer, February 2015

most. This survey will give some insight into what potential fans want to see. Often, less serious posts will be liked more, so keep content funny, personable, and entertaining.

To gain viewers for a page, put links on other websites and email signatures, business cards, and outgoing communications. To make the URL for the Facebook page easy to write and remember, it is important to "secure shorter 'vanity' URLs."[55] A customized URL makes the page more memorable, increasing the chance Facebook users will visit and become fans. Running contests or offering discounts to Facebook members are also good ways to convince people to follow a Facebook profile. Contests should be tailored to the product being offered. The risk is that if a contest goes poorly, it can be an embarrassment for the brand.[56] To avoid this, do not ask too much from members: pictures or stories are faster to submit than fully edited videos. More entries will be made if there are few or no barriers to joining the contest.

Groups are a classic and useful way to spread information about a product. However, on Facebook the groups' functionality presents some problems for marketing purposes.[57] Groups are very loosely organized and have many redundancies, overlaps, and competing groups on the same topics. Further, in groups beyond a certain size, mass messaging is blocked by Facebook, making communication with all the members difficult or impossible. In fact, most companies and brands have been guided to Facebook to the fan page. However, niche marketers and small firms might want to consider the group concept. The reason is because of the Facebook Edgerank algorithm, which means that unless the user engages with your page frequently, they may not see every one of your posts. A group will allow for more consistent communication.[58]

While few brands have successfully marketed with groups, a great number have used Facebook Places to expand their social presence. Aimed toward small- to medium-sized local businesses, Places is a location-based service that allows users to check in online before or after they visit. A relatively recent feature (launched in late 2010), many Facebook users are already engaged by checking in with their favorite businesses.[59] Companies have found that integrating their physical and online locations has increased traffic to both. Offering special deals when visitors check in online is a reliable way to draw more attention.[60] It is also possible to create local market events, or host a charity drive to bring visitors to a Places page.[61] With some creativity, integrating a business into Facebook Places is a strong SMM tool.

Facebook derives much of its revenue from advertising. It offers an advertising program that is designed to be approachable by small businesses as well as global corporations. Ad costs can be set very low (well under $100 per month) depending on the budget. There are multiple purposes for ads. They can direct more viewers to like a page or send them to an external website. Ads can display a picture as well as text; choose these carefully to attract more clicks. While Facebook ads can be useful to market a product, they also provide valuable information about users. The Facebook ad tool can be specified for demographics, including race, gender, interests, and location, and the "Estimated Reach" section can give an idea of how many users fit the target market.[62] This insight can be gained at minimal cost by employing the Facebook ads interface, and it can help to fine-tune other aspects of a marketing campaign even beyond Facebook and social networking.

While Facebook offers many technical tools to assist a social media marketer (and will doubtless continue to offer more in the future), do not lose sight of the service's social nature. Keep in mind that while people may have hundreds of page likes or friends, the trend on "Facebook is that most of its millions and millions of members communicate with relatively few people."[63] Having a large number of likes or fans is a good step but no guarantee of actual results if nobody pays attention or responds to page updates. To avoid this problem, focus on relationships. Facebook is about personal connections, so let some personality through in updates.[64] Giving a human voice to a brand is one of the most powerful advantages of this social networking platform. Engage with users to create an emotional connection; this tactic will build brand loyalty.[65] Used correctly, Facebook is an excellent tool for B2C marketing.

BUSINESS-TO-BUSINESS MARKETING

While most people might associate SMM exclusively with the consumer side, business-to-business firms have also made a huge impression with social networking. The most dominant platform for B2B marketing is the professional networking site LinkedIn: "according to a study by BtoB Magazine and the Association of National Advertisers, 81% of business-to-business marketers use LinkedIn."[66] While there are obviously other platforms available for B2B marketing, the current dominance of LinkedIn earns it the focus of this section.

LinkedIn is designed to facilitate interactions between business professionals. Users fill out profiles including their past education, job experience, skills, and so on. Like any social network site, people can connect with friends or colleagues, but the professional focus of LinkedIn causes many to take connections more seriously. As people are less prone to connecting with strangers or casual acquaintances, someone's connections can provide much more information about them. It is this "information about millions of people, including their connections, [that] makes LinkedIn such a powerful tool."[67] Before attempting to market on LinkedIn, complete the member profile in as much detail as possible. Unlike Facebook, putting more professional information on a profile can increase its chance of building connections.[68] Completing the profile signals seriousness and determination to use LinkedIn correctly.

Although some will screen their contacts, LinkedIn is still an enormously valuable networking or broadcasting tool to reach a huge audience. LinkedIn displays a broader network than just immediate contacts, including other people in the extended network. This "degrees-of-separation principle amplifies the value of contacts. A person who has only 100 direct contacts, for example, may have indirect access to over a million others."[69] LinkedIn recently implemented a status and newsfeed feature, which allows sharing of news topics or possibly marketing messages. Be aware, however, that LinkedIn is not as marketer friendly as some other social networks, and overt broadcasting is not generally rewarded by the user base.

To facilitate connections, LinkedIn has several useful features for an aspiring networker. InMail, the internal messaging service for the site, can be used to contact others. LinkedIn offers several premium, paid account options that include more usage of InMail and better messaging functionality. These options can be useful if LinkedIn is a substantial part of the social media strategy. However, the same function of the premium accounts—contacting others outside one's immediate network—can be accomplished in more subtle and less expensive ways as well. The introductions feature on LinkedIn allows users to mention others and to suggest potential contacts. Some people require potential contacts to know their email address before inviting them to connect; getting an introduction can avoid this problem if there is a valuable contact whose email is unknown. Use introductions to expand a network and broaden the base of connections available from which to draw.

To reach a broader B2B audience, some of the most useful LinkedIn features are groups and Answers. Groups can be set up as private or open allowing anyone to join. Nearly every profession or industry specialization has some form of associated group. Joining these can be a quick way to build contacts, as membership in a common group can be an excuse to connect with future business partners. Groups also have associated discussion boards for conveying information on relevant topics. These boards can be the best way to meet people in the group. Before posting a new topic or question, spend some time reading and responding to others' posts. While general rules of online etiquette apply (see Chapter 12 for more details), the expectations on LinkedIn are especially high. Show courtesy and respect for other users' time by posting only relevant, well-considered, and valuable thoughts to group discussion boards.

To find an even more targeted audience, participate on LinkedIn Answers. Members can pose questions for others to answer. Contributing valuable, well-considered answers can draw in business leads by highlighting personal expertise. Reading and responding to others' answers can also build a larger network; compliment someone on his or her good response, explain why it was useful, then ask that person to join as a contact. After asking a question, be sure to choose a best answer, and then follow up with that individual to give her or him personal thanks (through a private message). This is an effective way to build professional contacts with other experts in a field. Done well, networking through answers can generate revenue for a business.[70] The blogging feature can also help create a reputation for an individual or a company.

LinkedIn is targeted toward individuals, so interact under a personal account rather than a company or brand name. Instead of profiles, companies can set up pages, which LinkedIn members can follow in order to receive updates. These updates may include job openings, new positions, or similar information. At the time of this writing, there is no way to directly contact a company's followers on LinkedIn, limiting its applications for marketing. However, developing a large company following will raise awareness of a brand because more people will see that company as a suggestion based on their contacts' interests.

To channel more people toward following a company or being aware of a product, some firms are creating their own groups from the ground up. This is a highly involved process and should not be taken lightly. If this path is chosen, first create a descriptive group name, which should address a common issue or problem or otherwise make clear why someone would be influenced to join. Next, start formulating content, which should follow the group's theme but not be overly promotional. Ask contacts, past customers, industry analysts, and employees to join the group and/or follow the brand. The result can be a beneficial co-branding opportunity for all parties.[71] This co-branding is especially useful if coworkers or clients write recommendations for each other.

Having many contacts or followers for a company can build an image of being LinkedIn savvy, but on its own it will not generate new business leads. Even a high response rate can be misleading: many contacts may come from other marketers, consultants, or job seekers hoping for work.[72] While these contacts are not directly useful, they help to expand the extended network and open up more business options in the future. Be aware that the "most successful business users of LinkedIn focus on providing professional services."[73] While other industries or products can also successfully use this networking service, for some it may be an uphill battle. While LinkedIn is an excellent professional networking tool, as a way to market products, it requires more sophistication.

Much more can, and has been, said about marketing on LinkedIn. Out of necessity this textbook covers only the most essential elements. Other features of the platform, such as recommendations, LinkedIn advertising, and applications, are important, but their usage is so specific that no general treatment could do them full justice. A social media marketer who intends to specialize in LinkedIn as a career path should examine some of the many more-detailed trade books on the subject. However, for most purposes that matter, the lessons of other social networks will hold true here, albeit with minor modifications. Keep in mind that the primary purpose of LinkedIn is to find, and be found by, other professionals.[74] The standards for conduct and conversation are high due to the background of most LinkedIn members. By building goodwill, responding thoughtfully, and keeping the audience in mind, a social media marketer can employ LinkedIn or other B2B networks to achieve great results.

Google entered the social fray in early June 2011 with its network, Google+, which has grown at a rapid pace, reaching an estimated 50 million members by October 2011.[75] As Table 5.1 illustrates, Google+ now has 110 million users. However, it is estimated that less than 7% have more than 50 posts, indicating that most people have a profile, but don't use it. It also appears that Google+ is more suited to smaller brand communities. Dr. Zahay is active on the communities for the Google Online Marketing Challenge and Google Partners and keeps up to date in social media on the platform.[76] Eric Schmidt, CEO of Google, believes that there is room for multiple social networks and for more cooperation among them.[77] Although the usage statistics are impressive, Google+ has not really caught on as a marketing tool in the manner of Facebook and Twitter. There are a number of wonderful users on Google+ sharing excellent information, especially in the technical areas. In fact, Google+ can be thought of as a "thought network" for the sharing of pertinent information on a variety of topics. From a personal network standpoint, filling out a Google+ profile is a good way to be found on social media because the profile helps Google understand what is happening across platforms. Users can link YouTube, Gmail, and Blogger accounts in their profile. Google+ also has streams for content sharing and a highly versatile photo sharing application. Recently Google+ announced a separate manager for Photos and Streams, indicating the importance of such newer social media tools as Instagram and Snapchat which are photo based. Many have said Google+ is dead, but the emphasis appears to be changing at the executive level. With an executive in charge of Photos and Streams, perhaps that a more dramatic shift in the product is coming.[78, 79]

Why Use a White Label Social Network?

A white label social network is an online service that shares many, if not most, of the characteristics of a public social network like Facebook, with the key difference being the white label is privately run by a corporation or nonprofit organization. Hence, a white label social network is sometimes referred to as a corporate, private, or internal social network. A number of software vendors make platforms for organizations to use in constructing a white label social network. Some large corporations choose to build their own private social networks from scratch. However it is built, the chief purpose of a white label social network is to promote the goals of the organization that owns it.

White label social networks took off in popularity in the late-2000s. By 2007 there were dozens of services offering white label networking services to companies.[80] In 2008 ABI Research forecast that white label social networks would be a $1.3 billion industry within five years.[81] This forecast presaged a boom in white label social network companies until there were over 100 offering community management solutions.[82] These solutions are now called enterprise social networks or social business and the industry has continued to explode. The profusion of services contracted somewhat, as companies were sold and acquired, leaving fewer white label social network providers.[83] After the industry settled, the outcome left some services, such as Ning, RealityDigital, and Salesforce's Chatter, established as market leaders with large corporate clients. Some firms develop their own white label products. IBM Corporation's Developer Works helps the firm engage with its software partners. Developers can learn about the products and connect with IBM professionals who can answer their questions.[84]

However, there remain many competitive, low-cost white label social network solutions available and many not-for-profits take advantage of these solutions to communicate with their customers.

The Future of Social Networks

Interest in social networks has grown at a constantly increasing pace since 2005, with no indication of tapering off.[85] Although Facebook dominates the landscape today, this belief is evidenced by the many niche social networks that have survived and even thrived by catering to specific interests. One such example is Ravelry, which targets people with a passion for knitting, or My Own Car Show, which caters to hot-rod and antique car enthusiasts. These and other targeted social networks illustrate the power of specificity in audience selection.

However, Google+ and Facebook want to capture the masses, not small target markets. Schmidt is on record saying that Facebook, with over a billion users, may well have too many entrenched users to face competition. It's strategy seems to be to buy competitors and integrate the functions into Facebook.[86] Even though large networking sites are not always the best place to invest a marketing budget, they set social media trends and thus are worth developing a presence on.[87] Whatever the outcome, marketers who follow the precepts set forth in this chapter are likely to be the biggest beneficiaries of the competition and growth in social networking.

A new development is that the age of "social selling" has arrived. In some sense we might say that "stalking" is now a professional activity. LinkedIn Groups will provide ways to connect and interact with potential customers. Investing in the premium version to contact those with whom you do not have a first degree connection and get more metrics on your profile activity is a good way to start. Also, when building your network, start small and confine connections to those you know or to whom you are introduced. After you get started, consider open networking, where you accept invitations from those who share your professional interests. Use blog posts to draw attention to your area of expertise. Google+ can also be seen as a professional with its use of communites and platform with its use of communities and collections to share information on specific topics.

Table 5.6 indicates the features of various social platforms. The question often arises whether to market via a company page or a personal page. LinkedIn profiles are based on the user's particular skills. An independent digital marketing consultant or a salesperson might use just their personal profiles to make connections. They would make sure their profiles are properly filled out to the maximum, as per Appendix X.

They would also make sure that they were connected and engaged on appropriate groups. They might be associated with a company and contribute to that page, but personal connections would be made on LinkedIn.

It would be highly unlikely for a salesperson or independent consultant to market themselves personally on Facebook. However, it is quite common for such individuals to get together on Facebook around groups of mutual interest. Facebook clearly encourages the company page for brand promotion and the group for personal, shared interests. The Facebook company page can be an excellent source of brand promotion, especially combined with Facebook's targeted strategy.

BEST PRACTICES FOR SOCIAL MEDIA PLATFORM MARKETING

1. *Develop clear objectives. The first step is always picking an appropriate objective. Social media is all about engagement and developing relationships with customers. To do that, a company might use a social media site to collect an email address and then take it from there to use both social media and email marketing to develop the relationship.*

2. *Understand and monitor metrics. If engagement is the goal, establish clear metrics such as retweets, favorites, comments, sharing, and so on. Monitor the metrics frequently to chart progress to goal and make changes if needed.*

Year	Users	% of Population	% Change
2013	40.2 million	12.7	93.6
2014	64.2	20.1	59.9
2015	77.6	24.2	29.9
2016	89.4	27.6	15.1
2017	98.9	30.3	10.6
2018	106.2	32.2	7.4
2019	111.6	33.6	5.0

Source: http://www.mediapost.com/ publications/article/245711/instagram-fastest-growing-social-network.html? utm_source=newsletter&utm_medium= email&utm_content=comment&utm_ campaign=81061#reply. Retrieved February 2015

Table 5.6 **U.S. Instagram Users and Penetration** (millions; %change; %population)

Demographics of Leading Social Networking Platform Users
based on a survey of 1,907 US adults aged 18+
August 2015

Among internet users, the % who use:	Facebook	Pinterest	Instagram	LinkedIn	Twitter
Total	72%	31%	28%	25%	23%
Men	66%	16%	24%	26%	25%
Women	77%	44%	31%	25%	21%
White, Non-Hispanic	70%	32%	21%	26%	20%
Black, non-Hispanic (n=85)	67%	23%	47%	22%	28%
Hispanic	75%	32%	38%	22%	28%
18-29	82%	37%	55%	22%	32%
30-49	79%	36%	28%	32%	29%
50-64	64%	24%	11%	25%	13%
65+	48%	16%	4%	12%	6%
High school grad or less	71%	25%	25%	9%	19%
Some college	72%	37%	32%	25%	23%
College+	72%	31%	26%	46%	27%
Less than $30k/year	73%	24%	26%	17%	21%
$30-50k	72%	37%	27%	21%	19%
$50-75k	66%	41%	30%	32%	25%
$75k+	78%	30%	26%	41%	26%
Urban	74%	26%	32%	30%	30%
Suburban	72%	34%	28%	26%	21%
Rural	67%	31%	18%	12%	15%

MarketingCharts.com | Data Source: Pew Research Center's Internet & American Life Project

Source: http://www.marketingcharts.com/online/demographics-of-social-networking-platform-users-58488/attachment/pew-demographics-social-media-users-aug2015/

Figure 5.2 Demographics of Leading Social Networking Platform Users

3. *Know the audience. Understand where the target market you have in mind hangs out. Figure 5.2 shows the demographics of social media usage across platforms. Women migrate to Pinterest and men to LinkedIn. Instagram is the only platform that is inclined toward African-Americans and Hispanics. Twitter users are addicted to the latest news, so for news sites, Twitter is a natural fit.*[88]

4. *Communicate with your audience in the most appropriate way. On Facebook, shorter posts and visual images generate most engagement. Images also boost 'favorites' and 'retweets' on Twitter. Understand the platform and what can 'boost' customer engagement.*

5. *Keep search in mind. Now that tweets are showing up in Google search again, we must all be careful that we are using the most appropriate keywords and appropriate language and comments in social media communications. The world is a fishbowl today and we are the fish. Make sure you constantly monitor your brand and have a crisis management strategy should things go wrong.*[89]

Personal Branding: Optimizing Your LinkedIn Profile—for Students

Marketers frequently cite LinkedIn as one of the most valuable social networks to incorporate in a marketing strategy. But even marketers who have LinkedIn on their radar screens still wonder how to participate. What works, what doesn't, and what should you expect? Marketers usually engage on an individual basis on LinkedIn, although company pages can help build brand awareness and identify potential leads and levels of engagement.

Salespeople use LinkedIn for lead generation by joining Groups, sharing marketing collateral, and qualifying the leads that come through the channel.

Marketers increasingly use LinkedIn on a professional basis for something called "social selling". Marketers carefully create their LinkedIn Profile and then use the capabilities of LinkedIn to reach out to those with whom they would like to make a professional connection. There are also a number of tools available to help manage the data on LinkedIn and determine how effective the tool is for making social contacts. LinkedIn provides its own tools to help identify the best prospects as well as specialized tools for recruiting professionals.90 As individuals, we can do the same thing with our LinkedIn Profiles to market ourselves.

LinkedIn has become THE professional social network, with more than 332 million users, over 107 million in the United States. In fact, 40% of users check it daily and 89% of all recruiters report having hired someone through LinkedIn. Sadly, only about 13% of the Millennial population use LinkedIn, so students can distinguish themselves by marketing their personal professional brand on LinkedIn.91

Dr. Zahay employed best practices in LinkedIn Marketing to achieve extraordinary results for her students. Students planned, implemented, and measured their personal marketing campaigns in just eight short weeks, using the tips below.

Create a complete profile

Lesson #1. Figure out who you are. Since search, strategy, and branding are connected in developing the LinkedIn strategy, the first step is to go online and see "who am I" and what message you wish to present to the world. Put keywords describing yourself and what you do rather than a job title in the brief description section of the profile (under your name). Then these keywords should be used throughout the profile (particularly the summary) so you come up in the searches of those looking for people with your competencies and so LinkedIn can make suggestions about jobs that would be a good fit.

For example, Dr. Zahay suggested one student describe herself as a graphic designer (how she wants to be found) rather than an undergraduate student (her title). If you are adept at social media but your job title is Marketing Coordinator, put your skills and competencies in social media in the top part of your profile, throughout the summary, and in the skills for which you would like to be endorsed.

Lesson #2. Completely fill out your profile. Figure 5.3 shows what needs to happen to create a complete LinkedIn profile. This action will help you obtain All-Star status, which will get you displayed in search results. Students will need a nice "head" shot that looks professional and does not show too much skin. Dr. Zahay always tells her students not to display anything between the collar bone and the knees on any form of social media.

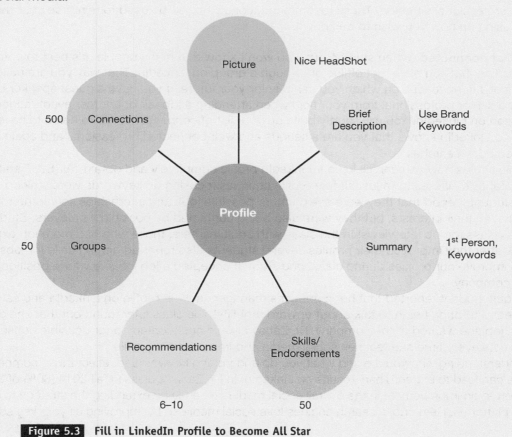

Figure 5.3 Fill in LinkedIn Profile to Become All Star

Again, your brief description, use the keywords that describe who you are and use every inch of the summary section, also with descriptive keywords. Also, use first person in your description; the LinkedIn profile is not a resume but a personal statement. Fill out your skills for which people can endorse you and use all 50 skills. Use every bit of "real estate" LinkedIn gives you to distinguish yourself and to be found by people who want to network with you and might hire you as well.

Lesson #3. Join up to 50 Groups and participate. LinkedIn gives you access to up to 50 Groups. Use them all. Social media is a two-way channel, which makes it especially important in a company to assign a point-person to oversee your social media initiatives, establish themselves as a community member, and respond to feedback. As a person, you also join LinkedIn Groups under your own name and title to establish a presence within the industry audiences. When you work for a company, you will find joining under a personal name also helps avoid the temptation to simply push company marketing into a community discussion group. Monitor ongoing conversations to find opportunities to comment on other people's topics. Include appropriate links and often share opinions or give feedback on other group members' comments. Be seen as a contributor and someone who can help. Not surprisingly, discussion group members are more interested in white papers or webinars that address industry trends, operational issues, and other educational topics than in hearing you are graduating soon and need a job.

After the relationship is established with individuals in a group, you can reach out and ask for help in your job search by requesting to "job shadow" for a day or meet for coffee to discuss career possibilities. Good personal branding is a mixture of online and offline activities. LinkedIn can be the foundation of your personal branding efforts.

Lesson #4. Get recommended. Get at least six to ten people to recommend you on LinkedIn to gain credibility. Recommendations are different from endorsements, which are just a click of a button. Someone recommending you takes the time to write a detailed paragraph about your skills and how they interacted with you in a professional situation. These recommendations can also be used to reinforce your personal brand by focusing on how you wish to be known.

Lesson #5. Get connected. When starting out, you won't know that many people. It's best to connect with people online that you have met offline or through a group on LinkedIn. That way you are building a network of solid connections on which you can rely for your future. If you have a guest speaker in class, or met a senior professional from your field when attending a job fair or another event, connect with that person on LinkedIn. You will shortly build up your list of connections. It also helps to have 500+ connections so LinkedIn knows that you are a serious and well-connected professional and again, will help you get served up in searches.

The graphic shows how you can fill in your LinkedIn profile completely and obtain "All-Star" status. The results in Dr. Zahay's classes from just simple profile changes focusing on keywords were striking. Not only did her day students report that they were seeing more possible jobs and internships served up to them that were a fit with their interests, but they were also being contacted by possible employers. Students began to miss class for job interviews! In the class with adult learners, those who had more job experience, the first week after they improved their profiles several students also reported getting calls for jobs. As we continued to improve our profiles during class, one student accepted a job interview for a position with a Fortune 500 company.

Another adult student reported that her manager's manager saw her profile on LinkedIn and said that the company needed to bring her in to talk about upward mobility! The class later found out that she got the management job she wanted at the company. Dr. Zahay always gets contacted for possible consulting and teaching projects every time she teaches social media and improves her profile.

Just by understanding who you are and what you do and putting keywords to reflect those competencies in your profile can lead to extraordinary results on LinkedIn. In Dr. Zahay's class in fall 2014, 80% of the students reported an improvement in the overall social media presence by extending the strategy to other social media platforms. Remember, search engines love social media so by improving all your key social media profiles, you will display a professional impression to the world in which you wish to work. In addition, 30% of Dr. Zahay's class became LinkedIn "All-Stars" in just eight weeks by completely filling in their profile.

These suggestions are just the first steps to creating a great LinkedIn profile. You can learn more from Melonie Dodaro and Mike O'Neill, LinkedIn experts that can be found on, LinkedIn! Don't forget to connect to Dr. Zahay at http://www.linkedin.com/in/drzahay

Dr. Zahay is an open networker and if you have a great LinkedIn profile, she just might accept your connection request.

Notes

1. http://decidedlysocial.com/13-types-of-social-media-platforms-and-counting/
2. Google Trends, (2011, July 13), "Searches on Google for Social Networks." Retrieved July 13, 2011, from http://www.google.com/trends?q=social+networks&ctab=0&geo=all&date=all&sort=0
3. Vik (2010, October 14), "What We Can Learn From Facebook's Success," There's Money Everywhere. Retrieved July 13, 2011, from http://theresmoneyeverywhere.com/what-we-can-learn-from-facebook%E2%80%99s-success/ and Morales, Mitchell (2011, July 11), "Why Facebook Succeeded." *Social Network Revolution Blog*. Retrieved July 13, 2011, from http://mitchellmessi.posterous.com/why-facebook-succeeded
4. eBizMBA (2011, July), "Top 15 Most Popular Social Networking Sites." Retrieved July 13, 2011, from http://www.ebizmba.com/articles/social-networking-websites
5. Rheingold, Howard (2000 [1993]), *The Virtual Community: Homesteading on the Electronic Frontier* (Cambridge, MA: MIT Press).
6. Weber, Larry (2009), *Marketing to the Social Web* (Hoboken, NJ: John Wiley), p. 198.
7. *Wikipedia* (n.d.), "Social Networking Service." Retrieved July 13, 2011, from http://en.wikipedia.org/wiki/Social_networking_service
8. Boyd, Danah M., and Nicole B. Ellison (2007), "Social Network Sites: Definition, History, and Scholarship," *Journal of Computer-Mediated Communication*, vol. 13, no. 1, article 11. Retrieved July 13, 2011, from http://jcmc.indiana.edu/vol13/issue1/boyd.ellison.html
9. WhatIs (n.d.), "Six Degrees of Separation." Retrieved July 13, 2011, from http://whatis.techtarget.com/definition/0,,sid9_gci932596,00.html
10. Prall, Laura (2010, September 15), "Sixdegrees.com—Social Networking in Its Infancy," *Afri Design Ad Blog*. Retrieved July 13, 2011, from http://blog.afridesign.com/2010/09/sixdegrees-com-social-networking-in-its-infancy/
11. Ryze (n.d.), "About Ryze." Retrieved July 13, 2011, from http://www.ryze.com/faq.php
12. Festa, Paul (2003, November 11), "Investors Snub Friendster in Patent Grab," CNET. Retrieved July 13, 2011, from http://news.cnet.com/2100-1032_3-5106136.html
13. Chafkin, Max (2007, June 1), "How to Kill a Great Idea!" *Inc.* Retrieved July 13, 2011, from http://www.inc.com/magazine/20070601/features-how-to-kill-a-great-idea.html
14. WebHostingReport (n.d.), "The History of MySpace." Retrieved July 14, 2011, from http://www.webhostingreport.com/learn/myspace.html
15. Boyd, Danah M., and Nicole B. Ellison (2007), "Social Network Sites: Definition, History, and Scholarship," *Journal of Computer-Mediated Communication*, vol. 13, no. 1, article 11. Retrieved July 13, 2011, from http://jcmc.indiana.edu/vol13/issue1/boyd.ellison.html
16. News Corporation press release (2005, July 8), "News Corporation to Acquire Intermix Media, Inc." Retrieved July 14, 2011, from http://www.newscorp.com/news/news_251.html
17. Ibid.
18. *Wikipedia* (n.d.), "MySpace History." Archived from the original on September 5, 2008, and retrieved July 14, 2011, from http://web.archive.org/web/20080905142107/http://profile.myspace.com/index.cfm?fuseaction=user.viewprofile&friendID=100000000
19. *The Telegraph* (2011, July 15), "MySpace Loses 10 Million Users in a Month." Retrieved July 14, 2011, from http://www.telegraph.co.uk/technology/myspace/8404510/MySpace-loses-10-million-users-in-a-month.html#

20. Seward, Zachary M. (2007, July 25), "Judge Expresses Skepticism about Facebook Lawsuit," *Wall Street Journal*. Retrieved July 15, 2011, from http://online.wsj.com/article/SB118539991204578084.html?mod=googlenews_wsj

21. Phillips, Sarah (2005, July 25), "A Brief History of Facebook," *The Guardian*. Retrieved July 15, 2011, from http://www.guardian.co.uk/technology/2007/jul/25/media.newmedia

22. Rosmarin, Rachel (2006, September 11), "Open Facebook," *Forbes*. Retrieved July 15, 2011, from http://www.forbes.com/2006/09/11/facebook-opens-up-cx_rr_0911facebook.html

23. Yadav, Sid (2006, August 25), "Facebook—The Complete Biography," Mashable. Retrieved July 15, 2011, from http://mashable.com/2006/08/25/facebook-profile/

24. Arrington, Michael (2005, September 7), "85% of College Students Use Facebook," TechCrunch. Retrieved July 15, 2011, from http://techcrunch.com/2005/09/07/85-of-college-students-use-facebook/

25. Abram, Carolyn (2006, September 26), "Welcome to Facebook, Everyone," *Facebook Blog*. Retrieved July 15, 2011, from http://blog.facebook.com/blog.php?post=2210227130

26. "Facebook Overtakes MySpace" (2008, May 7), Alexa. Retrieved July 15, 2011, from http://blog.alexa.com/2008/05/facebook-overtakes-myspace_07.html

27. Tsotsis, Alexia (2011, June 28), "Sean Parker on Why MySpace Lost to Facebook," TechCrunch, retrieved July 15, 2011, from http://techcrunch.com/2011/06/28/sean-parker-on-why-myspace-lost-to-facebook/ and Chmielewski, Dawn C., and David Sarno (2009, June 17), "How MySpace Fell off the Pace," *Los Angeles Times*, retrieved July 15, 2011, from http://articles.latimes.com/2009/jun/17/business/fi-ct-myspace17

28. Parr, Ben (2011, January 3), "Facebook Raises $500 Million in Funding, Now Worth $50 Billion," Mashable, retrieved July 15, 2011, from http://mashable.com/2011/01/03/facebook-raises-500-million-now-worth-50-billion-report/ and Goldfarb, Jeffery (2011, May 4), "Renren May Skew Facebook's Value," *New York Times* retrieved July 15, 2011, from http://www.nytimes.com/2011/05/05/business/05views.html. Kilgore,Tomi, (2015, March 25), "Facebook's Stock-marketing Valuation Tops $230 Billion," Market Watch. Retrieved April 23, 2015 from Facebook http://www.marketwatch.com/story/facebooks-stock-market-valuation-tops-230-billion-2015-03-20

29. Facebook Page Leaderboard (2011, July 6), "Top 100 Most Popular Facebook Pages in the World 2011." Retrieved July 6, 2011, from http://www.facebook.com/pages/Top-100-Most-Popular-Fac%E1%BA%BBbook-Pages-In-The-World-2011/165408200173753

30. Spertus, Ellen, and Mehran Sahami (n.d.), "Evaluating Similarity Measures: A Large Scale Study in the Orkut Social Network," *Google Papers*. Retrieved July 15, 2011, from http://static.googleusercontent.com/external_content/untrusted_dlcp/labs.google.com/en/us/papers/orkut-kdd2005.pdf. Jain, Sorav (2010, October 6), "40 Most Popular Social Networking Sites of the World," socialmediatoday. Retrieved July 15, 2011, from http://socialmediatoday.com/soravjain/195917/40-most-popular-social-networking-sites-worlds

31. Bonfils, Michael (2011, April 13), "Why Facebook Is Wiping Out Orkut in India & Brazil," Search Engine Watch. Retrieved July 15, 2011, from http://searchenginewatch.com/article/2064470/Why-Facebook-is-Wiping-Out-Orkut-in-India-Brazil "moderation social media management (2014, April 2), "Social media fast facts: Latin America." Retrieved April 22, 2015, from http://www.emoderation.com/social-media-fast-facts-latin-america/ Marketing Charts (2015, January 22), "Social Sharing Trends in 2014." Retrieved April 22, 2015, from http://www.marketingcharts.com/online/social-sharing-trends-in-2014-50697/

32. Spears, Lee, and Danielle Kucera (2011, May 4), "Renren Surges on First Day of Trading with Price-to-Sales Beating Facebook," *Bloomberg*. Retrieved July 15, 2011, from http://www.bloomberg.com/news/2011-05-04/renren-raises-743-million-in-china-social-networking-site-ipo.html

33. Steimle, Joshua J. (2015, January 4), "The State of Social Media in China." Retrieved April 22, 2015, from http://www.clickz.com/clickz/column/2383850/the-state-of-social-media-in-china

34. Digital Stats (2011, February 9), "Russian Social Network Vkontakte Has More Than 100M Registered Users." Retrieved July 15, 2011, from http://blog.gigya.com/tag/vkontakte/ and http://expandedramblings.com/index.php/russian-social-media-stats-yandex-vkontakte/

35. *Geeks Desk Tech Blog* (2011, March 28), "Top 10 Social Networking Websites." Retrieved July 15, 2011, from http://www.geeksdesk.com/top-10-social-networking-websites/

36. Weinberg, Tamar (2009), *The New Community Rules* (Sebastopol, CA: O'Reilly Media), p. 150.

37. Qualman, Erik (2009), *Socialnomics* (Hoboken, NJ: John Wiley), p. 122.

Marketing Charts (2015, January 22), "Social Sharing Trends in 2014." Retrieved April 22, 2015 from http://www.marketingcharts.com/online/social-sharing-trends-in-2014-50697/

38. Bolotaeva, Victoria, and Teuta Cata (2010), "Marketing Opportunities with Social Networks," *Journal of Internet Social Networking and Virtual Communities*, vol. 2010, article ID 109111. Retrieved July 13, 2011, from http://www.ibimapublishing.com/journals/JISNVC/2009/109111.pdf

39. http://www.agilemarketing.net/coca-colas-liquid-linked-content/, retrieved April 30, 2015

40. Golden, Michelle (2011), *Social Media Strategies for Professionals and Their Firms* (Hoboken, NJ: John Wiley), p. 213.

41. Weber, Larry (2009), *Marketing to the Social Web* (Hoboken, NJ: John Wiley), p. 217.

42. Barker, Melissa (2010, July 27), "5 Steps to a Winning Social Media Marketing Plan," EnzineArticles. Retrieved July 31, 2011, from http://ezinearticles.com/?5-Steps-to-a-Winning-Social-Media-Marketing-Plan&id=4748691

43. Sernovitz, Andy (2009), *Word of Mouth Marketing: How Smart Companies Get People Talking* (New York: Kaplan Publishing), p. 143.

44. Borges, Bernie (2009), *Marketing 2.0* (Tucson: AZ: Wheatmark), p. 195.

45. Halligan, Brian, and Dharmesh Shah (2010), *Inbound Marketing* (Hoboken, NJ: John Wiley), p. 89.

46. Gillin, Paul (2009), *Secrets of Social Media Marketing* (Irvine, CA: Quill Driver Books), p. 122.

47. Gannet, Kim Komando (2011, March 11), "Market Your Business on Facebook in 4 Easy Steps," *USA Today*. Retrieved July 14, 2011, from http://www.usatoday.com/tech/columnist/kimkomando/2011-03-11-komando-facebook_N.htm

48. Weinberg, Tamar (2009), *The New Community Rules* (Sebastopol, CA: O'Reilly Media), p. 159.

49. Golden, Michelle (2011), *Social Media Strategies for Professionals and Their Firms* (Hoboken, NJ: John Wiley), p. 211.

50. Ibid., p. 208.

51. Parker, Donna (2011, April 12), "10 Ways to Market to Women on Facebook," All Facebook. Retrieved July 14, 2011, from http://www.allfacebook.com/10-ways-to-market-to-women-on-facebook-2011-04

52. Weinberg, Tamar (2009), *The New Community Rules* (Sebastopol, CA: O'Reilly Media), p. 154.

53. Shaw, Sarah (2011, January 31), "How to Market Your Business (or Yourself) on Facebook," *Maria Shriver Blog*. Retrieved July 14, 2011, from http://www.mariashriver.com/blog/2011/01/how-market-your-business-or-yourself-facebook

54. Treadaway, Chris, and Mari Smith (2010), *Facebook Marketing: An Hour a Day* (Hoboken, NJ: John Wiley), p. 58.

55. Golden, Michelle (2011), *Social Media Strategies for Professionals and Their Firms* (Hoboken, NJ: John Wiley), p. 226.

56. Gillin, Paul (2009), *Secrets of Social Media Marketing* (Irvine, CA: Quill Driver Books), p. 223.

57. http://www.business2community.com/facebook/facebook-pages-vs-facebook-groups-whats-right-business-0932757, retrieved April 30, 2015.

58. Smith, Justin (2007, December 9), "The Facebook Marketing Bible: 24 Ways to Market Your Brand, Company, Product, or Service inside Facebook," InsideFacebook. Retrieved July 14, 2011, from http://www.insidefacebook.com/2007/12/09/inside-facebook-marketing-bible-24-ways-to-market-your-brand-company-product-or-service-in-facebook/

59. Howard, Justyn (2010, August 21), "A Local Business Guide to Facebook Places," Sprout Social Insights. Retrieved July 28, 2011, from http://sproutsocial.com/insights/2010/08/a-local-business-guide-to-facebook-places/

60. Axon, Samuel (2011, January 19), "How to List Your Business on Facebook Places," Sprout Social Insights. Retrieved July 28, 2011, from http://sproutsocial.com/insights/2011/01/how-facebook-places-local-business/

61. Ibid.

62. Halligan, Brian, and Dharmesh Shah (2010), *Inbound Marketing* (Hoboken, NJ: John Wiley), p. 91.

63. Weber, Larry (2009), *Marketing to the Social Web* (Hoboken, New Jersey: John Wiley), p. 208.

64. Shaw, Sarah (2011, January 31), "How to Market Your Business (or Yourself) on Facebook," *Maria Shriver Blog*. Retrieved July 14, 2011, from http://www.mariashriver.com/blog/2011/01/how-market-your-business-or-yourself-facebook

65. Parker, Donna (2011, April 12), "10 Ways to Market to Women on Facebook," All Facebook. Retrieved July 14, 2011, from http://www.allfacebook.com/10-ways-to-market-to-women-on-facebook-2011-04

66. MarketingProfs (n.d.), "LinkedIn Success Stories: How 11 Companies Are Using the Global Networking Site to Achieve Their Business and Marketing Goals." Retrieved July 29, 2011, from http://www.marketingprofs.com/store/product/37/linkedin-success-stories

67. Halligan, Brian, and Dharmesh Shah (2010), *Inbound Marketing* (Hoboken, NJ: John Wiley), p. 94.

68. Golden, Michelle (2011), *Social Media Strategies for Professionals and Their Firms* (Hoboken, NJ: John Wiley), p. 219.

69. Gillin, Paul (2009), *Secrets of Social Media Marketing* (Irvine, CA: Quill Driver Books), p. 123–24.

70. Schaffer, Neal (2009), *Understanding, Leveraging, & Maximizing LinkedIn* (Charleston, SC: Booksurge), p. 193.

71. Borges, Bernie (2009), *Marketing 2.0* (Tucson, AZ: Wheatmark), p. 193.

72. Marketing Sherpa (2009, July 29), "Using LinkedIn for Lead Generation: 6 Lessons." Retrieved July 29, 2011, from http://www.marketingsherpa.com/article.php?ident=31315#

73. Weinberg, Tamar (2009), *The New Community Rules* (Sebastopol, CA: O'Reilly Media), p. 164.

74. Schaffer, Neal (2009), *Understanding, Leveraging, & Maximizing LinkedIn* (Charleston, SC: Booksurge), p. 284.

75. Owyang, Jeremiah (2007, February 15), "Social Networking White Label Market Overcrowded, Reminiscent of CMS and Portal Craze of Yesteryear," Web Strategy. Retrieved July 31, 2011, from http://www.web-strategist.com/blog/2007/02/15/social-networking-white-label-market-overcrowded-reminiscent-of-cms-and-portal-craze-of-yesteryear/

76. McKay, Lauren (2008, July 23), " 'White-Label' Social Networking to Hit the Enterprise: ABI Research Predicts the Industry Will Reach $1.3 Billion Within Five Years," Destination CRM. Retrieved July 31, 2011, from http://www.destinationcrm.com/Articles/CRM-News/Daily-News/White-Label-Social-Networking-to-Hit-the-Enterprise--50038.aspx

77. http://www.forbes.com/sites/stevedenning/2015/04/23/has-google-really-died/, retrieved May 6, 2015.

78. http://mashable.com/2015/03/02/google-plus-changes/, retrieved May 6, 2015.

79. http://www.wired.com/2015/03/google-knew-dead-google-still-social-network/, retrieved May 6, 2015.

80. Owyang, Jeremiah (2007, February 12), "List of 'White Label' or 'Private Label' (Applications You Can Rebrand) Social Networking Platforms, Community Platforms," Web Strategy. Retrieved July 31, 2011, from http://www.web-strategist.com/blog/2007/02/12/list-of-white-label-social-networking-platforms/

81. Kanaracus, Chris (2008, February 11), " 'White label' Social Networking Set for Shake-up," InfoWorld. Retrieved July 31, 2011, from http://www.infoworld.com/d/developer-world/white-label-social-networking-set-shake-277

82. *SNAP Blog* (2010, June 23) "Internal Social Networks: Pros & Cons." Retrieved July 14, 2011, from http://snapblogger.wordpress.com/2010/06/23/internal-social-networks-pros-cons/

83. Meldrum, Scott (2010, October 28), "Fans Are Fickle: How to Inspire Loyalty after the 'Like.' " IMedia Connection. Retrieved July 31, 2011, from http://www.imediaconnection.com/content/27915.asp

84. https://www.ibm.com/developerworks/, retrieved May 6, 2015.

85. Owyang, Jeremiah (2008, June 3), "When Social Media Marries CRM Systems," Web Strategy. Retrieved July 31, 2011, from http://www.web-strategist.com/blog/category/white-label-social-network/page/3/

86. *SNAP Blog* (2010, June 23), "Internal Social Networks: Pros & Cons." Retrieved July 14, 2011, from http://snapblogger.wordpress.com/2010/06/23/internal-social-networks-pros-cons/

87. York, Emily Bryson (2010, February 22), "Starbucks Gets Its Business Brewing Again with Social Media," *Advertising Age*. Retrieved September 19, 2011, from http://adage.com/article/special-report-digital-alist-2010/digital-a-list-2010-starbucks-brewing-social-media/142202/

88. *YourDictionary* (n.d.), "Who Founded Starbucks?" Retrieved July 7, 2011, from http://answers.yourdictionary.com/business/who-founded-starbucks.html

89. BizAims (2009, July 8), "The History of Starbucks." Retrieved July 7, 2011, from http://www.bizaims.com/coffee%20break/curiosities%20events%20funny/the%20history%20starbucks

90. http://www.entrepreneur.com/article/243441, retrieved May 4, 2015.

91. http://expandedramblings.com/index.php/by-the-numbers-a-few-important-linkedin-stats/, retrieved May 4, 2015.

Microblogging

While many of the SMM tools discussed up to this point have had similar, historical mediums to draw guidance from, microblogging is almost entirely without precedent. Some other media encourage brevity, but microblogging positively enforces it. These changes present unique challenges for the modern marketing professional.

The popularity and growth of microblogging as a communication technology reflect broader social trends in how people view, consume, and digest information. The ability to focus on long messages or arguments has declined with access to digital technology: a 2002 BBC article reported that the average web browser's attention span was just seconds, comparable to that of a goldfish![1] In the decade since that column was written, consumers have become even more inundated with brief, catchy digital messages as advertisers try to capture those crucial few seconds.

In this short and fast environment, microblogging tools like Twitter are an increasingly relevant component for a marketing strategy. Companies are discovering that microblogging can play an important role in brand building, viral marketing, and increasing sales.[2] This chapter will explore a brief history of microblogging, some best practices for employing it in a SMM campaign, and how to leverage a microblogging presence to achieve the marketing objectives.

What Is Microblogging?

The term *microblogging* is not frequently used in conversation; instead, people typically refer to the name of their favorite microblogging platform, such as Twitter. However, for the purposes of this chapter, a definition to distinguish microblogging from other social media outlets is useful. Microblogging is a form of blogging, with the main difference being significant limits on the length of posts, typically consisting of short sentences and links.[3] Microblogging *"refers to broadcasting brief messages to some or all members of the sender's social network through a specific, Web-based, service."*[4]

The most essential aspect of microblogging is that messages are required to be short. *Platforms enforce a limit (most often 140 characters) to restrict the length of users' posts, and force ideas to be communicated succinctly.* To visualize how long is allowed, see the italicized sentence preceding this one; it is exactly 140 characters, including the period. Although many platforms exist, Twitter has led the way and become identified with the concept of microblogging. This chapter will focus on Twitter as the primary application for marketing via microblogging. A related concept is MWOM known as microblogging word of mouth, meaning that microblogging has the ability to accelerate word-of-mouth communications through social network, often called the "Twitter effect."

At the same time that Twitter dominates this category, the company has its share of challenges. Twitter was built for those can be thought of as "power" users, who use many of its features and really rely on the real-time aspect of the application. As of this writing, although Twitter is growing very fast in terms of revenue but its stock price has dipped since it went public. However, Google will now have full access to all tweets for search results, which should boost the profile of the platform. The platform will need to undergo some changes to grow and expand as many people find the real-time stream intimidating. It is interesting that many applications such as Hootsuite', TweekDeck, and Timehop have been developed to manage Twitter feeds. Presenting and managing the feeds presents a real opportunity for Twitter. New features such as "while you were away" highlight tweets that users not constantly glued to Twitter may have missed. Ultimately, the company may be purchased by a larger firm such as Facebook or Google, but as microblogging has its unique niche in social media, it might be difficult for these firms to integrate the application into their world.

A Brief History of Microblogging

Where did microblogging originate? The earliest ancestors of microblogs were referred to as "tumblelogs" and contained links or stream of consciousness posts, all in quick succession. Tumblelogs were first described by Jason Kottke in October 2005.[5] The concept of microblogging, as it exists today, leapt to prominence in 2006 with the launch of Twitter by its founder, Jack Dorsey. Originally an internal company service for Odeo, Twitter grew into a public sensation.[6] In February 2011 Twitter passed beyond 200 million accounts.[7] The latest estimate of the number of Twitter accounts is "about a billion" worldwide as of September 2013.[8] The more important metric is number of active users, and Twitter had 302 million as of March 2015.[9]

As noted before, Twitter has a solid lead in microblogging membership; a Pew Research report found that 23% of online adults now use Twitter, up from 13% in 2011.[10] However, other microblogging sites have gained an audience as well, as shown in Table 6.1. Some noteworthy sites include FriendFeed, Yammer, Posterous, and Soup.io to

Microblogging Sites	Alexa Global Traffic Rank*	Google Page Rank**
Twitter	8	10
Tumblr	36	8
FriendFeed	4660	8
Posterous	52062	8
Plurk	1784	7
Yammer	2753	7
Dipity	31043	7
Flattr	56247	7
Meetme	4268	6
Bentio	188442	6
Identi.ca	192511	6
Soup.io	4646	5
Twitxr	15825	5
Meemi	324576	4
Plerb	47154	4

Table 6.1 Popular Microblogging Sites, as of June 2015

*Alexa Global Traffic Rank estimates a site's popularity, with traffic data from Alexa Toolbar users and other diverse traffic sources, using an ascending scale where 1 represents the highest traffic rank.
**Google Page Rank uses the number and quality of links to a web page to determine its relative importance, using a scale of 0-10, with 10 indicating the highest rank and 0 the lowest.

name a few. In addition, social networking sites, such as Facebook, LinkedIn, and Yahoo Pulse, have a microblogging aspect in the form of status updates.

These sites offer varying features and post guidelines, and they also draw very different demographics; for example, Plurk (http://www.plurk.com) draws 55% of its traffic from India and 25% of its traffic from Taiwan. The company also recently received some new venture capital funding and is continuing to grow.[11] Other international microblogging sites are also rising in importance, such as Identi.ca, which is popular in India.[12]

From this plethora of sites, microblogging has evolved into an important source of news and citizen journalism. The ease of posting and sharing allows relevant news to reach interested groups quickly. The material covered can range from celebrity gossip to world events. During the Iranian elections, Twitter was frequently updated with news, making it possible to follow along with events in real-time.[13] When Osama bin Laden was killed by an American intervention in Pakistan, a Twitter user was the first to announce the operation. These and many other examples help to illustrate the power of microblogs for distributing information. The hashtag (#) feature of Twitter (discussed later in the chapter) makes news topics easily searchable so that important items can be found and shared.

Different Uses for Microblogging

While millions of people now participate in microblogging, the platform's usage is deceptively simple from a marketing perspective. Its purpose can be broken down into two main divisions: one is to convey information, and the second is to start a discussion or to participate in an ongoing conversation.[14] Both of these goals will be familiar from other social media platforms, but the special challenges of microblogging require a different format to accomplish them. The give-and-take nature of the format makes Twitter, and other microblogging platforms, a "very multidirectional communication medium."[15]

In his book *Twitter Power 2.0*, Joel Comm describes six different categories of microblog posts (written in context of Twitter, these are referred to as tweets). Different types of tweets include:

1. **Classic Tweets**: "This Is What I'm Doing Now."

2. **Opinion Tweets**: "This Is What I'm Thinking Now."

3. **Mission Accomplished Tweets**: "This Is What I've Just Done."

4. **Entertainment Tweets**: "I'm Making You Laugh Now."

5. **Question Tweets**: "Can You Help Me Do Something Now?"

6. **Picture Tweets**: "Look at What I've Been Doing."[16]

Depending on the industry, audience, and objectives, a different mix of these six components might be appropriate. Selecting the proper ratio between them is where much of the artistry behind microblog marketing is involved. While Twitter asks users to post "What's happening?" (the classic tweet), this may be one of the less-used categories employed by a marketing professional. Saying "I'm at the store" or "getting lunch" is not uncommon on a personal Twitter account but less useful for conveying a product-oriented message (unless the classic tweet is given some extra relevance or pizzazz). Indeed, sharing excess personal details can become a "mistweet" that is contrary to or does not serve the marketing objectives at all.[17]

While some personal "What's happening" posts are good to establish a human voice, for the purposes of SMM, the other five categories will probably be used more frequently. The following sections will offer guidelines for good microblog content and posting strategies. While reading, consider which category each tweet might fall into and how to balance all of the categories in a strategic way.

While other microblogging platforms offer unique benefits and target markets, Twitter remains the largest and best-known microblog site online, so in most cases it will be the starting point for establishing a brand's presence through microblogging. As such, the rest of the chapter will focus on Twitter, although similar strategies (with some intelligent modification) may likely be applicable to any other microblogging platform. This focus reflects not only Twitter's large market share for microblogging, but also the incredible utility of Twitter as a branding tool, especially for small businesses.[18] With the low start-up cost and speed of content creation, Twitter will be a common entry point for many SMM strategies.

Why is there so much focus on Twitter? The platform has a number of advantages for a clever SMM team. Unlike a blog or podcast, it takes less time to reach large numbers of readers on Twitter. The ability to directly contact other users with thoughts or questions invites a more interactive and engaging strategy. As a result, Twitter can draw attention from high-profile people and connect with opinion leaders in a variety of industries.[19] More and more celebrities, business leaders, and other public figures have become involved, deepening the pool of talented individuals with whom to communicate. In fact, Bruce Jenner/Caitlyn Jenner garnered a following of a million on Twitter in about 4 hours, breaking the record established by the President of the United States (@potus). An increasing number of CEOs are now active on Twitter in order to take advantage of these tangible benefits.[20]

The ease of connecting and the wide audience to reach caused one author to describe Twitter as "somewhat intoxicating."[21] Success from microblogging can indeed be a heady experience. However, failure is publicized and very sobering, so it is wise to enter with a plan and some basic guidelines to avoid mistakes.

Building Your Brand Online

SEARCH TO GATHER INFORMATION

One of the most powerful Twitter features is the ability to search users, posts, and subjects. For the former Twitter can operate as a "global human search engine."[22] In almost any field of expertise, it is possible to find someone on Twitter with relevant information to share. In a live conversation, listening is the best way to learn; on Twitter that function is filled by searching.[23] Developing good search skills is necessary to get familiar with the audience being addressed and to see what they will respond to.

Further, search can turn up information about specific topics. As tweets are displayed in reverse-chronological order, a researcher can look to see how frequently a specific topic is updated to get a feel for what the audience is interested in. A topic that receives many tweets is obviously important to more people. When beginning a SMM campaign, start using Twitter by looking up the brand's name, the competition, and what is being said about each.[24] This approach will give a feel for the social landscape and suggest intelligent future tactics.

The ease of topic searching is aided by hashtags. Included in the form of "#topic" in tweets, clicking on the word with "#" in front (the hashtag topic) will draw up a list of other tweets that have been tagged with the same topic. For example, if someone were looking for news about the economy and Federal Reserve, that individual could try searching *#economy* or *#Fed*. To find information about SMM, one could search *#socialmedia* or *#smm*. Users place hashtags in their tweets to make them more visible, so take advantage of this feature both when gathering information and attempting to pass messages on to others. Twitter users can also search topics without hashtags, although hashtags are still useful to track information at conferences and other live events.

KNOW THE AUDIENCE

Using the search function to navigate through Twitter is helpful for building a portrait of the target audience. Think back to Chapter 3 and the persona development cycle. Twitter, with its easily searched database of faces attached to personal interests and hobbies, provides an optimal arena to study and develop different user personas. To do this, find one person whose profile seems to exemplify a certain persona. Then, look at the list of similar people to follow, which Twitter provides. Make note of how their expressed interests are similar to or different from the first profile. Continue this process until a more fleshed-out persona emerges. Aggregating together different characteristics of Twitter users who all might be interested in a brand or product allows a picture of the target market to emerge.

A word of caution on using Twitter to estimate more general target audiences: the demographics on Twitter do not necessarily reflect those of the general public. Adoption of Twitter is more pronounced in some groups than others. For example, there tend to be more young (18- to 34-year-old) Twitter users and more African American and Hispanic Twitter users than would be found in a random sample of the population.[25] While this skewing introduces complications into statistical research, it should not affect the persona development process described in Chapter 3. Twitter is such a large and diverse community that many people can be found possessing any particular value or need that a social media marketer might be interested in. Focus on the segment that will be drawn to the marketed product, and then aggregate demographics become less important.

CUSTOMIZE THE PROFILE PAGE

When deciding whether or not to follow someone, the profile page (see Figure 6.1) plays an enormous role in a viewer's decision. Generally, looking at the profile is the most research that a Twitter user will do before deciding to follow or not. A good profile page will help to develop a solid following and also provide external benefits such as views to the main site and more interest in the marketed product.

Twitter offers many options to customize a profile's home page. Background, text color, avatar picture, and description are the most noticeable features that can be modified. The first, and perhaps most important choice, is selecting a good avatar picture, which will appear next to every tweet, so the avatar should be recognizable and eye-catching for best results. It is very common, and perhaps the best practice, to use a face picture as the avatar. Generally, people follow faces more readily than logos.[26] Consequently, putting a brand or corporate image as the avatar is less personable than a facial picture. The avatar picture does not have to be overly polished; casual photos can outdo studio photography by transmitting a more relaxed image.

The profile's description should complement the avatar by providing context and important details. Writing space is limited, so the description will have to be concise. The background image can fill in the rest that cannot be conveyed in the description.

A custom-made background image can display personality, longer explanation of the product or services, and past accomplishments. The background is also a place to put URLs for other social networking profiles, websites, or blogs.[27] The combined result in a profile page should both encourage viewers to follow and to give links to other social media platforms in order to allow deeper engagement.

TWEET CONTENT

On a Twitter feed, it is especially easy to miss tweets that do not immediately catch the eye. If an account does not provide appealing content, users will ignore it. As a golden rule, the best content is "interesting, fun, and valuable."[28] The first two are

Source: https://www.twitter.com/Debra Zahay-Blatz

Figure 6.1 Twitter Profile page Debra Zahay-Blatz

self-explanatory, but creating valuable content is more complex because it must be both timely and relevant. Think about the sorts of concerns, interests, or values that the target Twitter audience might have, and address those first. Also, refer back to the six types of tweets (covered earlier in the chapter). Keeping a balance between different categories will make the content fresher and more engaging. Companies like Zappo's have made their reputation by tweeting out various forms of content, everything from the personal plans of its CEO to the work of its customer service department.

While it is important to have varying content, do not cover too many different topics in quick succession. Having multiple streams of thought going at once can make replies from followers confusing and can prevent outside viewers from understanding the overall message(s). Even if several tweets are sent out each day, keep each day's tweets to a common theme or idea.[29] This practice will help prevent miscommunication.

With a limited space to write on Twitter, some content will be too large for a tweet, so it only makes sense to provide a link to another site. Distributing links to interesting articles, images, or websites can be valuable to readers and draw a positive response. However, sharing a link is no guarantee anyone will visit it, especially if the content is poorly described, is uninteresting, or seems untrustworthy. In particular, links without a title attached are unlikely to get a response.[30] To save room for describing the linked content, use shortened URLs. A few link-shortening services include tinyurl.com, is.gd, ow.ly, and bit.ly.[31] Some of these services also provide free analytics to determine how many people clicked each link, a metric that can be valuable feedback for choosing later content.

Aside from clicking on links, another way to know if followers listen or care about what is being discussed is to look at how many retweets are given.[32] Users can retweet a post, displaying its author on their own timeline, or they can use "RT @[author]" and mention for a similar effect. Twitter will show which posts are retweeted and who did the retweet. Twitter users retweet content they enjoy or are willing to vouch for, so it is a signal of approval when a retweet occurs. This process gives insight into which sorts of content are most popular.

Building a Twitter Following

Twitter is set up such that users only receive tweets in their feed from people they are following. Therefore, if a profile has no followers, then functionally no one will see what is being posted![††] Because of this, as well as the status some associate with a high follower count, many thousands of words have been written about the best ways to gather Twitter followers. This section will cover some basics.

Many different strategies have been employed to gain Twitter followers quickly. One classic is the mass follow strategy in which one follows lots of other profiles and hope they decide to follow back. Stefan Tanase, one researcher studying this issue, "found that simply following almost 50,000 people [gave] him nearly 8,000 followers in return, a follow-back rate of about 17 percent."[33] However, this approach has several pitfalls. The first is technical: Twitter implemented new rules that block users from following more than 2,000 profiles unless they are also being followed by a similar number.[34] A policy intended to deter automated accounts, mass marketing and spam, this reform makes mass following difficult. The second problem is practical: most of the users who follow back automatically will be mass marketers and spammers, who will never read the tweets from profiles they follow. This reality makes followers gained from the mass follow strategy largely worthless.

Another approach to gathering followers is the equal ratio strategy, which aims to keep the profile's following and follower counts as close to equal as possible. With this system the profile will only follow users who seem likely to follow back; it also follows back all followers. This strategy handily avoids Twitter's imposed ratio for those following over 2,000. However, the downside is that this approach is very slow to get off the ground. When starting a new Twitter profile, it may take weeks or months to gather even a hundred followers unless the brand is already well-known. For many SMM strategists, that period will be too long to wait.

A happy medium between the two methods above is the targeted follow strategy. The first step is to search for and follow a few (somewhere between 50 and 150) profiles with similar interests and ideas or those that already have members of the target audience following them. For a business this may mean following the competition! Ideally, choose accounts that have roughly equal following/follower counts, as such counts indicate these accounts are more likely to follow back. However, focus more on the content and interests, and do not be overly concerned about following some that are unlikely to return the favor immediately.[35]

To increase the chance of being followed back, consider sending a mention (perhaps also with the hashtag #NowFollowing or similar) to inform the person about gaining a follower. On Twitter, the mention feature makes directed messages very simple; a tweet with "@[name]" will be viewable on the @Mention section of that person's home page. Notifying someone she or he has been followed and promoting that individual's name with a tweet signals the follower is active and worth following back.

Even with best efforts, do not expect perfect results when gaining followers, especially early on. Not everyone will respond. Following an unknown Twitter account is somewhat like leaving an old-fashioned calling card.[36] If the person finds the "card" (the profile, avatar, and description) interesting enough, he or she may decide to follow also. From this starting point, some of those early follows can become core connections to draw from later. Strike up dialogue when appropriate, and begin developing relationships.

The advantage of following relevant accounts with similar topics of interest is granted by Twitter's "Suggested People" feature. Users see lists of similar accounts as well as suggested people to follow based on which profiles they view and follow. This feature can lead interested viewers back to related profiles. For example, consider a small café starting up a Twitter presence; it could follow other coffee companies (such as Seattle's Best and Starbucks), coffee wholesalers/retailers (such as Maxwell House and Folgers), as well as other local businesses in town. Then, if someone was searching through Twitter profiles related to either coffee or the local town, that person might find that small café's profile as a suggestion. In this way the suggestion feature can help to access the target audience.

The second stage of the targeted follow strategy is more passive: choosing which profiles to follow back. Hopefully, many followers will be interested in the brand or business, but others may be following indiscriminately in hopes of boosting their own numbers. Early on, with less than 500 to 1,000 followers, it is worthwhile to follow back nearly everyone.‡ Twitter accounts with few followers tend to lack credibility and draw in followers more slowly, so do not risk losing the first few! After the account has grown, one can afford to be more selective in choosing who to follow back. Ultimately, the goal of this targeted follow strategy is to draw in followers who will read and respond to messages or who will become future recommenders or sources of expertise. In this respect quality of followers is far more important than quantity.

While a targeted follow strategy is often the best match for the marketing objectives, it is not the fastest way of gaining Twitter followers. For those with less patience, there is the purchase option. Many different services offer to provide Twitter followers for a fee.

---

‡Why "nearly" everyone? Some Twitter accounts are overtly racist, sexualized, or otherwise in poor taste. For almost any industry, following a problematic Twitter account is a potential scandal waiting to happen. If a profile's background, tweets, or avatar image is offensive, it may be better to avoid association and not follow back.

While this option may be tempting in order to get an account started, it is *not* advisable. Much like the mass follow approach, bought followers will likely be some combination of automated accounts, inactive accounts, and accounts not in the target audience. Joel Comm observes that "the price to be paid for having a large number of followers is often a less-targeted market and a lower conversation rate of followers to customers or users of your own site."[37] This observation is especially true when there is no guarantee that all of the followers are real people! Although it takes time, this pitfall is the reason that a Twitter following must be built, not bought.[‡‡]

Finally, synergize with other communication media to draw existing contacts into the Twitter following. It is possible to easily integrate Twitter with Facebook, LinkedIn, Digg, and other social media platforms, but this tactic is just the beginning. Provide a link from the company website or blog requesting viewers to follow on Twitter. People browsing a page may be drawn to the attached Twitter account. When asking people to follow on Twitter, phrasing is important. According to one study,

> The way web sites tell users to follow them on Twitter has a dramatic effect on the clickthrough rate. Saying simply "I'm on Twitter" produces a click-through rate of 4.7 percent . . .
>
> Ordering users to "Follow me on Twitter" increased that clickthrough rate by 55 percent, pushing it up to 7.31 percent. Making the phrase more personal by saying "You should follow me on Twitter" increased the click-through rate to 10.09 percent, and providing a link for people to click in the phrase "You should follow me on Twitter here" was the most effective of all with a clickthrough rate of 12.81 percent.[38]

A higher click through rate indicates more people going from the linking website to the Twitter profile. On a high-traffic page, a well-worded Twitter follow request can bring in a large number of followers.

Twitter can be integrated into even more communication media. After a variety of content has been posted, consider assembling a string of tweets into a blog post; it will draw attention to the Twitter page as well as providing an easy, interesting blog update.[39] A Twitter account can also be promoted through personal contacts. Attach the Twitter handle to business cards, email signatures, and other outbound communications.[40] People who are already known from other interactions make great Twitter contacts because they might have some interest in the brand or business already. Collecting followers is especially fruitful when there is a prior relationship to build from.

Best Practices for Crafting an Effective Twitter Channel

The tips above provide a baseline of knowledge to start a Twitter account and begin using it successfully. Many businesses have developed a Twitter presence and have had positive results. One new derivative product is Twitter brand insurance, which will compensate companies for lost reputation on Twitter.[41] Intended to hedge against

---

[‡‡]There are also more subtle ways of "buying" followers on Twitter. Some companies do giveaways, offering a chance to win some new technology product for users who follow and then mention the company's Twitter profile. While this is a way to gain followers quickly, and is more likely to draw in actual people (instead of automated accounts), it suffers the same flaw of drawing an untargeted following. While giveaways can be useful for building community good will or awareness of a brand, they are still not the best way to gain valuable targeted followers.

unauthorized tweets or image smears online, this insurance (in million-dollar quantities) demonstrates how much businesses invest in microblogging as well as how easily those efforts can be ruined.

Twitter can become an extremely effective marketing channel, but only when it is used with forethought. Making a profile pay off over time will require a commitment of time, energy, and attention to detail. Keep the following in mind over the long-run execution of a Twitter SMM campaign.

1. SELF-PROMOTE CAUTIOUSLY

The first lesson in marketing on Twitter is to not market too much. In principle this advice may sound contradictory, but in practice it is essential in order to reach an audience and to keep that audience's attention. Do not assume that Twitter users will care about product announcements, updates, or promotions; there are thousands, if not millions, of obvious (sometimes automated) Twitter marketing accounts vying for their attention.

To distinguish oneself from the crowd of advertisers, focus on relationships first. Do favors for others, providing links or mentions, and they may reciprocate. A good ratio to keep in mind is 10:1.[42] In other words, promote others or share information ten times for each self-promotional tweet. The best Twitter "advertising" will come as a result of mentions or recommendations by contacts and followers, so foster those connections early on by generously promoting others.

2. CHOOSE OPTIMAL TWEET TIMES

Without a direct mention, someone will probably never see a tweet unless that individual is online and looking at his or her home page in the minute that it is posted. Especially for users who follow many people, it can take just minutes or seconds for a tweet to escape that person's view. Therefore, putting out updates when people are online to see them is essential for making an impact.

Some simple logic can illuminate when the best time to post is: people must sign on in order to make their own updates, so that is the time they are certain to be online. Therefore, in order to be seen, post updates at times that followers are also updating the most.[43] Some have found "midday and midweek tend to produce the best results." However, a well-timed tweet, like Oreo's "You Can Still Dunk in the Dark," posted during a blackout during the 2013 Super Bowl, can have life long after its initial post.[44] Also keep time zones in mind. Depending on where the audience is located, it might be asleep when a tweet is posted. Adapt the posting schedule to allow more viewers to see and react to each update.

3. RESPOND TO QUESTIONS

If the prior steps have been done well and if useful content and links have been shared, this air of expertise may lead other users to ask questions. This is one of the most frequent uses of Twitter for firms: quickly responding to consumer questions and comments. For example, Nike uses a separate Twitter handle @nikesupport to provide a single place to answer user questions quickly. Other firms rely on Twitter's speed and focus to create superior customer service.[45] As users can access Twitter from many different devices, engaging their questions in a forthright manner can create a sense of closeness unparalleled by other platforms.[46]

Microblogging encourages users to seek input from others, and in a business context, this practice means responding to comments, questions, or issues that potential customers might have. Providing useful information can build a brand's reputation and thought leadership (see the case studies in this chapter for some examples).

4. GATHER FEEDBACK

While it is possible to passively observe and respond on Twitter, a more proactive strategy is to request answers directly. Asking for opinions or product reviews is a cheap alternative to focus groups; Twitter users are generally happy to share their thoughts when asked politely. Take advantage of this impulse, and seek feedback whenever possible. If the following is interested and engaged, some are likely to respond.

In addition to gauging general sentiment, it is also possible to solicit expert advice through microblogging platforms.[47] For example, one real-estate agent asked his Twitter following whether a client could get a mortgage for a property where the well had not undergone a safety test.[48] After receiving a quick response of "Yes" from one of the agent's expert Twitter contacts, the client was able to get the loan. Instead of paying a lawyer or doing extensive research himself, the real estate agent was able to save time and money and ultimately serve the client better. This represents just one potential usage of microblogging to find useful advice, and undoubtedly far more applications also exist.

As feedback from Twitter can be very helpful, it is good to encourage and reward users who are willing to provide it. After asking a question, acknowledge the people who respond or provide an answer.[49] If followers are left feeling unappreciated, they will be less likely to help in the future. These give-and-take relationships, which may seem insignificant individually, can aggregate into a powerful machine for gathering input and information. Being kind, polite, and appreciative helps to grease that apparatus and keep it running smoothly.

5. PROVIDE UNIQUE VALUE

Implicitly, every successful Twitter marketing profile must answer the question "why follow and listen to the messages being offered?" If the answer to this question is unclear, it is unlikely that many users will pay attention to what is said. While stellar content can draw in viewers, even that alone may not be enough to guarantee results.

A simple way to keep viewers' attention that many companies have employed is to offer special deals on Twitter. These can include coupons, promotional discounts, special products, free shipping, and so on. The most important aspect is that the deal is only seen or available to Twitter users. Coca-Cola has been using advanced personalization techniques, a tactic borrowed from direct marketing. Coke buys promoted tweets and addresses the user by name as part of its "Share a Coke" campaign, which has personalized Coke bottles for purchase. The user is encouraged to go to the store and buy a Coke with their name on it.[50] Followers get a sense of exclusivity and privilege from the special bargain, and everyone has more reason to follow closely for future deals. Since Twitter is a real-time format, using the timeliest tweets is appropriate.

Not only is there value in time-sensitive events that are ideally suited to Twitter, it is interesting to note that multi-tasking, such as watching TV and being on social media simultaneously, is important with social media and Twitter in particular. The Super Bowl, Oscars, and Grammys typically top the list with the Super Bowl garnering millions of tweets. The famous "Ellen Selfie" at the Oscars in 2014 had 1.2 million retweets, demonstrating that people use Twitter to supplement their television viewing experience.[51]

Marketing with Microblogging

Due to its versatility, Twitter can assist in almost any marketing goal. Increasing brand awareness, connecting with customers, providing support, and distributing information are just some of the possible benefits. Twitter allows business leaders to "identify influential people . . . who have common interests and create potentially valuable relationships."[52] As part of a SMM campaign, Twitter makes every other social media tool more effective by providing a distribution outlet that can reach millions of consumers.

While most of this chapter has been about Twitter, the general principles may be applied to other microblogging platforms with only technical modifications. Other websites may have different conversations, news searching, or social mechanisms, but peoples' values and interests remain a constant factor across platforms. Provide content that is fun, interesting, and valuable, and people will come looking for more. Build reciprocal relationships with other members, and be able to call on their help in later need. These core aspects of microblogging remain a common theme.

Most of all, connecting microblogs with the marketing objectives takes creativity in order to use the briefest communication medium to persuasively convey much larger ideas. The best microblog operators combine creativity with experience and writing skills to keep their following engaged. Developing these talents is crucial to the successful social media marketer.

Best Practices: Building a Personal Brand with Twitter

Create a complete profile. Lesson #1: Figure out who you are. Lesson one is always figure out who you are and create a profile that emphasizes those changes. Whether you are a marketing or tax expert, your profile should reflect that emphasis. Use relevant hashtags (#) in your description so you can be found.

Follow those in your area. Lesson #2: Once you have your niche, follow those important to your interest(s). If you want to go into sports marketing, follow the top sports team. If graphic design is your thing, follow those individuals and companies.

Create lists around your interests. Lesson #3: A great feature of Twitter is the Twitter list. You can create lists around topics such as search engine marketing or a particular sports team. You can use lists to quickly see what others in your area are posting. You can also join or follow specialty lists created by others.

Create a follow strategy. Lesson #4: For most beginners, a targeted follow strategy aiming for those in your areas of interest works best. With a small number to manage, you can thank those who follow you and engage with them individually. This responsiveness will help you become an important person in the network revolving around your areas of interest.

Post at least three times a day. Lesson #5: Conventional wisdom says because of the real-time nature of the postings they will not always be visible to those who are on Twitter. You should post at least three times a day and one useful tool is klout.com. You can use Klout to find relevant content for you to post easily and also track your influence. Although the algorithm is not perfect, it can help you see how you are improving in your social presence. Remember: at least some of your content should be original, from your blogs, SlideShare, YouTube channel or other source of original content. Original content will help establish your influence.

Notes

1. BBC News (2002, February 22), "Turning into Digital Goldfish." Retrieved July 11, 2011, from http://news.bbc.co.uk/2/hi/science/nature/1834682.stm
2. Comm, Joel (2010), *Twitter Power 2.0* (Hoboken, NJ: John Wiley), p. 179.
3. Barker, Donald I., Melissa S. Barker, and Catherine T. Pinard (2013), Unit D, *Internet Research—Illustrated*, 6th ed. (Boston, MA: Cengage Learning), p. 12.
4. Thorsten Hennig-Thurau,Thorsten, Wiertz, Caroline, and Fabian Feldhaus, (2015). "Does Twitter matter? The Impact of Microblogging Word of Mouth on Consumers' Adoption of New Movies." Journal of the Academy of Marketing Science, 43:3, 375–394.
5. Kottke, Jason (2005, October 19), "Tumblelogs." Retrieved July 11, 2011, from http://www.kottke.org/05/10/tumblelogs
6. Arrington, Michael (2006, July 15), "Odeo Releases Twttr," TechCrunch. Retrieved July 11, 2011, from http://techcrunch.com/2006/07/15/is-twttr-interesting/
7. Johansmeyer, Tom (2011, February 3), "200 Million Twitter Accounts . . . But How Many Are Active?" Social Times. Retrieved July 11, 2011, from http://socialtimes.com/200-million-twitter-accounts-but-how-many-are-active_b36952
8. http://expandedramblings.com/index.php/march-2013-by-the-numbers-a-few-amazing-twitter-stats/, retrieved June 18, 2015
9. Twopcharts (n.d.), "What Does 300 Million Registered Twitter Accounts Mean?" Retrieved July 11, 2011, from http://twopcharts.com/twitter300million
10. Pew (2014, September), "Twitter Update 2014," Pew Internet. Retrieved June 3, 2015 from http://www.pewinternet.org/fact-sheets/social-networking-fact-sheet/
11. "Plurk.com" (n.d.), Alexa. Retrieved July 5, 2015, from http://www.alexa.com/siteinfo/plurk.com, http://www.adweek.com/socialtimes/plurk/476593
12. Alexa (n.d.), "Identi.ca." Retrieved June 5, 2015, from http://www.alexa.com/siteinfo/identi.ca
13. Kabani, Shama Hyder (2010), *The Zen of Social Media Marketing: An Easier Way to Build Credibility, Generate Buzz, and Increase Revenue* (Dallas: TX: BenBella Books), p. 76.
14. Comm, Joel (2010), *Twitter Power 2.0* (Hoboken, NJ: John Wiley), p. 117. Thurston, Michael (2015, June 3). "Jenner Debuts Post-Bruce Look, Breaks Twitter Record," http://sports.yahoo.com/news/call-caitlyn-jenner-debuts-post-bruce-look-181806811—oly.html.
15. Borges, Bernie (2009), *Marketing 2.0* (Tucson, Arizona: Wheatmark), p. 204.
16. Comm, Joel (2010), *Twitter Power 2.0* (Hoboken, NJ: John Wiley), p. 123–29.
17. Glaser, Mark (2007, May 15), "Your Guide to Micro-Blogging and Twitter," PBS, "Media Shift." Retrieved July 12, 2011, from http://www.pbs.org/mediashift/2007/05/your-guide-to-micro-blogging-and-twitter135.html
18. Kukral, Jim (2008, October 29), "How and Why to Use Twitter for Small Businesses," Small Business Trends. Retrieved July 12, 2011, from http://smallbiztrends.com/2008/10/how-why-twitter-small-businesses.html
19. Stelzner, Michael (2008, December 31), "How to Use Twitter to Grow Your Business," *CopyBlogger*. Retrieved July 12, 2011, from http://www.copyblogger.com/grow-business-twitter/
20. MacMillan, Douglas (2008, September), "CEOs' Take on Twitter," *Business Week*. Retrieved July 12, 2011, from http://images.businessweek.com/ss/08/09/0908_microblogceo/index.htm
21. Borges, Bernie (2009), *Marketing 2.0* (Tucson, Arizona: Wheatmark), p. 203.
22. Kabani, Shama Hyder (2010), *The Zen of Social Media Marketing: An Easier Way to Build Credibility, Generate Buzz, and Increase Revenue* (Dallas, TX: BenBella Books), p. 80.
23. Ibid., p. 87.
24. Brogan, Chris (2008, August 20), "50 Ideas on Using Twitter for Business." chrisbrogan.com. Retrieved July 12, 2011, from http://www.chrisbrogan.com/50-ideas-on-using-twitter-for-business/
25. Lee, Amy (2011, June 1), "Twitter Statistics: 13 Percent of Americans Tweet, Growth Led by African-Americans," *Huffington Post*. Retrieved July 13, 2011, from http://www.huffingtonpost.com/2011/06/01/twitter-pew-statistics_n_869790.html Pew Social Media Update (2015, January), Twitter Users. Retrieved June 7, 2015, http://www.pewinternet.org/2015/01/09/social-media-update-2014/pi_2015-01-09_social-media-new_01/
26. Warnke, Marc (2009, February 10), "Top 10 Things New People to Twitter Should Know," blog. Retrieved July 12, 2011, from http://www.marcwarnke.com/blog/marcwarnke/top_10_things_new_people_twitter_should_know

27. Borges, Bernie (2009), *Marketing 2.0* (Tucson, Arizona: Wheatmark), p. 206.

28. Comm, Joel (2010), *Twitter Power 2.0* (Hoboken, NJ: John Wiley), p. 76.

29. Rowse, Darren (2008, May 8), "5 Tips to Grow Your Twitter Presence," *ProBlogger*. Retrieved July 12, 2011, from http://www.problogger.net/archives/2008/05/08/5-tips-to-grow-your-twitter-presence/

30. Brantner, Eric (2009, January 11), "7 Ways to Get Your Twitter Followers to Click Your Links," SEOHosting. Retrieved July 12, 2011, from http://www.seohosting.com/blog/social-networking/7-ways-to-get-your-twitter-followers-to-click-your-links/

31. Ludwig, Sean (2009, February 16), "Top 10 Twitter Tips for Beginners," *PCMag*. Retrieved July 12, 2011, from http://www.pcmag.com/article2/0,2817,2341095,00.asp

32. Gage, Randy (2009) "Tweet This! A Twitter Manifesto." Retrieved July 12, 2011, from http://www.randygage.com/blog/tweet-this-a-twitter-manifesto/

33. Zappos (n.d.), "In the Beginning—Let There Be Shoes." Retrieved July 1, 2011, from http://about.zappos.com/zappos-story/in-the-beginning-let-there-be-shoes

34. FN Staff (2009, May 4), "Zappos Milestone: Timeline," *Footwear News*. Retrieved July 1, 2011, from http://www.wwd.com/footwear-news/zappos-milestone-timeline-2121760

35. Mitchell, Dan (2008, May 24), "Shoe Seller's Secret of Success," *New York Times*. Retrieved July 1, 2011, from http://www.nytimes.com/2008/05/24/technology/24online.html and Off the Grid PR, (2009, February 25), "Twitter: On Emerging Business Case Studies & Participatory Marketing." Retrieved July 1, 2011, from http://offthegrid-pr.com/socially-responsible-pr/2009/2/25/twitter-on-emerging-business-case-studies-participatory-mark.html

36. Lacy, Sarah (2009, July 22), "Amazon Buys Zappos; The Price is $928M, Not $847M," TechCrunch. Retrieved July 1, 2011, from http://techcrunch.com/2009/07/22/amazon-buys-zappos/

37. Griffin, Chris (2010, December 22), "Social Media Tips from the Major Players—Part One," WSI IMS. Retrieved July 1, 2011, from http://www.readwriteweb.com/archives/zappos_twitter.php

38. Off the Grid PR (2009, February 25), "Twitter: On Emerging Business Case Studies & Participatory Marketing." Retrieved July 1, 2011, from http://offthegrid-pr.com/socially-responsible-pr/2009/2/25/twitter-on-emerging-business-case-studies-participatory-mark.html

39. Comm, Joel (2010), *Twitter Power 2.0* (Hoboken, NJ: John Wiley), p. 78.

40. Twitter Help Center (2011), "Following Rules and Best Practices." Retrieved July 13, 2011, from https://support.twitter.com/entries/68916-following-rules-and-best-practices

41. Kabani, Shama Hyder (2010), *The Zen of Social Media Marketing: An Easier Way to Build Credibility, Generate Buzz, and Increase Revenue* (Dallas, TX: BenBella Books), p. 78.

42. Dykeman, Mark (2009, January 26), "Getting More Twitter Followers—or Losing Them." Pistachio Consulting. Retrieved July 12, 2011, from http://pistachioconsulting.com/twitter-followers/

43. Comm, Joel (2010), *Twitter Power 2.0* (Hoboken, NJ: John Wiley), p. 79.

44. Ibid., pp. 93–94.

45. Golden, Michelle (2011), *Social Media Strategies for Professionals and Their Firms* (Hoboken, NJ: John Wiley), p. 205.

46. Norgard, Brian (2009, February 24), "5 Ways to Find & Acquire Customers on Twitter," Shoe Money. Retrieved July 12, 2011, from http://www.shoemoney.com/2009/02/24/5-ways-to-find-acquire-customers-on-twitter/

47. Dell (n.d.), "Our Story." Retrieved July 1, 2011, from http://content.dell.com/us/en/corp/about-dell-our-story.aspx#

48. netbook fan (2011, March 23), "Dell Retakes Number-two Spot in Global PC Sales," Cheap Notebook Deals. Retrieved July 1, 2011, from http://www.cheapnetbookdeals.net/dell-netbook/dell-retakes-number-two-spot-in-global-pc-sales/

49. Rowse, Darren (2008, November 21), "How to Ask Effective Questions on Twitter," Twitip. Retrieved July 12, 2011, from http://www.twitip.com/how-to-ask-effective-questions-on-twitter/

50. Weinberg, Tamar (2009), *The New Community Rules: Marketing on the Social Web* (Sebastopol, CA: O'Reilly Media), p. 129. Heine, Christopher (2015, June 4). "Coke's New Twitter Ads Call Out Viewers by Name Social promos get personal." Retrieved June 7, 2015, from http://www.adweek.com/news/technology/cokes-new-twitter-ads-call-out-viewers-name-165174

51. Lansky, Sam (2014, March 4), "Oscars 2014: This Is the Most Retweeted Tweet Ever Is this the most star-studded selfie of all time?" *Time*. Retrieved June 7, 2015 from http://entertainment.time.com/2014/03/02/oscars-ellen-meryl-streep-selfie.

52. Borges, Bernie (2009), *Marketing 2.0* (Tucson, Arizona: Wheatmark), p. 208

Content Creation and Sharing: Blogging, Streaming Video, Podcasts, and Webinars

Twenty years ago, the terms *content marketing* or *blogging* did not exist. Today, blogs are an important source of news for millions, and professional blogging has been a path to wealth and fame for many people. For some companies, the corporate blog is the centerpiece of a well-developed content strategy that goes across all platforms. Understanding how to utilize blogging, streaming video, podcasts, and webinars to position a brand and to generate business is an essential skill for successful SMM.

Creating a Content Strategy

The key to successfully publishing content online is to have a clear and meaningful content strategy, based on the overall firm objectives and brand positioning. Curata defines content marketing as "The process for developing, executing and delivering the digital content and related assets that are needed to create, nurture and grow a company's customer base." Pulizzi and Barret (2008, p. 8) suggest that it is "the creation and distribution of educational and/or compelling content in multiple formats to attract and/or retain customers."[1] Spiller and Baier define content marketing as "providing useful information for free with the hope that people will search it out, consume it and trust the provider sufficiently to take whatever measurable action is being requested—order, visit, donate, vote, etc."[2] In short, content marketing as a strategy has three major components:

1. The *creation* of the content based upon target audiences and personas

2. The *dissemination* of the content through appropriate channels to achieve marketing objectives

3. The *measurement* of the success of the content through the analysis of results

In this context, all the social media channels discussed in this book are elements of an effective content strategy. As discussed in Chapter 3, a strong social media strategy starts with a clear understanding of how the marketing objectives relate to the target audience or buyer personas. To create content that will engage with the audience, the driving question is "what subject areas will interest members of the audience?" More importantly, as shown in Figure 7.1, how does the content reinforce your brand image or brand story? One of the advantages of publishing content as a part of an overall SMM strategy is that it can achieve a wide variety of marketing goals and objectives. Defining those goals clearly (as discussed in Chapter 2) will help to develop a content plan that will reach the target audience and deliver the most relevant results.

In fact, Wuebben suggests that all content marketing should reinforce the brand strategy through content deployed over multiple contact channels.[3] Zahay concurs by suggesting that after developing a clear brand story to reinforce the strategic positioning of the company, the next step is to select the type of content to reinforce that story. Should the firm tell stories about how people use its product or about the lifestyle its customers lead? The answer will be based on the audience and the selected personas and what resonates with those consumers of content. Finally, the marketer must then select the appropriate communications channels, based on the audience and content marketing objectives, to get that story out to the customer.

As the channels become more and more complex, it is important to develop a powerful story that can be told across channels. Chances are that the audience is less interested in the brand and the product than they are interested in a problem and a solution to that problem. Marketers must ask themselves, "About what subjects related to my brand is my audience passionate?" Intel offers behind-the-scenes insights on its products, technology, and human interest stories. Nonprofits, such as UNICEF, use content marketing brilliantly to tell the stories behind the children whom they are charged to help. Holliman and Rowley urge B2B marketers to create content that is "useful, relevant, compelling and timely" and suggest that KPIs must be developed and monitored to measure success.[4] How many times a blog is viewed is important, but whether that piece of content ultimately helped in the sales process is another more difficult question to ask. Content marketing also requires a significant advancement in multichannel attribution models

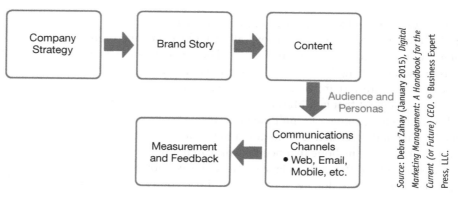

Source: Debra Zahay (January 2015), Digital Marketing Management: A Handbook for the Current (or Future) CEO. © Business Expert Press, LLC.

Figure 7.1 Developing the Company Strategy and Brand Story through Content Marketing

to really be able to tease out the purchase path from the analytics involved. In addition, Holliman and Rowley suggest the switch from selling to publishing has made the B2B sales relationship more consultative.

One additional key consideration in developing a content publishing strategy is to overcome the fear of being too specific. Many companies don't want to pigeonhole themselves into a small and specific niche of content that they will cover. However with the proliferation of content, the best strategy to building an audience is to be as niche and specific as possible.

In his book *The Long Tail*, Chris Anderson discusses how the web has created large opportunities for *Long Tail* content.[5] *The Long Tail* is small niche content that motivates smaller, highly specific audiences as contrasted with a generic *best seller*. For example, the *New York Times*, which produces generic news content with broad mass appeal, would not be in *the Long Tail*, whereas a small, locally focused newspaper or a newspaper focused on industry-specific news and updates might be. The evolution of the web has shown that there are consumers looking for that very specific *Long Tail* content. Combined with the low cost of online publishing, this highly specialized content can be developed efficiently and effectively.

The future of publishing and content creation lies in serving niche markets on a large scale. The lesson for bloggers is to keep in mind what specialized interests they might be able to market toward and to develop content that will appeal to such interests. Generalized content is commonly found elsewhere, and consequently, in order to build a blog's viewership and influence, the blogger must focus on specialized content that is not easily replicated.

Just a few short years ago, the mechanics of content marketing were simple. Upload a blog post or a white paper with an image and you were ahead of the game in content marketing. Nowadays, the strategy is sophisticated and telling. Marketers are nervous about content marketing because the challenge is to produce good content across multiple channels. The process of search engine marketing has also affected content marketing because search engines like blog posts, tweets, white papers, and other forms of content favor these items in search results. These contributions lend credibility to published content, but also create pressure to stoke the "content engine."

To help make sense of this process, the periodic table of content marketing as produced by Econsultancy has eight basic elements of contact marketing.[6] This table is reproduced in Figure 7.2.

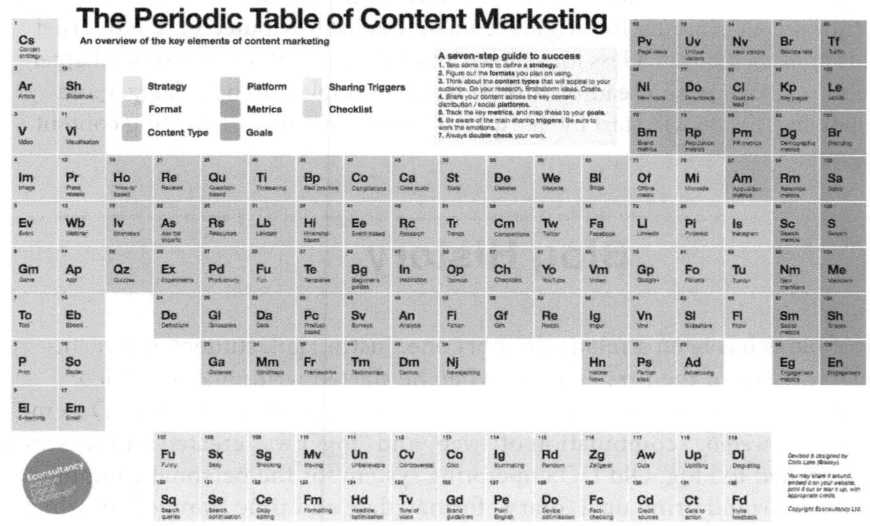

Source: Chris Lake (March 2015), "Introducing the Periodic Table of Content Marketing." © Econsultancy.

Figure 7.2 The Periodic Table of Content Marketing

1. **Strategy**—As stated in Chapter 3 and in this chapter, a strategy is key to any social media or content marketing effort. Strategy must be the key in developing strong content.

2. **Format**—A single piece of content can be deployed across many types, or repurposed. Email works well for entrepreneurs and small businesses, white papers for B2B, and so on.

3. **Content Type**—There are different types of content that work well for different businesses. Quizzes work well for B2C and testimonials for B2B.

4. **Platform**—Content distribution platforms can be overpaid, earned, or owned media, that is, over the company's website, over a social network, or through an advertising platform.

5. **Metrics**—Metrics help the marketer understand who is reading the content, when, the reach of the content, and a number of other useful pieces of information.

6. **Goals**—Content should support the business and brand strategy. If you want more people to view your content, that objective is brand awareness. An engagement objective involves having people interact with content on the web and create their own content around a brand.

7. **Sharing Triggers**—What marketers do to encourage sharing; marketers use emotional and other triggers to create responses in the audience (although consumers do not like it if they believe they are obviously being manipulated). Funny and disgusting both work as triggers for sharing video content.

8. **Checklist**—Before deploying, there should be a checklist ensuring that the content should be optimized for search, to support the company goals, and for other factors.

With all this content out there and so many factors involved, is it any wonder that jobs in SMM are booming. A recent survey on blogging by Orbit Media revealed that over half (57%) percent of bloggers are writing content for others.[7] Those writing for others are often getting paid to do so. Users like content and "content is king," but it is also a big challenge to keep the "content machine" fed and produce interesting content for a hungry and demanding content audience.[8]

This chapter looks at content marketing through the channels of blogging, podcasting, streaming videos, and webinars. What these ways of delivering content have in common is that they are all channels for original content that is distributed on the Internet primarily. It is *published* but in a less formal way than the content discussed in Chapter 11, such as ebooks. Any person reading this book, for example, can be a blogger and create the following. So we will start by discussing a fairly easy way of creating content, which is blogging.

Blog History

The history of blogs has been a relatively short one. Justin Hall, student at Swarthmore College, was one of the first bloggers when he started writing about video games and consoles around 1994. The term *blog* had not yet been coined; in December 1997, the word *weblog* (combination of "web" and "log") was created and was then eventually shortened to blog. Old DOS operating system for the personal computer, the command .log would bring up a "diary" format, date and time stamped, in which individuals could write down their personal or work-related thoughts and keep them in a centralized place.[9]

Blogging really took off after 1999 when LiveJournal and Blogger were launched. These sites allowed users with little or no technical ability to start their own blogs. At the middle of 2015, over 400 million people each month were reading blogs on WordPress alone, and 54 million posts are written each month.[10] This large number represents a potentially huge audience that can be reached through blogging.

What Is a Blog?

Most people who are active online have heard of blogs. Blogs are generally considered to be a collection of the blogger's personal thoughts and ideas around a particular topic and, as stated previously, are a less formal method of publication.[11]

Most importantly, a blog is a website that has regular updates (or blog posts) where the most recent updates are displayed first. Blogs often allow readers to leave comments and respond to the blog posts. A blogger is then a person who administrates, writes, and updates a blog.

What distinguishes a blog from other types of social media? In their oft-cited book, *Naked Conversations*, authors Robert Scoble and Shel Israel present Blogging's Six Pillars, which make blogs different from other communication methods.[12] To paraphrase, these pillars are:

- **Publishable**. It is cheap and easy for anyone to set up a blog. Posting is free and can be seen worldwide.

- **Findable**. People can find blogs with search engines. Typically, the more posts a blog has, the easier it will be to find.

- **Social**. Conversations about mutual interests can occur on blogs, either through direct comments or by linking to others with related content. These practices allow people to form connections with others regardless of their location.

- **Viral**. Blogs can often spread information faster than a news service. The more interesting people find a topic, the more rapidly they will spread it to others.

- **Syndicatable**. Viewers can easily subscribe to a blog using RSS and be notified about its updates in real time. This ability saves time in searching and makes content easily findable.

- **Linkable**. As blogs can link to each other, each blogger has access to a potentially huge audience.

Successful blogs take advantage of these six pillars to distinguish themselves and build influence on the social web. Blogs can be created for both personal and professional reasons, and they vary widely in topics and reader base. An individual may blog in order to develop his or her own position in relation to others in the field, or a company blog might help position a firm as an expert in its industry. In any case, sticking close to the core pillars of blogging is necessary for success.

Creating and Promoting a Blog

SETTING UP A BLOG

Creating a blog is almost always the easiest part of blogging. A starter blog can be created on WordPress, Blogger, or other free sites. These sites are examples of hosted blogs, which are run on some other company's website and server. Such blogs will typically have a suffix at the end of the URL address, indicating which service is hosting the blog. Businesses that want to invest more in blogging can self-host a blog on their website, usually for relatively little cost. Self-hosted blogs have the advantage of being taken more seriously because they require a larger time investment to create and maintain. They also lead search engines directly to your website instead of a third party.

Deciding how to set up the blog will depend on the circumstances; more information about hosted versus self-hosting can easily be researched online. The difficult parts of blogging are creating a compelling and relevant subject area for the blog, writing effectively, and improving the content over time based on reader feedback. For students, Google's Blogger is an easy choice because the blog can be easily linked to Google Analytics by placing the UA code from Analytics in Settings under Other.[13] We want to be able to easily monitor our blog and check analytics and that might be the best choice for a beginning blog.

PROMOTING A BLOG

INTRODUCTION AND EXAMPLE After creating a blog, it is the responsibility of the blogger to promote the blog to the target audience and gain readership. One way to increase readership to the blog is to request an email sign-up. Creating a list of readers who receive content on a regular basis and share it is a solid tactic for increasing blog readership. A good example of a well-promoted blog is *The Huffington Post*. The blog began life as just another liberal communication in an already crowded field; it aggregates news from other sources, but eventually it grew into a full-fledged news organization. The *Huffington Post* is an unlikely success story, built in large part on the notoriety of Arianna Huffington and her allies. According to a *Washington Post* article, "skeptics dismissed it as a vanity outlet for [Arianna Huffington] and her Hollywood friends.[14] But the Huffington Post has become an undeniable success, its evolution offering a road map of what works on the Web."[15]

Ms. Huffington's two objectives were obvious: drive traffic to the blog site and keep them coming back. The staff of the *Huffington Post* became adept as news aggregators in identifying the most compelling content on the web that matched its left-leaning editorial slant, as well as some juicy celebrity gossip, and reposting portions of these articles on the blog site. Ms. Huffington's editors are especially skillful at optimizing these story snippets "for search engine results, so that in a Google search, a Huffington Post summary of a Washington Post or a CNN.com report may appear ahead of the original article."[16] This practice is not without its critics. Indeed, Jack Shafer, who covers media for Reuters.com opinion section, characterized it this way: "Huffington glories in carving the meat out of a competitor's story, throwing a search-engine optimized (SEO) headline on it, and posting it."[17] The company site defends the practice as falling under the fair use doctrine. As the funding and ad revenues for the *Huffington Post* grew, the site eventually hired in-house reporters, columnists, and investigative journalists to create original news items to complement the content it aggregates.

To achieve *Huffington Post*'s second goal of retaining readership, it was clear from the start that it had to provide quality content from well-known political posters. Ms. Huffington led the way as a prolific blogger. In addition, she initially relied heavily on her impressive "rolodex of A-list celebrities and high-powered friends, soliciting early contributions from the likes of Larry David, Diane Keaton and Alec Baldwin."[18] Soon other notable voices followed, and, perhaps most importantly, the site threw open its doors to a legion of bloggers. Although bloggers received no remuneration, tens of thousands of posts poured in. This approach was not without its critics, as CNET writer Josh Wolf indicates, "[i]n most industries refusing to pay your labor force is not only unethical, it would likely border on slavery and be illegal as well. Apparently in the world of blogging it's considered good business practice."[19] The company justified the practice by saying they offer bloggers "visibility, promotion, and distribution with a great company" in exchange for their contributions.[20] Finally, Ms. Huffington's role in fund–raising played a key role in the blog site's success because it gave the site the capital necessary to rapidly expand its staff and infrastructure.

Today, the *Huffington Post* is still the number one blog in the blogosphere.[21] It has over 80,000 bloggers[22] with approximately 126 million visitors every month.

The viewership, content, and success of the *Huffington Post* have not gone unnoticed. The site won the Webby Award for the best political blog in 2006 and 2008 and was the People's Voice Winner in the political blog category in 2009, 2010, and 2011.[23] *Time* named it the second best blog in 2009.[24] In 2012, the blog won its first Pulitzer Prize.[25]

As with other successful blog sites, AOL snapped up the *Huffington Post* in February 2011 for $315 million.[26] However, there has been a dark cloud on the horizon for the blog site. In April 2011, Jonathan Tasini, a well-known labor advocate, filed suit against the *Huffington Post* in the United States District Court of New York on behalf of 9,000 uncompensated bloggers. He alleged damages of over $105 million from the sale of *Huffington post* to AOL, alleging it was the work of unpaid bloggers that created the value of the company.[27] Ms. Huffington was quick to counter, asserting the blog site is two things, "[a] journalistic enterprise, hiring hundreds of journalists with benefits, great salaries and we are a platform that is available to anyone who does quality work to disseminate their ideas, promote their books, movies, political candidacies or whatever it is they are engaged in."[28] The courts determined that the unpaid bloggers, although they contributed to the site's success, received their reward in terms of publication.[29]

CREATING A REPUTATION THROUGH BLOGGING

After setting up a blog with a nice niche format, students would be lucky to find themselves in the position of one of the most famous bloggers Robert Scoble. Scoble was the first prominent corporate blogger within a major corporation. Robert Scoble became a trailblazer in corporation communications by establishing a position as the first high-profile and influential corporate blogger. He accomplished this feat by telling the truth (as he saw it) in his blog posts, which often meant criticizing his employer, Microsoft Corporation, and its products while heaping praise on the company's fiercest competitors (Apple Computer and Google) and their wares. Scoble's brutal honesty and invitation to open communication with consumers endowed his employer with a renewed credibility, which Microsoft's much-maligned business practices had previously eroded.[30]

Scoble's corporate blog, called the *Scobleizer*, employed podcasts, RSS, and web video to give Microsoft, a company that had at that time a reputation as a ruthless competitor, a human face. He published his cell phone number and invited fans and critics alike to contact him directly or comment on his blog posts. This form of transparent and earnest corporate communication was more appealing to people than the bland press releases issued by the public relations department. Hence, Scoble's success quickly inspired other large companies to follow with their own corporate blogs (such as Sun, Adobe, and General Motors). Using his blog, Scoble "ushered in a new era of interaction among companies, customers, critics and the general public."[31]

Scoble used his blog to not only listen to the company's many constituencies but to build a network of resources so that he could help Microsoft respond appropriately to user needs.[32] At times, this practice meant criticizing poorly built Microsoft products and recommending competitors' offerings instead. Despite talking about some very touchy subjects (with legal implications), Scoble was never blocked from posting a blog by Microsoft.

Scoble knew more had to be done than listening. He garnered support from the highest levels, arguing that if Microsoft didn't improve its products based on feedback from the blogosphere, consumers would catch on that the company didn't value their input, and his efforts would be viewed as just a PR stunt. Senior management bought this argument, and Scoble began searching the web for any mention of Microsoft on blogs. He interacted with these bloggers, even if they had no readers and were just ranting.

The strategy was simple—let these bloggers know someone at Microsoft was listening and engaged. Over time, Scoble built an invaluable blog-based focus group.

Scoble confronted the appropriate product team leaders within Microsoft with these suggestions and criticisms, demanding to know what they were going to do about them. The responses he got from team leaders gave Scoble more to blog about, letting consumers know what Microsoft was going to fix, improve, make more secure, and so on. Scoble was also able get some Microsoft executives to blog within the company instead of sending out endless streams of email few had the time to read. These blogs later became a great repository of knowledge within the company for employees to search when necessary.

According to an article published in 2005 in *The Economist*, "[Scoble has] become a minor celebrity among geeks worldwide, who read his blog religiously. Impressively, he has also succeeded where small armies of more conventional public-relations types have been failing abjectly for years: he has made Microsoft, with its history of monopolistic bullying, appear marginally but noticeably less evil to the outside world, and especially to the independent software developers that are his core audience."[33]

A 2006 Northwestern University *Blogging Success Study* went further, quoting blogger Jeremy Pepper: "I can say without any issue that Robert Scoble has given Microsoft a friendly persona out there on the Internet. He's given a face to the organization that's different than Steve Balmer or Bill Gates. He's made it warm and fuzzy. It's no longer the evil empire. It's just, 'Oh this is the company Scoble works for!' It helps take off the taint that the company has had. . . . He doesn't talk about Microsoft all that much, but he is known as a Microsoft blogger."[34]

Although Robert Scoble left Microsoft in late 2006, he had accomplished the impossible: he made Microsoft not only approachable but likable—along with becoming a brand unto himself, with more than 20,000 subscribers to his *Scobleizer* blog. In addition, Scoble had shepherded in a new era in corporation communications, which he documented in a book, *Naked Conversations: How Blogs Are Changing the Way Businesses Talk with Customers*.[35]

Other corporate blogs soon sprang up to provide a human face to the corporation. The blog run by Marriott International's CEO, J. W. Marriott, has been praised for its accessibility and down-to-earth tone. Unlike many other corporate blogs, *Marriott on the Move*‡ does not focus on disseminating press releases. Instead, it provides the CEO an avenue to share stories and information on the business and to develop a likable public personality. The success of Marriott's blog is an instructive lesson for other social media marketers.

Marriott's blog has been a resounding success. Marriott employees make up about a fifth of the blog's readership, and they comment often. The blog gives a sense of camaraderie with the CEO that workers enjoy. The blog has also generated some tangible monetary gains, generating more than $5 million worth of revenue from bookings that originate from the blog.[36]

In the time since its creation, the Marriott blog has become a classic example of corporate blogging done well. J. W. Marriott himself has been highly praised for his blogging efforts. In 2008, he won the Excel Award given by the International Association for Business Communicators. When discussing his return on investment for the blog, Marriott said, "I would recommend it to any CEO. It's worth it." Mr. Marriott continues to blog to the present day.[37]

Everyone Is a Publisher

Bill Marriott realized early what few others did, that *Everyone is a Publisher*. The term *Publisher* used to be a term restricted to those who produced magazines, newspapers, and books. However, with the tools available on the web, anyone can become a publisher at minimal cost. This radical change poses both challenges and opportunities for the marketing professional.

Early in the Internet's development, creating a website required either strong HTML[†] coding knowledge or the hiring of a programmer and designer to do the work. Website development was time consuming and costly. Only the experts or the well-funded could create and publish content.

Today, a website can be created in under an hour with no expert coding knowledge using Weebly, Wix, WordPress, or other web-development tools. Editing websites has also become much easier. Even many large corporate websites are built on some Content Management System (CMS) that allows users with no programming knowledge to easily edit the site's content.

The online space has changed from a *read web*, where people would go to the Internet primarily to consume content and information, to a *read-write web*, where it is possible to create in addition to consuming content. Rather than passively taking in information, users can create and interact with the content they see.

CONTENT CLUTTER

With publishing tools so accessible, anyone can be a publisher, and as a result there are millions of blogs, websites, and podcasts published. There is such a proliferation of content online that even the highest-quality material has difficulty standing out and building an audience.

According to a 2008 survey by Universal McCann, there were 26 million blogs and about 60 million blog readers in the United States, each of whom read about three blogs.[38] If total, that would mean about six blog readers per blog if divided evenly, but that is not the case. Realistically, a few blogs have lots of readers while many blogs have almost no readers. That trend is likely to continue, as shown in Figure 7.3.[39] Most companies consider their blog as part of their business strategy and consumers increasingly look to blogs to make business decisions. Blogs are a good source of inbound links, which raise the search engine profile of a site and consumers trust information and content from blogs.

This reality sets a higher bar for publishers and content creators. In addition to creating interesting and relevant content to publish, part of the strategy must include how to

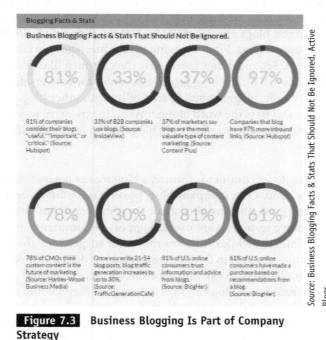

Figure 7.3 Business Blogging Is Part of Company Strategy

[†]HTML stands for HyperText Markup Language; it is the most frequently used markup language for websites.

build an audience and where to syndicate content online. Many of the social media tools covered elsewhere in this book (Facebook, Twitter, social news sites, etc.) can be excellent syndication platforms to build a following for a blog.

In addition to leveraging social media to find an audience, consider ways to connect with current customers, direct mail subscribers, email newsletter readers, and so on with whom to blog content. An existing client base will generally be more interested in viewing the related blog, so finding ways to draw them into reading blog content is a valuable way to build readership.

Marketing Benefits of Blogging

As one of the oldest and best-known social media outlets, blogging has several unique advantages. The potentially large audience and strong focus on content produces several benefits for blogging being part of an active SMM campaign.

COMMUNICATING WITH (POTENTIAL) CUSTOMERS

More so than the audience of most other social media platforms, that of blogs rewards thoughtful posts and fully developed ideas. As Brian Solis explains, "blog posts inherently boast the ability to share expanded content, text, video, audio, images, tags, links, to more effectively and deeply express, explain, and support the ideas and context related to any given topic."[40] This attribute makes blogs valuable in a broad variety of industries (as the case studies in this chapter demonstrate). Every business entails some form of expertise that can potentially be shared with and interest online viewers. In this context blogging can help to both position a company's brand as well as bring in new leads.

WORD-OF-MOUTH MARKETING

Some recent studies have found that word of mouth may be more than twice as effective as traditional marketing; it results in more new customer acquisitions and has longer-lasting results.[41] While many social media platforms can be valuable in creating buzz about a product or service, blogs are especially important. Blogging facilitates word-of-mouth marketing in several ways. First, blogging makes messages portable and easy for others to link to or share. Second, blogs create new topics, much like mini-press releases, that spur public discussion. Third, a blog provides a center for conversation via comments or replies. And finally, blogging builds credibility with other bloggers, making it more likely that others will pass the word along.[42] As an inexpensive way to tap into the powerful marketing method of word of mouth, blogs are an invaluable tool for a social media marketer.

RECEIVING FEEDBACK Due to its comments feature, a blog makes it easy for viewers to respond to the topic at hand. On a company blog, posting recent news or questions to the community can bring valuable insights about the public mood on relevant issues. Both positive and negative responses are useful; supportive comments may influence other viewers to feel similarly, while criticisms may offer suggestions about potential changes. Some companies are able to develop new product ideas based on blog comments or to make improvements to existing goods. As an accessible and informal way for customers to provide feedback, a blog can save time and money a company would otherwise have to spend seeking out that same information.

Communicating with customers, word-of-mouth marketing, and getting feedback are just a few potential benefits from a blog. As a social media campaign develops, more creative uses can certainly be found.

Linking a Blog to Marketing Objectives

While there are many blogs on the Internet, a much smaller fraction of them generate tangible returns for the blog's creator(s). Many blogs are personal and function like an online journal; their authors do not generally expect an outside return. However, there are also many professional or corporate blogs that do not accomplish their objectives or are unclear even on what objectives should be accomplished! The difficulty of blogging successfully is why over 50% of blogs are abandoned within the first 90 days.[43]

When deciding on whether to start a blog and what the goals of blogging should be, it is important to consider the overall marketing goals and objectives. Such consideration will help to determine the right type of content to create based on the audience being reached. It will also make following up on and maintaining a blog more achievable. Indeed, "the single biggest risk in business blogging is setting the wrong strategy, resulting in discouragement and abandonment" of the blog.[44] A half-hearted blogging attempt may be worse than nothing at all, so it is crucial to set a long-term strategy before creating a blog for SMM.

Monitoring the Blogosphere

One of the primary benefits from blogging is to learn about the "tone" of the online community with regard to certain subjects, but the problem is that relevant comments are likely to be dispersed through a huge number of different blogs. While staying current on important blogs in the industry and looking at reader comments is a good start, you must mount a monitoring effort that goes considerably farther in order to see a broad segment of opinions, especially if a blog is still in its infancy and has few active commentators.

One crude metric for public sentiment is a look at how many views that posts on different topics generate (number of blog views or visits is typically easily available on hosted blogs). In theory the more that people enjoyed a certain post, the more likely they are to pass along or recommend it to others, boosting the number of views. However, view counts alone give no insight on whether overall sentiment is positive or negative or if any of these people will ever become potential leads.

The difficulty of determining what people think about a brand has driven an enormous growth in social media monitoring software, much of which is directed toward blogs. While many paid software suites exist for this purpose, they can cost hundreds of dollars a month in order to license and run. There are free tools available to monitor a blog such as the metrics in Blogger and the links to Google Analytics. How many resources you should dedicate toward monitoring blog chatter will depend on your industry, your marketing budget, and the size of your existing blog following as well as how widely dispersed online opinion is on the relevant topics, to name just a few factors. However, time and money spent in monitoring general opinion is almost always well spent; it is impossible to finely tune a blogging strategy without some feedback on what needs to be changed or which content people find most attractive. Developing knowledge about public sentiment and response on other blogs makes SMM efforts through blogging much more fruitful.

Video Streaming in the Social Media Mix

There are many ways to publish content on the social web. As the bandwidth of the Internet has increased, it has made it possible to publish audio and even large video files. The challenge has been to create the means to encode, deliver, and receive these files in a user-friendly manner. As these technologies have come together, new forms of publishing online were born. One of these publishing options is streaming video.

Unlike blogging, which is interactive through comments but not live, streaming video is a live video broadcast that is shared over the Internet. Marketers have begun to incorporate streaming into their social media plans as apps like Periscope (owned by Twitter) and Meerkat have allowed easy sharing of video streams. Of course video streaming is best-suited to live, interactive content. Viewers can comment on the video they are seeing and interact with a brand not only through still photographs but with what is happening at the moment. Streaming is best done when shared online and when other forms of social media are used to interact also. For example, GE on Periscope broadcast the flight of a GE drone as it flew from coast to coast. Using the hashtag #droneweek, brand interaction was also conducted on Twitter, using the #GeneralElectric and @GEDronePilot accounts.

Another good example is Doritos, which hosted live giveaways on Periscope of "roulette" bags, in which every sixth chip is quite spicy. Viewers were chosen as contestants and the host spun a roulette wheel to choose prizes. There was also use of a team game on Twitter and a promotional YouTube Video, and winners were announced on Vine. The hashtag used was #DoritosRoulette. Contestants had to tag other friends on social media to participate. There are some outstanding legal issues from these services as they open the door to video piracy and other questionable practices. Their benefits for marketers in these situations, however, are clear. Video streaming is yet another way to build a brand.[45]

MARKETING THROUGH PODCASTING

When the technologies of increased bandwidth and audio came together in the early 2000s, another new publishing platform was born—podcasting.

The word *podcast* was "*Oxford American Dictionary's* Word of the Year in 2004" but not everyone knows its precise definition.[46] Speaking generally, podcasts are media files distributed via subscription on the Internet. According to *Wikipedia,*

> [a] podcast (or non-streamed webcast*) is a series of digital media files (either audio or video) that are released episodically and often downloaded through web syndication. . . . The mode of delivery differentiates podcasting from other means of accessing media files over the Internet, such as direct download, or streamed webcasting. A list of all the audio or video files currently associated with a given series is maintained centrally on the distributor's server as a web feed.[47]

To distill the core aspects of podcasting, this definition from the *Journal of Information Technology & Politics* is also helpful: "A podcast is a digital audio or video file that is episodic, downloadable, and program-driven, mainly with a host and/or theme; and convenient, usually via an automated feed with computer software."[48] The client software used to check web feeds and download new podcasts is occasionally referred to as a podcatcher.

A podcast may contain only audio or audio and video recording together. Podcasts that have both audio and video recording are sometimes called a vodcast.[49] Podcasts can be consumed one of three ways: (1) played directly off the website on a computer (clicking the play button), (2) downloaded to a computer and listened to offline, and (3) downloaded to portable MP3 players for listening offline.[50] Note that podcasts are not usually streaming content; they are recorded and then published on the Internet for later access by listeners.

---

*Note that the word *webcast* is functionally a synonym of *podcast* in most circumstances, except that webcasts may use streaming audio or video, while podcasts are almost always downloaded in their entirety before viewing. We will use the term *podcast* in this text exclusively in order to reflect common usage and avoid excessive jargon, but note that webcasts may also be a useful SMM tool and should not be discarded out of hand due to their omission here.

A Brief History of Podcasting

From the mid-1990s to the early 2000s, key pieces of technology were being developed to improve the encoding, delivery, and reception of audio and video files via the Internet. One of the key breakthroughs came in the form of a technology called an RSS (Really Simple Syndication), which enabled users to subscribe to content for automatic delivery.

Although RSS was initially developed by the Netscape Communication Corporation in 1999, it wasn't until around 2000 that innovator Dave Winer extended the protocol to handle audio files, creating the forerunner to podcasting, the audioblog. These audioblogs were recorded on MP3 files. By the mid-2000s, entrepreneur Adam Curry, nickname "The Podfather" because of his pioneering work in this area, became heavily involved in developing podcasting technology. [He is] credited with coming up with the idea to automate the updating and delivery of audioblogs. Curry's idea is the manifestation of the podcast. Working together, Curry suggested to Winer that he rethink the RSS feed so that when a new MP3 file was posted it would automatically be updated via the RSS feed. Winer added a "file enclosure," which told a computer where to download a new audio file that had been posted. With that innovation, the modern podcast was born.[51]

In February 2004, Ben Hammersley, writing an article for *The Guardian*, coined the term *podcasting* in reference to audioblogging.[52] The word *podcasting* was a combination of "iPod" and "broadcasting." Numerous companies struggled to establish a variety of different names for audio and video downloads, such as AudioBlogs, Blogcasts, Nano-Casts, vlogs, and NetCasts. It wasn't until Apple put audio and video together in their iTunes's podcast directory that the term *podcast* became the standard for both formats.[53] Today, it is much easier to create and disseminate podcasts. One useful free tool for creating podcasts is Audacity, which provides audio recording and editing tools that are accessible to all.

Creating and Sharing Podcasts

Like blogging, podcast production is inexpensive. Creators using podcast equipment "costing less than $100 have produced podcast content viewed by thousands."[54] Video podcasts are also possible now with the low cost of video production. The low cost makes podcasts a boon to start-up companies and marketing departments that are on a tight budget. It is no wonder that podcasts are being utilized more in SMM, given the low cost of entry and the opportunity to reach thousands of viewers or listeners.

Due to the growth in the industry, sites have popped up to make creating audio podcasts easier than ever. Podcasts can now be created with just a phone: call a number, enter a personal identification number, and record. Creating a podcast can be as simple as leaving a voice mail.[55] The more challenging aspect is choosing a podcast's format and its content and then persuading listeners to subscribe.

CHOOSE A FORMAT

Typically, podcasts are one of three lengths: 10 minutes, 30 minutes, or 60 minutes. The length of the presentation will influence how much can be said in each segment. However, regardless of the length and whether the goal is to create an audio or video podcast, there are three primary formats to choose from:

- **Presentation**. Record a live monologue or give a simple talk on a subject. If a recording is made of a live presentation in hopes of turning it into a podcast, keep in mind that audio editing will be necessary to avoid having dead time or static in the final product.

- **Q&A.** A question-and-answer session can be set up with one or more individuals in order to give the listener or viewer more information.

- **Co-hosted.** When a podcast is co-hosted, it essentially becomes an on-demand talk radio show. Conversation should be kept organic and as unscripted as possible, but it is recommended that "the speakers choreograph their format and approach so they don't step on each other's words or create awkward pauses."[56]

Certain formats may lend themselves to different lengths more easily. For example, a Q&A session on a complex subject may seem rushed or overly simplified if it is crammed into 10 minutes. Or a co-hosted show on a simple topic might become repetitive or forced if the podcast aims to fill a full hour. Of course, the specifics will depend on the content being produced. Before starting to podcast as part of a SMM campaign, create a mental estimate of which format will be the most common so that the podcast can ideally be kept at a consistent length of time for each segment.

PODCAST CONTENT

In deciding the content focus for a podcast, there are three different possibilities: *instructional*, *informative*, or *entertainment*. While these three can be combined to some extent, it is best to stay with a common theme that connects the entire series of podcasts. While some podcasters choose to rotate between the different themes, such rotation may lose listeners if done incorrectly. A particular target audience is more likely to be drawn by a unique and distinctive theme, so regularity in content can help to draw more subscribers. For example, Dan Schawbel, the personal branding expert, used podcasts as well as blog content to connect with his audience when he released his new book, *Promote Yourself: The New Rules for Career Success*.[57] These podcasts helped audiences connect with the book's content to facilitate purchase and sharing.[58]

Recall the advice on content about blogging: specificity is valuable. This advice holds true for podcast content as well. Do not attempt to create a one-size-fits-all content; focus instead on the interests of a specific target audience. The benefit of podcasts from a listener's point of view is the enormous variety and minimal cost of subscribing. In a medium with so few entry barriers, the content being offered must have tangible appeal to some subset of the online audience, or it will be ignored in favor of more exciting presentations.

PRODUCING PODCASTS

While a podcast can theoretically be recorded in minutes, producing polished content that will draw an audience takes more time and effort. Many factors can contribute to a podcast's success or failure. Especially for a business using podcasts to demonstrate thought leadership or expertise, an amateurish-sounding podcast can be embarrassing. When creating podcasts, it is important to keep in mind the following:

- **Choose an articulate moderator.** Recorded audio often amplifies people's speaking quirks. When creating audio podcasts, it is especially important to find a moderator who has minimal verbal static (such as "um," "ah," or "like") and who has a strong vocal presence.

- **Create talking points, not scripts.** It is a difficult balance to strike but an important one. Having a full script can make the audio recording sound wooden or overly rehearsed, while having no outline can cause the speaker to lose focus. Ideally, the podcast should be presented in a relaxed and conversational manner.

- **Brevity.** When creating a podcast, determine the content first and the length second. Avoid the temptation to stretch out content to make keep people listening. Listeners value their time, so do not take up any more than necessary to cover the topic.

- **Avoid overediting.** Verbal static like "um" can be removed. However, if significant editing would be required to remove bad phrasing, consider rerecording instead. Too much editing can make the podcast sound choppy and forced, and consequently, the less audio editing, the better.

- **Include music.** Introducing the podcast with a brief clip of music lends a professional air to the production and keeps the audience engaged. It also makes the podcast more memorable. To avoid infringing on copyrights, look for music that has a Creative Commons-type license or is podsafe licensed.

Of course, following all of these tips is still no guarantee of attracting a large audience. Gaining subscribers will depend on a combination of engaging content, a charismatic presentation, and consistent updates. For a podcast to be successful, new content must be posted with some regularity (i.e., daily, weekly, or biweekly), similar to a radio show. Mainstream news channels (such as CBS, CNN, and MSNBC) have jumped on board with this format and are regularly releasing podcasts to disseminate information.[59] Competition from professional news outlets has raised the bar for small-time podcasters and has increased podcast audiences' expectation of frequent updates with interesting content.

DELIVERING PODCASTS TO CONSUMERS

The advantage of podcasts is that they exploit the ways in which public media-viewing habits have changed in recent years. People desire information and entertainment to be available on demand, commercial free, and anywhere. Podcasts are a perfect fit in that they allow the listener to download the audio file and listen at her or his convenience. With the ease of finding and downloading podcasts, they cost almost nothing for consumers to access. Podcasts can be shared at no cost on iTunes, Zune, Sony, and Phillips, to name just a few.[60]

Delivering podcasts to listeners is the easiest part. The more difficult aspect of distributing podcast content is ensuring that it is found by the target audience. There are a host of directories available for listing podcasts; "[a]mong the best are Podcast Alley, and iPodder. org."[61] In addition to directories, there are separate search engines for finding podcasts, because they are more difficult to index. One of the first search engines for podcasts was Podscope. Digital Podcast helps with news and reviews and also tips for podcasters, both audio and video.[62] The most notable directory of podcasts is iTunes itself. Stitcher, CastRoller, and Learn Out Loud can also be valuable resources. Since podcasts are more difficult to index than text-based websites and media, specialized search engines became a necessity.[63]

To assist a search engine in finding podcasts, it is important to fill in the ID3 tag. ID3 is a file data tagging format that is recognized by most media-playing software.[64] It includes the title, author's name, description, and running time of the media file. Music devices, which are often used to listen to podcasts, can show this information to the listener. Since editing software does not require that these fields be filled in, it is important to remember to enter this information manually. Search engines read and index the information provided in ID3 tags, making it more likely that an online viewer will see the podcast in search results.[65]

Marketing with Podcasting

While many possible goals can be accomplished by podcasting, choosing which to focus on will depend on the larger marketing objectives being pursued. Podcasts have the advantage of both sharing information and putting a human voice or face on a brand. As such, podcasts can complement a broad variety of other social media efforts as part of a SMM campaign.

A podcast can be a strategic component of the marketing plan, but it requires a strong commitment to creating content that is tailored to the marketing objectives. This commitment will not only provide focus when developing content, but it helps ensure some payoff from the effort. As an example, suppose one is promoting a catering business, and the objective is to gain new clients from the podcast. The focus could be to demonstrate expertise, by creating a vodcast of the owner assembling delicious hors d'oeuvres. Additionally, it could teach the audience about the ingredients being used without giving away the exact recipe, building up demand for the service and product. A list of podcasts by subject is available on podbay.fm.

In addition to indirect marketing, podcasts can bring in independent revenue. There are two very different methods to monetize podcasts. The first option is to recruit paid sponsors to advertise on the podcast, much like with any radio or television station. This model of advertising is well established but has potential negative side effects on subscribership. Advertisements that interrupt content will annoy people and may cause them to stop listening. The second method to monetize podcasts is to offer fee-based content. Taking this approach requires the creator to produce top-notch content that viewers will find worth paying for. With so many free podcasts floating around, it may be difficult to convince consumers to pay for one unless it is truly unique and superior. While monetizing is a fine ultimate goal in a podcast-based strategy, it should not be pursued from the start, or there may never be enough subscribers to accomplish anything at all!

Perhaps more important than direct revenue are the advantages a brand can gain from regular podcasting. Speaking persuasively about a field demonstrates confidence and expertise, helping to distinguish a company as a thought leader in the industry. While setting up a website and blog is relatively easy, podcasting well requires both more determination and talent. Still, while it requires a significant commitment of time and energy, podcasting can be a valuable tool in a SMM campaign.

In the late 1990s, the *Harry Potter* series of fantasy novels, written by British author J. K. Rowling, made reading fashionable again for children and spawned a series of blockbuster films based on the books. Over the years *Harry Potter* has become a fixture of the pop-culture landscape. Not surprisingly, "a flurry of podcasts sprung up to report *Harry Potter* news, debate *Harry Potter* theories and celebrate beloved (or despised) *Harry Potter* characters."[66] *MuggleCast* emerged from the pack to not only become one of the most popular podcasts with Potter fans but one of the most popular podcasts, period.

The *MuggleCast* show covered a wide variety of subjects about *Harry Potter*. According to Andrew Sims' LinkedIn profile, "[he] produces, hosts, and edited this semi-monthly podcast for MuggleNet."[67] The *MuggleNet* fan site originally hired him to manage its content, but in 2007 it made him president. Andrew Sims was the main host for *MuggleCast* and took part in every episode except one, which was aptly named, "Andrew-less."[68] The show also regularly featured a variety of other cast members, guest hosts, and *MuggleNet* staffers and continues until this day.[69]

The biggest challenge for *MuggleCast* was to convert the massive *Harry Potter* fandom into loyal listeners. The show had to come up with a format and content that would draw in the fans and keep them coming back for more. In addition, the podcast faced competition from other fan-based podcasts, especially the popular *PotterCast*. The show was looking for a way to gain a competitive advantage but still remain fan friendly because many of the same listeners might become subscribers to both podcasts.

MuggleCast sought to create superior programming and content that featured a unique mixture of interviews, breaking news, and give-and-take with fans by reading fan email and responding to it. *MuggleCast* personalized the listening experience by the reading of fan email (MuggleMail), which typically consists of listeners arguing with statements made by the hosts. Fans were encouraged to submit audio questions for a panel of Potter experts to answer.[70] Character analyses and a discussion on a theory of the week provoked audience participation, keeping the interaction between hosts and fans lively.[71]

MuggleCast, hosted by Andrew Sims

The hosts of the podcast made their commentaries entertaining by frequently interjecting wit and humor. The show segment, "Spy on Spartz," featured a phone call to *MuggleNet*'s founder Emerson Spartz, asking him where he was and what he was doing. A British joke of the week and highlights of the weird email sent to the show, often with strange or incoherent requests, added humor.[72] As one fan wrote, "I simply can't put into words how funny these people are."[73]

Finally, one of the most important strategic decisions was to list *MuggleCast* on Apple's iTunes, which provided a sizeable potential audience for the podcast.[74] In the words of Andrew Sims, "[t]he day I saw MuggleCast finally up on iTunes I couldn't believe my eyes that we were actually published—that's when I realized we could really make something out of this."[75]

Underscoring the success of the show's podcasting strategies is the significant public and media industry recognition that it received: it won the Podcast of the Year from the Weblog Awards in 2005;[76] the People's Choice Award in 2006 at the Second Annual Podcast Awards in Ontario, California; the Best Entertainment Podcast in 2008; and the Best Entertainment Podcast at the 2009 Podcast Awards.[77] Although the *Harry Potter* book and movies series have ended, new generations of readers appear to be developing an appetite for Pottermania, which is likely a good omen for this podcast, which has recently been reinitiated.

Hosting Webinars

While podcasts can be analogized to an online radio show, video streaming to an online television show, and blogging to an online newspaper column, webinars more resemble a conference or seminar. A webinar, or teleseminar, is a seminar that is conducted live over the web and (unlike a podcast) is designed to be interactive.[78] The term *webinar* was coined from the phrase "web-based seminar."[79] To attend a webinar, the listener can call a phone number (much like a conference call) or listen live on a computer's speakers by accessing the webinar through the Internet. The specifics depend on how the webinar is set up by the host. Webinars are typically B2B marketing activities, although anyone can set them up to convey content on any topic. There are even billing systems that make it easy to deliver paid content.

Webinars sometimes contain a visual aspect such as a slide show presentation or livestream video. There are even technologies that allow the presentation of all the material as a streaming video. They require scheduling in advance so that people can make time to participate. Since webinars are often a live experience, it is important to post and promote the date and time that the webinar will be held. On average the duration of a webinar is one to two hours. Many webinars are free, but some companies charge a fee to attend their webinars.

Webinars are still relatively new as a SMM tool. Up until fairly recently, webinar software was expensive and not very reliable with large numbers of participants. Now, many companies offer webinar services: Adobe Connect Pro, WebEx, GoToWebinar, and iLinc, to name just a few. Webinar technology has evolved over the past few years, making the medium an effective, low-cost marketing solution.

HOW TO SET UP A WEBINAR

Webinar services vary in their abilities, but their webinars are relatively easy to set up and run. There are a number of free to low-cost webinar sites available, and so the first step is selecting the right webinar service. When selecting where to host the webinar, one should consider the following factors: the number of attendees, the visual content, and the frequency with which the webinar is held. Because some webinar hosting sites have a cap on the number of attendees, it is important to get an estimate beforehand. If there will be visual content, it will be necessary to have a website host the webinar rather than using a conference call system. Lastly, establishing the frequency with which the webinar will be held will determine if it is better to pay a monthly subscription fee or if a one-time webinar fee will be most economical.

There may be some other technical details to decide on after a webinar service has been chosen. Webinar hosting sites often allow the creation of multiple choice questions (polls) for attendees to answer during the webinar; the results will be displayed. The poll can provide information about the attendees' general sentiments, as well giving the webinar participants a feeling of interaction. Through the survey, the webinar can also mimic a focus group and provide valuable information to the webinar's creator and participants.

The next step is creating the webinar outline, which contains a list of the main points to be covered during the webinar. These points should be kept brief to avoid any temptation of reading directly off the outline. Having a clear schedule for the talk will help avoid going off on unnecessary tangents and will ensure that the relevant material gets covered.

After an outline has been created for the webinar, the event must be scheduled. Most services have a simple user interface that allows a webinar to be scheduled in under 10 minutes. Webinar sites like the ones listed above require the host name, email, company, webinar title and description, date and time, reoccurrence information, and category.[80] Today, webinars are often recorded so listeners can hear the information when it is convenient.

Once the webinar is scheduled and listed online, it is time to start promoting it on other social media channels. As webinars are not usually available after they are presented, promoting the webinar to ensure a sufficient number of attendees is essential.

PREPARING FOR AND EXECUTING THE WEBINAR

While webinars can be a valuable component in a SMM campaign, they also carry some risks and dangers. One downside is that when hosting a webinar, there is no way to gauge the audience's reaction. Without faces or expressions to read, feedback may be hard to immediately assess. Another potential problem is that webinars are live with no chance to rerecord if the speaker is stumped or misspeaks. Because of these risks, time spent preparing for the webinar will be very well spent indeed.

Some webinar hosting sites have a moderator monitoring the webinar. If that is the case or if there are several speakers planned, coordination will be needed regarding introductions, which person will begin the call, and so forth. A few minutes of planning can avoid an awkward start to a webinar.

Webinars need to remain focused on the core content while still providing openings for listener participation and questions. Decide in advance if questions will be answered as they arise or held until the very end. Either approach can work, but it should be determined beforehand in order to avoid wasted time. Also, take steps to prevent interruptions. Be sure the speaker's surroundings will be quiet with little background noise. Simple measures like closing the door, turning off phones and alarms, and a "Do Not Disturb" sign are important matters to consider in advance. Finally, keep any relevant materials to be used during the webinar within easy reach so that there will be no unnecessary distractions.

Once preparations have ended and the webinar's scheduled beginning has arrived, be sure to start on time! As it is a live event, starting late leaves the audience waiting. Being inconvenienced makes it less likely that attendees will sign up for another webinar by the host.

When taking questions, answer them concisely and avoid rambling. It is difficult to anticipate the number of questions that will be asked, so leave enough time to cover them by giving brief but informative responses whenever possible. If there is extra time at the end, it is possible to readdress an earlier question, but if time runs out, people whose questions were not addressed will be frustrated.

Even if the ultimate goal of the webinar is to get business leads, avoid selling a service or product overtly during the webinar. People attend webinars to learn, and it is critical to meet that expectation or the audience may go elsewhere. If the content provided is valuable enough, then the presenter's expertise will signal a high quality of work, inspiring the audience to seek that person's services.

At the conclusion of the webinar, always invite the attendees to make contact with further questions or to connect on networking platforms after the webinar is completed. This is the time when business leads can be generated. Take advantage of the expertise that conducting a webinar conveys to accomplish other marketing goals. Keep the webinar around in an archived form for those who missed it and send a link to participants and registrants so they can find the content again. Some companies and organizations use webinar archives; YouTube is also an excellent choice for archiving for future access.

Marketing with Webinars and/or Podcasts

One of the biggest advantages of using webinars is the ability to gather an enormous audience (in some cases over 500 people) in a seminar-type format without anyone needing to travel.[81] This characteristic of the webinar makes it an ideal format for training sessions or information sharing. Yet another benefit to webinars is that the audience can ask questions and get immediate answers. Unlike prerecorded podcasts, the audience can engage directly with the speaker, making webinars an ideal way to establish expertise and impress customers.

Clever social media marketers have also used webinars to gather information about potential clients. Webinars typically require participants to provide an email address in order to participate. This email list can later be used to send targeted messages based on the person's interest in the webinar. To gather further insight on the audience, a number of lead qualification questions can be asked prior to webinar registration. Especially if the webinar is popular, it can accumulate a large amount of data to better reach the target audience.

How does one decide between podcasts and webinars as components in a SMM strategy? While clearly not mutually exclusive, many campaigns choose to focus their efforts on either one or the other or to emphasize one medium more than the other. This choice may reflect available technology and resources (podcasts are typically less expensive to produce than webinars) or, more likely, a difference in the content or product being marketed.

With their interactive focus, webinars are highly valuable as a tool for learning or collaboration. The primary disadvantage of webinars is that they require planning and coordination beforehand because the event is live and must be attended at the time of its presentation. Podcasts, on the other hand, are less interactive because the viewer downloads and then listens to the file at leisure. While this may restrict the use of podcasts as a teaching tool, the advantage is broader access by viewers and less effort on coordinating because a podcast can still be accessed many months after it has been recorded. This continuing accessibility makes podcasts a natural fit for opinion, information, or entertainment products and services.

Depending on the industry, some organizations use both webinars and podcasts in their SMM campaign; others use just one or the other. Both offer valuable opportunities to engage consumers on a more personal level than text-based communication. Marketing strategies that leverage that deeper connection can be highly successful in using webinars and/or podcasts. Often B2B marketers are successful with webinars. The company MPi (www.mpiworldclass.com), which helps dealerships across North America create vehicle inspection programs, has successfully used webinars to develop leads and close sales by providing meaningful content and getting the right participants to the webinars. Meaningful content means industry leaders and experts and providing a solution to a current challenge. The right attendees were also solicited through social media, primarily through LinkedIn connections. Another B2B firm, a document management company named Recall, generated a $290,000 pipeline from one webinar that targeted small business owners alone.[82]

Best Practices for Blogging, Podcasting, Video Sharing, and Webinars

While no "secret formula" exists for becoming a popular blogger or podcaster or other online creator and disseminator of content, the following tips provide advice for maximizing the chances of success. Keep in mind that these are only guidelines and success in blogging can be attained in many ways. The same emotional triggers for video sharing and those listed in the periodic table of content marketing apply to other types of shared content as well. Positive emotions such as exhilaration have been shown to increase the level of video sharing and are important with other types of content as well.[83]

1. USE CATCHY TITLES

A great title attracts attention and gives people a reason to read, listen, and attend, while a mediocre title either goes unnoticed or actually discourages people from reading the post, listening to the podcast, or attending the video streaming broadcast. Although there are no hard and fast rules for writing great titles, there are useful guidelines. First, use the title to communicate a benefit.[84] In other words, people search for blogs and other content that provide information about topics of interest (e.g., "10 Ways to Write Great Blog Titles"). Second, ask a question in the title. Readers love to be challenged. This is one of the most effective ways of drawing readers into the post and also helps elicit comments, especially if the question is personalized (e.g., "How Should You Ask for a Raise?").[85] Finally, be sure to include keywords in the title so that search engines will pick them up, hence, improving the search engine ranking of the post so people can find it.[86] Catchy titles also work when marketing a webinar.

2. UPDATE FREQUENTLY

The most common advice for successful blogging, podcasting, and streaming is that content should be updated at least once a week, sometimes daily. Webinars should occur on a regular basis so they develop a loyal following as well, although weekly and daily updating is probably not necessary. Online audiences can quickly lose interest if content is spaced too far apart. Before creating a blog or podcast, you should be sure that you will have enough interesting posts for the blog, perhaps even writing some up in advance to be posted later. If updates occur less than once a week, expect to be perceived as disengaged and expect the possibility of losing blog viewers. Streaming video for marketing tends to be more event-focused. For more hope in creating a loyal viewership, attend to the YouTube channel information posted in Chapter 8.

3. KEEP CONTENT FOCUSED

People will often find a blog or podcast while browsing or researching other topics. Generally, net surfers do not want to sift through a rambling post or podcast to find the bits of information they might be of interest. Blog updates should be long enough to cover one topic with sufficient depth but should avoid using filler or trying to combine several topics into one post. If one blog post covers two topics, a person who is looking for information on just one of the topics will find half of the material superfluous. Concise, focused blog posts are easy to read and will keep readers coming back for more. Webinars should also keep to the point.

4. INVITE COMMENTS

Perhaps the best way to encourage interaction on a blog, podcast, or streaming video is to end each post with a question that asks for help or is provocative. For example, "What other tips have I missed?" or "Is the social media about to bust?" Be sure to reply to comments in order to make readers feel they are part of the blog and help shape its direction. Interaction is often essential in creating an avid and involved readership.[87] Webinar viewers are often asked to participate via chat or phone call questions to stimulate engagement. Streaming video allows for a high level of interaction, as our examples showed.

5. PROMOTE THE BLOG, STREAMING VIDEO, PODCAST, OR WEBINAR

With so much content out there, it takes effort to be seen in the crowd. For podcasts, getting listed on search engines helps. Look around at other blogs, check to see what blog communities they are involved in, and join ones that look reputable. These initial actions will make it easier for search engine users to find the blog. However, this step is only the beginning: developing a blog presence takes time, so never overlook an opportunity to subtly self-promote (in a tactful fashion, of course). Webinars are usually B2B and can be easily incorporated into a content marketing strategy to help the consumer along the purchase cycle or as a tool for customer retention. Opt-in email marketing is a good way to promote all of these content tools to other businesses.

6. ENGAGE WITH OTHERS

As a content creator, make thoughtful comments on other relevant blogs or video or audio content and respond to comments that others make. Developing an online "personality" for a brand is important for any online content to be successful, and that requires a high degree of interaction with others. Take advantage of the two-way nature of online communication by engaging those with related interests or with companies having products complementary to yours. Offering to provide a link or a review to someone else in exchange for their doing the same is a tried-and-true method for building blog connections, and it remains a useful strategy. However, the most valuable engagement will often come from unplanned interactions, so be open to those possibilities.

7. AVOID NEGATIVITY

Do not make insulting or aggressive statements toward other people, brands, or companies in any format. It may be true that conflict draws a crowd, but that group is unlikely to become a productive part of the target market. Negative comments also invite others to respond in turn, potentially harming both sides' reputations. Even worse, it could result in a lawsuit if taken too seriously. Criticism can be given without being offensive, but you should be sure that any controversial comments are heavily researched, well-founded in fact, and presented in an even tone that is not accusatory or aggressive. In general, sticking to positive and constructive comments is both safer and more effective for building standing as a content creator and disseminator.

8. STAND BY THE CONTENT

Not every blog post, podcast, webinar, or streaming video event will be well received. Sometimes, one episode or situation may generate controversy or negative attention. If that happens, deleting the affected content is *not* a solution. Once content is published online, it will be viewable through syndication services even if the original post is taken down. Trying to hide the evidence, so to speak, may draw attention to the controversy and make dissatisfied viewers even more determined to spread the word. Instead, stand by what was written (which should not be too difficult if the original content was well conceived). If it is necessary to make a correction, consider leaving the original text with a strike-through mark if it is a blog post and an explanation of why the revision was made. Internet controversies can either blow over quickly, or they can linger indefinitely in the public consciousness. Whenever possible, avoid compounding the situation by going back on what was said because it will make the mistake memorable and generate more negativity.

9. CROSS PROMOTE

Use other social media channels to get word out about the content. When a new post is made, webinar or podcast produced, or video event streamed, provide links to it on other platforms. Keep in mind that not every member of the target audience will be on every platform, so provide as many opportunities as possible for them to stumble over the content. Blogs probably offer the best opportunity for sharing thoughts and information, so use other, less content-heavy platforms to promote the deeper ideas found in blog posts.

10. ARCHIVE THE CONTENT

Good content can continue to drive consumers to a site, reinforce the brand, and encourage action after the moment has passed. It is important to have a place where content can be stored and retrieved for those who missed the live event. Libraries, publishers, and trade associations actively keep archives of content. Public sources such as YouTube and iTunes help keep content accessible to potential consumers.

11. USE METRICS

Most of the platforms we are discussing have metrics associated with them to see who is coming to your site. Use these tools to track page views, time on site, visits, and unique visitors. Another useful tool is Google Analytics, which can be easily embedded in Blogger to display additional traffic details, such as the geographic location of the audience. Analyzing posts, comments, and number of re-shares can also help gauge the popularity of particular content and indicate which content is resonating with your audience. Tracking email sign-ups and subscriptions to RSS feeds will help connect with and monitor the audience for your content. Seeing who leaves the broadcast early will help craft future content. This activity should be helping with search rankings, as search engines love content, so track search rankings over time. If using the content to generate revenue, track the response to specific calls to action as well as revenue generated from specific content.[88]

Blogging to Build Your Personal Brand: Optimizing Your Online Brand by Blogging— for Students

Blogs are the easiest form of content discussed in this chapter to use, so we suggest students start there. Although there are many blogs, with a good niche and some targeted promotion a student can create a loyal blog following. Particularly if the blog is to be used to create a personal brand for the purpose of getting a job or internship, keep the content professional. Here are some good lessons in starting a blog for professional purposes.

Lesson #1. Find your niche. Remember *the Long Tail* of marketing to a niche? Figure out what you are good at and how you can contribute in the blogosphere, but make it specific. Your topic could be blogging about a sports team or fashion or another passion or interest. You could also blog about digital marketing and what you are doing in your classes. I had a student who loved fantasy baseball, found a niche, and had a good following after just a few weeks of blogging.

Lesson#2. Reserve your niche. Create your unique blog, reserve the URL, create unique hashtags and twitter handles that you can use to cross-promote your blog. Make sure you get found by search engines by using "keyword rich" posts and tag your pictures and videos because otherwise search engines can't find them.

Lesson #3. Create meaningful blog content for your audience. It sounds easy but can be difficult. Determine the target audience for your blog and create meaningful content accordingly. Creating a persona and looking where that type of person "hangs out" on line can be quite useful. Red Bull does a great job of producing content around the active lifestyle without actively promoting its product. Red Bull's blogs discuss movies, music, sports, and other topics outside of the brand itself to reinforce the image as a product for those with an active lifestyle.

Lesson #4. Observe good formatting rules. Remember that people process information in bits and bytes so use small (three sentence) paragraphs, headings, and subheadings. Short posts are good, with a minimum of 500 words. A post of a approximately 1500–1700 words will increase the chances of being read and shared.[89]

Lesson #6. Blog regularly. Blog *at least* twice a month and use email sign ups so that those who are interested know when you have a new blog coming on stream.

Since the trend is toward longer posts, committing to twice a month may be much more realistic than a once a week schedule. Regular posts are the best way to achieve a loyal leadership. There is no hard and fast rule when it comes to blogging but it is important to have a rhythm so readers know when to expect content.[90]

Lesson #7. Promote your blog. It is the responsibility of the blogger to promote the blog through the appropriate audience and channels and to encourage and incent sharing. If you are being paid to blog, make sure that you disclose all financial relationships.

Lesson #8. Respond to your audience. Comments can be useful feedback and be sure to acknowledge someone who has made a meaningful comment on your blog. I also remove posts that are obviously spam or self-promotional. Make sure to keep an eye on the comments on your posts so that you remain in charge of the content.

Lesson #9. Use metrics to refine the approach. Metrics don't have to be complicated. For one of her own blogs, which is centered around teaching, Dr. Zahay noticed that posts where she talked about recruiting and hiring students and interns received the most views and comments. She used that information to create some other, related posts, including one coaching students on how to find a job or internship.

Notes

1. Pulizzi, Joe and Newt Barrett (2005), *Get Content Get Customers: Turn Prospects into Buyers with Content Marketing* (Bonita Springs, FL: McGraw-Hill).
2. Spiller, Lisa and Martin Baier (2012), *Contemporary Direct and Interactive Marketing* (Newport News, Virginia: Racom Communications).
3. Wuebben, Jon (2012), *Content Is Currency: Developing Powerful Content for Web and Mobile* (Boston, MA: Nicholas Brealey).
4. Holliman, Geraint and Jennifer Rowley (2014), "Business to Business Digital Content Marketing: Marketers' Perceptions of Best Practice," *Journal of Research in Interactive Marketing*, vol. 8, no. 4, pp. 269–293.
5. Anderson, Chris (July 11, 2006), *The Long Tail: Why the Future of Business Is Selling Less of More* (New York, NY: Hyperion).
6. Lake, Chris (March 18, 2014), "Introducing the Periodic Table of Content Marketing," *Econsultancy*. Retrieved September 23, 2015, from https://econsultancy.com/blog/64539-introducing-the-periodic-table-of-content-marketing/
7. Crestodina, Andy (September 10, 2015), "Research Reveals Success Tactics of Top Bloggers: 11 Trends," *Orbit Media Studios*. Retrieved September 21, 2015, from http://www.orbitmedia.com/blog/blogger-research/?utm_source=sept20-newsletter&utm_medium=email&utm_campaign=blogger-research-2015
8. Chang, Stephanie (December 19, 2013), "The Future of Content: Upcoming Trends in 2014," *Moz*. Retrieved September 14, 2015, from https://moz.com/blog/future-of-content-upcoming-trends-in-2014
9. Zarrella, Dan (2010), *The Social Media Marketing Book* (Sebastopol, CA: O'Reilly Media), p.11.
10. (n.d.). "Stats," WordPress. Retrieved September 14, 2015, from https://wordpress.com/activity/
11. (n.d.). "Blog," *Wikipedia*. Retrieved September 14, 2011, from http://en.wikipedia.org/wiki/Blog
12. Scoble, Robert and Shel Israel (2006), *Naked Conversations: How Blogs Are Changing the Way Businesses Talk with Customers* (Hoboken, NJ: John Wiley), p. 28.
13. Zahay-Blatz, Debra and Todd Kelsey (September 20, 2013), "Linking Search and Social through G+ and Blogging," *LinkedIn Slide Share*. Retrieved September 20, 2015, from http://www.slideshare.net/zahayblatz/teaching-analyticws-through-g-and-blogger

14. Kurtz, Howard (July 9, 2007), "A Blog That Made It Big," *Washington Post*. Retrieved June 7, 2011, from http://www.washingtonpost.com/wp-dyn/content/article/2007/07/08/AR2007070801213.html

15. (February 7, 2011). "The Huffington Post," The *New York Times*. Retrieved June 7, 2011, from http://topics.nytimes.com/top/reference/timestopics/organizations/h/the_huffington_post/index.html

16. Stelter, Brian (March 1, 2009), "Copyright Challenge for Sites That Excerpt," *The New York Times*. Retrieved September 30, 2015, from http://www.nytimes.com/2009/03/02/business/media/02scrape.html

17. Maneker, Marion (February 8, 2011), "AOL-Huffington Post: Why the Heavy Breathing?," *Big Picture*. Retrieved June 9, 2011, from http://www.ritholtz.com/blog/2011/02/aol-huffington-post-why-the-heavy-breathing/

18. Sarno, David (February 7, 2011), "A Brief History of the Huffington Post," *Los Angeles Times*. Retrieved June 8, 2011, from http://articles.latimes.com/2011/feb/07/business/la-fi-huffington-post-timeline-20110207

19. Wolf, Josh (September 26, 2007), "Huffington Post Doesn't Plan to Pay Its Bloggers," *CNET News*. Retrieved June 9, 2011, from http://news.cnet.com/8301-13508_3-9785908-19.html#ixzz1Oe4oLZ3y

20. Ibid.

21. (2015). "Top 15 Most Popular Blogs—September 2015," eBizMBA. Retrieved September 14, 2015, from http://www.ebizmba.com/articles/blogs

22. (2014). "The Huffington Post," LinkedIn. Retrieved September 20, 2015, from https://www.linkedin.com/company/the-huffington-post

23. The Webby Awards (2006–2011). Retrieved June 8, 2011, from http://www.webbyawards.com/webbys/current.php

24. McNichol, Tom (n.d.), "25 Best Blogs 2009," *Time*. Retrieved June 8, 2011, from http://www.time.com/time/specials/packages/article/0,28804,1879276_1879279_1879302,00.html

25. Bercovici, Jeff (April 16, 2012), "The Huffington Post Wins Its First Pulitzer Prize," *Forbes*. Retrieved September 20, 2015, from http://www.forbes.com/sites/jeffbercovici/2012/04/16/the-huffington-post-wins-its-first-pulitzer-prize/

26. Ho, Erica (February 7, 2011), "AOL Acquires Huffington Post for $315 Million," *Time*. Retrieved June 9, 2011, from http://newsfeed.time.com/2011/02/07/aol-acquires-huffington-post-for-315-million/

27. Peters, Jeremy W. (April 12, 2011), "Huffington Post Is Target of Suit on Behalf of Bloggers," *The New York Times*. Retrieved June 7, 2011, from http://mediadecoder.blogs.nytimes.com/2011/04/12/huffington-post-is-target-of-suit-on-behalf-of-bloggers/

28. Noronha, Charmaine (May 11, 2011), "Huffington Post Launches Canadian Site," *Chicago Sun Times*. Retrieved June 9, 2011, from http://www.suntimes.com/business/5654972-420/huffington-post-launches-canadian-site.html?print=true

29. Tasini et al. v. AOL Inc et al., U.S. District Court, Southern District of New York, No. 11-02472.

30. (n.d.). "Embrace, Extend, and Extinguish," *Wikipedia*. Retrieved June 1, 2011, from http://en.wikipedia.org/wiki/Embrace,_extend_and_extinguish

31. Cone, Edward (October 3, 2006), "Robert Scoble: Life after Microsoft," *CNET*. Retrieved June 1, 2011, from http://www.pcmag.com/article2/0,2817,2023650,00.asp

32. Ibid.

33. (February 10, 2005). "Chief Humanising Officer," *The Economist*. Retrieved June 1, 2011, from http://www.economist.com/node/3644293?story_id=3644293

34. (November 6, 2006). *Blogging Success Study*, Northwestern University. Retrieved June 2, 2011, from http://www.scoutblogging.com/success_study/

35. Scoble, Robert and Shel Israel (2006), *Naked Conversations: How Blogs Are Changing the Way Businesses Talk with Customers* (Hoboken, NJ: John Wiley)

36. Halzack, Sarah (August 25, 2008), "Marketing Moves to the Blogosphere: Business Model Shifts to Engage Customers Online," *Washington Post*. Retrieved June 10, 2011, from http://www.washingtonpost.com/wp-dyn/content/article/2008/08/24/AR2008082401517.html

37. Fernando, Angelo (June 23, 2008), "Marriott CEO Blog: 'A Cool Way to Tell Stories,'" *Social Media Today*. Retrieved June 10, 2011, from http://socialmediatoday.com/index.php?q=SMC/38200

38. Universal McCann (March 2008), "Power to the People: Wave 3 Social Media Tracker," *Scribd*. Retrieved June 9, 2011, from http://www.scribd.com/doc/3836535/Universal-Mccann-on-Social-Media

39. Dube, Mark (n.d.), "Blogging Facts and Stats," *ActiveBlogs*. Retrieved September 21, 2015, from https://www.activeblogs.com/blogging-facts-stats/

40. Solis, Brian (2010), *Engage! The Complete Guide for Brands and Businesses to Build, Cultivate, and Measure Success in the New Web* (Hoboken: NJ: John Wiley), p. 168.

41. Trusov, Michael, Randolph E. Bucklin, and Koen Pauwels (September 2009), "Effects of Word-of-Mouth Versus Traditional Marketing: Findings from an Internet Social Networking Site," *Journal of Marketing*, vol. 73, no. 5.

42. Sernovitz, Andy (2009), *Word of Mouth Marketing: How Smart Companies Get People Talking* (New York: Kaplan Publishing), pp. 140–41.

43. Meyerson, Mitch (2010), *Success Secrets of the Social Media Marketing Superstars* (Irvine, CA: Entrepreneur Media), p. 166.

44. Borges, Bernie (2009), *Marketing 2.0: Bridging the Gap between Seller and Buyer through Social Media Marketing* (Tucson, AZ: Wheatmark), p. 174.

45. Ueland, Sig (August 15, 2015), "8 Brands That Live Stream Video for Innovative Marketing," *Practical Ecommerce*. Retrieved September 21, 2015, from www.practicalecommerce.com/articles/91805-8-Brands-That-Live-Stream-Video-for-Innovative-Marketing

46. Brogan, Chris, and Julien Smith (2009), *Trust Agents* (Hoboken, NJ: John Wiley), p. 20.

47. (n.d.). "Podcasts," *Wikipedia*. Retrieved June 14, 2011, from http://en.wikipedia.org/wiki/Podcast

48. Gil de Zúñiga, Homero, Aaron Veenstra, Emily Vraga, and Dhavan Shah (2010), "Digital Democracy: Reimagining Pathways to Political Participation," *Journal of Information Technology & Politics*, vol. 7, no. 1, p. 47.

49. Weber, Larry (2009), *Marketing to the Social Web: How Digital Communities Build Your Business* (Hoboken, NJ: John Wiley), p. 181.

50. Borges, Bernie (2009), *Marketing 2.0: Bridging the Gap between Seller and Buyer through Social Media Marketing* (Tucson, AZ: Wheatmark), p. 221.

51. Martell, James (April 5, 2011), "The History of Podcasting—How'd We Get Here?" *TheHistoryOf.net*. Retrieved July 8, 2011, from http://www.thehistoryof.net/the-history-of-podcasting.html

52. (n.d.). "History of Podcasting," *Voices.com*. Retrieved July 8, 2011, from http://www.voices.com/podcasting/history-of-podcasting.html

53. (September 28, 2010). "A Podcast by Any Other Name Is Still a . . . ," PostCast411's Podcast (originally posted in *Blogger and Podcast Magazine* in June 2007). Retrieved June 12, 2011, from http://podcast411.libsyn.com/a-podcast-by-any-other-name-is-still-a-

54. Meyerson, Mitch (2010), *Success Secrets of the Social Media Marketing Superstars* (Irvine, CA: Entrepreneur Media), p. 251.

55. Ibid., p. 254.

56. Gillin, Paul (2009), *Secrets of Social Media Marketing* (Fresno, CA: Quill Driver Books). pp. 212–13.

57. Schawbel, Dan (2013), *Promote Yourself* (New York: St. Martin's Press).

58. (April 8, 2013). "Podcast #14: Facebook Home, Wellness & Gene Simmons," *Dan Schawbel*. Retrieved on September 21, 2015, from http://danschawbel.com/podcasts/podcast-14-facebook-home-wellness-gene-simmons/

59. (n.d.). "Podcasts," CBS News. Retrieved June 14, 2011, from http://www.cbsnews.podcast.com/" http://cbsnews.podcast.com/; "Audio & Video Podcasts" (n.d.), CNN, retrieved June 14, 2011, from http://www.cnn.com/services/podcasting/; and "Get Podcasts from NBC News, MSNBC and msnbc.com" (n.d.), MSNBC, retrieved June 14, 2011, from http://www.msnbc.msn.com/id/8132577/t/get-podcasts-nbc-news-msnbc-msnbccom/

60. Meyerson, Mitch (2010), *Success Secrets of the Social Media Marketing Superstars* (Irvine, CA: Entrepreneur Media), p. 259.

61. Gillin, Paul (2009), *The New Influencers* (Fresno, CA: Quill Driver Books), p. 166.

62. (n.d.). "Digital Podcast," *Digital Podcast*. Retrieved September 21, 2015, from http://www.digitalpodcast.com/

63. Basu, Saikat (December 20, 2013), "What is the Best Way to Find New Podcasts?," *makeuseof.com*. Retrieved September 20, 2015, from http://www.makeuseof.com/tag/what-is-the-best-way-to-find-new-podcasts/

64. (n.d.). "Welcome," ID3.org. Retrieved June 14, 2011, http://www.id3.org/

65. Gillin, Paul (2009), *Secrets of Social Media Marketing* (Fresno, CA: Quill Driver Books), p. 215–16.

66. Maltese, Racheline (August 25, 2006), "The Weird, Wacky World of Harry Potter Podcasts," Associated Content from Yahoo! Retrieved June 11, 2011, from http://www.associatedcontent.com/article/53830/the_weird_wacky_world_of_harry_potter.html?cat=9

67. (n.d.). "Andrew Sims Profile," LinkedIn.com. Retrieved June 15, 2011, from http://www.linkedin.com/in/sims89

68. (n.d.). "MuggleCast," *Urban Dictionary*. Retrieved June 15, 2011, from http://www.urbandictionary.com/define.php?term=MuggleCast

69. (n.d.). "Muggle Cast," tvtropes.org. Retrieved June 15, 2011, from http://tvtropes.org/pmwiki/pmwiki.php/Main/MuggleCast

70. (n.d.). "MuggleNet, Podcast," *Wikipedia*. Retrieved June 16, 2011, from http://en.wikipedia.org/wiki/MuggleNet#Podcast

71. (n.d.). "Harry Potter Fandom," *Wikipedia*. Retrieved June 16, 2011, from http://en.wikipedia.org/wiki/Harry_Potter_Fandom

72. Ibid.

73. (December 8, 2006). "MuggleNet's Harry Potter Podcast!," *Electrify My Life*. Retrieved September 14, 2011, from http://stellarnostalgia.multiply.com/reviews/item/8

74. (September 8, 2005). "Secret Podcasting," Book Corner, Apple. Retrieved June 11, 2011, from https://www.apple.com/enews/2005/09/08enews1.html#top

75. Holmes, Julian Bennett (March 19, 2007), "Interview with Andrew Sims of Mugglecast," *GigaCom*. Retrieved June 11, 2011, from http://gigaom.com/apple/interview-with-andrew-sims-of-mugglecast/

76. McWilliams, Ryan (June 24, 2009), "Mugglecast: The #1 Harry Potter Podcast," Associated Content from Yahoo! Retrieved June 16, 2011, from http://www.associatedcontent.com/article/1830661/mugglecast_the_1_harry_potter_podcast.html

77. (n.d.). "What Is MuggleCast: Awards Won," *The LeakyPedia*. Retrieved June 16, 2011, from http://www.the-leaky-cauldron.org/wiki/index.php?title=MuggleCast

78. Weber, Larry (2009), *Marketing to the Social Web: How Digital Communities Build Your Business* (Hoboken, NJ: John Wiley), p. 31.

79. Brown, Georg (2008), *Social Media 100 Success Secrets* (Newstead, Australia: Emereo Publishing), p. 110.

80. Webinarlistings.com (n.d.). Retrieved July 8, 2011, from http://www.webinarlistings.com/calendar/events/index.php?com=submit

81. Karten, Naomi (2010), *Presentation Skills for Technical Professionals* (United Kingdom: IT Governance Publishing Company), p. 208.

82. Agron, Mike (June 20, 2013), "Demand Generation Webinar Case Study: How MPi Beat Their Audience Recruitment Goals by More than 200%," *WebAttract*. Retrieved September 13, 2015, from http://www.webattract.com/blog/?p=1499 Arketi Group (n.d.). "Core: Winning Webinar Results in Revenue." Retrieved November 1, 2015, from http://arketi.com/thinking/newsletter-on-btob-marketing/2015-10-recall.html

83. Kuchinskas, Susan (December 16, 2013), "The Emotions That Trigger Video Sharing," *Contently*. Retrieved September 13, 2015, from http://contently.com/strategist/2013/12/16/the-emotions-that-trigger-video-sharing/

84. Rowse, Darren (August 20, 2008), "How to Craft Post Titles That Draw Readers into Your Blog," *Problogger*. Retrieved August 20, 2011, from http://www.problogger.net/archives/2008/08/20/how-to-craft-post-titles-that-draw-readers-into-your-blog/

85. Morrison, Gwen (February 18, 2011), "You Had Me at 'Hello World' or How to Write a Killer Blog," *Endurance Marketing*. Retrieved August 20, 2011, from http://endurancemktg.com/you-had-me-at-hello-world-or-how-to-write-a-killer-blog-title

86. Noguchi, Yo (June 1, 2011), "6 Tips for Writing Outstanding Blog Titles," *Techshare*. Retrieved August 20, 2011, from http://jimgrey.wordpress.com/2011/07/25/six-ways-to-build-blog-readership/

87. Grey, Jim (July 25, 2011), "Six Ways to Build Blog Readership," *Down The Road Blog*. Retrieved August 20, 2011, from http://endurancemktg.com/you-had-me-at-hello-world-or-how-to-write-a-killer-blog-title

88. Cohen, Heidi (February 2, 2011), "21 Real Blog Metrics Your Company Needs to Track," *Content Marketing Institute*. Retrieved August 20 2011, from http://contentmarketinginstitute.com/2011/02/blog-metrics/

89. Brown, Tim (November 14, 2014), "What'll Be the Best Length for a Blog Article in 2015 for SEO?," *Snap Agency*. Retrieved September 21, 2015, from http://www.snapagency.com/blog/whatll-best-length-blog-article-2015-seo/

90. (n.d.). "What is the Best Blogging Frequency? The Complete Answer," *i-scoop.com*. Retrieved September 21, 2015, from http://www.i-scoop.eu/corporate-blogging-business-blogging/best-blogging-frequency-complete-answer/

Video Marketing

Videos are highly engaging to customers and consequently have become an important marketing tool. Marketers find success with captivating videos on various platforms that welcome both long- and short-form creations. When a video goes viral, the marketer experiences a huge windfall.

Video platforms have proliferated on the Internet, although YouTube, owned by Google, is the largest player by most measures. In early 2015 YouTube offered the following factoids:

1. "YouTube has more than 1 billion users

2. The number of hours people are watching on YouTube each month is up 50% year over year

3. 300 hours of video are uploaded to YouTube every minute

4. Half of YouTube views are on mobile devices

5. More than a million advertisers are using Google ad platforms, the majority of which are small businesses."[1]

6. GlobalWebIndex added that in April 2015, despite competition from Facebook and Twitter, more Internet users visited YouTube.[2]

7. Google added that Millennials are twice as likely to be focusing on the content while watching video on a mobile screen than while watching TV. Mobile is the first screen for Millennials, not the second or third screen.[3]

LEARNING OBJECTIVES

After completing this chapter, students will be able to:

- Explain the place video marketing can play in the digital marketing mix
- Discuss the pros and cons of viral videos
- Describe how consumer use of television and video are changing
- Explain benefits of marketing with online videos
- Discuss some of the major video platforms

(Continued)

And YouTube is only one of thousands of video platforms worldwide, used by consumers and marketers alike!

Viral Videos—Numa Numa and the Old Spice Guy

What is said to be the first viral video was posted on December 4, 2004. It was created for his own amusement by a nineteen-year-old New Jersey resident Gary Brolsma. He was lip-syncing to a song from an obscure Moldavian pop group that was popular in Europe at the time. The name of the song was Dragostea Din Tei; the video is known by the translation Numa Numa. It is important to recognize that this was before YouTube, which was introduced in February 2005. Even so, according to CNET, as of December 2014 the video had been viewed over 700 million times, some of those views are on YouTube where someone other than Gary uploaded it.

How could a video like this possibly go viral? An early fan, Tom Fulp, posted it on his creative community website, Newsgrounds. He says, "Gary looked like a fun guy having a good time. It made you smile and feel happy when you watched it."[4] The public took it from there. That is the essential problem with making a marketing video go viral; it is not in the control of the marketer! It does sometimes happen, though, as in the case of Gillette's Old Spice Guy.

Gillette introduced its first men's body wash product in 2003. By 2009 the category was crowded and highly competitive. Worse, Gillette became aware that Dove was launching a campaign for its product during Super Bowl 2010. Dove was a particularly troublesome competitor because it was a female-oriented brand and over 60% of men's body wash purchases were made by women.[5]

When Wieden + Kennedy, the advertising agency working on Old Spice, began designing the Old Spice campaign, they drew on the heritage of the brand. The "Old Spice Guy" campaign centered on former NFL player Isaiah Mustafa (the "Old Spice Guy") in a video that was over-the-top in masculinity. The commercial opened with, "Hello, Ladies. Look at your man. Now back at me. Now back at your man. Now back to me. Sadly, he isn't me, but if he stopped using ladies scented body wash and switched to Old Spice, he could smell like he's me."[6]

The agency used pre- and post Super Bowl promotion to build buzz. The video got social media attention before and after the game, and by the time it debuted on TV, the day after the Super Bowl, many people assumed that they first saw in on the game.

Courtesy of The Advertising Archives

In June 2010 the agency launched a social media campaign to leverage the attention the ad had achieved. To achieve this, the team created over 180 response videos, where the "Old Spice Guy" recorded video replies to comments left by online influencers and celebrities.[7]

As part of the campaign the agency ran a Twitter ad promotion, which featured the product as a trending topic.[8] The campaign was also supported by traditional media buys in targeted environments, as well as discount coupons to further help encourage sales of the product.[9] Hence, Old Spice did not rely solely on word of mouth to spread the video. They produced a powerful video, but seeded it with traditional marketing as well.

"The Man Your Man Could Smell Like" video quickly became a cultural phenomenon. In the first day of the Old Spice campaign, the video received 6 million views, 20 million views by the third day, and 40 million views by the end of the week. As a consequence, the Old Spice Twitter account shot up to over 43,000 followers and the company's YouTube channel was viewed over 58 million times.[10] This traction drove a 300% increase in traffic to the website: OldSpice.com and increased the number of interactions on the company's Facebook page by 800%.[11] Clearly, the video's success had a significant impact on engagement in other social media channels for Old Spice.[12]

Furthermore, the Old Spice campaign spurred hundreds of parody videos, including one by Grover on Sesame Street, as well as invitations for the actor, Isaiah Mustafa, to appear on popular TV talk shows, such as "The Oprah Winfrey Show" and "Ellen," to discuss the ad.[13] Most important, the videos were successful in driving sales of the Old Spice Body Wash. Nielson estimated that sales of the product jumped 55% in the three months during the campaign, with a 107% lift in July 2010 alone, when the social media campaign was launched.[14] And the Old Spice videos were effective in reaching the target demographic—women. Old Spice accounted for 75% of the conversations in the category during 2010 and half of those conversations came from women.[15]

It is worth noting that the immense success of the Old Spice video campaign is difficult to replicate. The basic concept of the "Old Spice Guy" had been tested a number of times by Procter & Gamble without success. The right creative aspects, which took many years to hone, were what made the campaign so effective. Even so, the videos that followed attracted less attention, although Gillette credited them with lifting sales.[16]

As David Hallerman of Advertising Age so clearly puts it, "the most clever marketers saw a major sticking point in making the Old Spice [Guy] into a model for their own campaigns: its success depended on excellent, compelling creative. And while every brand would like to think all its video assets are compelling, that's clearly not the case. Making advertising videos that consumers want to watch is, in truth, very, very difficult."[17]

The key take-away from these two case histories? A video that goes viral is, in large part, luck. Even without that kind of infrequent luck, however, video has become a key part of the marketer's content portfolio and thoughtful strategy and careful planning are essential. Its continuing growth underscores the need for good video marketing.

Consumer Use of Video

Anyone who was looking at marketing predictions for 2015 would have found many prognosticators saying it was going to be the "year of mobile" and many more saying it was going to be the "year of video." Who was right? Both were!

Mobile use is growing rapidly as we will discuss in Chapter 12. Video is growing by leaps and bounds. Adobe research showed that unique visitors to video sites rose 146% between June 2013 and June 2014.

Figure 8.1 shows that, while traditional TV still leads in time spent viewing, an increasing amount of time is spent viewing videos—as time-shifted TV, on the Internet, and on mobile devices. Mobile and time-shifted video are the trends marketers must

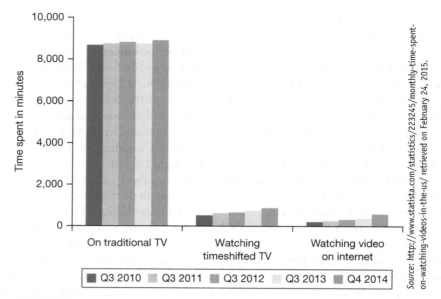

Source: http://www.statista.com/statistics/223245/monthly-time-spent-on-watching-videos-in-the-us/ retrieved on February 24, 2015.

Figure 8.1 Time Spent Viewing Video Content by Medium

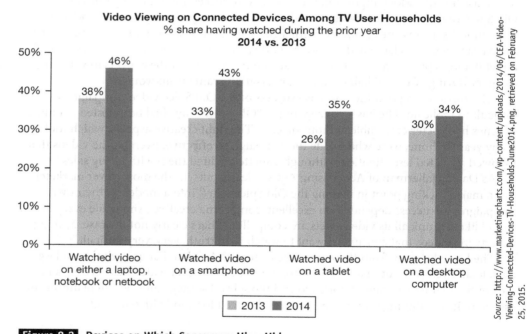

Source: http://www.marketingcharts.com/wp-content/uploads/2014/06/CEA-Video-Viewing-Connected-Devices-TV-Households-June2014.png, retrieved on February 25, 2015.

Figure 8.2 Devices on Which Consumers View Video

accommodate. Figure 8.2 shows another aspect of the video revolution, the trend toward mobile devices with desktop video viewing still growing, but more slowly.

Google, owner of YouTube, also asserts that U.S. consumers who view branded video content on smartphones are "significantly more likely to watch, share, and feel personally connected to ads and branded video content than their counterparts watching on desktop or television are."[18]

The same study indicated that not only do retail shoppers like to use smartphones for information while shopping but at least a third of them prefer to use their smartphones rather than ask a store employee for assistance. The data in Figure 8.3 show that consumers are more likely to take the actions that marketers desire as a result of branded videos seen on smartphones. In addition to actually making purchases, shoppers also

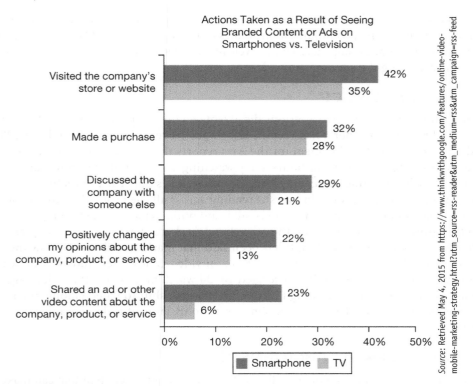

Source: Retrieved May 4, 2015 from https://www.thinkwithgoogle.com/features/online-video-mobile-marketing-strategy.html?utm_source=rss-reader&utm_medium=rss&utm_campaign=rss-feed

Figure 8.3 Video Motivates Consumers to Take Action

visited the brand website for more information, improved the favorability of their attitudes, and shared their positive perceptions with others in multiple ways. All are very desirable outcomes for marketers!

Data on business to business (B2B) video marketing is harder to come by, but as early as 2010 Forbes found senior executives watching more video, more often, sharing with colleagues and taking action based on video content.[19] In 2014 Digital Sherpa stated that 75% of executives watch business videos at least once a week.[20]

Remember two things about B2B video marketing:

1. Video can be especially useful for the small business that needs awareness and reach but lacks a large media budget.

2. Executives are people too! The growth of video viewing among the general population makes a strong case for corresponding growth in the business community.

Benefits of Marketing with Online Videos

Three of the main advantages of marketing with online videos include the ability to engage viewers, reach large audiences, and showcase products. Each of these benefits is explained in detail below.

ENGAGING VIEWERS

Video is a very popular medium because it can create a stronger connection with consumers. It is particularly good for storytelling that is enjoyable to most viewers. For many people video stimuli are more appealing than dry text or listening to a podcast. Also, "[t]he more senses that are involved in gathering information, the more engaging the process becomes."[21] Viewers become more vested in the content when a human face is attached to it. Further, communication studies estimate that 50% to 80% of meaning is conveyed through body language. Thus, a well-made video deepens the communication experience, making the message more persuasive.

LARGE AUDIENCES

Most online or print ads have a serious disadvantage: they require the viewer to read them, and reading in general has become less popular over time. For example, "a 2007 study by the National Endowment for the Arts reports that 'on average, Americans aged 15 to 24 spend almost two hours a day watching TV, and only seven minutes of their daily leisure time on reading.' And… web video is only further fueling this difference in time spent watching versus reading across all age groups."[22] More people choose to consume their information visually, and online video marketing taps into this growing trend. Video, on the other hand, is skyrocketing in popularity, as indicated in the previous section. It has been said that marketers always "follow the eyeballs" and the eyeballs of all age groups are on video. Study after study has shown that young consumers, generally those aged 18–34 watch more video than older age groups. Now studies are beginning to show a noticeable shift to video among older age groups 50 and over. The video audience is not only large, it is demographically diverse.[23]

BUILDING BRAND AWARENESS

Some brands seem to have an obvious link with stories and other content that can make compelling video. Red Bull has created such a link between its energy drink and extreme sports. If you are a skier, you may watch its double pipe or snowboarding series. If you like racing, they offer everything from motocross to Indycars. If you like running the offerings range from steeplechase to mountain running to sponsorship of road races for charitable fundraising. The events and the videos get a great deal of press attention, further increasing the brand reach. And, by the way, there are some product videos thrown into the mix. It's a virtuoso performance!

SHOWCASING THE PRODUCT

Demonstrating how to use a product has several benefits as a video marketing strategy. Viewers with no experience with the product may watch the video, be impressed with its quality or other appealing features, and consider making a purchase. In this respect an online video can function much like an old-fashioned infomercial. However, instructional videos also have the advantage of assisting those who have already bought the product. By providing value to the existing customer base, it may cause them to write positive reviews or otherwise participate in the social media campaign and/or to share the video with their contacts. Even if the viewership is limited, this factor makes videos demonstrating a product's utility potentially highly profitable.

Home Depot, the world's largest home improvement retailer, produces a wide variety of product use videos (Figure 8.4). The company started as a discounter but came to understand that its consumer base needed more than low prices. Customers wanted good customer service and they needed lessons in do-it-yourself home repairs and improvement. In 2011 the company acknowledged that, "do-it-yourselfers made up more than 60 percent of the building supply industry's sales volume, but the majority of them did not have the technical knowledge or expertise to accomplish most home repair or improvement projects."[24] This recognition caused Home Depot to hire knowledgeable do-it-yourselfers and professional tradespeople, who then underwent thorough product knowledge training. They were able to provide more helpful customer service than the minimum-wage personnel common throughout the industry.

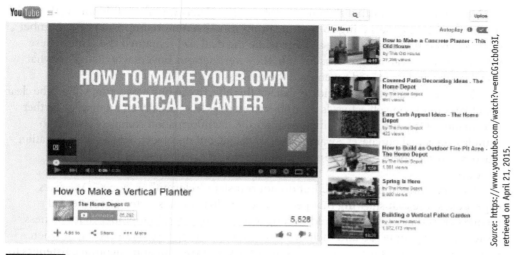

Source: https://www.youtube.com/watch?v=emCG1cb0n3I, retrieved on April 21, 2015.

Figure 8.4 The Home Depot Consumer Video Channel

The effectiveness of one-on-one customer service lead to in-store workshops on subjects, often seasonal, of particular interest to that store's customers that proved to be very effective. How do you reach more customers with this type of project- and product-specific knowledge? Video, of course!

According to YouTube, Home Depot's consumer video channel has over 85,000 subscribers.[25] The business has another important market segment—home contractors. The Home Depot Pro Channel on YouTube has almost 2,500 subscribers who can access everything from informational videos to a contractor loyalty program.[26]

GENERATING BUSINESS LEADS

The conventional B2B wisdom has suggested that business videos are good for demonstrating products and help to build trust in the brand and product. Recent research indicates that videos actually work to sell products. In B2B terms, video is effective in converting leads to sales. Moreover, they attract and convert at a lower cost than other favored B2B lead generation activities like trade shows that work but are extremely expensive. In late 2014 the Aberdeen Group conducted a study that demonstrated the effectiveness of video in B2B lead generation. Figure 8.5 shows some of the results.

Lead stage	Without Video	With Video	Increase in Marketing Generated Revenue
Web site Visitors	400,00	400,000	_____
Responses	11,600	19,200	_____
Qualified Leads	2,587	4,282	_____
Opportunities	936	508	_____
Closed Deals	89	147	_____
Average Deal Size	$12,000	$12,000	_____
Marketing-Generated Revenue	$1,068,869	$1,769,163	$700,294

Source: http://v1.aberdeen.com/launch/report/research_report/9788-RR-Video-Hidden-SalesCycle.asp, retrieved on April 29, 2015.

Figure 8.5 Use of Videos Increases B2B Revenues

Notice in particular that the number of *qualified* leads was almost double with the use of video in the marketing communications mix. Even more important, the number of *closed deals* was almost twice as large while the deal size remained the same. These were not people watching videos for fun; they were serious buyers who acted on what they learned and produced revenue in the process!

How does a marketer make videos that are this effective in business settings? First, be clear about your marketing objective. Is your objective a sales lead, usually an inquiry for further information? Or is the product simple enough and the information complete enough to stimulate an actual purchase? Awareness is important, but the objective of a lead-generation video is to bring about some type of behavior, not to develop awareness and favorable attitudes.

Relevant content is essential. But do not translate "relevant" as "long." One sales expert cites research showing that people begin to lose interest after 1 minute and recommends that no video should be longer than 3 minutes. Remember that business customers are people too and include music and appealing visual effects. Then when you have a great, persuasive video, post it everywhere you can and encourage listeners to share. In fact, committing to sharing a video with a colleague may be the first step on the way to revenue-generating behavior![27]

LEADING VIDEO PLATFORMS

Marketers post their branded videos on multiple platforms, including their own websites. The cost involved in making a good video and the potential for reaching various target markets dictates multiple platforms. The list of largest platforms in Table 8.1 makes it clear that these marketing videos compete for attention in a complex ecosystem.

Some platforms, YouTube for example, do not intentionally accept videos over 15 minutes in length, but do accept videos from anyone, business or individual, with a legitimate account. NetFlix was originally a movie rental site, but it added TV shows and, later, its own original content. Amazon—not on the list—rented videos from its beginning. Later it entered streaming. It supports its quest for original content with a site called Amazon Studios that seeks original concepts and offers production funding.[28]

YouTube	User-generated content uploaded by both consumers and businesses; owned by Google
NetFlix	Movies and TV shows plus original content
Vimeo	Video sharing site; channel for video sales by creators; owned by consumer media company IAC
Yahoo Screen	On demand streaming of videos including movies and TV shows
Daily Motion	International site with consumer-generated and commercial videos from many producers
Hulu	Features both movies and TV shows on demand and live streaming of popular TV shows
Vube	Hosts viral, user-generated content
Twitch	Features games and videos about gaming
LiveLeak	User-generated news videos from around the world
Vine	Features looping videos approximately 6.5 seconds in length uploaded by both consumers and businesses; owned by Twitter

Source: http://www.ebizmba.com/articles/video-websites

Table 8.1 Largest Video Platforms Ranked by Estimated Number of Monthly Unique Visitors as of March 2015

How many of the platforms listed in Table 8.1 have you used to post your own videos? Conversely, are there platforms in this list of ten largest that you have never heard of? Those questions begin to sketch out the complex nature of the video space.

And as you look at the different types of platforms, and who owns them, bear in mind that there are other powerful players in this space. Facebook allows videos on both posts and Facebook Pay per Click (PPC) ads. Facebook videos allow functionality like tagging people, just like posts do. Until recently Facebook users were likely to share their videos by linking to YouTube. However, by one estimate in November 2014 views of videos uploaded directly to Facebook overtook views of YouTube videos on Facebook for the first time. Advertisers like Facebook ads because they generate more viewer interaction than videos on other platforms, perhaps because they are embedded in a content-rich context. At least one British retailer, home furnishings supplier John Lewis, uploaded its 2014 Christmas ad directly to Facebook for the first time. Even on a single platform, Facebook, the video ecosystem is complex.[29]

Facebook is well established with great market power. However, newer players are receiving considerable attention.

Snapchat was founded in 2011 as a messaging app with little desktop presence. By May 2014 users were sharing over 700 million photos and videos each day. It represents "ephemeral" video and photo sharing. A photo or video is viewable for only 10 seconds, then it self-destructs. The platform is inherently social, linking with contacts upon sign-up.

The 10-second life span is important to viewers but equally important to marketers is the fact that each post lives for only twenty-four hours. That puts great pressure on marketers to tell a compelling story and Snapchat has moved quickly to meet their needs. Self-destructing pictures were the only option at first. Video was quickly added. The most recent service that appeals to marketers is Snapchat's Our Stories.[30] This feature allows users who are attending an event to contribute their own snaps to the live feed of the event. Friends, both those who are attending and those who are not, can watch the snaps.

One reporter says he received a screenshot of a friend's contribution to New York City's February 2015 "Snowmageddon" Our Story event. The friend's app showed that the shot was viewed 25 million times and 5,000 screenshots were taken. The reporter expressed skepticism over the numbers but found other events with viewership in the millions. Snapchat assured the reporter that the numbers reported represent unique views of the content. With over 100 million monthly active users, viewership in the millions is not impossible, but there is considerable doubt about the viewership numbers being reported by Snapchat.[31]

Questions about the metrics are not preventing marketers from experimenting with Snapchat and many seem pleased with the results. Taco Bell knows that it has over 200,000 friends on the app although the exact number is not clear. Taco Bell executive Nicholas Tran describes them as "crazy engaged." He estimated that up to 80% of Taco Bell's followers open its Snaps and 90% of them view them in their entirety. Tran says that, "The platform is one of the most engaging places for us to play."[32] As of this writing that play takes place on the platform features that are available free to any registered user. If a platform has that many users, can commercialization, perhaps in the form of paid/promoted posts, be far behind?

Notice that of the ten leading video platforms listed in Table 8.1, only one, Twitter's Vine, represents short-form video. Twitter does not allow long-form video, only the 15-second videos accepted by Vine, which has been quite successful. It is worth thinking about the role short-form and ephemeral video may play in the future of the medium.

This list of most-visited video sites only begins to suggest the diversity of platforms. That means that marketers must learn to create and promote videos that appeal to audiences of all kinds.

How to Create Appealing Video Content

Creating a video to share online is fairly easy, but making the *right* video that will be widely viewed and will accomplish marketing objectives is much more difficult. The challenge may vary depending on the industry or sector being promoted. Some organizations lend themselves especially well to video marketing: "For example, many churches routinely shoot video of weekly services and offer it online for anybody to watch. . . . Many amateur and professional sports teams, musicians, and theater groups also use video as a marketing and PR tool."[33] For other products that are more technical and perhaps less immediately engaging, more creative approaches may be necessary.

A variety of authors have offered recommendations for developing online video content to be posted on YouTube and other video-sharing sites. Perhaps the most authoritative advice comes from conversations with accomplished online video creators, which author Paul Gillin used to develop the AEIOU rule: video content should be *a*uthentic, *e*ntertaining, *i*ntimate, *o*ffbeat, and *u*nusual.[34]

AUTHENTIC

Use real people in actual locations. The Home Depot video channels, both consumer and professional, provide many good examples of using real people, often in their own homes and work settings, to offer authentic advice. Online viewers sometimes see high production values as a sign of slick professional marketing and may be more skeptical of the content. Plenty of viral videos are recorded using just a webcam. Viewers will not only forgive, but they will also frequently reward a "homemade" feel in online video because the content appears more believable. This is especially true if the videos are shot during an activity or an event, not in a studio.

ENTERTAINING

Put simply, people want enjoyable fun content. At times it can be valuable to focus less on company branding and more on entertainment value. Red Bull is a master at creating videos that engage viewers with all kinds of sports, from extreme and exotic to professional and celebrity. The emphasis is on the sports and the athletes, not on the energy drink, although the tie-in is obvious. In early 2015 Red Bull celebrated 1 billion YouTube views with—what else—a recap of its videos![35] If a video is viewed millions of times because it is crammed with thrilling action, the brand will be carried along for the ride even if it is mentioned very briefly. Entertaining videos make news, are shared on social networks, and can even spawn imitations and spinoffs, which further expand the brand's influence.

INTIMATE

It is part of human nature to follow stories or personal drama experienced by peers. A video that tells a story, perhaps focusing around one person and showing how others react, is more appealing because it creates a connection with the viewer. Dove launched the "Real Beauty" social media campaign in 2012 with personal and compelling videos designed to bolster the self-esteem of tweens, teens, and young adult women. Their ad agency said this Facebook campaign increased their number of fans by 75% in just three months. In 2015 they added another social channel with the #SpeakBeautiful campaign on Twitter. This effort went a step further in attempting to lessen the personal negativity often found in social media. Not all industry pundits liked the campaign, but it meets the criteria of personal and compelling and features the brand in a flattering light.[36] The campaign integrated Facebook and website video with other social platforms for maximum impact.

A different kind of personal campaign that caught on is Burger King's (BK's) Whopper Freakout campaign in which customers' reactions were secretly filmed when they were told that BK had discontinued the Whopper. Run as both a TV ad and a longer web video, this highly personal (some would say voyeuristic) campaign created a huge response for the company.[37]

OFFBEAT AND UNUSUAL

Offbeat and unusual tend to work together, as underscored by the Old Spice Guy viral videos. A video needs to be distinct and memorable to stand out among the millions uploaded regularly. Videos that challenge a taboo or that seem otherwise strange and unlikely can be highly popular. Most viral videos feature these qualities. Bland content is easily skipped or ignored, so video marketing teams have to constantly innovate and find new ideas. An unusual image or clip may be further edited by other content creators, an action that amounts to free advertising for the company.

This discussion sounds as if viewers watch videos all the way through. In fact, relatively few videos are viewed in their entirety. Adobe studied consumer video viewing on entertainment and media sites from 2013 through 2014 (Figure 8.6). They reported that the type of device mattered, with videos viewed on the desktop having the highest completion rate at 20%—not very high. Video viewed on smartphones had the lowest—10%.[38] Does size make a difference in the viewing of consumer videos?

Completion gives people an opportunity to comprehend the entire video message, so it has long been considered important. Receptivity to video advertising is a more specific concept, and its importance to marketers seems obvious. Another study found that people were more receptive to video ads when they were in public places. Perhaps more surprising than the finding relative to size is another study that found that location, mood, and content also matter. Video viewers were most receptive in public places like restaurants and gyms or while commuting. In addition, a mood of excitement increased receptivity and business was the most compelling content category.[39]

These studies show that marketers' use of both content videos and video advertising must be tailored to the audience and also to usage factors. Consumers must first be interested in viewing the video, hopefully to completion. Then if they can be induced to share videos, their effectiveness increases.

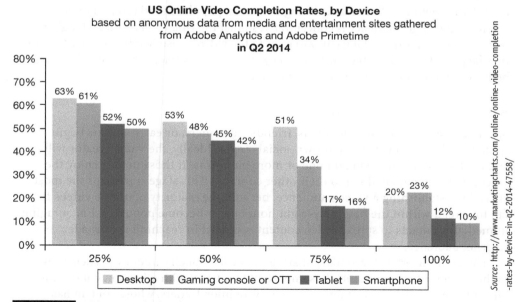

Figure 8.6 Video Completion by Device

SHARING ONLINE VIDEOS

Creating strong video content is challenging, but that is only the beginning. In order to influence, videos must be found online and watched. While some content is so creative, funny, or engaging that it spreads organically, not all online video producers are so fortunate. Especially when the topic is a more serious company, brand, or organization, finding the best way to share an online video so that it reaches the target audience can be a significant obstacle to marketing success.

Author Mark Schaefer says people share content for three basic reasons. They share:

1. As an act of altruism, to help or to share information

2. To express their own identity

3. Because they have an emotional connection with the brand

According to Mark, here's the big lesson: "People share content for intrinsic and emotional reasons. But businesses are trying to get people to share content for economic reasons."[40] Marketers must understand the issues involved in getting viewers to share their videos.

In order to overcome this barrier and successfully distribute an online video, there are several different levels of sharing that must occur. Sharing occurs in several stages and marketers can take steps to encourage sharing in each stage. First, the primary sharing occurs when the video creator posts it online; then, the secondary sharing happens as insiders or friends of the creator share the video; and finally, tertiary sharing occurs when online viewers begin sharing the video of their own accord. To be widely disseminated, an online video must pass through all three stages, so each will be discussed in turn.

PRIMARY SHARING

Primary sharing is perhaps the simplest step, as it can be done by just one person. A video must be posted online, often on several different video-sharing sites, so that more people will have the opportunity to find and watch it. The poster can also use other social networking, link sharing, or microblogging websites to distribute links to the video as well as the brand website. Even if the video is posted at multiple locations, consider funneling all link traffic through the most popular portal (YouTube) or wherever the target audience is concentrated so that the video will be ranked higher by search engines. Posting a blog entry to refer to the video is also helpful because the post may be picked up and further distributed by syndication services and shared by other bloggers or by commercial content sharing sites.

SECONDARY SHARING

Secondary sharing occurs when fans, friends, customers, or early viewers begin spreading the video within their own social circles. Ideally, the video creator will already have some following on one or more platforms. If those people enjoy the video, they will pass it along to their other contacts. This stage is perhaps the most crucial in establishing a video's audience, because the majority of online videos that fail to spread within the first forty-eight hours never become popular.[41] Encouraging immediate contacts to spread video content is crucial in reaching the broader Internet audience.

The groundwork for secondary sharing can be laid much earlier by participating in the online video community. It is important to interact with other content creators. Like other online networks, there are YouTube opinion leaders, whose content has more influence than that of the average user. It is possible to "identify opinion leaders by their behavior" because they are more likely to have rated an online video or posted comments regarding an online video.[42] These are the people who are likely to lead general opinion, influence others toward specific content, and perhaps determine the success of a video marketing campaign.

In order to encourage fans to spread their video content, some companies use contests or incentives or feature user-submitted videos on the corporate website or blog. For example, Doritos has run contests for a video ad to be shown on the Super Bowl for a number of years. The contest gets a great deal of publicity that enhances the value of Doritos paid advertising.

Even less dramatic incentives like a free burrito can allow a company to leverage user-generated videos. Offering to share content created by outsiders makes those people more likely to reciprocate by sharing the company's content, or telling others about the contest. Even small, informal fan competitions have proved a successful way to facilitate secondary sharing.

TERTIARY SHARING

Lastly, tertiary sharing is when content is spread on the Internet by people who likely do not know or have connections with the original video's creator. It is in this stage that most viral videos are found. Of course, viral videos are just the examples when primary and secondary sharing were highly successful, making the final stage of distribution huge and often global. To reach anything close to that scale, however, a video's creator likely spent considerable effort on the earlier stages. The Q4 2014 ShareThis study found that Facebook accounted for a large majority of the shares (81%) just as it has for several years. Far behind came Pinterest with 7% of the shares and Twitter with 6%. No other channel, not even email, accounted for as much as 2%.[43] Keep in mind that sharing of online information, particularly videos, happens on more than just social networks but the decline of email as a channel for sharing shows just how powerful social media has become.

In order to make tertiary sharing easier, be sure that each video has a descriptive and memorable title. Those words may be all that someone has for reference when she or he sees a link or recommendation from a friend, especially if it comes through email. Also consider having different titles, tags, or keywords associated with the video on each online video-sharing website. The more ways there are to find and share a particular video, the more likely it will be widely viewed and influence the target audience.

What, then, are the best practices that will result in your video being disseminated to the appropriate target audience, shared widely, and fulfilling the established marketing objectives?

BEST PRACTICES FOR VIDEO MARKETING

1. **Match the production techniques to the intent of the video.** Videos from conference speeches or interviews, for example, can be shot casually, even with smartphones. It doesn't matter whether it is a Star Wars convention or a gathering of chip designers for computers that process big data. The production values can be casual.

On the other hand, videos that are not shot in a live setting should be professionally produced. Good production values do not necessarily translate to high cost, however. Professionally produced videos are accessible to even small businesses today and they are worth their cost in the effectiveness they can have in achieving business goals.

2. **Design and produce videos for mobile—first and always.** A Google video executive estimates that mobile video viewing has grown by 400% in just the past two years. He describes mobile viewers as today's "captive audience" and indicates that mobile viewers may be more engaged in the content than other viewers, especially television.[44]

3. **Design and produce videos for the platforms on which they are to appear.** A 10-second teaser shot for a new product on Snapchat is obviously going to be very different from a 9-minute product use demonstration posted on YouTube. Either of these videos, however, may have important roles in a single campaign or in various campaigns for the same brand. The product, the audience, and the marketing objectives all play a part in deciding what type of video on what platform.

4. **Post your videos on multiple platforms and on your own website.** Create as many opportunities for viewing and for sharing as possible.

5. **Optimize your videos to be found in search.** Optimization techniques are beyond the scope of this text, but they are readily available on the Internet. Or call in an expert. All agencies have search engine marketing (SEM) experts today and so do many businesses. It is also a field that is rampant with freelance workers and they can be asked to demonstrate tangible achievements from past campaigns.

6. **Encourage viewers to share your videos.** Incentives work; so does simple recognition in many instances. Many studies have shown that people share all kinds of content simply to provide information to others, so appeal to their altruism. Most video-sharing sites include a share bar. The call to action can be for the viewer to use one or more of the share icons to share with their friends. Shares can be powerful.

7. **Finally, a don't! Don't make a sales video.** Leave those for the infomercial pitchmen. Make videos that entertain, inform, and encourage people to engage in desired behavior. You can be almost sure that a hard sell video will not be shared and probably will not be acted on.

These video best practices, along with the detail presented in the chapter will help marketers of all kinds add effective videos to their marketing communications mix.

Notes

1. (n.d.). YouTube, "Statistics." Retrieved April 29, 2015, from https://www.youtube.com/yt/press/statistics.html
2. Global Web Index, "What to Know about YouTube on Its Tenth Anniversary." Retrieved April 29, 2015, from https://plus.google.com/+GlobalWebIndexNet/posts/jQKL1jcLRKV
3. (April 2015). Think with Google, "Why Online Video Is a Must-Have for Your Mobile Marketing Strategy." Retrieved May 4, 2015, from https://www.thinkwithgoogle.com/features/online-video-mobile-marketing-strategy.html?utm_source=rss-reader&utm_medium=rss&utm_campaign=rss-feed
4. (December 9, 2014). CNET, "How 'Numa Numa' Invented the Viral Video." Retrieved April 26, 2015, from http://www.cnet.com/news/why-did-that-video-go-viral/
5. "The Man Your Man Could Smell Like," (2011), Effie Awards. Retrieved April 26, 2015, from http://apaceffie.com/docs/default-source/resource-library/oldspice_case_pdf.pdf?sfvrsn=2
6. (2010, February 4). YouTube, "Old Spice | The Man Your Man Could Smell Like." Retrieved November 6, 2011, from http://www.youtube.com/watch?v=owGykVbfgUE
7. Newman, Andrew Adam (2010, July 15), "Old Spice Argues That Real Men Smell Good," *The New York Times*. Retrieved November 6, 2011, from http://www.nytimes.com/2010/07/16/business/media/16adco.html?scp=1&sq=old%20spice%20video&st=cse
8. Brian Morrissey (2010, July 14), "How Old Spice Ruled the Real-Time Web," *Adweek*. Retrieved November 6, 2011, from http://www.adweek.com/news/technology/how-old-spice-ruled-real-time-web-102823?page=2

9. Mauro (2011, July), "Old Spice Responses Campaign," Vimeo. Retrieved November 6, 2011, from http://vimeo.com/25187993

10. Brian Morrissey (2010, July 14), "How Old Spice Ruled the Real-Time Web," *Adweek*. Retrieved November 6, 2011, from http://www.adweek.com/news/technology/how-old-spice-ruled-real-time-web-102823?page=2

11. Wieden + Kennedy (2010, August 11), "Old Spice Social Campaign Case Study Video," Digital Buzz Blog. Retrieved July 26, 2011, from http://www.digitalbuzzblog.com/old-spice-social-campaign-case-study-video/

12. Neff, Jeff (2010, July 26), "How Much Old Spice Body Wash Has the Old Spice Guy Sold?" *Advertising Age*. Retrieved November 6, 2011, from http://adage.com/article/news/spice-body-wash-spice-guy-sold/145096/

13. Gibson, Ellen (2011, June 24), "Cannes Ad Prize Asks Novel Question: Did It Work?" Huffington Post. Retrieved November 6, 2011, from http://www.huffingtonpost.com/huff-wires/20110624/us-ads-that-work/

14. (2010, July 28). "Old Spice Viral Campaign Translates into Sales—Lots of Them," MarketingVox.com. Retrieved November 6, 2011, from http://www.marketingvox.com/old-spice-viral-campaign-translates-into-sales-lots-of-them-047427/?utm_campaign=newsletter&utm_source=mv&utm_medium=textlink

15. Morrissey, Brian (2010, August 4), "Old Spice's Agency Flexes Its Bulging Stats," *Adweek*. Retrieved November 6, 2011, from http://www.adweek.com/adfreak/old-spices-agency-flexes-its-bulging-stats-12396

16. Roberts, Mary Lou (February 17, 2011), "Old Spice Guy Is Back—Quietly," DIY Marketing. Retrieved April 26, 2015, from http://diy-marketing.blogspot.com/2011/02/old-spice-guy-is-back-quietly.html

17. Hallerman, David (2010, August 26), "What Marketers Can Learn From the Old Spice 'Your Man' Campaign," AdAge Digital. Retrieved November 6, 2011, from http://adage.com/article/digitalnext/marketers-learn-spice-man-campaign/145603/

18. Tweney, Dylan, (October 20, 2014), "Adobe Report Finds Massive 43% Growth in Online Video Watching," VB. Retrieved March 24, 2015 from http://venturebeat.com/2014/10/20/adobe-report-finds-massive-43-growth-in-online-video-watching/

19. "Why Online Video Is a Must-Have for Your Mobile Marketing Strategy," (April 2015), Think with Google. Retrieved May 4, 2015 from https://www.thinkwithgoogle.com/features/online-video-mobile-marketing-strategy.html?utm_source=rss-reader&utm_medium=rss&utm_campaign=rss-feed

20. "Video in the C-Suite," (2010), Forbes Insights. Retrieved April 26, 2015, from http://images.forbes.com/forbesinsights/StudyPDFs/Video_in_the_CSuite.pdf

21. Mincher, Sarah (January 9, 2014), "25 Amazing Video Marketing Statistics." Retrieved April 26, 2015, from http://www.digitalsherpa.com/blog/25-amazing-video-marketing-statistics/

22. Safko, Lon and David K. Brake (2009), *The Social Media Bible: Tactics, Tools & Strategies for Business Success* (Hoboken, NJ: John Wiley), p. 237.

23. Dixon, Colin (March 11, 2015), "Young Millennials Watch 16% Less TV, 21% More Internet Video." Retrieved April 27, 2015, from http://www.nscreenmedia.com/young-millennials-watch-16-less-tv-21-internet-video/

24. (n.d.). "The Home Depot, Inc." Funding Universe. Retrieved June 18, 2011, from http://www.fundinguniverse.com/company-histories/The-Home-Depot-Inc-Company-History.html

25. "The Home Depot," YouTube. Retrieved on May 8, 2015, from https://www.youtube.com/user/homedepot/about 4/21

26. "The Home Depot Pro Channel," YouTube. Retrieved on May 8, 2015, from https://www.youtube.com/user/TheHomeDepotPro

27. Heynes, Karen (September 1, 2014), "5 Tips for Creating Videos That Generate Sales Leads." Retrieved April 29, 2015, from http://www.sales-initiative.com/toolbox/selling/5-tips-for-creating-videos-that-generate-sales-leads/

28. (n.d.). "Amazon Studios," Amazon. Retrieved April 29, 2015, from http://studios.amazon.com/

29. O'Reilly, Lara (December 9, 2014), "Facebook Video Is Driving YouTube Off Facebook." Retrieved April 29, 2015, from http://www.businessinsider.com/facebook-video-v-youtube-market-share-data-2014-12

30. Jarboe, Greg (March 23, 2015), "Snapchat: How Ephemeral Video Marketing Is Engaging Viewers." Retrieved March 17, 2015, from http://www.reelseo.com/snapchat-video-marketing/

31. DeAmicis, Carmel (February 24, 2015), "Snapchat's 'Our Stories' Are Generating Tens of Millions of Views." Retrieved May 1, 2015, from https://gigaom.com/2015/02/24/snapchats-our-stories-are-generating-tens-of-millions-of-views/

32. Sloane, Garett (August 22, 2014), "Snapchat's 'Crazy Engaged' Fans Can't Resist a Message from Taco Bell." Retrieved April 1, 2015, from http://www.adweek.com/news/technology/snapchats-crazy-engaged-users-cant-resist-message-taco-bell-159677

33. Li, Charlene and Josh Bernoff (2008), *Groundswell: Winning in a World Transformed by Social Technologies* (Boston, MA: Harvard Business Press), p. 41–62.

34. Gillin, Paul (2009). *Secrets of Social Media Marketing* (Irvine, CA: Quill Driver Books), p. 216–219.

35. McAvoy, Kevin and Khalil Garriott (January 27, 2015), "Red Bull's YouTube Channel Hits 1 Billion Views." Retrieved April 20, 2015, from http://www.redbull.com/us/en/stories/1331701991361/red-bull-youtube-one-billion-views

36. Nudd, Tim (February 19, 2015), "Dove and Twitter Team Up to Address Hateful Tweets about Beauty on Oscar Night." Retrieved on April 20, 2015, from http://www.adweek.com/news/advertising-branding/dove-and-twitter-team-address-hateful-tweets-about-beauty-oscar-night-163040

37. (May 14, 2008). "2008 Creativity Award Winner: Burger King: Whopper Freakout." Ad Age, Retrieved December 15, 2015, from http://adage.com/article/the-creativity-awards/2008-creativity-award-winner-burger-king-whopper-freakout/127035/

38. (October 21, 2014), "Online Video Completion Rates, by Device, in Q2 2014." Retrieved March 17, 2015, from http://www.marketingcharts.com/online/online-video-completion-rates-by-device-in-q2-2014-47558/

39. (October 2, 2014), "Video Viewers' Ad Receptivity Most Influenced by Location." Retrieved March 17, 2015, from http://www.marketingcharts.com/online/video-viewers-ad-receptivity-46595/

40. Stelzner, Michael (April 10, 2015), "Social Sharing." Retrieved on April 20, 2015, from http://www.socialmediaexaminer.com/social-sharing-with-mark-schaefer/

41. Jarboe, Greg (2009), *YouTube and Video Marketing: An Hour a Day* (Hoboken, NJ: John Wiley), p. 47.

42. (January 22, 2015), "Social Sharing Trends in 2014." Retrieved on May 8, 2015, from http://www.marketingcharts.com/online/social-sharing-trends-in-2014-50697/

43. Ibid.

44. Mohan, Neil (April 3, 2015), "How to Win the Moments That Matter in Mobile Video." Retrieved on May 1, 2015, from http://www.adweek.com/news/technology/how-win-moments-matter-mobile-video-163822

Marketing on Photo Sharing Sites

Photo sharing is a relatively nascent and sometimes overlooked area of social media marketing. Some companies find it hard to believe that sharing pictures on the web can be an effective marketing strategy. However, photo sharing is experiencing an unprecedented growth surge, in large part due to the ubiquity of smartphones equipped with constantly improving cameras. In addition, photo marketing has risen in prominence. Simply put, consumers respond to visual images. Pinterest and Instagram are classified as social network platforms in Chapter 5 but rely heavily on visual images and will be discussed here.

Visual images have changed in their meaning from the beginning of photographic records. Instead of preserving images for posterity, photos are now seen as visual representations of fleeting moments, often quite small and trivial, to be captured and put aside. In fact, Snapchat has thrived on this fact. Its images are supposed to "disappear" after a few seconds.

The Growing Importance of Visual Marketing

What these trends mean is that marketers must be aware of the importance of visual images to consumers and be constantly changing and updating their images and encouraging consumers to do the same. In fact, most companies today realize the importance of visual images. For example, Google is

LEARNING OBJECTIVES

After completing this chapter, students will be able to:

- Define photo sharing
- Describe a brief history of photo sharing
- Explain the benefits of marketing with online photos and other images
- Detail how to market on photo sharing sites

(Continued)

de-emphasizing Google+ and emphasizing the photo sharing capabilities associated with that social media platform. Facebook purchased Instagram in recognition of the importance of photo sharing and is itself an important site for photo sharing by its consumers. To underscore the growing importance of photo sharing, realize that on the business-to-business side of the equation Salesforce recently announced Instagram integration in the form of its Social Studio. The site allows its customers to publish content to Instagram and share the most successful images across social platforms. Advertisers can use a single platform for Facebook, Instagram, Twitter, and LinkedIn on social.com to place and monitor their advertising as well as to engage customers and respond to customer service issues.[1]

The growth trend in marketing through photo sharing, as evidenced by Salesforce's recent actions, is a response to the growth in the sharing of visual images worldwide. This trend will only increase with the rise of cell phones, particularly smartphones. According to eMarketer, one in two people in the United States have smartphones; by 2017 65% of the population will have one. Globally, one in four people have a smartphone today; this figure will grow to one in three worldwide by 2018.[2] With almost 2 billion people snapping pictures with smartphones and tablets and mobile applications that make it easy to instantly upload and share these pictures, people are flocking to photo sharing sites for personal and business use. Photo sharing is, by its very nature, a social activity. Hence, for companies, nonprofits, and government agencies, photo sharing sites now represent a wealth of SMM opportunities. In addition, the nature of how images are perceived is changing. Instead of a way to provide documentation for posterity, photographic images in particular are seen as a way to capture fleeting aspects of the day, or the Instagram "moment."[3]

The bottom line is that photos and images encourage us to share and interact with posts, which is a common definition of engagement. People will typically like and comment more on posts when these include a visual image. This phenomenon has made marketing through photo sharing extremely popular as marketers are constantly seeking to identify and engage with their consumers. Figure 9.1 shows the different types of Facebook content and number of Facebook likes and comments for each.

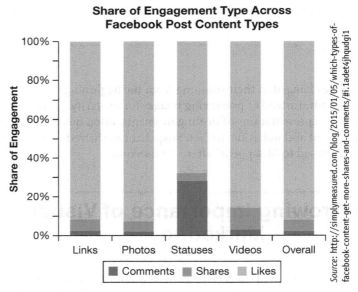

Figure 9.1 Facebook Engagement Varies When Photos and Videos Are Included

Status updates attract the greatest number of comments and therefore get the highest engagement score. When the objective is to start a conversation, status posts are the clear winners. However, other types of engagement are increased when photos and videos are added. Videos encourage shares, which is a good way to get the marketing message out. Photos in particular encourage likes and actually achieve the highest engagement per fan per post. Good, compelling content is important for engagement but can be boosted by powerful images.[4]

To understand the technology of sharing images, we need to define some terms. A digital photo album, or the more modern term *image hosting site*, is a place where a user can store pictures from a device such as a phone, tablet, computer disk or drive in a central database and retrieve and print pictures. Many applications such as Snapfish and Walmart began simply by recreating the old photo album concept, charging for printing of hard copies of pictures. These days, most image hosting sites have developed into sites for photo sharing. In contrast to a digital photo album, a photo sharing site is more robust. A photo sharing site lets users upload photos and other images for public or private consumption, allowing others to comment, rate, and tag the pictures.[5] These sites provide permanent and centralized access to a user's images (and usually video clips, too). Most photo sharing sites create albums or galleries, where visitors can view all the works of individual authors on the site. Many provide desktop-like photo management applications for organizing and presenting images. Photo sharing sites typically permit registered users to comment on the images and tag them with descriptive keywords, which the site uses to group the images by topic, making it easier to locate similar graphics. Prices vary and sites may charge fees, although the trend has been toward free sites. The most popular and well-visited photo sharing sites include those shown in Table 9.1.

Photo Sharing Sites	Alexa Global Traffic Rank*	Google Page Rank**	Estimated Unique Monthly Visitors ebiz|MBA July 2015	Date Started
Instagram	37	9	100,000,000	October 2010
Imgur	52	6	87,500,000	2009
Flickr	85	9	80,000,000	February 2004
DeviantArt	141	7	45,000,000	August 2001
Photobucket	219	7	60,000,000	June 2003
Image Shark	667	3	8,000,000	December 1999
WeHeartIt	818	6	8,100,000	2007
TinyPic	1,073	6	9,000,000	November 2002
Image Venue	1,340	4	5,750,000	August or November 2004
Shutterfly	1,605	6	20,000,000	1999
Snapfish	4042	7	NA	2000

Table 9.1 Popular Photo Sharing Sites, as of July 2015

*Alexa Global Traffic Rank estimates a site's popularity, with traffic data from Alexa Toolbar users and other diverse traffic sources, using an ascending scale where 1 represents the highest traffic rank.
**Google Page Rank uses the number and quality of links to a web page to determine its relative importance, using a scale of 0–10, with 10 indicating the highest rank and 0 the lowest.
***The eBiz|MBA site produces a monthly report on site visits that is an updated average of each website's Alexa Global Traffic Rank, and its U.S. Traffic Rank from both Compete and Quantcast.

Figure 9.2 The Twitterverse Was Fascinated by the Monkey Selfie

One of the issues of using images is who owns the image. The copyright protection afforded to users varies among photo sharing sites. In general, copyright holders of photos, artwork, and other images can grant users the right to use their creations without fees or royalties and still retain their copyrights.[6] It is critical to check the copyright policy of a photo sharing site before posting images to it or using images from it for commercial or personal purposes.

In general, a copyright attaches to that image as soon as a photo is taken and the copyright applies to the taker of the photo. Only the copyright holder can then reproduce, display and distribute, and create derivative works. Copyright law can be interpreted fairly strictly. In 2011, a nature photographer was taken unawares when a monkey took a "selfie" with his camera by picking the camera up and snapping a picture. The photographer then posted the picture on social media. This incident is famously known as the "monkey selfie." The photographer then tried to claim copyright of the image but the copyright was denied because only a human being can legally hold a copyright (see Figure 9.2). The image went viral and the photographer did not own the rights to the image.[7]

These days with the ease of sharing, the question of who owns the copyright to the image comes up frequently. In general, it is best to err on the side of caution when creating images. Creating your own images with tools such as SmartArt in Word or PowerPoint or taking your own photographs (being careful to get permission to post pictures of individuals) is often the best way to go for blogging or social media efforts on your own behalf.

For a corporation, Social Media Examiner notes there are five things to think about before posting an image.

> "#1: Do you understand the term fair use? Just because you provide attribution and/or a link back to the original doesn't mean you're free and clear. Fair use has nothing to do with attribution. That's an issue related to plagiarism, which is different from copyright.

Fair use basically means you're allowed to infringe on someone's copyright and they can't do anything about it. If your use is covered by fair use, you don't have to provide attribution anyway (although it would be nice).

#2: Why are you using the image? If it is " . . . for purposes such as criticism, comment, news reporting, teaching (including multiple copies for classroom use), scholarship, or research . . . " you're on the right track.

If you're just using the image to pretty up a post, then think twice; or better yet, get permission or buy a stock image.

#3: Have you transformed the image? If the new work which incorporates the copyrighted image is a "transformative work"—what you created no longer resembles the original—there is a greater likelihood of finding an exception to copyright infringement.

Are you taking an image and incorporating it into an infographic? Is the image now part of a video used for one of the reasons set forth in the Copyright Act?

#4: How much of the image are you using? If you're using a thumbnail and linking to the original location, there is greater likelihood of finding fair use than if you just post the original image. If you're doing a post about facial features and are just using a portion of the face from an image, you stand a better chance of arguing fair use than if you used the entire image.

#5: Are you willing to risk your site being taken down, getting a cease and desist/bill/DMCA or being sued? The Digital Millennium Copyright Act (DMCA) provides very powerful options for a copyright owner to protect his or her works in the digital space. By hitting "publish," you may be opening a can of worms."[8]

In other words, be sure to understand that you are using the image appropriately before posting. Especially for corporations, images must be posted legally. Is it really worth the hassle if a company is unsure of the source of the image?

A Brief History of Photo Sharing

Launched in September 1995, Webshots was one of the first photo sharing sites.[9] Webshots began life as a sports-oriented screen saver sold at retail for PCs, but in 1999 it morphed into a social network, which by April 2000 became the most popular photo sharing destination online[10]. A number of similar sites were founded in the late 1990s, although the two photo sharing sites that would come to dominate the field, Photobucket and Flickr, didn't come into existence until the early 2000s, as shown in Table 9.1.

Photobucket was founded on June 1, 2003, by Alex Welch and Darren Crystal.[11] This photo sharing site is well known for personal photo albums and (more recently) as a way to store and share videos, as depicted in Figure 9.3. Since the acquisition of Photobucket by News Corp. in 2007, the site has gained a more social networking feel similar to MySpace (formerly a News Corp. property).[12] Although News Corp. divested its majority stake in both Photobucket (December 2009) and MySpace (June 2011), Photobucket's

Figure 9.3 Photobucket Categorizes Images to Make Browsing and Searching Easier

image storage facilities continue to serve as a place for MySpace members to store photos.[13] Users may keep their photo albums private, permit password-protected guest access, or open them to the public.[14]

By June 2006 Photobucket had become the most popular photo sharing site, capturing 44% of the market.[15] However, starting in 2007, complaints began surfacing about not enough free storage, photo editing tools, and options in pro accounts, as compared with Flickr.[16] In August 2009 Photobucket reduced free storage space from 1 GB to 500 GB, further angering users, who were unable to upload more images to their accounts unless they were willing pay the upgrade fee.[17] Eventually these missteps were corrected, and Photobucket now offers new members 2 GB of free storage in addition to premium plans.[18]

Flickr was founded in February 2004 by Stewart Butterfield and Caterina Fake, pictured in Figure 9.4. The Vancouver-based parent company, Ludicorp, was originally launched to develop a social network-based massively multiplayer online game. As the funding began to run low, the only portion of the game fully developed was the user-interface. So Ludicorp opted to use the game's user interface as the basis for a photo sharing service dubbed Flickr.[19]

Martin Klimek/ZUMAPRESS.com/Newscom

Figure 9.4 Flickr cofounders Stewart Butterfield and Caterina Fake take a photo of themselves during a photo shoot in San Francisco

The game's user-interface provided a chat room on Flickr. Fake recalls that "George Oates [a Flickr employee] and I would spend 24 hours, seven days a week, [in the chat room] greeting every single person who came to the site. We introduced them to people, we chatted with them. This is a social product. People are putting things they love—photographs of their whole lives—into it. All of these people are your potential evangelists. You need to show those people love."[20]

Over time the chat room was dropped, as new versions of the site did away with the original gaming codebase and as the focus shifted to file uploading and sharing. The site's growing popularity attracted the elite of Silicon Valley, including Google and Yahoo!, as potential buyers of the fledgling company. In March 2005 Yahoo! acquired Ludicorp and Flickr for a reported $35 million.[21] In a move to take advantage of Photobucket's storage restrictions, Flickr lifted the previous size upload limits for free accounts on April 9, 2008.[22]

In spite of their success, the founders of Flickr, husband-and-wife team Butterfield and Fake, were experiencing a growing frustration in working for a large enterprise like Yahoo![23] According to Butterfield, "Yahoo failed to provide some resources needed during the first couple of years [after the acquisition]. Decision-making slowed because of bureaucracy."[24] In June 2008 both founders resigned from the company. In fact, "Stewart Butterfield and Caterina Fake had already distanced themselves from Flickr, with Fake working in another Yahoo! division and Butterfield on an extended paternity leave."[25]

Despite the departure of the founders, the photo sharing site continued to gain popularity, fostering an environment where professional photographers felt comfortable posting and discussing their work.[26] In May 2009 White House official photographer Pete Souza began using Flickr as a conduit for releasing White House photos.[27]

In September 2010 Flickr announced its 5 billionth photo upload.[28] By January 2012 Flickr had 17.6 million unique monthly visitors,[29] and just a month later, the site announced its 6 billionth photo upload.[30]

The year 2010 also saw the rise of Instagram, which has rapidly overcome many other sites in terms of marketing impact. Kevin Systrom and Mike Krieger created Instagram in October 2010. Instagram is almost purely visual, with very few comments. The platform was a success from the beginning and had one million users by its second month. Two years later, Instagram was purchased by Facebook, which has launched sponsored photos and videos.[31] Many brands from Starbucks to Target to CBS use Instagram to market effectively by creating fan engagement. Mercedes, for example,

Figure 9.5 Applebee's #fantographer Campaign Showcased Products and Engaged Customers

allowed users to create their own customized vehicle, with a price tag to match, by featuring its own virtual custom shop on Instagram.[32]

In October 2015 the Instagram stats page showed 400 million active users worldwide, 80 million photos uploaded daily, and 3.5 billion likes daily.[33] Instagram is expected to comprise more than 10% of Facebook's global ad revenues by 2017, including 28% of all its U.S. mobile revenues.[34] Instagram itself still does not directly generate revenue. However, advertising videos created in Instagram can be posted on Facebook and "boosted" to create advertising revenue on the Facebook platform. What Instagram photos and videos can do is pull people in and involve them with the brand. Applebee's, for example, encouraged its customers to tag images of food in its "fantographer" campaign (Figure 9.5), effectively turning its Instagram site over to its fans.[35] The company increased its Instagram following by 35% and its engagement by 24% with this campaign.[36]

While Instagram is a way to "share the world's moments," Pinterest offers to ""connect everyone in the world through the 'things' they find interesting" via a global platform of inspiration and idea sharing.""[37] Like Instagram Pinterest has grown rapidly since its founding, also in 2010. According to stats summarized in October 2015 Pinterest has 100 million global users with 30% of all U.S. Internet users on the platform. Use by gender is skewed, with 42% of U.S. online women using it as opposed to 13% of online men,[38] although Pinterest said in January 2015 that men were its fastest-growing demographic.[39] One billion boards have been created and 50 billion items Pinned. It is a hugely popular mobile site with 75% of its daily traffic coming through mobile apps. It is a valuable platform for brands that use it well with 45% of online shoppers having bought something as a result of a Pinterest recommendation. The brand with the most engagement on Pinterest? Nordstrom![40]

One digital marketer says that "Instagram is about sharing your own photos. Pinterest is about curation."[41] What implications does that have for brands that use these wildly popular sites?

As Figure 9.6 shows, the primary audience for both sites is women, but beyond that there is considerable difference. The Instagram audience is looking for authentic,

Source: http://blogs.constantcontact.com/difference-pinterest-and-instagram/

Figure 9.6 What Marketers Should Know about Using Instagram and Pinterest

personal experiences with a brand and nonprofits as well as B2C brands can use this to their benefit. The craft-oriented audience on Pinterest is looking for ideas and reacts by visiting websites and engaging in other purchase-related behaviors, making it ideal for B2C brands who are able to translate their brand story into appealing visuals.

Another popular photo-sharing site is Imgur. Founded in an Ohio University dorm room in 2009, this site is one of the top sites on the Internet and is a self-styled "storytelling community." Its motto is "Explore Share Discuss."[42] A user might post a picture of his hands and explain his occupation and others will comment on the person's hands and how they relate to that particular profession and other remarks. The stream of comments creates a story around the image. Each day popular images are displayed, shared, and commented upon by Imgur's users. According to Forbes in late 2015 the platform had more than 150 million unique users each month, more than 5.5 billion pageviews and saw 45 million new images uploaded to the site. This storytelling approach is so popular that the site received its first round of external funding in 2014 and is beginning to use display advertising to monetize the site.[43] One of the test clients for promoted posts is eBay, which has been having success with Imgur Promoted Posts.[44] Creative images are proving to work well to drive traffic, even though the cat in Figure 9.7 does not look particularly happy about the whole thing.

Clearly photo sharing is a trend that cannot be ignored by marketers. However, using visual marketing is new and it is important to understand why and how it should be done.

Benefits of Marketing with Online Photos and Other Images

Photo sharing sites function much like other social networks. Users must be active in the community in order to produce results. Indeed, the social communities surrounding image sharing sites are the most important factor because they will circulate and share the content.[45] On Imgur, for example, the most influential users not only share photos but interact with others, commenting on many pictures. Users in turn vote on comments

Source: http://www.adweek.com/news/technology/heres-how-advertisers-are-learning-market-imgurs-geeky-millennials-166201

Figure 9.7 A Promoted Post on Imgur

on the photographs with up and down arrows for "like" or "not," pushing popular comments to the top of the list. Staying connected will draw people back to connect or to look at other targeted content. An early campaign for Canon, a leading camera brand, created a "photochain" for its EOS camera series to emphasize the creativity and inspiration in taking great photos. The brand wanted to stand for "creative inspiration" in photography. Each photographer in the chain took a picture, selected a detail, and made that detail the emphasis for the next photo, connecting photographers and ideas across Australia. Photographers could upload their pictures to Canon's website, start their own photochains, and have an opportunity to have their work highlighted in Canon's advertising campaigns in various media. The website then connected photographers to tutorials, blogs, and products to spark creativity and increase the conversation with the brand. The tracking allowed Canon to see how the company was connecting its customers to each other and to monitor brand conversations.[46]

From a marketing standpoint, there are several advantages to photo sharing campaigns.

1. Showcase the product. Photos can be used to showcase a product, document offers, and influence buyer mood.[47] Most directly, images of the product can generate interest and online buzz, leading to sales. Showcasing a product is most effective when the presentation is highly detailed. Some companies shy away from distributing product images and specifications, fearing that their trade secrets will be uncovered. While this is a legitimate worry, the potential risk is often outweighed by the sales benefits of sharing product information. Giving detailed specifications and technical details in photo form can draw press attention and build confidence with potential customers.[48]

2. **Reinforce the brand message.** Company pictures can be highly persuasive for potential buyers even when they are not directly about the product. A company's values and social presence can affect customers either positively or negatively; in an age of online transparency, some consumers expect to know the faces behind the final product. Posting photos can give "a strong sense of culture and provide a human face to the company."[49] The old saying that a picture is worth a thousand words remains true in an online world. Pictures demonstrate an institution's values and beliefs far more vividly than written description.

3. **Drive web traffic.** While visual marketing can help draw traditional press attention, it is perhaps even more effective at driving web traffic toward a product website. Photo sharing websites (and images and videos in general) are treated kindly by search engines such as Google.[50] Photo results often show up on the first page of results, bringing many to view that content. This reality makes photo sharing a natural complement to other tools in a SMM campaign.

4. **Create awareness and encourage sharing.** Andy Crestodina, Founder and Strategic Director of Orbit Media Studios, says that "a blog post without an image is like a postcard without a stamp."[51] He also points out that posts with images are more likely to be shared on Facebook and that Tweets with images get retweeted more often than those without. Posts with images are also retained in memory longer. He goes on to discuss best practices for optimizing both photos and images created by the marketer. Best practices include having the model look at the product, not at the camera, and creating infographics that contain an embed link.[52]

5. **Leverage opportunities to market with low costs.** Finally, the cost, in both money and effort, is low when pursuing an image sharing strategy. While there are initial setup costs, such as purchasing equipment and possibly online storage space, that small investment can be sufficient to propel a photo marketing campaign forward. Taking pictures at company events is quick and easy. This type of activity makes the time commitment for maintaining a photo sharing presence less demanding than a social networking site, such as Facebook or LinkedIn.[53] Compared to the benefits of spotlighting a business and its products for online viewers, photo sharing is indeed very inexpensive.[54] The low cost of executing an image sharing campaign makes it attractive to many companies.

Building Your Personal Brand through Photo Sharing

Photo sharing can be a great way to tell people about yourself. Some individuals have two separate photo sharing accounts, one professional and one personal. The problem with this approach is that anyone can find you on the Internet so you might want to consider being judicious in your postings. The following approach is suggested:

1. **Tie your photo sharing strategy into your professional goal.** If you want to be a professional photographer, pick a professional site like 500px and post regular samples of your work. If you want to be a digital marketer, create a board in Pinterest to keep photos and infographics on the subject and start sharing.

Picking just one or two photo sharing sties will help you to focus. Of course make sure this site is where the people you want to know about you hang out.

2. **Keep the pictures linked to your professional brand, but have fun.** "Headshots" like those on LinkedIn show your best side, but candid shots in your work environment will convey who you are. Photos that might not be appropriate for LinkedIn might work well in Facebook or Instagram. For photo sharing sites that are highly visual, it is fine to have a sense of humor, as long as you are modest and display good taste.

   For example, Dr. Zahay posts pictures of her classrooms and the interaction she has with her students. She is known for her hands-on classes, often taught in the lab. In this case, she uses a picture that reinforces that part of her brand. The picture in Figure 9.8 shows Dr. Zahay and her class in fanciful Halloween garb, "scarified" using a tool from Google photos. The picture received a lot of positive attention on Dr. Zahay's social media circles and helped reinforce her message that students work hard in her classes but also have fun.

   Show yourself at work or in a volunteer capacity that reinforces your personal brand message.

3. **Focus on engagement.** Post pictures that will encourage commenting and sharing. This way your brand will be known beyond your circle of friends and contacts.

4. **Be sure not to overshare.** Monitor which pictures get the most attention and with which frequency. Post others like them and be sure to respond to those who comment, engage, or connect with you.

Courtesy of Debra Zahay

Figure 9.8 Dr. Zahay's Social Media Class in Halloween Garb Created Facebook Engagement

Marketing with Photo Sharing Sites

Once the decision is made to market with photo sharing, there are several steps involved in marketing with photo sharing sites.

1. Determine the target market. The first step in marketing on photo sharing sites is to determine the target market for the images because different photo sharing sites cater to different clientele. Identifying the demographics and behavioral characteristics of the target market enables the marketer to select an optimal series of photo sharing sites on which to upload images. Check out the sites to determine whether they are primarily trafficked by, for example, college-age viewers, women, or professional photographers and artists.

In addition, consider the nature of the images to be offered. If many pictures are humorous, instructional, or quirky in nature, then place them on photo sharing sites that have similar offerings. Selecting a single photo sharing site necessarily limits a company's target market. By using multiple photo sharing sites for uploading images, marketers can expand their reach to different audiences.

2. Select the photos to upload. Selecting the photos to upload is both the most basic and most crucial aspect of image sharing. The content of photos intended for sharing will likely be different from those used in websites or as part of product content. While professional photography or stock photos (produced by picture agencies or photo libraries) may be useful for ad campaigns, these staged images are less helpful for photo sharing. The most popular shared images tend to be unplanned or spontaneous in appearance. Further, detailed, up-close photographs draw more interest than landscapes. Still, while landscape photos can be interchangeable, there are many aspects that are unique as details change throughout the day. Take advantage of this variety when creating photo content. The Library of Congress used Flickr to select historical photographs, increasing the reach of the library to many who would not visit the library website itself. These discussions resulted in the launch of Flickr Commons, where cultural heritage institutions can showcase and preserve photos online. Today dozens of historical and arts organizations from all over the world participate in this effort to "catalog the world's public photo archives."[55]

3. Use photos to demonstrate knowledge, involve users, not to sell. Photos can be used to demonstrate knowledge about a business or industry. For example, a person selling cars might post pictures from the most recent car show he or she attended.[56] As direct advertising is banned on some photo sharing sites, doing indirect promotion can be the most effective way to market a product. Talk about the product in image descriptions but avoid overt sales talk.[57] A link back to the company blog or website is subtle, but it is enough to draw interested viewers to the product. Getting users involved is critical, especially in such an interactive activity such as taking pictures. The success of platforms like Instagram, Pinterest, and Imgur show how brands as well as individuals can engage consumers through visual marketing,

4. Market the content. Posting photos, in itself, is no guarantee that the images will be seen. A significant component of sharing images is to market the content being posted. While some shared images will go viral and be spread widely with little effort by their creators, this experience is not the most common. Even popular, catchy images may take time to disseminate if they are not publicized well early on. To avoid such delay, employ social networking tools, both on the image sharing website and on external social networks. Social media platforms such as Facebook and Google+ with their photo and video sharing capabilities can be an important part of an image sharing strategy. Integrate with these platforms to help spread images to more viewers.

Another set of tools that can be used to help distribute online images is the internal search engines on photo sharing sites. Photo search engines direct users to images that interest them based on keywords. Most search engines rely on tags or descriptions to decide which photos to show when a person searches. To help more people find a photo, include highly detailed tags that facilitate photo searching. Mentally ask whether a customer would be able to easily find each image if he or she were looking for information.[58] What search terms might the individual employ? With this in mind, choose tags that are memorable, descriptive, and commonly used. The format of tags may vary depending on the photo sharing site. Flickr tags are space separated so that "salt lake city," for example, might become *saltlakecity* or *slc*.[59] When starting on a new platform, see what format and style popular offerings have chosen, and use that as a starting point for creating tags and descriptions.

5. Secure permissions. Not every photo post must be original content. Creating adaptations, parodies, or tributes to other artistic creations is common and even encouraged among many online audiences. However, when sharing repurposed images, it is important to keep legal issues in mind and to avoid taking material without permission or attribution. Some photo content is governed by extremely strict license agreements that limit third-party sharing. Seek out photos that use Creative Commons licensing, which is used by many Internet publishers. These licenses allow photo creators to retain rights to their images, even if the images are used commercially or otherwise shared. The details will depend on which photo sharing portal the images have been posted to, so do the research in advance to avoid legal problems later.

In addition to legal permissions, image sharing requires personal permission as well, especially if casual or unplanned photos are taken. Not everyone is comfortable seeing him- or herself posted online, especially if the person is caught in an awkward moment. Acquire permission from people in photos (especially customers or employees) before uploading or tagging them in images.[60] This permission is especially needed if the picture could cause harm or hurt feelings later on—for example, a picture of someone drinking or appearing overly familiar with someone other than a significant other. Online, the context of a picture is not always clear, so always check with the people featured in photos so that later they will not be unhappy or embarrassed.

Best Practices in Marketing through Photo Sharing

1. Determine your brand story and your target market and corresponding objectives and metrics. Do you wish to increase the number of posts, engagement, improve your audience size or rate of growth? Is your audience likely to be on Instagram, Facebook, Pinterest?

2. Benchmark against others in your brand category to see how they are using images. Make sure your approach is unique and resonates with your audience.

3. Optimize your content by not posting the same content the same way on every site. Realize that one platform may be important to your audience and gauge the analytics. Do your customers respond better to videos or short images? What time of day do they post and comment?

4. **Realize that the customer is the center of your efforts.** If all the photos are posted by the company or brand, the consumer will be less likely to be involved. The goal should be to get customers to share information themselves. If one customer shares images that are pertinent to your brand, other consumers will follow suit. If you put customer photos on your page customers will be more likely to promote your brand. One way to encourage sharing is to use contests and other means to encourage photo sharing. For example, if consumers can get some sort of prize or recognition, particularly based on the number of shares or "likes." In 2014, Starbucks sponsored a contest to redesign its cup on Instagram "#WhiteCupContest" and received over 4,000 applications.[61] Not only was there recognition for the winner, but the other participants felt challenged to increase their creativity.

5. **Don't just display products**; show products in context of how they are used. Instead of showing a coffee cup, show people enjoying coffee.

6. For sharing your own photos, **use images that express your brand's personality.** Don't just use images that are static but ones that evoke the brand.

7. **Use each major platform to its best advantage.** Instagrammers like to show off the latest trends, while Pinterest users often develop elaborate boards over time.

8. **Find and develop your brand influencers.** These individuals can help you tell your story and achieve your goals. Some simple searches around your brand or using a social media monitoring tool will help build relationships with these key brand advocates.

9. **Above all, measure and respond.** See which photos posted by both you and your customers generate the most interest to determine how consumers want to interact with your brand. Use hashtags, descriptive titles a help measure the popularity of specific content.

Notes

1. Corselli, Andrew (August 4, 2015), "Salesforce Announces Instagram Integration," Direct Marketing. Retrieved August 4, 2015, from http://www.dmnews.com/social-media/salesforce-announces-instagram-integration/article/430302/?utm_source=feedburner&utm_medium=feed&utm_campaign=Feed%3A+NewsDMNews+(DMNews+News)
2. "Over Half of Mobile Phone Users Globally Will Have Smartphones in 2018," eMarketer (December 11, 2014). Retrieved July 14, 2015, from http://www.emarketer.com/Article/2-Billion-Consumers-Worldwide-Smartphones-by-2016/1011694#sthash.RfoCW8aR.dpuf
3. Susan Murray (August 2008), "Digital Images, Photo-Sharing, and Our Shifting Notions of Everyday Aesthetics," *Journal of Visual Culture*, vol. 7, no. 2, pp. 147–163.
4. Thomason, Michael (January 5, 2015), "Which Types of Facebook Content Get More Shares and Comments?" Retrieved July 14, 2015, from http://simplymeasured.com/blog/which-types-of-facebook-content-get-more-shares-and-comments/#i.vw7q03hepcsktv
5. Barker, Donald I., Melissa S. Barker, and Catherine T. Pinard (2012), Unit D, *Internet Research—Illustrated*, 6th ed. (Boston, MA: Cengage Learning), p. 15.
6. "Explore/Creative License" (n.d.), Flickr from Yahoo! Retrieved July 16, 2011, from http://www.flickr.com/creativecommons/
7. "Monkey Selfie on Wikipedia Drives Photographer Bananas," NBC News (August 6, 2014). Retrieved August 2, 2015, from http://www.nbcnews.com/tech/internet/monkey-selfie-wikipedia-drives-photographer-bananas-n174251

8. Hawkins, Sara (November 22, 2013), "Copyright Fair Use and How it Works for Online Images," Social Media Examiner. Retrieved August 3, 2015, from http://www.socialmediaexaminer.com/copyright-fair-use-and-how-it-works-for-online-images/

9. "Webshots Celebrates 15 Years!," *Webshots Blog* (September 22, 2010). Retrieved July 16, 2011, from http://blog.webshots.com/?p=1376

10. Excite@Home's Webshots Ranked #1 Online Photo Destination, Excite@Home, Press Release (April 20, 2000). Retrieved September 16, 2011, from http://www.webshots.com/corporate/index.cgi?h=PRESS&t=press_release03.html

11. Arrington, Michael (August 3, 2009), "Photobucket Founders to Leave News Corp.," TechCrunch. Retrieved July 17, 2011, from http://techcrunch.com/2009/08/03/photobucket-founders-to-leave-news-corp/

12. Huang, Gregory T. (February 5, 2010), "It's Official: Ontela Bought Photobucket from News Corp," xconomy. Retrieved July 17, 2011, from http://www.xconomy.com/seattle/2010/02/05/it%E2%80%99s-official-ontela-bought-photobucket-from-news-corp/

13. Ibid.

14. Sheehy, Ryan (n.d.), "Photobucket," You are 1 in 7 billion. Retrieved July 17, 2011, from http://youare1in7billion.com/2011/04/05/photobucket/

15. Prescott, LeeAnn (June 21, 2006), "Hitwise US: PhotoBucket Leads Photo Sharing Sites; Flickr at #6," Hitwise. Retrieved July 17, 2011, from http://pic.photobucket.com/press/2006-06-HitwiseBlog.pdf

16. Schroeder, Stan (May 7, 2007), "Photobucket Gets MySpaced—Time to Switch to Flickr?" Mashable. Retrieved July 17, 2011, from http://mashable.com/2007/05/07/photobucket-myspaced/

17. Photobucket (n.d.), *Wikipedia*. Retrieved December 10, 2011, from http://en.wikipedia.org/wiki/Photobucket#cite_note-6

18. (n.d.). "Free Accounts," Photobucket. Retrieved October 10, 2015, from http://support.photobucket.com/hc/en-us/articles/200724044-Free-Accounts

19. Graham, Jefferson (February 27, 2007), "Flickr of Idea on a Gaming Project Led to Photo Website," *USA Today*. Retrieved July 17, 2011, from http://www.usatoday.com/tech/products/2006-02-27-flickr_x.htm

20. Ibid.

21. (n.d.). "Butterfield, Stewart and Fake, Caterina—Creators of Flickr, Career, Sidelights," *encyclopedia.jrank*. Retrieved July 17, 2011, from http://encyclopedia.jrank.org/articles/pages/3928/Butterfield-Stewart-and-Fake-Caterina.html

22. "Video for all + HD!" *Flickr Blog* (March 2, 2009). Retrieved July 17, 2011, from http://blog.flickr.net/en/2009/03/02/video-for-all-hd/

23. Butterfield, Stewart, and Caterina Fake (December 1, 2006), "How We Did It: Stewart Butterfield and Caterina Fake, Co-founders, Flickr," *Inc.* Retrieved July 17, 2011, from http://www.inc.com/magazine/20061201/hidi-butterfield-fake.html

24. Kopytoff, Verne B. (January 30, 2011), "At Flickr, Fending off Rumors and Facebook," *New York Times*. Retrieved July 17, 2011, from http://www.nytimes.com/2011/01/31/technology/31flickr.html?_r=1

25. Robinson, Gavin (June 19, 2008), "Flickr Founders Resign from Yahoo!" Geek. Retrieved July 17, 2011, from http://www.geek.com/articles/blurb/flickr-founders-resign-from-yahoo-20080619/

26. Pormit, Jack (May 20, 2011), "War of the Networking Sites Pt. 2: Flickr vs Photobucket," *Wordpress Blog*. Retrieved July 17, 2011, from http://jacopormit.wordpress.com/2011/05/20/war-of-the-networking-sites-pt-2-flickr-vs-photobucket/

27. (n.d.). "Flickr History," *Wikipedia*. Retrieved September 16, 2011, from http://en.wikipedia.org/wiki/Flickr#History

28. Sutter, John D. (September 20, 2010), "5 Billionth Photo Uploaded to Flickr," CNN. Retrieved July 16, 2011, from http://articles.cnn.com/2010-09-20/tech/flickr.5.billion_1_photo-sharing-site-flickr-facebook?_s=PM:TECH

29. (n.d.). "Number of Unique U.S. Visitors to Flickr from January 2012 to July 2015 (in Millions)," Statist. Retrieved October 11, 2015, from http://www.statista.com/statistics/252566/number-of-unique-us-visitors-to-flickrcom/

30. 6,000,000,000, Flickr Blog (August 4, 2011). Retrieved December 10, 2011, from http://blog.flickr.net/en/2011/08/04/6000000000/

31. Geoff (January 3, 2014), "The Compete History of Instagram," WERSM. Retrieved August 4. 2015, from http://wersm.com/the-complete-history-of-instagram/

32. Gibson, Rebecca (December 9, 2014), "The 14 Best Instagram Campaigns of 2014," Postano Blog. Retrieved August 4, 2015, from http://www.postano.com/blog/the-14-best-instagram-campaigns-of-2014

33. (n.d.). "Stats," Instagram Press Page. Retrieved October 11, 2015, from https://instagram.com/press/

34. "Instagram Mobile Ad Revenues to Reach $2.81 Billion Worldwide in 2017," eMarketer (July 27, 2015). Retrieved August 4, 2015, from http://www.emarketer.com/Article/Instagram-Mobile-Ad-Revenues-Reach-281-Billion-Worldwide-2017/1012774

35. "Applebee's Turns Its Instagram Over to Foodies for the Next Year," AdWeek (July 22, 2014). Retrieved August 4, 2015 from http://www.adweek.com/news/technology/applebee-s-turns-its-instagram-over-foodies-next-year-159048

36. Gibson, Rebecca (December 9, 2014), "The 14 Best Instagram Campaigns of 2014," Postano Blog. Retrieved August 4, 2015, from http://www.postano.com/blog/the-14-best-instagram-campaigns-of-2014

37. Cass, Jacob (n.d.), "Pinterest: What, Why, How and Who? + Tips & Pin Optimisation," Just™Creative. Retrieved October 11, 2015, from http://justcreative.com/2012/04/24/pinterest-guide/

38. Smith, Craig (October 8, 2015). "By the Numbers; 90+ Amazing Pinterest Statistics (September 2015)," DMR. Retrieved October 11, 2015, from http://expandedramblings.com/index.php/pinterest-stats/

39. Latifi, Sadia (January 21, 2015), "Reach men, the fastest-growing demographic on Pinterest," Pinterest for Business Blog. Retrieved October 11, 2015, from https://business.pinterest.com/en/blog/reach-men-fastest-growing-demographic-pinterest

40. Smith, Craig (October 8, 2015), "By the Numbers; 90+ Amazing Pinterest Statistics (September 2015)," DMR. Retrieved October 11, 2015, from http://expandedramblings.com/index.php/pinterest-stats/

41. Zimmerman, Sue (April 1, 2015), "Should You Go on Pinterest or Instagram for Your Business? 7 Facts to Consider," Agora Pulse. Retrieved October 10, 2015, from http://www.agorapulse.com/blog/pinterest-or-instagram-for-business

42. (n.d.). "Our Story," Imgur. Retrieved August 4, 2015, from http://imgur.com/about

43. Bertoni, Steve (March 25, 2015), "Can Imgur Turn Its 150 Million Users into a Booming Business?" Retrieved October 12, 2015, from http://www.forbes.com/sites/stevenbertoni/2015/03/25/can-imgur-turn-its-150-million-users-into-a-booming-business/

44. Sloan, Garett (August 3, 2015). "How Advertisers Are Getting on Board With Imgur, a Pinterest for the Millennial Male," AdWeek. Retrieved August 5, 2015, from http://www.adweek.com/news/technology/heres-how-advertisers-are-learning-market-imgurs-geeky-millennials-166201

45. Solis, Brian (2010), *Engage! The Complete Guide for Brands and Businesses to Build, Cultivate, and Measure Success in the New Web* (Hoboken, NJ: John Wiley), p. 63.

46. "Canon 'Photochains' Case Study," YouTube (June 22, 2010). Retrieved August 4, 2015, from https://www.youtube.com/watch?v=wS1dO8ydngE

47. (n.d.). "Use Photos as Part of Your Marketing Arsenal," Fun Careers. Retrieved July 17, 2011, from http://www.funcareers.com/work_at_home_articles/49/Use-Photos-as-Part-of-your-Marketing-Arsenal.html

48. Scott, David Meerman (2009), *The New Rules of Marketing & PR* (Hoboken, NJ: John Wiley), p. 185.

49. Borges, Bernie (2009), *Marketing 2.0* (Tucson, AZ: Wheatmark), p. 85.

50. Bard, Mirna (May 11, 2011), "Are Photo-Sharing Sites Overlooked?" *SmartBlog*, Social Media. Retrieved July 18, 2011, from http://smartblogs.com/socialmedia/2011/05/11/are-photo-sharing-sites-overlooked/

51. Crestodina, Andy (n.d.). "15 Blog Images: Best Practices for Adding Great Pictures to Every Post," Orbit Media Studios. Retrieved October 12, 2015, from http://www.orbitmedia.com/blog/blog-image-best-practices/

52. Ibid.

53. Golden, Michelle (2011), *Social Media Strategies for Professionals and Their Firms* (Hoboken, NJ: John Wiley), p. 307.

54. Safko, Lon, and David K. Brake (2009), *The Social Media Bible: Tactics, Tools & Strategies for Business Success* (Hoboken, NJ: John Wiley), p. 194.

55. (n.d.). "The Commons," Flickr. Retrieved October 12, 2015 from https://www.flickr.com/commons/institutions/

56. Gillin, Paul (2009), *Secrets of Social Media Marketing* (Irvine: CA: Quill Driver Books), p. 210.

57. Safko, Lon, and David K. Brake (2009), *The Social Media Bible: Tactics, Tools & Strategies for Business Success* (Hoboken, NJ: John Wiley), p. 198.

58. (n.d.). "How to Market on Photo Sharing Sites," Stepforth.com. Retrieved July 17, 2011, from http://www.stepforth.com/resources/web-marketing-knowledgebase/diysmm/smm9-photo-sharing-sites/

59. Weinberg, Tamar (2009), *The New Community Rules: Marketing on the Social Web* (Sebastopol, CA: O'Reilly Media), p. 271.

60. Golden, Michelle (2011), *Social Media Strategies for Professionals and Their Firms* (Hoboken, NJ: John Wiley), p. 292.

61. (n.d.). "Starbucks Announces the Winner of Its White Cup Contest," Starbucks. Retrieved October 12, 2015, from https://news.starbucks.com/news/starbucks-announces-the-winner-of-its-white-cup-contest

Discussion, News, Social Bookmarking, and Q&A Sites

Social conversation and sharing of information are basic elements of human discourse that have assumed even more importance in the digital age. Sites where users can discuss, become better informed, and catalog the information that most interests them are an important part of the social media scene and have growing importance to brand marketers.

This chapter will discuss social media networks as a source of information for users and as a means to organize information. Discussion boards, social news, social bookmarking, and question-and-answer (Q&A) sites provide opportunities for marketers to engage with consumers in a social marketing campaign. In the early days of social media, the different social sites served a specific purpose; however, as social media sites have evolved, many have integrated new trends into their existing platforms. For example, Facebook promotes the use of Pages, which serve essentially the same purpose as a discussion board, and also has incorporated a trending feature for social news. Rather than focusing on which social media sites fit within a specific category, this chapter will discuss the tools available to social media marketers and use currently available platforms as examples.

This chapter contributed by Janna Parker

- Describe how to market with Q&A sites
- Discuss the future of discussion boards, social news, social bookmarking, and Q&A sites

People can find a variety of ways to meet other like-minded people and to carry on discussions. There are a number of types of social media platforms whose primary role is to facilitate discussions. In this chapter we will cover discussion boards, social news sites, social bookmarking sites, and Q&A sites. Some types of discussion forums are in decline and others are gaining popularity. Major change is occurring in this space because many platforms, from Facebook and Twitter to brand sites to government sites, have discussion boards that cater to the specialized interests and needs of their users.

The Evolution of Online Discussions

One of the earliest types of social media is the discussion board. A discussion board is a service where participants can exchange messages with each other. Organization of these messages may vary or be customizable by the individual user. Often a sense of community develops around discussion boards, which have regular members that share common interests. This sense of community can motivate either online friendships or feuds, depending on the tone and topics being discussed.

A discussion board is typically organized into groups based on topics of interest. A discussion group is made up of forums, which frequently arrange posts and replies about a specific subject in an indented hierarchical fashion so that users can easily follow the flow of a conversation. The treelike structure of a forum is called a thread because it reveals the chronological order of posts and replies in a forum. A moderator monitors and facilitates forum discussions, enforcing discussion board policies and rules. If users engage in abusive exchanges, known as flaming, or post inappropriate material, the forum moderator acts as an arbitrator to settle disputes and remove disallowed content and an administrator handles technical details.

Many of the major portal sites, such as Google Groups, Yahoo! Groups, and Microsoft's Windows Live Groups, have discussion boards. Social media platforms such as LinkedIn have active discussion groups, but they usually require the user to join the site to search for groups and/or participate in them. LinkedIn now requires that a person be a member of a group to be able to participate in or even view a discussion thread. In addition, there are branded discussion boards, which are hosted by companies and nonprofits and which attempt to build online communities of brand enthusiasts and evangelists, facilitate customer support by answering user questions, and increase brand awareness. Government agencies also use discussion boards to answer questions and disseminate information. Specialized search services exist to help locate discussion groups, such as groups.google.com, groups.yahoo.com, and boardreader.com.[1]

Traditional discussion boards have declined in popularity over recent years. A popular discussion board for women iVillage was found in 1995 and by 2006 claimed 14.5 million unique visitors per month when NBCU bought iVillage for $600 million with the strategy of promoting the website on *The Today Show*. Unfortunately, for NBCU, many women started turning to other social media networks and iVillage is no longer in business.[2] The decline of discussion boards has received attention for several years. In an opinion column for *The New York Times*, Virginia Heffernan comments on the demise of iVillage and several other popular discussion boards. She also attributed the demise to the expansion of social media sites.[3] There are those who predict that discussion boards will see a revival in popularity. On socialmediatoday, Chris Abraham predicted that 2015 would be "The Year of Message Boards and Forums";[4] due to concerns over cyber-bullying and privacy, thus, using a message board allows an organization to own the content as opposed to being in a community on Facebook. It allows the owner to have more control with guidelines and moderators who can address problematic discussants.

A large scale revival of discussion boards would require a big shift in consumers' online habits and by the end of 2015, there was no indication that his prediction was correct.

Discussions on topics now take place in many different forms on the Internet. Facebook Groups allow any person (administrator) to create a group that is focused on a topic and serves as a discussion board or forum. The administrator can set the group as open to all on Facebook or closed, which requires either an invitation or approval to join from a member. In a secret group, all posts can only be viewed by members of the group and members must be added by the administrator. These groups have been created for causes, political groups, movie lovers, and so on. Another alternative form of discussion board is provided by Twitter. Twitter Chats are sponsored by an organization during a specific time period during which people use a hashtag to comment on topics or answer questions provided by the organizer. Hootsuite recommends that the chats be curated using a platform such as Storify for future reference. Hootsuite hosts a #HootChat on Thursdays at 1 p.m. EST.[5]

Within the realm of higher education, discussion boards are growing especially for classes that are online. Professors use discussion boards to simulate a classroom environment for students who can't meet due to geographic differences. Even classes set in a traditional setting are using discussion boards. This may be due to class size or content but regardless of the reason, professors have found that by using discussion boards they can require all students to engage in the conversation. Popular online learning management systems such as Blackboard have built in features that allow instructors to set up discussion boards. Some universities provide pedagogical instruction to professors who want to incorporate discussion boards into the classroom. Cornell University provides not only the resources but also recommendations for effective use of online discussion boards.[6]

Marketing with Social News and News Aggregation Sites

A social news site lets users submit links to news stories or other web pages to be ranked and displayed. Although every social news site permits users to submit content, sites differ in how they rank and display it. For example, Reddit and Newsvine organize content based on votes by readers, with the most popular articles appearing on the front page, while Slashdot and Fark use human editors to determine which articles show up on the front page.

Most social news sites also provide the means for readers to discuss and comment on articles. Several social news sites even let users vote on comments and then they rank and display the most popular comments first. As a consequence of user involvement in shaping the content of social news, these sites appear to be fundamentally altering the way news is consumed.[7] Today, instead of journalists or editors, readers are taking control of the news they view. News comes from many more sources than in the past, popularizing stories that traditional media outlets might not have deemed newsworthy. Since some social news sites let readers create custom views of the news or automatically personalize the news for them, users now have access to individualized news that features content relevant to that person. While social news sites share some characteristics, like any product or service, it is necessary to differentiate from the competition. While not an exhaustive list, the evolution of some of these social news sites will be discussed next with an emphasis on major changes.

Fark, which started in mid-1997 but which didn't become active until February 1999, targeted a more general audience with what is often a humorous view of the news.[8] According to founder Drew Curtis, "[t]he idea was to have the word Fark come

Site	eBizMBA Rank among All Sites	Number of Estimated Monthly Visitors
1. Facebook	3	900,000,000
2. Twitter	12	310,000,000
3. Pinterest	23	250,000,000
4. Google+	26	120,000,000
5. Tumblr	33	110,000,000
6. Reddit	105	110,000,000
7. StumbleUpon	300	28,000,000
8. Digg	1,278	6,000,000
9. MetaFilter	2,066	4,500,000
10. Newsvine	2,082	4,000,000
11. Folkd	2,093	3,000,000
12. Fark	3,106	2,500,000
13. Scoop.it	5,654	2,000,000
14. Slashdot	6,024	1,600,000
15. Delicious	6,113	1,500,000

Table 10.1 Top 15 Most Popular Social Bookmarking Websites | October 2015*

* The 15 Most Popular Social Bookmarking Sites as derived from the *eBizMBA Rank*, which is a continually updated average of each website's *Alexa* Global Traffic Rank and U.S. Traffic Rank from both Compete and *Quantcast*.

to symbolize news that is really Not News. Hence the slogan 'It's not news, it's Fark.' "[9] However, when major events occur, such as 9/11, the site's traffic spikes, and its discussion forums and news aggregation take the role of a more serious news outlet.[10] As shown in Table 10.1, Fark still numbers among the leading sites in the sector now generally referred to as social bookmarking instead of just news sites. In addition to the free site, Fark has launched two different forms of a subscription service. TotalFark has several additional benefits including content solely for subscribers and only these subscribers can vote. BareFark eliminates the sponsored ads for subscribers. The site now receives about 2.5 million visitors each month (Table 10.1).

Digg, which started in December 2004, was the first social news site to introduce voting on articles. The site lets users "digg" or "bury" articles, equivalent to voting up or down, respectively, causing the articles with the most Diggs to appear at the top. Burying an article does not decrease its popularity, but if an article accumulates enough buries, it will be automatically deleted.[11] Digg's pioneering interface helped it become the dominant social news site during the last half of the 2000s. As you can see from Table 10.1, it far exceeds the older Fark site in terms of estimated monthly visitors.

Longtime rival to Digg, Reddit, was launched in January 2005. The site styles itself as "the front page of the Internet."[12] Unlike Digg, the up- and down-votes of the community directly affect an article's ranking. An "upvote" increases an article's score, while a "downvote" decreases it. Top scoring articles appear on the front page of Reddit keeping it always fresh and interesting. Reddit was acquired by Condè Nast, owner of *Wired* and other magazines and websites, in October of 2006.[13] As shown in Table 10.1, Reddit is larger than both Fark and Digg as measured by estimated monthly visitors.

Reddit has faced some criticism for the rules regarding discussion boards and their content. The social news site allows users to create subreddits, which serve as discussion boards in the community. Over the years, there have been many criticisms of subreddits due to content that have included misogynistic or racist themes. In June 2015, CEO Ellen Pao announced that five subreddits had been deemed "hateful" and would be shut down. Reddit users did not respond well to what was considered a shutdown of free speech. This coincided with the firing of a popular Reddit employee, Victoria Taylor, who was responsible for overseeing several popular subreddits. Many subreddits went "dark" out of protest and the site went down significantly in the number of page views in less than a month.[14] By early July, Ellen Pao agreed to resign. In the technology world, some wondered if this would be Reddit's "Digg moment." The Digg moment occurred in 2010 after a major site redesign and policy changes caused a crash in site traffic from which it has never fully recovered.[15]

Reddit seems to have avoided major damage and in late 2015 responded by announcing the launch of a new website called Upvoted (Figure 10.1). The website features articles and videos that are based on popular Reddit posts curated by the website's staff reporters and further developed. Upvoted will also feature branded content as advertising similar to what can be found on BuzzFeed. Unlike Reddit, Upvoted readers will not be able to post content, vote, or make comments on any stories.[16] This departure from the voting system that has contributed to Reddit's success shows that social news is an ever evolving form of social media. It is too early to tell if Upvoted will be a success

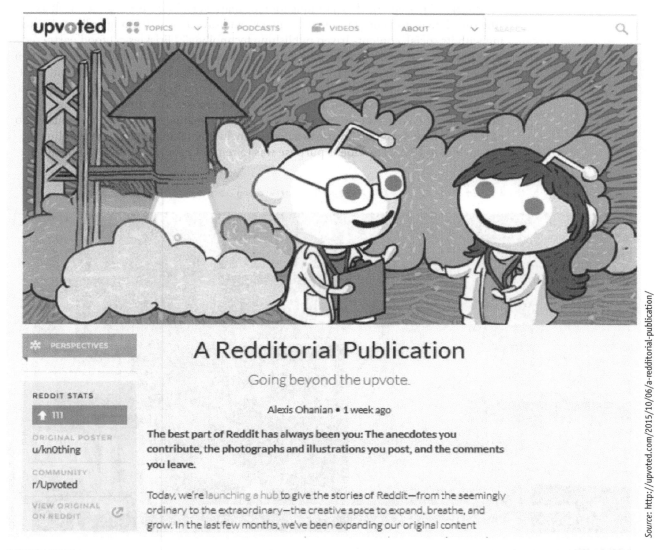

Figure 10.1 Reddit Announces New Publication Upvoted

for Reddit or if this is a misstep. The history of social news sites indicates that readers will turn elsewhere if format changes are not well received and Digg serves as a good example. Digg was purchased by Betaworks in 2012 and is no longer considered a social news site, rather, it is a news aggregator with an editorial staff that curates the news and readers no longer vote.[17] News aggregators have staff that look for news from a variety of sources around the web, whereas a social news site depends on news from readers or use software with proprietary algorithms for searching for and curating content.

As with other forms of social media, social news is constantly evolving and is being incorporated into sites not solely dedicated to one form of information. BuzzFeed and Upworthy are two websites that have a hybrid form of social news. Alexa.com lists both as viral marketing sites with BuzzFeed at number 1 with an estimated 150,000,000 unique visitors per month and a global traffic rank of 129.[18] BuzzFeed and Upworthy have incorporated some of the features from social news sites into their platforms. BuzzFeed, a news and entertainment site that originally only posted content created by its staff, has added a community section that allows registered users to submit content. Readers vote using yellow buttons with labels such as LOL and WTF or with gifs. Upworthy focuses solely on news that has a societal impact. Articles are located by Upworthy curators as well as submitted by readers but readers don't rank the stories.

BuzzFeed has emerged as a unique tool for marketers. The site describes itself as "the social news and entertainment company" and says it "is redefining online advertising with its social, content-driven publishing technology."[19] Friskies cat food partnered with BuzzFeed to create videos that features an older cat explaining life in the home to a new kitten in a series called "Dear Kitten." The videos have been very popular but what makes these videos so unique is that they are essentially a long commercial for Friskies. On BuzzFeed, the video authorship is attributed to Friskies as a "Brand Publisher."[20] BuzzFeed has even partnered with President Barack Obama to create a humorous video of the president engaging in various activities including taking selfies and doodling on paper (Figure 10.2). The video's purpose was to remind people that the deadline for

Source: https://www.whitehouse.gov/blog/2015/02/12/president-obama-selfie-stick-and-healthcaregov

Figure 10.2 The President Partners with BuzzFeed for Health Care Ad

enrolling in health insurance was approaching. The video was posted on BuzzFeed and was shown on television during the health care insurance sign-up period. It can be found within a press release on the WhiteHouse.gov site along with links that encourage the visitor to explore heath care options.

Perhaps the most powerful draw of marketing on social news sites is the incredible payoff to stories that become popular or end up on the front page.[21] Top stories may receive tens of thousands of views by a targeted, relevant audience. However, for every influential social news story, there are thousands that languish in obscurity with very few up-votes at all. Stories that remain on the bottom will receive little if any traffic. The feast-or-famine nature of social news can be either exhilarating or frustrating, so learning from the experience of others is essential to boost the chance of marketing success.

On social news sites, perhaps the most important determinant of an article's success or failure will be the title. Many hurried users will vote a story up or down based solely on the title and never view the attached content. Make the title appeal to short attention spans because those tend to dominate the space on social news sites. To see what sorts of titles have generated a response, look at items from the Top News or front page of a social news site. What attributes do those titles have? Emulate the form of other successful headlines to hopefully draw traffic to new offerings.

In addition to a catchy title, some sorts of content are favored more by social news readerships. In particular, lists are a popular format because they are easy on the eyes and quick to read. BuzzFeed is generally credited with inventing the "listicle." According to no less than the Oxford Dictionary a listicle is "a piece of writing or other content presented wholly or partly in the form of a list: *a recent BuzzFeed listicle called '21 Pictures That Will Restore Your Faith in Humanity' has attracted more than 13 million views.*"[22] So popular are lists that they have become recognized as short-form content by many types of publications and have even stimulated research at the prestigious Poynter Institute, a journalism research and training organization. One of their researchers studied 10,000 BuzzFeed posts and found that 29-item lists got the most readership. He pointed out that in spite of this, BuzzFeed sells 10-item lists to advertisers along with video posts and other ad formats. The researcher asked BuzzFeed Editor-in-Chief Ben Smith whether the site used this type of data when creating posts. He answered that BuzzFeed doesn't "engineer from a number" but instead tries to make posts exactly the right length for the content.[23]

In every case, whether a list or another format, content should be well spaced so that it can be skimmed easily and highlight the main points. Much like a successful blog or microblog post, social news content should be relevant, entertaining, and informative. These are the factors that may lead other members to up-vote a story.

Good content alone is not enough to reach the top of social news sites. The sheer volume of articles submitted is a barrier because the vast majority will never be seen. To increase an article's visibility, having a good relationship with a power user, who can influence many others to view a story, is a big help. The article volume makes networking with other members a top priority on social news sites. Vote up submissions by other users with similar interests, and they may return the favor. Without genuine participation, it is unlikely a marketer will achieve her or his goals from social news; users who only submit their own content are quickly identified as spammers and ignored.[24] Avoid this pitfall by supporting others' content frequently and building relationships with users to create a springboard for marketing messages.

Even if an article becomes popular and generates tens of thousands of visits to the website, not every one of those viewers will stay to look at the rest of the site or consider purchasing a product. Luckily, web traffic is only one potential benefit of social news as a marketing strategy. By providing space for discussion and comment by a wide reader base, social news can draw comments and input (much like a discussion board). It can also build an organization's thought leadership by contributing valuable content to the community.[25]

Many conversations occur on social news sites, regarding breaking news and hot products, which cannot be found anywhere else. Observing and engaging in these discussions can provide an edge to any business.

In addition to broadly popular general-purpose social news sites that have been discussed above, there are also platforms targeted toward narrower audiences. New niche social news sites are being developed constantly. With some research a social media marketer can find social news platforms that will be receptive to almost any product. A combined approach, which uses both the large, mainstream platforms as well as specialty social news sites, will have the best chance of reaching target audiences. As with the other social media websites, many social news sites have incorporated social advertising in their platforms. This offers marketers another opportunity to use targeted advertising as well as sponsored content. BuzzFeed has shown that it is possible for brands to create content that is technically advertising but still appeals to social media users.

Marketing with Social Bookmarking and S-Ecommerce

"Social bookmarking is a way for people to store, organize, search, and manage 'bookmarks' of web pages."[26] Most services allow users to organize their bookmarks using tags, which are simply single word descriptors that assist in categorizing the bookmarks. Users can search social bookmarking sites using the descriptor in order to find content and then can bookmark that content within their own accounts. Other terms for social bookmarking include folksonomy, collaborative tagging, social classification, social indexing, and social tagging;[27] however, social bookmarking is the term most commonly used by social marketers. A site called New Social Bookmarking Sites List contains a list of sites that accept external content according to the rules of each site. The entries are verified by the site and the list indicates whether they have pop-ups or they are sponsored sites. It also accepts new bookmarking sites.[28]

Many social media sites are dedicated solely to this purpose; however, as social media evolves, many other sites are incorporating the concept. You may have been surprised to see Facebook, Twitter, and Pinterest as numbers 1, 2, and 3 in Table 10.1, since they are not primarily social bookmarking sites. Their inclusion and high ranking is interesting since Facebook does allow users to see previous posts but it does not allow users to easily organize anything other than their own notes, photos, and videos. Twitter's favorite's feature also serves as a bookmark but also doesn't make it as easy to locate a specific favorite. As the number 3 company on the list, Pinterest is the website that more people associate as a social bookmarking site, although it represents bookmarking of photos, not of textual content. Pinterest has made bookmarking even simpler by providing an easy to install button for toolbars.

As social bookmarking has become more popular, various social media sites have attempted to find additional ways to monetize their traffic. Social commerce or s-ecommerce is a subset of ecommerce that incorporates selling within social networks.[29] Various forms of s-ecommerce have been tried since ecommerce started but have not been successful. In 2012, Facebook launched Gifts. People could send their friends a gift through the site. Problems with suppliers led Facebook to switch to gift cards only format but eventually Facebook shut down Gifts.[30] In June 2015, Pinterest introduced a limited number of buyable pins for specific retailers, which allow users to purchase products from pins without leaving the site.[31] The buying opportunities are indicated by the price printed in blue as shown in Figure 10.3a. By July Facebook was testing the addition of a buy button, simply the word Buy[32] as shown in Figure 10.3b.

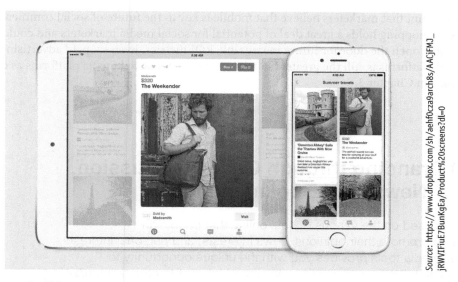

Source: https://www.dropbox.com/sh/aehf0cza9arch8s/AACjFMJ_jRWV1FiuE7BunKgEa/Product%20screens?dl=0

Figure 10.3a Pinterest Buy Screen

Source: https://www.facebook.com/business/news/Discover-and-Buy-Products-on-Facebook-Test

Figure 10.3b Facebook Buy Screen

In September Twitter began to test its own buy button, a blue Buy Now bar at the bottom of the Tweet screen.[33] Other platforms are expected to participate in the move toward social selling.

Notice two things about these developments. First, all three examples were of tests, not full-scale rollouts to all business users of Facebook, Twitter, and Pinterest. The intent was to ensure that all systems were working properly and could handle the expected volume of transactions before the social commerce opportunity was offered to a larger set of brands on each platform. Second, the emphasis was initially on mobile. That is a strong hint that marketers believe that mobile is key to the future of social commerce. Social shopping holds a great deal of potential for social media marketers and could possibly open the door for future measurable ROI metrics. Even so, paid advertising on social platforms is still the greatest source of revenue for social media platforms as discussed in Chapter 3.

Personal Branding through Online Discussion, News, and Bookmarking

This chapter has focused on the various outlets online that people and organizations use to promote their opinions, news interests, and personal interests. Using these social media tools provides you with the unique opportunity to present yourself as an influencer or expert in an area of interest to others. In order to effectively position yourself, you should be careful when engaging in social conversations. Additionally, remember that as you make your personal brand more visible online, you need to be careful not to tarnish your brand by careless posting.

Lesson #1: Engage in professional discussions related to your career interests. The social media industry has many discussion forums that allow people to discuss current trends in social media and digital marketing. Consistent participation in a Twitter Chat is a good way to engage in a current conversation with industry experts. A thoughtful tweet could be a great way to impress someone within the industry. LinkedIn groups have discussions on specific topics. Discussions are only available to members. Join a group and over time, you could possibly find that your carefully written comments could even lead to current opportunities.

Lesson #2: Be careful of participating in discussions on controversial topics. Many people are very passionate about their political or personal beliefs. When you see a post or Tweet on a controversial topic, think twice before engaging in the discussion. If you decide to participate, make sure to be respectful of others in the discussion. Remember that even if you go back and delete comments, nothing is completely erased from the Internet.

Lesson #3: Your username will be associated with your post and you can't control the comments of others. When uploading a story on a social news site think first about the content. Of course, there will always be those who write inflammatory comments, but some stories will be more likely to attract this type of user. Social issues and political viewpoints are very likely to lead to a hostile dialog among those commenting. Do you really want this type of discussion to be linked to your brand?

Lesson #4: Your bookmarks on your registered accounts are available for others to see. Bookmarking is a great way to save information for later. Bookmarking recipes, DIY ideas, and other interesting web pages is a great way to build a following. There is plenty of more "adult" type content available through bookmarking and avoid bookmarking this type of information. You will not be regarded as a professional if you link this type of information to your user name or account.

Lesson #5: Properly attribute the source of any content that you pin to your Pinterest or other bookmarking account. Always link back to the original.[1] An overview of U.S. copyright laws can be found on the website of Purdue University. Although it was written for their faculty and staff for educational purposes, their copyright tutorial is an excellent resource for anyone who is looking to use material created by others. Purdue University has an excellent resource for the layperson on copyright law.[2]

Lesson #6: Follow the rules of the bookmarking site. Know the rules of the sites that you are using. Pinterest will kick you off if you don't follow their rules. Copyright infringement, spamming, and pornographic posts are just some of the posts that can get you kicked off of Pinterest.[3] It is your responsibility to know the rules of the different sites that you use.

Lesson #7: Show your expertise by using content curation. Creating content is not the only way to demonstrate your expertise. Finding content written by others and reposting it with proper attribution is a good way to establish your reputation. You can re-post the content within your own post to start a discussion. Many social media strategists will send a tweet with a link to a relevant article and add a comment at the beginning of the post. Posting an article to LinkedIn along with a meaningful comment is a good way to show your professional connections that you are staying current with your field.

---

1. Lee, Kevin (March 2, 2015), "The 29 Most Common Social Media Mistakes: Which Ones Are Real? Which Ones Are Breakable?" Retrieved October 15, 2015, from https://blog.bufferapp.com/social-media-rules-etiquette
2. University Copyright Office (n.d.), "Copyright Basics," Purdue University. Retrieved on October 15, 2015, from https://www.lib.purdue.edu/uco/
3. (n.d.). "About Pinterest: Terms of Service," *Pinterest*. Retrieved on October 15, 2015, from https://about.pinterest.com/en/terms-service

Marketing with Q&A Sites

Q&A site lets people pose questions and receive answers back from anyone willing and (hopefully) knowledgeable enough to reply. Most Q&A sites can also provide fast answers by looking up questions that have already been asked; the other option is waiting to see if someone answers the query. While Q&A sites are primarily intended to deliver information, they can also be an avenue for SMM. However, Q&A sites are not an appropriate place to promote a product (unless, by some amazing coincidence, the marketed product happens to be the answer to someone's question). Instead, members of Q&A sites gain a reputation for providing detailed and useful answers.[34] This process can be a natural way to demonstrate thought leadership and build trust in a brand through the knowledge of its spokespeople.

Sharing information through Q&A sites builds an aura of expertise especially because many services provide points or rankings to members who provide the best answers (either decided by community vote or chosen by the question's asker). In order to build your reputation on Q&A sites, simply share answers in a thorough, detailed way. In addition to building a reputation, there are some tangible benefits as well. Q&A sites can help build links back to a personal profile or a product page, drawing more attention from the target audience. Beware, however, of many sites that offer to help build links through Q&A sites. These links may, at best, not be considered good quality by search engines and can harm the ranking of the site, not help it.

Some of the long-established sites in this space that are still active include Yahoo! Answers, Ask.com, and Answer.com. However, due to its distinct target market and format, the relatively young Q&A site Quora deserves mention. A combination of professional networking and an advice service, Quora presents unique opportunities for a social media marketer. Brands, however, cannot be directly involved on Quora. They might find a way to be indirectly involved as did President Obama, who in his continuing effort to promote health care insurance became a Verified Profile on Quora so he could answer health care questions there.[35]

Upon joining Quora, users are encouraged to follow areas and people of interest. The site is integrated with other social networking platforms such as Facebook and will suggest trends and contacts to follow based on prior connections. After following topics of interest, start observing what other users have posted. Members are encouraged to establish areas of expertise by answering questions and posting news. This practice makes Quora an excellent platform to get breaking information about specific industries.[36] Do not rush into asking questions immediately; first tap into the resources. Quora makes all of this as easy as possible by maintaining an active email program to inform users about trending issues in their areas of interest and, in general, to encourage them to participate. Providing valuable answers is the core of any successful Q&A site member's strategy, and Quora is no exception. By communicating about topics with expertise and insight, social media marketers can establish themselves as thought leaders online.

Sprout Social pointed out that "as of April 2013, 83 percent of the top 100 brands had at least one discussion thread dedicated to them on the Q&A site."[37] That makes Quora an excellent place for marketers to listen and perhaps to identify influencers or brand advocates. Be careful here, as on all sites, not to engage in overt self or brand promotion. Remember that Quora describes its mission as "The best answer to any question"[38] and conduct your participation accordingly.

Future of Discussion Boards, Social News, Social Bookmarking, and Q&A Sites

In their original form of stand-alone discussion sites, discussion boards are generally in decline. However, in a broader sense discussion boards have become a mainstay of many sites. For instance, online gamers love to discuss the gaming scene and their own play. Some companies have found discussion boards a great source of product innovation. Most online retail sites include discussion boards for posting consumer opinions and receiving company feedback for the benefit of their customers as well as for their own use.

Social news sites continue to gain ground over traditional news media outlets as new generations move from traditional news media to the Internet. In 2011 online news readership overtook newspapers for the first time[39] and for the most part that trend continues. Key findings from the Pew State of the News Media report for 2015 reflect a still-changing media scene both online and offline. These were the major points:

- Thirty-nine percent of digital news sites (which include the online properties of traditional media like CBS and the New York Times) get more of their traffic from mobile than from desktops. However, mobile users remain on the site longer.

- Traditional newspapers continue to struggle and cable news also showed a significant decline in prime-time viewership.

- Viewership is up for evening network news and for early evening and early morning local TV news.

- Downloads of podcasts were up a whopping 41%.

- Digital news ad revenue continues to grow but the traditional offline brands receive little of that revenue.[40]

As often happens Facebook and Twitter reflect these media trends. The proportion of their news that users get from these two sites is growing rapidly as shown in Figure 10.4. The fact that 63% of respondents got news from Twitter and Facebook is a surprise to many and a source of concern to some. It perhaps comes as no surprise, however, that many people keep up with so called breaking news on Twitter as it happens. This chapter has demonstrated that these two sites and others are moving aggressively to become major players in the social news and social bookmarking ecosystems.

For better or worse, news has not only become more digital but it has also become more personalized and social. As this chapter has pointed out, there are two basic types of digital news sites. One is driven by user contributions and user voting. Facebook and Reddit both provide examples of this type of news. The other type bears superficial resemblance to traditional news media in that employees who are professionals, usually either journalists or Internet experts, select the news to be published. It is not clear if one approach or the other will win out. Indeed, it is likely that both approaches will continue to thrive on various platforms. As of this writing, Twitter has a product called Moments in beta. It is "a feature that curates the day's trending topics and news items into slideshows of image and video tweets with the occasional text posting." According to the Twitter product manager, "It's a way to explore content on the platform and not feel like you have to commit to following these people."[41]

This chapter has shown that sites that help users catalog and keep track of content they care about are enjoying explosive growth. However, once again it is not

Facebook and twitter News Use is on the Rise

% of___users who get news there

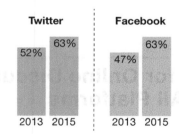

Twitter: 2013 52%, 2015 63%

Facebook: 2013 47%, 2015 63%

Of those who get news from___ in 2015, percent who have kept up with a news event as it was happening

Twitter 59%
Facebook 31%

Social Media and News Survey, March 13-15 & 20-22, 2015. Q2, Q4, Q7, Q11.

PEW RESEARCH CENTER

Source: http://www.journalism.org/2015/07/14/the-evolving-role-of-news-on-twitter-and-facebook/

Figure 10.4 Percent of Respondents Who Get News from Facebook and Twitter

the early bookmarking sites, which focused on individual productivity that are enjoying the growth. The growth is occurring on sites that allow users to share their favorite Internet content and to comment on it. That includes sites like Facebook and Pinterest as well as sites known for bookmarking like Reddit and Digg. Loren Baker, writing in Search Engine Journal says, "The positive effects of social bookmarking for publishers of news sites, blogs, and other web sites is outstanding. Social bookmarking can introduce sites to others with relevant tastes, drive traffic to your site, and [generate] valuable backlinks." He points out that the data produced by social bookmarking is valuable to search engines, and he encourages marketer activity on sites selected for their relevancy.[42] Also writing about SEO, Deepak Panwar says that bloggers should always submit their posts to well-regarded bookmarking sites. It increases their brand awareness, improves their search engine rankings, and leads to higher Google Page Rank and domain authority, a measure of the name's power.[43]

The original Q&A sites seem to have been undergoing traffic decreases in recent years. Whether newer sites like Quora can revive the Q&A sector is still an open question. Social media marketers must not forget, however, that whatever the platform used they must listen to customers' issues and respond to them. They can also use sites like the ones described in this chapter to develop a reputation for expertise that will lend credibility to the companies they represent. Whatever the type of site, there are a set of basic best practices for approaching online discussions.

One problem that social media marketers are trying to solve is how to track shares of content that fall within dark social. Any website traffic that can't be attributed to either a search engine or some other referral that includes a referrer tag is considered dark social.[44] When a person copies and pastes a link into a text, email, instant message, or even another app, the referral site tag is lost and the share isn't tracked. People have many reasons for doing this that may range from wanting to keep the share to just one person, not wanting that particular story associated with personal social media or just convenience. A study by RadiumOne found that 32% of people only share through dark social.[45] Focusing on analytics can create a sense that every visit must be tracked; however, social media marketers should sometimes just be grateful that the content is being shared and that traffic to the website is occurring. At this point in time, there are no known methods for stopping dark social and even if one is found, consumers with privacy concerns will always find ways to keep their sharing private.

Best Practices for Online Discussions on All Platforms

While all the types of communications forums discussed in this chapter are generally open and welcoming to newcomers, there are some basic guidelines that all participants are expected to follow. Sometimes known as "netiquette" (a contraction of Internet and etiquette), these largely unspoken rules define interactions in online communities. In some cases the rules are enforced by a forum moderator or administrator and in others the community is self-policing. For those not observing these guidelines, the response from discussion board veterans is likely to be both swift and harsh. While different forums have variations on these general rules, what follows are some commonly accepted pillars of discussion etiquette, no matter which of the types of forums you are using.

STICK TO THE TOPIC

Discussions, or threads, always have a title and general topic that is obvious from reading just a few posts. This focus is essential for people to quickly gather specific information. Avoid tangents, chit-chat, or diversions from the main topic because they inconvenience other users. For general comments or discussion, seek out forums in the "off topic" section.

SEARCH BEFORE POSTING

Some forums see frequent repeats of common questions or have dealt with an issue in depth before. Prior to asking the community for an answer, search the forum to see if the topic has already been discussed. Most discussion boards have extensive archives that can be mined for information. Asking questions that have been answered before makes the poster seem lazy or inexperienced.

USE GOOD GRAMMAR AND CAPITALIZATION

Many forum users will employ Internet shorthand, loose grammar, or generally poor writing in their posts. For a social media marketer, however, this practice can damage a professional image or reduce credibility of the information presented. While minor grammar errors are easily forgiven, they should not impact readability. Having solid grammar, good spacing, and proper punctuation all makes a post easier and more enjoyable to read. For a similar reason, do not use ALL CAPITALS when posting; it is interpreted as shouting by forum users and will generate negative responses.

NO FEEDING THE TROLLS

In online conversations, a troll is someone who attacks or personally insults another user, driving a thread off topic with negative comments. Similarly, "trolling" may refer to posting unsupported, controversial claims intended to anger others and provoke a response. It should go without saying that a good social media marketer never resorts to trolling in order to get a point across. It is also best to avoid interacting with other users who are acting like trolls. The most effective response is to ignore them and refuse to give them the attention they are seeking. Without a response or someone taking the bait, users who troll usually become bored in time and go away.

DO NOT POST REPETITIVELY (OR DOUBLE-POST)

If a question or comment does not receive a response on one thread, it is unwise to post it elsewhere. If both posts eventually generate comments, it splits the conversation and is inconvenient to view. Users find it annoying when someone litters a forum with comments that disrupt the flow of discussion. If a post has not generated immediate response, just wait. It is possible that no one is interested in responding at the time, and posting again will only aggravate those who were ambivalent to start with.

NO SOCK PUPPETS

According to *The New York Times*, a sock puppet is "the act of creating a fake online identity to praise, defend or create the illusion of support for one's self, allies or company."[46] Several large companies have attempted this tactic and have been caught. For savvy forum users, it is fairly easy to spot sock puppets or other fake accounts. It is better to endure some negative comments than destroy a brand's credibility online by creating fake accounts. Platforms are also taking more notice, as when Reddit shut down some domains or Quora set up verified profiles.

None of these guidelines is groundbreaking, and many will likely seem obvious to the reader. Most online etiquette issues can be resolved with some common sense and by reading the rules of the discussion board before posting messages. With focus on relevant sites and content and with due respect for best practices of online conversations, marketers can make this platform a useful part of their digital media strategies.

Notes

1. Barker, Donald I., Melissa S. Barker, and Catherine T. Pinard (2013), Unit D, *Internet Research—Illustrated*, 6th ed. (Boston, MA: Cengage Learning), p. 8.
2. Moses, Lucia (October 31, 2014), "How One-Time Dot.Com Darling iVillage Fell to Earth," Digiday. Retrieved on October 6, 2015, from http://digiday.com/publishers/ivillage/
3. Heffernan, Virginia (July 10, 2011), "The Old Internet Neighborhoods," *The New York Times*. Retrieved on October 6, 2015, from http://opinionator.blogs.nytimes.com/2011/07/10/remembrance-of-message-boards-past/?_r=0
4. Abraham, Chris (January 7, 2015), "2015: The Year of Message Boards and Forums," Social Media Today. Retrieved on October 6, 2015, from http://www.socialmediatoday.com/content/2015-year-message-boards-and-forums
5. Deidrichs, Matt (May 2015), "Everything You Need to Know to Set Up Your First Twitter Chat," HootSuite Blog. Retrieved on October 6, 2015, from http://blog.hootsuite.com/a-step-by-step-guide-to-twitter-chats/
6. (n.d.). "Online Discussions," Cornell University Center for Teaching Excellence. Retrieved October 6, 2015, from http://www.cte.cornell.edu/teaching-ideas/teaching-with-technology/online-discussions.html
7. Baekdal, Thomas (June 1, 2009), "What the Heck Is Social News?" Baekdal. Retrieved July 20, 2011, from http://www.baekdal.com/media/social-news-explained
8. (n.d.). "Fark Frequently Asked Questions (FAQ): Random Stuff," Fark. Retrieved July 20, 2011, from http://www.fark.com/farq/misc/
9. (n.d.). "About Fark," Fark. Retrieved on October 13, 2015, from http://www.fark.com/farq/about/#What_is_Fark.3F
10. McBride, Kelly (June 22, 2009), "Archived Chat: Frat House Meets Debate Club When It's News and It's Fark," Poynter Institute for Media Studies. Retrieved July 20, 2011, from http://www.poynter.org/latest-news/everyday-ethics/96384/archived-chat-frat-house-meets-debate-club-when-its-news-and-its-fark/
11. Spiliotopoulos, Tasos (n.d.). "Votes and Comments in Recommender Systems: The Case of Digg," Madeira Interactive Technologies Institute, University of Madeira. Retrieved July 20, 2011, from http://hci.uma.pt/courses/socialweb/projects/2009.digg.paper.pdf
12. (n.d.). "We Power Awesome Communities," Reddit. Retrieved October 16, 2015, from https://www.reddit.com/about/
13. (n.d.). "Reddit," CrunchBase. Retrieved July 20, 2011, from http://www.crunchbase.com/company/reddit
14. Poletti, Therese, (July 8, 2015), "Is Ellen Pao Snafu Beginning of Reddit's end?" *New York Post*, Retrieved on October 10, 2015, from http://nypost.com/2015/07/08/is-ellen-pao-snafu-beginning-of-reddits-end/
15. Francis, Nathan (July 3, 2015), "Will Reddit Have Its 'Digg Moment' after Firing Popular IAMA Employee Victoria Taylor?" *Inquisitor*. Retrieved on October 10, 2015, from http://www.inquisitr.com/2221512/will-reddit-have-its-digg-moment-after-firing-popular-iama-employee-victoria-taylor/
16. Greenberg, Julia (October 5, 2015), "No Comments Allowed on Reddit's New News Site Upvoted," *Wired*. Retrieved on October 10, 2015, from http://money.cnn.com/2015/10/06/technology/reddit-new-site-upvoted/
17. Kelly, Samantha Murphy (July 20, 2012), "Digg Is Being Rebuilt from Scratch and Needs Your Help," *Mashable*. Retrieved October 13, 2015, from http://mashable.com/2012/07/20/digg-rebuild/#_TOCjHoDTEql
18. "Top 15 Most Popular Viral Sites, October 2015," eBizMBA.com (October 2015). Retrieved October 10, 2015, from http://www.ebizmba.com/articles/viral-sites

19. (n.d.). "About," BuzzFeed. Retrieved October 18, 2015, from http://www.buzzfeed.com/about

20. BuzzFeed, "Dear Kitten: Regarding Friendship" (August 7, 2015). Retrieved October 13, 2015, from http://www.buzzfeed.com/friskies/dearkittenregardingfriendship#.rdVMPNMnE

21. Halligan, Brian, and Shah, Dharmesh (2010), *Inbound Marketing: Get Found Using Google, Social Media, and Blogs* (Hoboken, NJ: John Wiley), p. 110.

22. (n.d.). "listicle," Oxford Dictionaries. Retrieved October 16, 2015, from http://www.oxforddictionaries.com/us/definition/american_english/listicle

23. Beaujon, Andrew (July 1, 2014), "Why 29 Is the Best Number for BuzzFeed listicles," Poynter Online. Retrieved October 16, 2015, from http://www.poynter.org/news/mediawire/257470/why-29-is-the-best-number-for-buzzfeed-listicles/

24. Garrett, Chris (2010), "Using Social Bookmarketing to Improve Your Traffic, Links, and Visibility," in Mitch Meyerson, ed., *Success Secrets of the Social Media Marketing Superstars* (Irvine, CA: Entrepreneur Media), p. 266.

25. Go, Gregory (n.d.), "Six Reasons Why You Should Care about Social News," About.com. Retrieved July 18, 2011, from http://onlinebusiness.about.com/od/onlinecommunities/a/whysocialnews.htm

26. (n.d.). "Social Bookmarking—What Is It and How Can I Use It for My Site?" *Network Solutions.* Retrieved on October 13, 2015, from http://www.networksolutions.com/support/social-bookmarking-what-is-it-and-how-can-it-help-promote-my-site/

27. Ibid.

28. (n.d.). "New Social Bookmarking Sites List 2015," New Social Bookmarking Sites List. Retrieved October 17, 2015, from http://new-social-bookmarking-list.com/

29. Cohen, Heidi, (November 2, 2011), "What Is Social Commerce?" *Heidi Cohen: Actionable Marketing Guide.* Retrieved on October 13, 2015, from http://heidicohen.com/what-is-social-commerc/

30. Holmes, Ryan (August 2015), "For Impulse Shoppers, a Brave New World on Social Media," *HootSuite.* Retrieved on October 13, 2015, from http://blog.hootsuite.com/?s=social+shopping&lang=en

31. (n.d.). "Buyable Pins," Pinterest. Retrieved October 19, 2015, from https://business.pinterest.com/en/buyable-pins

32. Constine, Josh (June 10, 2015), "Facebook Challenges Pinterest with News Feed Buy Button for Shopify Merchants," TechCrunch. Retrieved October 19, 2015, from http://techcrunch.com/2015/06/10/never-leave/

33. Jain, Tarun (September 8, 2015), "Testing a Way for You to Make Purchases on Twitter," Twitter Blog. Retrieved October 19, 2015, from https://blog.twitter.com/2014/testing-a-way-for-you-to-make-purchases-on-twitter

34. Weinberg, Tamar (2009), *The New Community Rules: Marketing on the Social Web* (Sebastopol, CA: O'Reilly Media), p. 189.

35. Beese, Jennifer (March 25, 2014), "Quora Just Got Better for Brands, Here Are Some Getting-Started Tips," Sprout Social. Retrieved October 19, 2015, from http://sproutsocial.com/insights/quora-just-got-better-brands-getting-started-tips/

36. Sundar, Mario (n.d.), "How Can You Use Quora Professionally?" Quora. Retrieved July 18, 2011, from http://www.quora.com/How-can-you-use-Quora-professionally

37. Beese, Jennifer (March 25, 2014), "Quora Just Got Better for Brands, Here Are Some Getting-Started Tips," Sprout Social. Retrieved October 19, 2015, from http://sproutsocial.com/insights/quora-just-got-better-brands-getting-started-tips/

38. (n.d.). Quora. Retrieved October 19, 2015, from https://www.quora.com/

39. Choney, Suzanne (March 14, 2011), "Online News Readership Overtakes Newspapers," Technolog, MSNBC. Retrieved July 20, 2011, from http://technolog.msnbc.msn.com/_news/2011/03/14/6267015-online-news-readership-overtakes-newspapers

40. Barthel, Michael (April 29, 2015), "5 Key Takeaways from State of the News Media 2015," Pew Research Center. Retrieved October 16, 2015, from http://www.pewresearch.org/fact-tank/2015/04/29/5-key-btakeaways-from-state-of-the-news-media-2015/

41. Baldwin, Roberto (October 6, 2015), "Twitter's Curated Moments Slows Down the Newsfeed for New Users," Engadget. Retrieved October 16, 2015, from http://www.engadget.com/2015/10/06/twitter-moments/

42. Baker, Loren (December 6, 2007), "50+ Social Bookmarking Sites: Importance of User Generated Tags, Votes and Links," Search Engine Journal. Retrieved October 16, 2015, from

http://www.searchenginejournal.com/50-social-bookmarking-sites-importance-of-user
-generated-tags-votes-and-links/6066/

43. Panwar, Deepak (August 31, 2015), "Top 65 High PageRank Social Bookmarking Sites List,"
SEO Tricks. Retrieved October 19, 2015, from http://www.wpseotricks.com/top-pagerank
-social-bookmarking-sites-list/

44. Sorokina, Olsy (December 6, 2014). "Everything You Need to Know about Dark Social,"
Hootsuite. Retrieved October 20, 2015, from http://blog.hootsuite.com/everything-you-need
-to-know-dark-social/

45. Ibid.

46. Stone, Brad (July 16, 2007), "The Hand That Controls the Sock Puppet Could Get Slapped,"
New York Times. Retrieved July 19, 2011, from http://www.nytimes.com/2007/07/16
/technology/16blog.html?ex=1342238400&en=9a3424961f9d2163&ei=5088&partner=rssnyt&
emc=rss

11

Content Marketing: Publishing Articles, White Papers, and E-Books

This chapter will discuss several *conventional* publishing methods, which have been adapted and expanded for online distribution and SMM. Articles, books, and white papers all existed long before the Internet. However, as technology has advanced, the reach and application of these media has broadened substantially. In the context of content marketing, these types of publications can be the basis for a strong program. Articles, books, and white papers can represent the "long-form" version of the company's brand story. From a long article, the company can *repurpose* the content across various "short forms" of social media.

Blog posts, Twitter campaigns, and LinkedIn updates all represent the various social channels across which this derivative content may be disseminated. These types of shorter form of content often start with a solid article or white paper. A best practice is to then distribute content in different forms depending on the objectives. Content distributed at the appropriate time can encourage purchase or facilitate other SMM objectives, such as customer retention.

One example of this approach to content distribution comes from Kristin Jones from Jones PR, a public relations firm that takes a content marketing approach. Ms. Jones practices what she preaches by using longer form content like white papers along with blog posts and video marketing. Jones's version of the marketing sales funnel as shown in Figure 11.1 focuses on both long-form and short-form content discussed in this book and

After completing this chapter, students will be able to:

- Describe the sales funnel and its role in content marketing
- Detail the major article directories and the benefits of article marketing
- Explain how to create a well-written article to be disseminated online

(Continued)

- Describe the role of e-books in content marketing
- Explain how to use the content sharing capabilities of LinkedIn for personal branding
- Identify some of the key issues in marketing with articles, white papers, and e-books
- Detail best practices in marketing with articles, white papers, and e-books

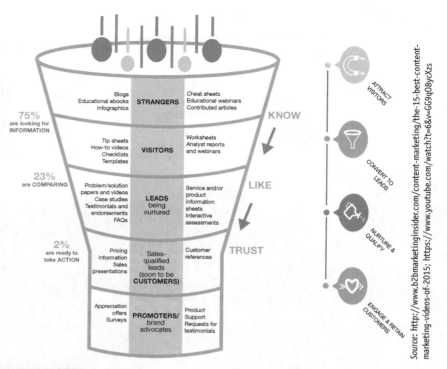

75% are looking for INFORMATION

23% are COMPARING

2% are ready to take ACTION

STRANGERS
Blogs
Educational ebooks
Infographics
Cheat sheets
Educational webinars
Contributed articles
KNOW

VISITORS
Tip sheets
How-to videos
Checklists
Templates
Worksheets
Analyst reports
and webinars

LEADS being nurtured
Problem/solution papers and videos
Case studies
Testimonials and endorsements
FAQs
Service and/or product information sheets
Interactive assessments
LIKE

Sales-qualified leads (soon to be CUSTOMERS)
Pricing information
Sales presentations
Customer references
TRUST

PROMOTERS/ brand advocates
Appreciation offers
Surveys
Product Support
Requests for testimonials

ATTRACT VISITORS
CONVERT TO LEADS
NURTURE & QUALIFY
ENGAGE & RETAIN CUSTOMERS

Source: http://www.b2bmarketinginsider.com/content-marketing/the-15-best-content-marketing-videos-of-2015; https://www.youtube.com/watch?t=6&v=GG9q08ycXzs

Figure 11.1 The Sales Funnel and Appropriate Types of Content for the Stages

includes a sound track from attraction, conversion, nurturing to engagement. Different types of content are encouraged depending on the stage of the funnel and the desired objectives. The concept is to provide appropriate content when the customer is looking for information versus when the objective is product comparison or post-purchase support. Whereas short articles and blogs might be interesting to complete strangers to a firm's offerings, those customers who are qualified as solid leads would be more likely to respond to the in-depth information of a white paper or even an e-book. This chapter will discuss how to create and disseminate these more in-depth forms of content.

Publishing and Distributing Articles

One type of in-depth content, long-form articles, can be listed in an article directory. An article directory is a website where users submit original articles for approval and syndication (free distribution to other websites with proper attribution).[1] The articles are organized into categories, such as technology, business, and health, so that they can be more easily found by readers and website owners for dissemination. See Table 11.1 for a list of the largest article directories and their Google Page Rank and Alexa Global Traffic Rank.

An article submission generally runs 400 to 500 words in length with a 2–3% keyword density (the percentage of times a word appears in an article).[2] A directory article also tends to have a highly descriptive title. Article brevity, appropriate keyword density, and careful titling are done to optimize the chances the piece will be ranked at the top of search engine results. However, directory articles lack the copyediting and editorial oversight of professional publications, such as magazines or newspapers.

Article Directory	Alexa Global Traffic Rank (TR)	Google Page Rank (PR)	No Follow (NF)
1. ehow.com	843	7	NF!
2. hubpages.com	1,184	6	
3. seekingalpha.com	1,380	7	NF!
4. examiner.com	1,767	8	NF!
5. ezinearticles.com	2,609	6	
6. apsense.com/article/start	4,839	4	
7. articlesbase.com	7,628	6	NF!
8. biggerpockets.com/articles	8,291	4	NF!
9. goarticles.com	9,209	2	
10. buzzle.com	9,919	6	

Table 11.1 Ten Largest Article Directories

Source: http://www.vretoolbar.com/articles/directories.php

These directories are typically meant to not only inform but also to promote an author, business, brand, website, or issue.

Although less important because of other forms of content today, the creation of articles that state a business' point of view, develop a case study, or otherwise highlight the firm's capabilities can be important sources of information. The first step in article-based marketing is to produce article content that the target audience will be interested in reading. Shirley Slick, a dedicated, experienced math educator, falls into this category of someone who produces in-depth articles. Slick uses EzineArticles to raise awareness about the problems with the way math is being taught in the United States along with suggesting possible solutions to the problem. Since 2010, she has become a Diamond Level Expert Author with 241 articles to her credit and has gained a worldwide following. She has become an expert by creating article content that is detailed and meaningful to her audience.

In many ways the requirements for strong article content are very similar to those for blogs, as discussed in Chapter 5. Most of the advice found there will apply just as much when writing an article as a blog. Indeed, some blog posts can be adapted and transformed into articles with very little modification. What really distinguishes an article from a blog is the length of the piece and the depth of content. A good article can range in length from several hundred to several thousand words, depending on the topic and the target audience. Blog post readership tends to fade after 1,500 to 1,700 words, whereas articles can often be 5,000 to 10,000 words in length. While readers may be forgiving of a typo, offhand reference, or colloquialism in a blog, the expectations for an article are higher. As an article takes time and forethought, readers will typically expect more research, fact checking, and polish than they do from blogs.

The power of article marketing comes from the many easy syndication services that exist to share online articles. A few of the more popular article directories are listed in Table 11.1. Many of the article websites have dramatically decreased in terms of their Alexa global traffic rank in recent years as other forms of content marketing have emerged and evolved. Still, a well-written and topical article appearing on one (or more) of these sites can garner a significant viewership.

Note the "No Follow" (NF) column, which identifies the article directories that prevent search engines from following article links. Marketers are among the heaviest contributors to article directories, and a site that automatically inserts the no-follow attribute in article links defeats the objective of gaining a higher placement in search engine ranking because it blocks search engines from associating articles with that site. Hence, most marketers favor article directories without the no-follow requirement; however, some are willing to submit articles to NF directories to improve awareness and establish their authority on highly-trafficked sites.

There are other rewards to be had from writing online articles. Some article directories offer "Expert" or "Frequent Contributor" status to their best authors and feature these writers' works more prominently. Much like print, where authors can develop a following for their work, online article directories make further writings available to readers interested in a particular author. However, Google's search engine appears to provide no real ranking benefit in organic search for distributing articles because many of these articles have become rampant with "spammy" content. For search engine optimization purposes, write the article and post it on a blog or the company website.[4]

One of the most important steps to creating successful article content is to choose a good title. As most viewers will see the title first and have to decide from that whether to read the rest of the article, creating an appealing title can make or break an article's distribution success. To draw in readers, the title should be concise and descriptive, as well as give a solid idea about the topic. To generate interest, the title should bring to mind a question that the reader wants to have answered. This need creates an incentive to view the content. If the title is boring or does not bring to mind any interesting questions, it is unlikely that readers will take the time to view the article.

Above all, the article itself should deliver on the promise made by the title. It is important to adequately address the question or issue being discussed. Attempting to trick readers with a title that does not match the article body is a sure way to disappoint, frustrate, or annoy the viewer. Finally, some article directories have specific guidelines that titles must meet for publication; for example, capitalizing the first letter of every word or avoiding certain forms of punctuation.[4] Follow these rules to avoid unnecessary complications on the path to publication, and produce articles that people will be willing and able to read.

Creating White Papers and E-Books

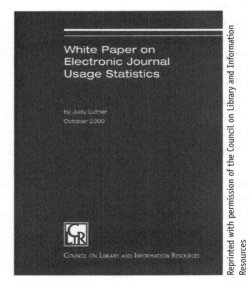

Reprinted with permission of the Council on Library and Information Resources

Figure 11.2 **Example of a White Paper**

A more popular form of content marketing is the white paper. The term *white paper* is derived from *white book*, an official publication by a national government.[6] In public policy, white papers are delivered to policy makers to inform them on important issues. Businesses eventually began to adopt the term, referring to informative documents for important clients as white papers. In this context a "good white paper is written for a business audience, defines a problem, and offers a solution, but it does not pitch a particular product or company."[7] Marketing messages in a white paper should be as subtle as possible, if they appear at all. According to Michael Knowles, a white paper "is a technical document that describes how a technology or product solves a particular problem. It's a marketing document and a technical document, yet it doesn't go too far in either direction"[8] (see Figure 11.2 for an example). Most white papers are sponsored by particular companies to help market their products. In digital marketing, the email marketing firm Exact Target and the outbound marketing firm Marketo make extensive use of white papers to market their brands along with many other companies like Adobe and BrightEdge, which are included on this list of top-performing white papers of 2014.[9]

Table 11.2 Top White Papers in the Digital Marketing Depot in 2014

What will be an effective white paper is defined mostly by its audience's expectations. A white paper is expected to have at least six pages of text and to provide useful information about a business or technical issue. A white paper should contain sources, facts, and figures.[10] Further, white papers are typically intended for the reader to review before making a purchase, in which case they may be referred to as technical support documents. For example, Table 11.2 illustrates the top white papers in the Digital Marketing Depot for 2014. These topics include some original content but are mostly the product of companies seeking to sell their products by demonstrating competence in a particular area. Online distribution, which avoids warehousing and printing costs, has made white papers both easier to access and more popular for businesses and not for profits, so we will continue to see the form grow in popularity.[11]

Another growing form of content distribution is the e-book (which stands for electronic book and is also sometimes called a digital book, ebook, or eBook) is defined by the Oxford English Dictionary as "an electronic version of a printed book that can be read on a computer or handheld device designed specifically for this purpose."[12] While precise, this definition does not add much for a social media practitioner. For the purposes of SMM, David Meerman Scott "define[s] an e-book as a PDF-formatted document that identifies a market problem and supplies an answer to the problem. . . . Well executed e-books have lots of white space, interesting graphics and images, and copy that is typically written in a lighter style than the denser white paper."[13] However, both e-books and white papers require strong written communication skills, content, and great presentation to be implemented successfully.

While the growth for e-books in the general marketplace has slowed, the market for self-produced e-books for promotional purposes appears to be growing and may be about 30% of all e-books. The Content Marketing Institute itself produces e-books that other firms can use to guide their content marketing strategy.[14]

Personal Branding through Content Marketing on LinkedIn for Students

While it is not likely that students will market themselves through the creation of white papers, articles, and e-books, it is likely that students will want to take advantage of the content marketing capabilities of LinkedIn. Previously, we have discussed the importance of creating a profile on LinkedIn and creating a network of contacts. Contacts on LinkedIn will want to know who you are and what you do and will expect you to post not only the content that others have created, but also some of your own. LinkedIn has made it easier to create such content in recent years.

Lesson # 1. Create content for your audience. LinkedIn has made it easier to create and publish short articles by allowing anyone to create a blog and publish the content to followers. While there are special rules to being designated a LinkedIn Influencer, someone who has deep knowledge of a particular subject, anyone can create and publish blog posts. The posts should follow the rules of good blogging and include visuals and make use of subheadings. Once completed, these pieces can be immediately shared with your contacts. As with other blogs, make sure you pay attention to comments and respond accordingly. These posts can help you toward a goal of sharing at least some portion of your content as original content.

Lesson # 2. Use photos and videos. It is possible also to add photos, videos, and presentations to your profile to showcase work you have done. LinkedIn now owns SlideShare and it is easy to put a SlideShare presentation on a LinkedIn profile with a click of a button. Students may think they don't have anything to share in terms of original content but student presentations can be relevant to business professionals. A presentation about a company's social media strategy, a critique of a website or mobile app design, and a number of other topics might be of interest to your LinkedIn connections. Adding a video or SlideShare will increase the number of profile views, which will tell LinkedIn you are influential to your network. This content will also attract others to you and help you form valuable connections in your field.

Lesson #3. Monitor the work of your network. LinkedIn has also purchased Newsle, a site which allows the user to create electronic newsletters based on network connections. By monitoring content of those in your network more closely, you can understand what is important to them and tailor the content you create accordingly. LinkedIn Pulse provides a daily view of news based on your connections and also suggests other relevant content. Both tools can be used to monitor content from your network, influencers, and other sources to best determine how to position your personal brand. These applications are also a great way to keep current in a chosen field.[1,2,3]

---

[1] Etherington, Darrell (June 14, 2014). "LinkedIn Acquires Newsle to Deliver More Relevant News about Your Connections," TechCrunch. Retrieved October 14, 2014, from http://techcrunch.com/2014/07/14/linkedin-acquires-newsle-to-deliver-more-relevant-news-about-your-connections/

[2] Roslansky, Ryan (June 14, 2014). "Stay in the Know on Your Network: Newsle Joins the LinkedIn Family," LinkedIn. Retrieved October 14, 2015, from http://blog.linkedin.com/2014/07/14/newsle-joins-the-linkedin-family/

[3] Kothari, Akshay (June 17, 2015). "Introducing the New LinkedIn Pulse: Your Daily News, Powered By Your Professional World." LinkedIn. Retrieved October 1, 2015, from http://blog.linkedin.com/2015/06/17/introducing-the-new-linkedin-pulse-your-daily-news-powered-by-your-professional-world/

Lesson #4. Curate Content for Your Network. Now that you are monitoring the work in your field, you can engage in "content curation" for your network. Quite simply, content curation means taking content that already exists and organizing it for your audience. For example, you could write a blog post on content curation practices referring to the work of leaders in the field. You can also ask influencers in the field to contribute to your content or ask your audience for feedback and then report back on what they said. There are many ways to take original content and make it your own to create value for your audience. This approach saves time and avoids the appearance of constant self-promotion.[4]

Lesson #5. Plan and schedule. It will be easier to create and share content if you have specific goals, like one blog post and one SlideShare presentation or video per month. Not having a plan will make it more difficult to create a loyal following. Try to set goals that are reasonable and can be achieved each month. It is useful to set aside a specific time each week for blogging or creating content. Using a social media management and monitoring tool like Hootsuite allows you to send curated and original content to all your networks on a periodic basis.

These acquisitions by LinkedIn clearly signal that creating content will be valued in how your profile is categorized and served to others during searches. It is important to create content to stay ahead of the pack. Besides, content is a great way to create a personal brand on any social media network.

---

[4] Cohen, Heidi (December 8, 2014). "How To Curate Content Like A Pro: 8 Lessons (Examples Included)," Content Marketing Institute. Retrieved October 1, 2015, from http://contentmarketinginstitute.com/2014/12/how-to-curate-content/

Marketing with Articles, E-Books, and White Papers

In most cases, the ultimate goal for article, white paper, or e-book marketing will be the same: draw attention and develop a company's reputation for thought leadership and then use that expertise to generate sales. In order for this strategy to be successful, however, the audience must not perceive the content to be overt marketing material. Keeping a distinction between overt and covert goals is crucial to marketing with this type of content..

One example of an organization that uses long-form and in-depth content in its marketing strategy is the Soroptimist International of the Americas (SIA). In 19 countries and territories, SIA works to improve the lives of women and girls. SIA club members strive to accomplish this goal by participating in a wide variety of programs and local projects that involve education, employment, healthcare, disaster recovery, and the prevention of domestic violence, sexual assault, and sex trafficking.[15] The term *Soroptimist* is a combination of the Latin words *soror* meaning "sister" and *optimus* meaning "best," which loosely translates to "best for sisters." The organization has made a distinctive niche in part through white papers focusing on women's issues, such as human trafficking and domestic violence. These white papers help to educate the community and raise funds for the group.[16]

If the end goal is to sell a product, doing so effectively with an article, white paper, or e-book will require more subtle framing than with a standard advertising pitch. Do not include the product name in the description or title.[17] Instead, describe a problem, some common solutions, and then finally discuss what special benefits the product being marketed has in solving that problem. In every instance, "solutions are only introduced after a significant case has been established, demonstrating a clear need."[18] Put valuable, general information first and then specific details about the product's advantages toward the end (if they need be mentioned at all). The real benefit of publications may be much greater than a few sales leads; indeed, a "single well-written white paper can propel a business to the thought leadership position and lead to enormous business opportunities."[19] Keep an open mind, and be prepared for unexpected benefits from authoring content-heavy material.

The style of white papers, articles, and e-books has evolved over time. Tighter budgets due to recent economic conditions have caused a shift to shorter white papers, with more sales-oriented content and less information.[20] In order to compete in this environment, new white paper publishers would do well to include pictures and easily read information in order to keep up with the flood of brief documents that now exist online. However, it is still a wise move to avoid overt sales pitches in order to help distinguish from less sophisticated white papers that confuse information delivery with direct marketing. Do not miss the larger opportunity to advance a brand's image and reputation by making the mistake of treating these publications as purely a marketing platform.

Another question now arises. How many white papers or e-books should be published as part of an SMM campaign? According to Gordon Graham, who has built a reputation around his expertise on white papers, there are five factors to consider: experience, market segments, problems solved, competition, and budget.[21] A company with little experience should write one or two white papers and then evaluate what the firm has learned before writing more. If there are many market segments, more white papers may be required in order to cover all of them. Depending on how many different problems the company can solve and depending on the degree of differences between these problems, more white papers may be needed for each problem area. If there are many competitors in the field publishing white papers, it can also influence the optimal amount of publishing to do. Finally, the budget available will determine how much research and publishing an organization can afford to fund.

An advantage of e-books and white papers is that they have high-perceived value to the recipients, and they typically require the reader to provide an email address or other information to download or access. Sometimes e-books or white papers are only available for purchase and are directly monetized in this fashion. However, for most marketing purposes, the goodwill and customer information that can be gained from giving these publications away for free is much more valuable. Collecting email addresses through the distribution of a white paper gives valuable leads to the sales team and can also generate information on customer demographics, common areas of interest, and more.

White papers are primarily used by business-to-business marketers because the tone and content is designed for business executives with a strong component of technical or professional information. E-books are more commonly used in the consumer market and are expected to be entertaining as well as informative. However, there can be substantial overlap between the two forms. For example, a bicycle shop might publish a white paper on how to find the right-sized bike, a beginner's guide to cyclist lingo, bicycling etiquette, or tips for new riders. These white paper topics might be valuable to general readers and help generate new customers. To connect with seasoned riders, the white papers could contain more advanced topics. As always the most important part in any marketing effort using this type of content is to find relevant content for the marketing goals and to target audiences and then put that content into a clear and useful format as either a white paper, an article, or an e-book.

Best Practices in Crafting Articles, White Papers, and E-Books

While the process described below is tailored toward white papers, it can also be applied, with minor modification, to writing e-books or lengthier articles. In many ways the steps to writing either will be similar. As e-books have existed for less time than white papers, there is much more flexibility of opinion as to the "correct" way to write an e-book. On the one hand, this flexibility is a disadvantage because e-books convey less prestige and authority than the official-sounding white paper. On the other hand, the flexibility of e-book formatting makes it a useful platform for creative authors to showcase their thoughts. In any case, applying a level of organization and detail that would be found in an industry white paper or detailed articles toward writing an e-book is sure to generate better results than a haphazard approach to authoring.

Most of all, writing content-heavy but appealing marketing content, such as white papers, takes strong writing skills and practice. Having a solid process to guide the writing effort will make these potentially daunting publications more manageable. Business owner and white paper author Al Kemp lays out his nine-step process for writing white papers.[22] In order, these steps are Assess Needs; Plan; Acquire Information; Organize Content; Design the Look and Feel; Write; Illustrate; Review, Revise, and Approve; and finally Publish. A brief description of the process, along with insights from other white paper authorities, appears below. Again, this process applies to the other types of content discussed in this article as well.

STEP #1. ASSESS NEEDS

In order to make decisions about the structure and content, it is necessary to have a clear vision of the goals one is attempting to achieve. These may be *overt* goals that are clear to the reader (such as educating the public about a product or providing information about a problem) or *covert* goals that might not be directly mentioned (such as increasing sales or creating doubts about the capabilities of competing products).

After considering the goals, define the audience that the content is being written for. It is generally agreed that to write successful articles, white papers, and e-books, it is necessary to understand the audience.[23] What are the personal characteristics, jobs, and work responsibilities of the audience members? How large a company is each associated with and in what sector of the economy? Ideally, identify different segments of the audience based on job descriptions because such knowledge will provide more specific insight about audience members' behavior. Further, having a clear idea of the ideal audience will help later when deciding which material to include and what to leave out. It is possible that several pieces of content on similar subjects must be produced, each tailored to a different set of readers.

STEP #2. PLAN

After or during the first step, start planning how the content will be constructed. Consult with the sales department to see how the content will be integrated into the sales process, and determine how the material will be distributed. This process will help to further define the audience and to inform the structure and tone of the final. Next, decide responsibilities and estimate costs. A polished white paper, article, or e-book will require research, writing, illustration, editing, and review. Calculate out-of-pocket expenses as well as labor costs in order to provide a rough figure for the time and resources needed. Then prepare a schedule and project plan to lay out when the white paper will be completed.

STEP #3. ACQUIRE INFORMATION

In order to write a good article, white paper, or e-book, expertise is necessary. The relevant knowledge can be gained from reading and research or through interviews with authorities in the field. Interviews are especially valuable for unearthing information that may not yet be broadly available. After gathering the facts, analyze how they can support the goals set for the content. Obviously information about functionality of the product will be important, but that should be supplemented with other, less product-specific facts as well.

STEP #4. ORGANIZE

It is likely that step number three may have uncovered an unmanageable amount of information, or at least more than will be needed for the content being written. To determine what is most important, one option is to create a simple outline with groups and subgroups to represent different themes or strands of information. Too many subgroups can make later organization complicated, so do not create too many specific groups. After this process is complete, hopefully the outline that has been created will become a roadmap for the final case study. Choose the starting point for the case study (perhaps a story or anecdote that will draw in the reader), and then put the major topics in order to follow.

STEP #5. DESIGN THE LOOK AND FEEL

Different audiences may have varying expectations for document presentation and formatting. Think about what the model reader would prefer. If a graphic illustration professional is available, he or she should be able to create the "look" after being given some general guidelines. If no professional is available, consider using one of the preconstructed page templates that come with many word processing programs.

Almost always, the page layout should center on ease of browsing. Keep in mind, most readers will not go word by word through an article, white paper, or e-book. Instead, online viewers tend to scan over text quickly and may read more slowly online.[24] This reading practice makes informative headings, visual aids, and short paragraphs serious advantages. Big blocks of text are less pleasant to read and may turn off a reader altogether. While white articles, white papers, and e-books should convey a lot of information, they should also be easy on the eyes and appealing to online consumers. Most articles, white papers, and e-books will not be printed, so be sure that the final product will look good on a computer screen.

Remember to create a catchy title page. In the planning stage, some sort of rough title should have been considered. Choose a layout that is aesthetically pleasing and draws the reader further into the paper. Also, consider including an abstract on the first page to give a general idea of the topic and conclusions. Further, in this stage, select the font, line length, spacing, page size, and color scheme that will be applied to the document. Avoid cramped layouts; keep some white space to make the text more readable.

STEP #6. WRITE

Fill in the content that was outlined earlier using details gathered through research. Audiences for these types of content expect to be educated, but they want technical elements to be combined with narrative and other interesting content. If the product is technology based, some space to explain how the item works is necessary, but do not become bogged down in technical details. To inspire action, this type of content needs to move beyond purely technical topics.[28] Ultimately, most readers want to see what the benefits of a product are, not just its functionality. Make sure the article, white paper, or e-book fulfills both objectives. Whenever possible, quantify costs and benefits in specific ways, and estimate amounts of money that can be gained or lost by certain problems or solutions. Tangible information that assists in decision making will draw the most significant viewers toward the communication.

Prevent miscommunication with readers by explaining all acronyms and by using consistent wording when defining each concept. Articles, white papers, and e-books may be accessed by people with a broad range of familiarity with the topic at hand. Readers expect to learn and be challenged but are not generally excited to read a condensed user's manual. Use examples whenever possible to illustrate ideas as well as any other means to avoid losing the audience in obscure technical discussions.

When writing, keep the style direct and uncomplicated. For the first draft, focus on explaining the material well, and worry about eloquence during the revisions. At all stages, avoid excessive jargon or puffed-up marketing rhetoric. When studying news releases for word usage that David Meerman Scott refers to as "gobbledygook," he finds that that the phrases "next generation," "flexible," "world class," "scalable," and "easy to use" are employed thousands of times.[25] Other overused marketing phrases include "industry standard," "groundbreaking," and "user friendly." When employed in this type of content, these words call to mind a marketing press release, not an educational document. Such usage sacrifices the main advantage of white papers, articles, and e-books, which is that they can "penetrate most organizations' anti-marketing defenses because they are sought after and brought into the organization by decision-makers."[26] Be sure to eliminate unhelpful buzzwords to convey the correct impression about the content to the audience.

Forming an article, white paper, or e-book around a list can occasionally be a helpful design and catch the reader's attention.[27] While more detailed than a list of tips, a list-based piece of content can provide valuable information in an easily digested fashion for the hurried reader. The danger is that a list may seem too shallow or overly simplified and thus alienate the audience. The term *white paper* implies a level of information and analysis that must be upheld or risk disappointing readers. However, keeping a white paper light and readable by using bullet points or lists is an intelligent tactic. The same tactic can apply to articles and e-books.

STEP #7. ILLUSTRATE

Good articles, white papers, and e-books contain a visual as well as textual element to keep readers engaged. Especially with more complicated material, visual aids are essential in order to focus the audience's attention and to explain complicated concepts. Creating visual elements should occur at the same time as the writing process so that both elements complement each other.

Keep in mind that some viewers will skim through the content before deciding to read it in full. To draw in these readers, ensure that the illustrations convey the primary content and selling points of the material. Using charts to display data, well-chosen pictures to illustrate examples, and documenting the sources will help convince an unsure reader that the paper contains valuable material that is worth the reading time.

STEP #8. REVIEW, REVISE, AND APPROVE

In a first round of reviewing, the article, white paper, or e-book should be evaluated by experts in the field or ideally by some of the people interviewed during step three. These reviewers can catch factual errors or correct imprecise explanations. The final draft should also be reviewed by the senior management of the company who is sponsoring the content. As a result of these reviews, there may be changes to both organization and content. Improvements for the final draft might include writing style revision, improved flow of the text with images, a grammar check as well as a check of the spelling of names, and so on. Before sending the white paper to publication, also check with the legal and accounting departments to avoid later conflicts.

STEP #9. PUBLISH

Most likely, the article, white paper, or e-book will be published electronically, so this step can be rather simple. Before publishing, always check the final output to ensure that it correctly transferred from final draft to final product version. If a print version is to be produced, check for errors in the proofs before printing, and avoid the potential high cost of reprinting to correct errors.

This nine-step formula for crafting an article, white paper, or e-book may seem overly exhaustive. However, it reflects an industry standard and the very high expectations of this type of content. Making a half-hearted attempt at writing the material may be worse than doing nothing at all: while an excellent article, white paper, or e-book signals expertise, a poor one demonstrates just the opposite. White papers have existed for many years, and the process for creating them is well established. Applying this process to online articles and e-books can help ensure their success. Failing to meet the standards across these types of content shows a lack of understanding of the role of this content and is an easy way to lose credibility with social media professionals.

Notes

1. Barker, Donald I., Melissa S. Barker, and Katherine Pinard (2012). *Internet Research Illustrated*, 6th ed. (Boston, MA: Course Technology/Cengage Learning). Retrieved September 7, 2011, from http://www.cengage.com/search/productOverview.do?N=+16+4294922451&Ntk=P_Isbn13&Ntt=9781133190387
2. (n.d.). "Article Directory," *Wikipedia*. Retrieved July 3, 2011, from http://en.wikipedia.org/wiki/Article_directory
3. (n.d.). "Shirley Slick," EZine @rticles. Retrieved September 28, 2015, from http://ezinearticles.com/expert/Shirley_Slick/820954
4. Slegg, Jennifer (January 30, 2014). "Matt Cutts: Using Article Directories for Links? Just No," Search Engine Watch. Retrieved September 26, 2015, from http://searchenginewatch.com/sew/news/2326161/matt-cutts-using-article-directories-for-links-just-no#
5. "The EzineArticles.com Article Writing: Article Title Training" (2008), EzineArticles. Retrieved June 26, 2011, from http://media.ezinearticles.com/pdf/ezinearticles/training/full/article-title.pdf
6. Stelzner, Michael A. (2009). "How to Write a White Paper—A White Paper on White Papers." Retrieved June 22, 2011, from http://www.stelzner.com/copy-HowTo-whitepapers.php
7. Scott, David Meerman (2009). *The New Rules of Marketing & PR* (Hoboken, NJ: John Wiley), p. 135.
8. Knowles, Michael (2002). "How to Write a White Paper," Michael Knowles Consulting. Retrieved June 22, 2011, from http://www.mwknowles.com/free_articles/white_paper/white_paper.html
9. "2014 Content: Top Ten Whitepapers at Digital Marketing Depot," Digital Marketing Depot (December 23, 2014). Retrieved September 26, 2015, from http://digitalmarketingdepot.com/2014-content-top-10-whitepapers-digital-marketing-depot-12364
10. Graham, Gordon (July 7, 2009). "When Is a White Paper NOT a White Paper?" WhitePaperSource. Retrieved June 21, 2011, from http://www.whitepapersource.com/writing/when-is-a-white-paper-not-a-white-paper/

11. Kantor, Jonathan (September 9, 2009). "Understanding White Paper Longevity: Why White Papers Survive in the Midst of a Printing Industry Downturn," WhitePaperSource. Retrieved June 21, 2011, from http://www.whitepapersource.com/writing/understanding-white-paper-longevity-why-white-papers-survive-in-the-midst-of-a-printing-industry-downturn/

12. e-book (2011), Oxford Dictionaries. Retrieved June 22, 2011, from http://oxforddictionaries.com/definition/e-book?region=us

13. Scott, David Meerman (2009). *The New Rules of Marketing & PR* (Hoboken, NJ: John Wiley), p. 136.

14. Harris, Jodi (May 28, 2015). "7 Tips We Learned Analyzing 75 Content Marketing Examples," Content Marketing Institute. Retrieved September 28, 2015, from http://contentmarketinginstitute.com/2015/05/content-marketing-examples-ebook/

15. *Soroptimist International of the Americas Program Impact Report* (2009–2010), Soroptimist. Retrieved July 2, 2011, from http://www.soroptimist.org/members/program/ProgramDocs/GeneralInformation/English/ProgramImpactReport.pdf

16. (n.d.). "Soroptimist White Papers," Soroptimist. Retrieved September 28, 2015, from http://www.soroptimist.org/whitepapers/whitepapers.html

17. Kranz, Jonathan (March 9, 2010). "Do the Flip: How to Turn Product/Service Features into White Paper Topics," WhitePaperSource. Retrieved June 21, 2011, from http://www.whitepapersource.com/writing/do-the-flip-how-to-turn-productservice-features-into-white-paper-topics/

18. Stelzner, Michael A. (2006). *Writing White Papers: How to Capture Readers and Keep Them Engaged* (Poway, CA: WhitePaperSource), p. 4.

19. Ibid., p. 1.

20. Kantor, Jonathan (January 5, 2010). "The Recession's Impact on White Papers," WhitePaperSource. Retrieved June 21, 2011, from http://www.whitepapersource.com/writing/the-recessions-impact-on-white-papers/

21. Graham, Gordon (August 11, 2009). "How Many White Papers Are 'Enough'? Some Thoughts for Marketers," WhitePaperSource. Retrieved June 24, 2011, from http://www.whitepapersource.com/marketing/how-many-white-papers-are-enough-some-thoughts-for-marketers/

22. Kemp, Al (2005). *White Paper Writing Guide: How to Achieve Marketing Goals by Explaining Technical Ideas* (Arvada, CO: Impact Technical Publications). Retrieved June 22, 2011, from http://www.impactonthenet.com/wp-guide.pdf

23. Graham, Gordon (January 5, 2010). "The First Key to White Paper Success," WhitePaperSource. Retrieved June 21, 2011, from http://www.whitepapersource.com/writing/the-first-key-to-white-paper-success/

24. Golden, Michelle (2011). *Social Media Strategies for Professionals and Their Firms* (Hoboken, NJ: John Wiley), p. 265.

25. Scott, David Meerman (2009). *The New Rules of Marketing & PR* (Hoboken, NJ: John Wiley), p. 145.

26. Stelzner, Michael A. (2006). *Writing White Papers: How to Capture Readers and Keep Them Engaged* (Poway, CA: WhitePaperSource), p. 5.

27. Graham, Gordon (April 3, 2010). "How to Write a White Paper, by the Numbers," WhitePaperSource. Retrieved June 21, 2011, from http://www.whitepapersource.com/writing/how-to-write-a-white-paper-by-the-numbers/

Mobile Marketing on Social Networks

The mobile era has arrived and it finds marketers striving to keep up with the rapidly changing habits and needs of consumers. Mobile has a growing role in shopping activities so content, location and the technologies that enable instantaneous communication are all important factors.

LEARNING OBJECTIVES:

After completing this chapter students will be able to:

- Discuss the growth of mobile connectivity and device use globally and in the United States
- Explain where social networking fits into the mobile environment
- Identify main issues related to using apps and to purchasing on mobile devices
- Discuss the emergence of buy buttons and location identification on social sites

(Continued)

The huge ecosystem loosely known as "mobile" has been growing with dizzying speed according to any number of metrics including number of users, types of devices, and the activities users are carrying out on social networks from their mobile devices. In the few short years since the first edition of this book was published this growth has brought about fundamental changes in the way marketers think about mobile marketing. Those changes include:

- The growing number of people who are mobile only or at least mobile first in terms of many daily activities.
- The dominant role of apps in mobile use.
- The decreasing popularity of consumer check-in apps.
- The ability to include location data in postings on most social platforms.
- Increasing use of location-based technology in retail applications.
- The growing importance of social platforms and activities on mobile.

Marketers have responded by introducing a "mobile first" strategic approach. Whether mobile first is the correct approach, as we will discuss later in the chapter, one certainty is that mobile is not the only consideration. The term "audience first" has been suggested as a more desirable approach. Many marketers advocate omnichannel strategy as the correct way to deal with fragmented markets and communications channels.

Whatever term marketers choose to use, however, it is clear that, while social is an increasingly important part of mobile marketing strategy, it is not the entire solution. Retailer Home Depot has already been singled out in Chapter 8 for its skill in reaching DIY home owners with video. In that chapter we also acknowledged the important role of mobile viewership in video marketing. Home Depot has recently combined many of these strategic themes in a new app that aims to improve customers' ability to visualize how a paint color will look in their home. Put another way, it integrates the in-store and in-home experiences with a mobile app that is being advertised on TV.

The Home Depot Project Color app complements its Color Center page on the corporate website. All the retailer's paint brands are participating in the project even though most of them also have their own color choice app. The Home Depot app uses a variety of technologies including augmented reality to give a realistic depiction of what a paint color will look like in a particular room. This makes choosing paint color a much less stressful and time-consuming decision for the consumer. According to the company's manager of online merchandising, Samara Tuchband,

> "Our real objective is that we were looking to help our customers with a best-in-class omnichannel experience," . . ."The app was really launched as a complementary product to [the Color Center] experience so that regardless of how I decide to engage, the app becomes a complement to that by saying, hey I want to experience color in my own space – the app now allows for that," she said.[1]

The TV commercial was posted on YouTube, but Figure 12.1 was taken from the website of an advertising metrics platform.[2] iSpot.tv uses its own technology to "connect

- Distinguish between social first, audience first, and omnichannel marketing strategies
- Explain the use of beacons in retail stores
- Discuss the importance of satisfying customer experience on mobile devices

Figure 12.1 The Project Color App TV Commercial

Source: https://www.iSpot.tv, Inc.

the dots" between a TV commercial and resulting earned activity on social, video, and search channels.[3] That alone is a sign of the times. The posting also features a social sharing bar.

The Home Depot app story is interesting in its own right. However, it makes a deeper point. Just as mobile is part of overall marketing strategy, social is part of overall mobile marketing strategy. Social media makes up part of a mobile campaign or strategy, not all of it. It is therefore not correct to talk about a social mobile strategy.

In this chapter we will discuss the important considerations involved in using social media as part of a mobile marketing campaign. As we do so, we will continue to acknowledge that mobile is most often a part of an omnichannel marketing campaign that supports an overall marketing strategy.

In this chapter we will cover:

- The role mobile is playing in the lives of customers
  - o Usage, devices, activities, and market segments
  - o How social has become part of that picture
- Social media platforms and their mobile popularity
- Location marketing technologies and platforms and their use in mobile marketing campaigns
- Omnichannel marketing strategy
- Customer experience in mobile marketing campaigns
- Best practices for the social aspect of mobile marketing

Mobile in the Lives of Global Consumers

The world is well on its way to being digital and mobile is quickly becoming the main avenue of access to digital technology including the Internet. In order to understand the main outlines of the mobile economy, let's look at a few key questions about growth and use.

How Many People Use Mobile to Access the Internet and Social Platforms?

Primarily as a result of access to affordable technology, mobile has taken hold around the world although growth remains uneven. Data published in 2015 shows that over half the world's 7.2 billion people use mobile, over 40 percent use the Internet and over 20 percent have active social media accounts (Figure 12.2a). According to Figure 12.2b that's over 1.6 *billion* people (23% of the population) accessing more than 2 billion social media accounts on their mobile phones each month.[4]

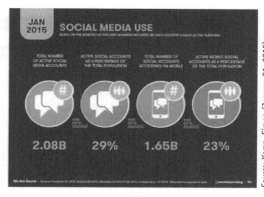

Source: Kemp, Simon (January 21, 2015). "Digital, Social & Mobile Worldwide in 2015," We Are Social, Retrieved August 1, 2015 from http://wearesocial.net/blog/2015/01/digital-social-mobile-worldwide-2015/

Source: Kemp, Simon (January 21, 2015). "Digital, Social & Mobile Worldwide in 2015," We Are Social, Retrieved August 1, 2015 from http://wearesocial.net/blog/2015/01/digital-social-mobile-worldwide-2015/

Figure 12.2a and b Global Internet and Social Media Use

Which Networks Do They Access?

One answer is the same the world over—Facebook. Beyond that, the answer differs according to the popularity of platforms in various countries and regions. Figures 12.3a and 12.3b show a striking difference between the next most popular networks globally and in the United States. Globally four of the six top platforms are messenger apps.[5] WhatsApp in particular has received a great deal of attention in recent years for its exploding popularity and for its acquisition by Facebook in 2014. WhatsApp is not widely used in the United States but it is the leading messenger app in India, Brazil, and Mexico among others. The introduction of cheaper devices has greatly increased the use of smartphones and for many consumers in these countries the phone is their first and

Active Users by Social Platform
Most Recently Published Monthly Active User Accounts by Platform, in Millions

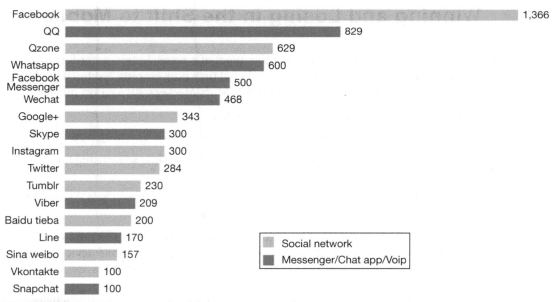

Platform	Users (Millions)
Facebook	1,366
QQ	829
Qzone	629
Whatsapp	600
Facebook Messenger	500
Wechat	468
Google+	343
Skype	300
Instagram	300
Twitter	284
Tumblr	230
Viber	209
Baidu tieba	200
Line	170
Sina weibo	157
Vkontakte	100
Snapchat	100

Legend:
- Social network
- Messenger/Chat app/Voip

Figure 12.3a Leading Social Media Platforms Globally

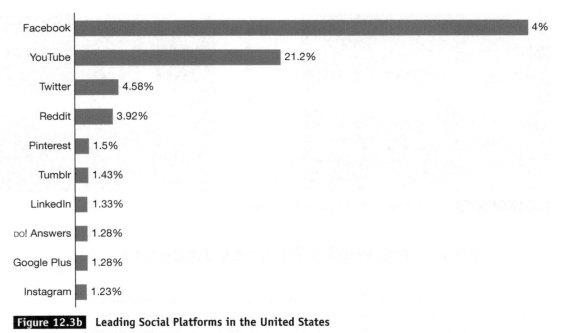

Facebook — 4%
YouTube — 21.2%
Twitter — 4.58%
Reddit — 3.92%
Pinterest — 1.5%
Tumblr — 1.43%
LinkedIn — 1.33%
DO! Answers — 1.28%
Google Plus — 1.28%
Instagram — 1.23%

Figure 12.3b Leading Social Platforms in the United States

only access to the Internet. They have no inherent loyalty to platforms like Facebook and Twitter and they like WhatsApp's ease of use and the fact that it provides cheaper communications than SMS.[6]

In the United States the most popular mobile social networks are the usual suspects—Facebook, Twitter, Blogger, LinkedIn, Google+, and Pinterest along with news and blogging sites Reddit and Tumblr.[7] Notice that Instagram shows up on this top ten list, a tribute to its rapid growth.

Which Devices and Which Services Are Winning and Losing in the Shift to Mobile?

Desktop and even TV are losing share to other types of screens. In fact, according to data from venture capital firm KPCB mobile digital time now exceeds desktop digital time by 51% to 42%. Other highlights from consultant Mary Meeker's 2015 report include:

- 55% of mobile data traffic comes from video
  - o Facebook gets 4 billion video views each day with 75% coming from phones
- The amount spent on mobile ads grew 34% in 2014 while advertising for desktops grew only 11%.
  - o Mobile advertising is still behind the curve. Mobile represents 24% of digital time but only 8% of advertising dollars spent.[8]

The trend to mobile has come at the expense of desktop use. Figure 12.4 shows that a total of 61% of digital time of the average U.S. adult user is on a mobile device, either smartphone or tablet, with only 39% on the desktop.[9] Younger consumers are more mobile than older consumers—no surprise there.

Many social networking platforms have benefitted substantially from mobile activity. Data from 2013 indicates that the largest social platforms vary in the amount of their usage time that comes from mobile (Figure 12.5).[10] However, the overwhelming question is, how many of these platforms—from Twitter to Snapchat—are accessed primarily by mobile?

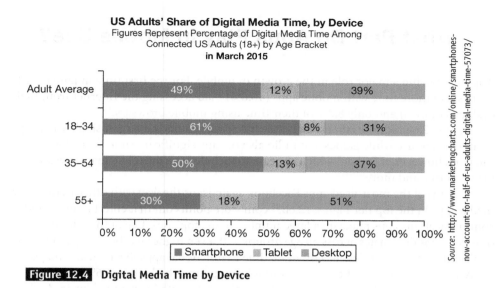

US Adults' Share of Digital Media Time, by Device
Figures Represent Percentage of Digital Media Time Among
Connected US Adults (18+) by Age Bracket
in March 2015

	Smartphone	Tablet	Desktop
Adult Average	49%	12%	39%
18–34	61%	8%	31%
35–54	50%	13%	37%
55+	30%	18%	51%

■ Smartphone ▨ Tablet ■ Desktop

Source: http://www.marketingcharts.com/online/smartphones-now-account-for-half-of-us-adults-digital-media-time-57073/

Figure 12.4 Digital Media Time by Device

Mobile vs. desktop: 85% of time Twitter users spent on Twitter happened on a mobile device. on.wsj.com/1gSsENd

Social Network Activity: Mobile vs. Desktop
% of time spent on social networks in the United States, by platform*

■ Desktop ▨ Mobile

- Facebook: 32% / 68%
- Twitter: 14% / 86%
- Instagram: 2% / 98%
- LinkedIn: 26% / 74%
- Pinterest: 8% / 92%
- Tumblr: 46% / 54%
- Vine: 1% / 99%
- Snapchat: 100%

THE WALL STREET JOURNAL. * December 2013, Age 18+   Source: comScore ©①③ statista ◪

Source: Dow Jones & Company, Inc/Twitter

Figure 12.5 Amount of Platform Traffic from Mobile

LinkedIn, used primarily by professionals, gets a significant majority of use from mobile while popular blogging platform Tumblr gets a bare majority. Otherwise, mobile dominates.[11]

Some of this growth, however, is coming at the expense of other platforms. Location-based platforms Foursquare and Gowalla were experiencing major growth just a few years ago with Foursquare growing 50% to about 30 million users in 2012.[12] Gowalla, with about 1 million users at the end of 2011,[13] was acquired by Facebook. Many of the top employees at Gowalla moved to Facebook to create the ability to add location data to Facebook posts.[14] In late 2014 Foursquare announced that it would change its focus from consumer check in to selling its location database to app developers that wish to include location services in their apps[15] That strategy continued to unfold when Foursquare added Twitter to its list of business partners. The partnership allows Twitter to include specific locations in tweets—Time-Life Building instead of New York City, for example.

What Part Do Apps Play in Mobile Use?

Apps are playing a major role in the growth of mobile. For the first time in January 2014 users spent more time with mobile apps (46.6%) than accessing the Internet from their desktops (45.1%) and only 8.3% of their time using mobile browsers.[16]

Figure 12.6a indicates that social networking represents the largest single category of mobile app use while games and radio also occupy significant time.[17] The largest category, however, is "other," which appears to include categories like maps, weather, news, sports, and more.

In terms of the most-used apps Facebook again leads the way with other well-known media apps in the top tier Figure 12.6b.[18] comScore points out that entertainment and communications apps make up a large number of the top apps. Use of these leisure-oriented apps dominates across all age groups with even higher use by younger age groups while older consumers devote a bit more time to functional apps like mail and maps.

A study at the end of the year reported that app usage had grown 76% in 2014, with shopping apps showing the highest growth.[19] News site Marketing Unwired asks an important question. Look at your own mobile phone—how many apps are those of a brand you patronize? It's likely that you, like most other consumers, will find that relative few of yours are "branded apps." Experts suggest that most branded apps are not sufficiently useful to warrant the space they occupy on users' phones.

An exception is Starbucks. The company has been working on its mobile app since 2011 and it now has an impressive array of services. Earning and tracking loyalty rewards was an early and popular service. Users can now get free music downloads as well as browse drink and food menus. Its payment service has enjoyed huge growth. MIT Technology Review reports that:

> Twelve million active users now pay for their Frappuccino with a wave of a phone. Of the $1.6 billion spent via smartphone in U.S. stores in 2013, the company claims, a full 90 percent went to Starbucks, and most payments experts don't doubt it. Starbucks's mobile wallet is actually a digital stored-value card more akin to its popular gift card. Its success—the app now accounts for 16 percent of Starbucks's 47 million weekly transactions (up 50 percent from a year ago)—makes it both a model and a target for payment apps from other retailers and tech companies alike.[20]

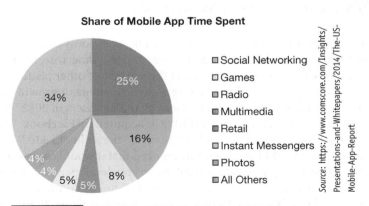

Share of Mobile App Time Spent

- Social Networking
- Games
- Radio
- Multimedia
- Retail
- Instant Messengers
- Photos
- All Others

25%
34%
16%
8%
5%
5%
4%
4%

Source: https://www.comscore.com/Insights/Presentations-and-Whitepapers/2014/The-US-Mobile-App-Report

Figure 12.6a Time Spent With Categories of Mobile Apps

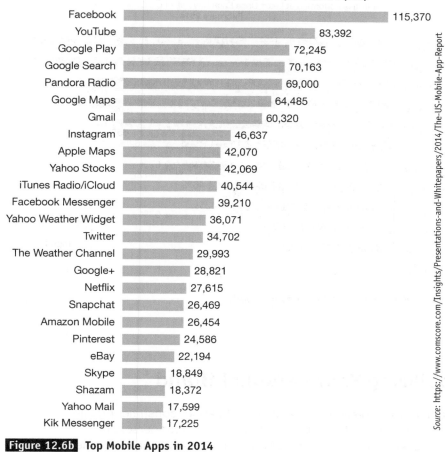

Top 25 Mobile Apps by Unique Visitors (000)

App	Unique Visitors
Facebook	115,370
YouTube	83,392
Google Play	72,245
Google Search	70,163
Pandora Radio	69,000
Google Maps	64,485
Gmail	60,320
Instagram	46,637
Apple Maps	42,070
Yahoo Stocks	42,069
iTunes Radio/iCloud	40,544
Facebook Messenger	39,210
Yahoo Weather Widget	36,071
Twitter	34,702
The Weather Channel	29,993
Google+	28,821
Netflix	27,615
Snapchat	26,469
Amazon Mobile	26,454
Pinterest	24,586
eBay	22,194
Skype	18,849
Shazam	18,372
Yahoo Mail	17,599
Kik Messenger	17,225

Source: https://www.comscore.com/Insights/Presentations-and-Whitepapers/2014/The-US-Mobile-App-Report

Figure 12.6b Top Mobile Apps in 2014

In 2015 Starbucks introduced the ability to order and pay in advance at stores in selected cities. Would you have guessed that mobile would become a large part of the strategy of a bricks and mortar coffee shop chain? Starbucks intends to keep it that way with a continuous stream of mobile innovations.[21]

What Kinds of Activities Do Consumers Conduct on Mobile?

The top two activities are communications—email and text messaging. However, Figure 12.7, which shows both smartphone and tablet use, indicates that email's historical dominance of Internet users' activities has almost vanished.[22] It has been overtaken by text messaging, even in the United States. The rest of the top five activities include search and participating in social networking. The fifth most popular activity is described as "while watching TV." Many of us think of that as multitasking and the degree to which users are on mobile at the same time they are watching TV is striking—about 70% of both smartphone and tablet users are using mobile devices while watching TV. They are doing various other things including playing games and watching movies and videos. Notice that the final activity on this list is using a tablet and a smartphone at the same time. Our reliance on our devices seems to have permeated almost all aspects of our life.

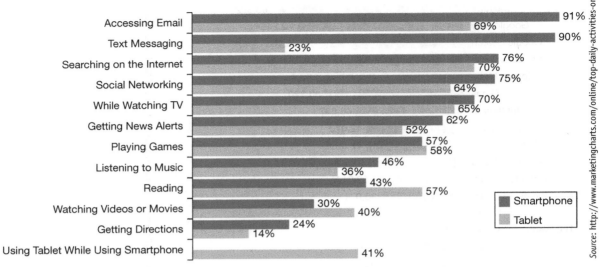

Daily Activities on Smartphones and Tablets
Activities Performed at Least Once Each Day / % of US Device Owners Surveyed
February 2014

Activity	Smartphone	Tablet
Accessing Email	91%	69%
Text Messaging	90%	23%
Searching on the Internet	76%	70%
Social Networking	75%	64%
While Watching TV	70%	65%
Getting News Alerts	62%	52%
Playing Games	57%	58%
Listening to Music	46%	36%
Reading	43%	57%
Watching Videos or Movies	30%	40%
Getting Directions	24%	14%
Using Tablet While Using Smartphone		41%

Figure 12.7 Activities Performed at Least Once Each Day on Mobile

Mobilizing Your Personal Brand

Having read this chapter, which presents a wealth of data about consumer mobile use, you may not yet be convinced that it is important to have your personal branding content available in a mobile format. Would managers expect to be able to access this content on mobile devices or would they expect to work from their desktops?

The answer is that managers are people too and they are using mobile in their professional lives just as they use it in their personal ones. Internet Retailer quotes a 2014 survey of B2B buying practices as finding that "85% of respondents say they require content on B2B sites to be optimized for mobile devices, up from 69% a year earlier."[1] AdWeek's Social Times adds that Facebook, Twitter, and LinkedIn are the networks of choice for B2B users.[2] That data is talking about general business use. We can assume that LinkedIn is especially important in learning about job applicants but that managers can find their way around Facebook and Twitter to learn more—hopefully things that reflect well on the applicant. It is easy to imagine that research like this is often done on the go—during the commute, a flight, and so forth. That means a good mobile presentation is vital.

How does one go about mobilizing personal branding content?

Lesson #1. Be sure that your website and/or blog are optimized for mobile.
This is not as difficult as it may sound. When establishing a website use a responsive template, one that will display equally well on desktop and mobile devices. Blogs may require you to choose a separate mobile template for your blog because there are many presentation options. Either way, the responsive templates have become more reliable in recent years but be sure to check from different devices. Then verify that your sites measure up to Google's mobile standards by

using the Google Mobile-Friendly test.[3] Having your site meet Google's mobile standards means it will be identified as mobile-friendly in search results. You can find more information about this at http://googlewebmastercentral.blogspot.com/2014/11/helping-users-find-mobile-friendly-pages.html

Lesson #2. Create a variety of personal branding content. You have been encouraged to do that throughout this book. When you think about it from the standpoint of mobile, it quickly becomes apparent that viewers of your content are likely to watch a short video or page through a presentation on mobile. Reading a 20-page strategy paper on mobile seems somewhat problematic.

Lesson #3. Pay attention to sharing and following on social media and subscribing on email. Give mobile viewers the opportunity to share and to follow your work on mobile just as you do on the traditional web. Number of likes, shares, and followers add to your credibility, whether their source is mobile or traditional.

Lesson #4. Consider a low-key text campaign if you can get the contact information. It is helpful to politely call attention to new content, especially if you think it is potentially useful. If necessary, do this on LinkedIn or Twitter where it is easier to get people to follow you.

Lesson #5. Double down on monitoring. In the case of mobile, add to your monitoring regimen checking all your content on mobile as you post it and spot check older items from various devices from time to time.

> Think of mobile as another way for people to access your personal branding content and give it the importance it deserves. As your career progresses and mobile becomes even more ubiquitous the effort you make to mobilize is likely to be well rewarded.

Sources:

1. Tambor, Zak (January 29, 2015). "B2B buyers demand mobile-optimized content," Internet Retailer, Retrieved August 15, 2015, from https://www.internetretailer.com/2015/01/29/b2b-buyers-demand-mobile-optimized-content

2. Bennett, Shea (February 25, 2015). "The Potential of Social Media (for #B2B Marketers)," Ad Week. Retrieved August 15, 2015, from http://www.adweek.com/socialtimes/social-media-b2b-stats/615931

3. (n.d.). "Mobile Friendly Test," Google. Retrieved August 16, 2015, from https://www.google.com/webmasters/tools/mobile-friendly/

Are Consumers Making Purchases on Mobile?

The short answer is, "Consumers are doing a lot of shopping on mobile devices but not yet a lot of purchasing, at least in the U.S." In July 2015 MediaPost quoted a study that found 26% of consumers who owned mobile phones making purchases on them, up from 23% in 2013. That is a rather low rate of growth compared to other activities in the mobile space and appears to be the result of security concerns.[23]

However, the answer that marketers need to understand is more complex. eMarketer describes mobile commerce activities as "upper funnel," activities like searching, comparing, and finding vendors and locations. This is especially true of smartphone users, less true of tablet users who may proceed to purchase. eMarketer points out tablet users are usually not mobile. They are more likely to be at home on their couch, more like a desktop user.[24]

The amount of shopping time on mobile devices has been steadily growing, with mobile (smartphone and tablet) retail traffic outpacing nonmobile (desktop and laptop) traffic for the first time.[25] The implication is still that purchases are made in other channels, not mobile.

What products are digital purchasers most likely to buy on mobile? The answer to that question varies by product, with a 2015 study reported by Business Insider (12.8a) finding groceries the most likely to be purchased on mobile and, perhaps surprisingly, electronics the least likely.[26] Figure 12.8b helps to explain the purchase decisions by showing that local searches are much more likely to result in a purchase than are more generic searches.[27] Seventy-eight percent of local searches on mobile phones in 2013 actually resulted in a purchase.

Why did those mobile customers complete their purchases? A 2014 study shows that the right price was the top purchase consideration for telecom, autos, and entertainment while restaurant decisions were most influenced by a nearby location.[28] Many potential mobile purchases are abandoned, however. A 2015 study found that 56% of smartphone owners who responded had abandoned a transaction, down from 66% the year before. The main reasons were general uncertainty about the purchase, slow loading times, difficulty using the app or site, difficulty typing in information on a small screen, and complicated payment process.[29]

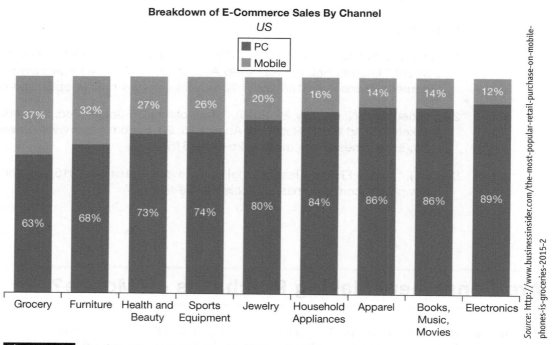

Breakdown of E-Commerce Sales By Channel

US

Figure 12.8a   Purchase Channels Used by Desktop and Mobile Purchasers

Source: http://www.businessinsider.com/the-most-popular-retail-purchase-on-mobile-phones-is-groceries-2015-2

Percentage of Searches that Resulted in a Local Purchase

PC/Laptop   **Mobile Phone**   **Tablet**

61%   78%   64%

Source: https://blog.kissmetrics.com/surprising-mobile-ecommerce/

Figure 12.8b   Local Searches More Likely to Result in Purchases

The picture painted by this plethora of statistics is complex, but there are clear indications of the directions in which mobile shopping is evolving:

- Mobile (smartphones and tablets) is becoming increasingly dominant at the expense of personal computers (desktop and laptop).

- Social networking is an important mobile activity.

- Communications, both on social platforms and traditional digital platforms, are still more prevalent on mobile than shopping.

- Shopping activities tend to represent the upper (earlier) part of the purchase funnel where purchases are unlikely to take place but the opportunities for influencing the ultimate purchase are great.

- Purchasing is increasing, albeit slowly, in the mobile arena.

- The likelihood of a mobile purchase varies significantly from one product category to another.

What Will the Impact Be of Having a Buy Button on Social Networking Sites?

We are all familiar with the "buy it now" buttons on websites. Many of them are shopping cart icons, some are just the words; they are many different colors, but the intent is clear. They are a direct call to action on the part of the visitor to the site. Buy something, right now, on this site!

Social networks are joining in with their own buy buttons. In summer 2015 Pinterest announced a blue Buy It button next to the familiar red Pin It button.[30] Facebook participated in the parade with its test of a simple blue Buy button on selected brand pages.[31] Twitter quickly announced an expansion of its own buy button test.[32] Instagram's offer was slightly different—ads with a buy button.[33]

At this writing it is too soon to know how successful direct purchasing on social sites will be. What is your prediction?

It is pretty easy to predict that, if the original efforts are not as successful as the platforms and brands wish, the programs will be tweaked until they are successful. Direct sales on social platforms appear to be an activity whose time has come. Will many of those sales be mobile? Probably so!

Does this statistical portrait of growing mobile dominance validate the idea of mobile-first strategy or are there other approaches that can be more valuable in an increasingly mobile world?

Mobile-First Strategy

The growth of mobile that we have just chronicled has caused marketers to rethink traditional digital approaches. One answer has been "mobile first," the concept of designing mobile products first, then designing for desktop and laptop environments.[34] The cry of "mobile first" is generally attributed to then-Google CEO Eric Schmidt. In a 2010 speech he "urged application developers inside and outside of Google to "work on mobile first, ahead of desktop computers."[35] The term "mobile first" caught on, but Schmidt's reference was to IT development activity, not to marketing strategy. Marketers have picked up the term without careful examination of what Schmidt and other technical experts are saying.

Other marketers have responded with a competing concept—audience first. Proponents of this approach recommend using the massive amounts of data produced by digital media to precisely define target audiences—their needs, wants, and behaviors in both online and offline contexts. Strategy then follows audience definition. According to advertising technology company Turn, "Instead of focusing on channels or complex technical solutions, you can concentrate on telling the story of your brand and products—and reach customers at precisely the moments they'll be most receptive to your message."[36] The main theme—define your audience then develop marketing strategies that appeal to it—is Marketing 101. The difference in the mobile age is reaching people at precise moments when they are receptive. We will return to that subject later in the chapter.

Both approaches have some merit. If mobile screens are first for a majority of customers, shouldn't they come first for marketers also? Marketers have always been told to put their customers first. What has changed today is commonly referred to as "big data," the ability to capture every click on every device with the hope of creating a comprehensive view of each individual customer.

Both approaches have merit, but both fail to fully recognize the impact of all the channels available to the consumer—especially offline ones that recognize the primacy of the retail store in consumer purchasing. Hence the term *omnichannel marketing*. Figure 12.9 portrays the omnichannel perspective of mobile, social, online, and physical stores.[37] The purchase channels are supported by big data that profiles individuals and CRM capabilities that facilitate reaching them at receptive moments.

Google Now is a deceptively simple example of the big data and CRM elements of the concept. It is a Google service that provides reminders and alerts in the form of cards that appear at the bottom of the smartphone screen. The image in Figure 12.10 is from Google's tutorial for the service.[38] It shows a family of happy campers who have tapped the command to show local events and are finding out what is happening in the local area.

Google Now is not a separate app; it is part of the Google search app. Start by thinking about how much Google can learn from your search history if you allow the service to access that. It can also search your Gmail for information like airline and hotel reservations. When it finds them it will send reminders.

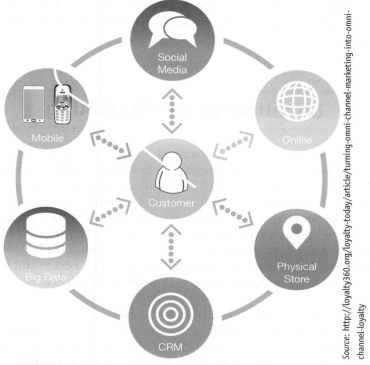

Source: http://loyalty360.org/loyalty-today/article/turning-omni-channel-marketing-into-omni-channel-loyalty

Figure 12.9 Elements of an OmniChannel Strategy

Source: https://www.google.com/landing/now/

Figure 12.10 The Google Now Landing Page

Other information must be provided by the user. If you have the Google Maps app on your phone it probably has already identified your home address. You can enter your work address and get traffic updates on your commute (by car, by bike, walking, or public transit). You can enter your favorite sports teams, your stocks, and much, much more. Google sends you news, reminders, and updates when relevant events warrant them.[39] Google seems to decide what is timely and relevant. Right now mine says, "Check back soon; More cards will appear when the time is right."

The Google Now service combines behavioral data with user-supplied preferences to provide information which has a good chance of being useful at a time which has a good chance of being relevant. Is it a sign of mobile services to come?

In one way it clearly is showing the way. Location-based services have changed from check-in apps to other ways of reporting location and other technologies for location-based marketing.

Location-Based Marketing

Earlier in the chapter we pointed out that check-in apps, which people use to report their location and activities to their friends, are in decline and that, in fact, Gowalla was purchased by Facebook. Since 2012 Facebook users have been able to add their location to posts. Twitter enables location services through your smartphone so it can deliver content and trends based on your current location and so you can geotag your posts.[40] Instagram users can create a photomap for their images. Pinterest allows users to add a map to their boards so they can pinpoint the location of pins. Using location in a different way, LinkedIn encourages members to add location to their work experience in their profiles, making their experience searchable by location.

Allowing social media users to reveal their locations is one way to use location technologies. Marketers then have the data to target platform users by location that can be very useful, especially to local marketers. Physical retail stores remain an important part of the omnichannel world (Figure 12.11). Retailers are using technology to find when their customers are near or inside the store and provide relevant information to them.[41]

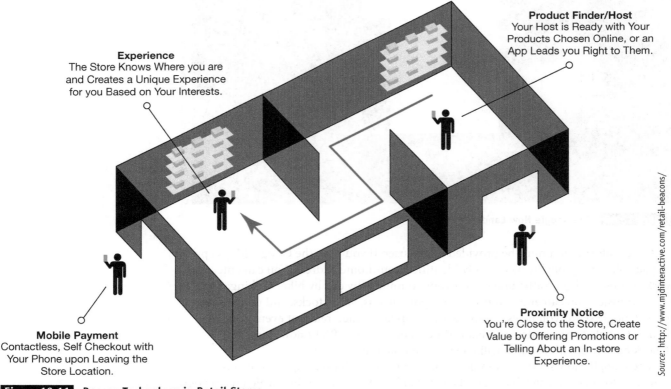

Product Finder/Host
Your Host is Ready with Your Products Chosen Online, or an App Leads you Right to Them.

Experience
The Store Knows Where you are and Creates a Unique Experience for you Based on Your Interests.

Mobile Payment
Contactless, Self Checkout with Your Phone upon Leaving the Store Location.

Proximity Notice
You're Close to the Store, Create Value by Offering Promotions or Telling About an In-store Experience.

Source: http://www.mjdinteractive.com/retail-beacons/

Figure 12.11 Beacon Technology in Retail Stores

Figure 12.12a The Tesco Express Lunch Promotion

Figure 12.12b Checkout QR Code

The retail-level technology that has received the most notice in recent years is the beacon—a small, inexpensive Bluetooth device that can communicate with the smartphones of nearby customers. As suggested in Figure 12.11 the retailer can send personalized promotions including coupons to entice them into the store, offer product information and in-store navigation guides, promote loyalty and reward programs, provide mobile payment options, and more.[42] All of this is aimed at delivering a seamlessly satisfying customer experience, one that has due regard for the customer's privacy. One estimate has 37% of large retailers deploying beacons in 2015[43] and another forecasts those beacons will drive over $4 billion in sales in the first year with a tenfold increase in the second year.[44]

British supermarket chain Tesco has long been a leader in loyalty programs and has been an early mover in using mobile technologies. In late 2014 Tesco conducted what it termed a live experiment at a Tesco Metro (urban convenience) store.[45] It was an experiment, not a full-fledged test, because the beacon technology was not integrated into the Point of Sale system. Consequently it involved only a select group of products and a separate payment option.

One technology analyst who tried the system explained how it worked.[46] First the customer must download the app, in this case the Powatag app. The app asks for the customer's contact and credit card information, making this an opt-in situation. Cards explaining the promotion were handed out as customers entered the store (Figure 12.12a). Customers were invited to choose a sandwich, crisps (chips) and a drink, then to pay by scanning a giant QR code on a nearby table or the one on the floor that is pictured in Figure 12.12b. This allowed the customers to avoid the usual long lunch time queue at the checkout counter. Overall, it sounds like a good way to pick up a quick lunch. Notice that it uses a manufacturer app, not a Tesco app, making it usable by many retailers. The analyst who described his experience said it would be even more useful as a checkout option in restaurants.

The beacons use customer data and produce a great deal more. That makes it essential that retailers and beacon manufacturers fully inform customers of how data is collected and used and that they ensure the security of customer data. Although there may be millions of beacons already deployed in stores, shopping malls, stadiums, airports, and other public places, a 2015 study found that 70% of respondents did not know what a beacon was. When asked if they would shop in a retail store that used another technology, facial recognition, for marketing purposes an overwhelming 75% said they would not.[47]

Location-based technology offers great opportunities for marketers but it carries with it great risks. Marketers need to deploy the technology with due regard for the privacy and security of their customers or they may face significant backlash. Most important of all, marketers need to ensure that every mobile service they deploy adds to the quality of the customer experience.

Mobile Customer Experience

First, what exactly do we mean by customer experience? Here is a simple explanation of what it is and is not:

Customer experience (CX)—is not a single event.

It is the sum of all customer interactions and the resulting perceptions of the brand.[48]

That definition implies that CX is an omnichannel phenomenon. All channels used by a consumer are important in creating the overall experience. By the same reasoning, any channel can be important in degrading the experience. Satisfying experience, like trust, takes time and effort to build but it can be destroyed by a single unsatisfactory event.

Second, if mobile is the first screen for many people or many activities, the mobile experience becomes paramount. Marketers must take all possible steps to make the mobile experience a satisfactory one and to integrate mobile and all other channels to the overall experience so as to make it equally satisfactory.

Third, a reminder that good customer experience drives customer loyalty, which in turn drives customer lifetime value.[49]

A study conducted by Forrester Consulting for Google argues that mobile customer experience is created in micro-moments throughout the day. They identify moments and give examples:

- Want to know. Smartphone users turn to their phones for brief but important sessions from everything to getting a weather report to chatting with friends on social media.[50]

- Want to go. Searches for nearby products, services, and stores are increasing. 50% of those searches result in a store visit within a day and 18% lead to purchases.

- Want to do. 91% of smartphone users turn to their phones for information while completing tasks.[51]

- Want to buy. 82% turn to phones to help them make purchase decisions.[52]

The study says that brands need to understand the moments that matter to their customers and how to react to those moments. Searches for nearby restaurants go up near the dinner hour, for example. Then ask what information will be most helpful in making the decision easier and faster. Diners want to know where the restaurant is and what menu items they offer. Marketers also need to use contextual clues like time of day and location to provide the most relevant information. All the information must be based on the customers' needs. Diners would be happy to be able to find out if a table for four is available 30 minutes from now.

Then, of course, the diners want to have good food and a pleasant dining experience at the restaurant. And, oh yes, they'd like fast checkout also! Marketers can and should measure how well they are meeting customer needs at each step in the purchase journal.

That is a brief summary of the customer experience task facing marketers today, but it gives a sense of the magnitude of that task. The Google study warns that 98% of brands are not yet ready to identify, deliver on, and measure these moments that are rich with purchase intent.[53]

What are the best practices that will allow marketers to meet the challenges of mobile marketing and to optimize the role of social media in it?

Best Practices for Social Mobile Marketing

1. **Understand the brand's target audience and the role mobile plays in their daily lives and their shopping habits.** While identifying and understanding audience behaviors and needs is a cardinal rule of marketing, it takes on special importance in the mobile environment. Mobile is still evolving and significant differences exist in areas like age demographics and purchasing of specific product categories.

2. **Give consumers complete control of the data they share with brands.** Brands need to strive for complete transparency about how they collect and use consumer data. This is difficult in an environment where consumers do not have a deep understanding of some of the technology they use on a daily basis.

3. **Ensure that information provided to consumers is relevant to their current circumstances and has the potential to be immediately useful.** Even though consumers have opted in to mobile communications from marketers, the communications must occur at a time that is relevant to the consumer, not at the time that is convenient to the brand.

4. **As search becomes increasingly important in the mobile arena, marketers need to take special care that their sites are optimized for mobile search.** Consumers tend to search when they need something and tend to act on the results of the search.

5. **Remember that B2B customers are also using mobile and expect content to be available in mobile formats.** Use of mobile devices and social networks is nearly ubiquitous among business professionals. B2B brands and products must be ready to meet their needs.

6. **Mobile experience is a key part of overall customer experience. It is often the entry point to the customer purchase journey and is likely to come into play at various touchpoints along the journey.** The customer journey is under the customer's control, not the marketers'. Brands must orchestrate their marketing activities so they provide satisfying customer experience at each customer touchpoint at each stage of the purchase journey. Although it is very important, mobile is only one part of overall customer experience.

Customer use of mobile devices will continue to evolve over the coming years. So will the technologies marketers have to interact with mobile customers. Social networks themselves and the way social platforms are used in the mobile environment are also likely to undergo change. Staying abreast of developments and using them in a way that pleases customers and fulfills marketing objectives will continue to be a major challenge.[54, 55]

Notes

1. Tode, Chantal (July 29, 2015). "Home Depot's Project Color app paints best-in-class omnichannel experience," Mobile Commerce Daily. Retrieved July 29, 2015, from http://www.mobilecommercedaily.com/home-depots-project-color-app-paints-best-in-class-omnichannel-experience

2. N.d. "The Home Depot Project Color App TV Commercial, 'Virtual Test Drive,' " iSpot.tv, Retrieved July 30, 2015, from http://www.ispot.tv/ad/74kj/the-home-depot-project-color-app-virtual-test-drive

3. N.d. "Real-time TV Advertising Metrics Platform," iSpot.tv. Retrieved July 30, 2015, from http://www.ispot.tv/our-platform

4. Kemp, Simon (January 21, 2015). "Digital, Social & Mobile Worldwide in 2015," We Are Social. Retrieved August 1, 2015, from http://wearesocial.net/blog/2015/01/digital-social-mobile-worldwide-2015/

5. Kemp, Simon (January 21, 2015). "Digital, Social & Mobile Worldwide in 2015," We Are Social. Retrieved August 1, 2015, from http://wearesocial.net/blog/2015/01/digital-social-mobile-worldwide-2015/

6. McMillan, Robert (February 20, 2014). "You May Not Use WhatsApp, But the Rest of the World Sure Does," Wired. Retrieved August 1, 2015, from http://www.wired.com/2014/02/whatsapp-rules-rest-world/

7. N.d. "Most popular social media websites in the United States in June 2015, based on share of visits," Statista. Retrieved August 18, 2015, from http://www.statista.com/statistics/265773/market-share-of-the-most-popular-social-media-websites-in-the-us/

8. Sloan Garett (May 27, 2015). "These Are the Digital Trends Everyone in Tech and Advertising Needs to Know," AdWeek. Retrieved August 1, 2015, from http://www.adweek.com/news/technology/these-are-digital-trends-everyone-tech-and-advertising-needs-know-165017

9. (July 21, 2015). "Smartphones Now Account For Half of US Adults' Digital Media Time," Marketing Charts. Retrieved August 9, 2015, from http://www.marketingcharts.com/online/smartphones-now-account-for-half-of-us-adults-digital-media-time-57073/

10. (April 3, 2014). "Mobile vs. Desktop," Twitter. Retrieved August 3, 2015, from https://twitter.com/wsjd/status/451886622788055040

11. Mandese, Joe (July 31, 2015). "Next Year Will Be The 'Year Of' Mobile: For Video, Anyway," MediaPost. Retrieved August 9, 2015, from http://www.mediapost.com/publications/article/255212/next-year-will-be-the-year-of-mobile-for-video.html?utm_source=newsletter&utm_medium=email&utm_content=readmore&utm_campaign=84918

12. Smith, Cooper (January 14, 2014). "Foursquare's New Big Data Initiative Is Going To Help It Thrive, Even As The Check-In Withers," Business Insider. Retrieved July 28, 2015, from http://www.businessinsider.com/foursquare-surpasses-45-million-registered-users-and-begins-collecting-data-in-new-ways-2-2014-1

13. Siegler, M.G. (February 10, 2011). "Nearing a Million Users, Gowalla Moves Forward On The 'Social Atlas' Path," Tech Crunch. Retrieved July 28, 2015, from http://techcrunch.com/2011/02/10/gowalla-users/

14. Constine, Josh (December 5, 2011). "Gowalla Confirms It Will Shut Down As Founders and Team Members Join Facebook," Tech Crunch. Retrieved July 28, 2015, from http://techcrunch.com/2011/12/05/gowalla-acqhire/

15. Sloane, Garett (June 27, 2015). "Foursquare Starts Selling All That Data," AdWeek. Retrieved July 28, 2015, from http://www.adweek.com/news/technology/foursquare-starts-selling-all-data-158628

16. (March 5, 2014), "In the US, Time Spent With Mobile Apps Now Exceeds Desktop Web Access," Marketing Charts. Retrieved August 12, 2015, from http://www.marketingcharts.com/online/in-the-us-time-spent-with-mobile-apps-now-exceeds-the-desktop-web-41153/

17. Lipsman, Andrew (August 21, 2014). "The U.S. Mobile App Report," comScore. Retrieved August 12, 2015, from https://www.comscore.com/Insights/Presentations-and-Whitepapers/2014/The-US-Mobile-App-Report

18. Ibid.

19. Perez, Sarah (January 6, 2015). "App Usage Grew 76% In 2014, With Shopping Apps Leading The Way," Tech Crunch. Retrieved on August 12, 2015, from http://techcrunch.com/2015/01/06/app-usage-grew-76-in-2014-with-shopping-apps-leading-the-way/

20. Hof, Robert D. (January 26, 2015). "Starbucks Bets the Store on Mobile," Technology Review. Retrieved on August 12, 2015, from http://www.technologyreview.com/news/534016/starbucks-bets-the-store-on-mobile/

21. (June 18, 2014). "Top 10 Branded Apps that are Actually Useful," Marketing Unwired. Retrieved on August 12, 2015, from http://www.mobext.ph/blog/top-10-branded-apps-that-are-actually-useful-

22. (February 27, 2015). "Top Daily Activities on Smartphones and Tablets," Marketing Charts, Retrieved on August 7, 2015, from http://www.marketingcharts.com/online/top-daily-activities-on-smartphones-and-tablets-41027/

23. Loechner, Jack (July 24, 2015). "Mobile Shopping To $217.4 Billion By 2019," Media Post. Retrieved August 7, 2015, from http://www.mediapost.com/publications/article/254311 /mobile-shopping-to-2174-billion-by-2019.html#reply?utm_source=newsletter&utm_ medium=email&utm_content=comment&utm_campaign=84610

24. (February 12, 2015). "Mobile Is Still for Upper-Funnel Shopping Activities," eMarketer. Retrieved August 3, 2015, from http://www.emarketer.com/Article/Mobile-Still-Upper-Funnel-Shopping-Activities/1012048

25. (September 2014). "The Ascension of Mobile Commerce," Internet Retailer. Retrieved August 3, 2015, from https://www.internetretailer.com/trends/mobile-commerce/ascension-mobile-commerce/

26. Smith, Dave (February 23, 2015). "More people use mobile devices to buy groceries than any other retail category," Business Insider. Retrieved August 7, 2015, from http://www .businessinsider.com/the-most-popular-retail-purchase-on-mobile-phones-is-groceries -2015-2

27. Patel, Neil (n.d.). "Surprising Mobile Ecommerce Statistics that Will Change the Way You Do Business." Retrieved August 7, 2015, from https://blog.kissmetrics.com/surprising-mobile-ecommerce/

28. Lee, Jessica (June 3, 2014). "60% of Consumers Use Mobile Exclusively to Make Purchase Decisions [Study]," Search Engine Watch. Retrieved August 7, 2015, from http:// searchenginewatch.com/sew/study/2348076/60-of-consumers-use-mobile-exclusively-to-make-purchase-decisions-study#

29. Shaut, Brady (August 18, 2015). "Survey: 56% of U.S. Consumers Have Abandoned a Mobile Transaction." Retrieved August 18, 2015, from http://www.adweek.com/socialtimes/survey-56-of-u-s-consumers-have-abandoned-a-mobile-transaction/625265

30. DeAmicis, Carmel (June 2, 2015). "Pinterest Launches the Buy Button," re/code. Retrieved August 10, 2015, from http://recode.net/2015/06/02/pinterest-launches-the-buy-button/

31. Matney, Lucas (July 15, 2015). "Facebook Adds Buy Button Integration As It Continues To Reinvent Pages," Tech Crunch. Retrieved August 10, 2015, from http://techcrunch .com/2015/07/15/cant-buy-me-love/#.pwdk8b:ZgyS

32. Addady, Michael (August 6, 2015). "Twitter expands 'Buy' button to more than 100,000 merchants," *Fortune*. Retrieved August 10, 2015, from http://fortune.com/2015/08/06/twitter-buy-button/

33. Sloan, Garett (June 1, 2015). "Instagram Unleashes a Fully Operational Ad Business," AdWeek. Retrieved August 10, 2015, from http://www.adweek.com/news/technology/instagram-just-unleashed-fully-operational-ad-business-165117

34. (n.d,). "Mobile First Strategy," Techopedia. Retrieved August 10, 2015, from http://www .techopedia.com/definition/29153/mobile-first-strategy

35. Hamblen, Matt (February 17, 2010). "Google CEO preaches 'mobile first'," Computerworld. Retrieved August 11, 2015, from http://www.computerworld.com/article/2520954/mobile-wireless/google-ceo-preaches--mobile-first-.html

36. (2014). "Building an Audience-First Digital Marketing Strategy," Turn. Retrieved August 11, 2015, from https://www.turn.com/livingbreathing/assets/089259_Smart_Market_Vol_3_ Building_Audience-First_Digital_Marketing_Strategies.pdf

37. (December 24, 2013). "Turning Omni-Channel Marketing into Omni-Channel Loyalty," loyalty360. Retrieved August 10, 2015, from http://loyalty360.org/loyalty-today/article /turning-omni-channel-marketing-into-omni-channel-loyalty

38. (n.d.). "Google Now," Google. Retrieved August 10, 2015, from https://www.google.com /landing/now/

39. Patterson, Ben (June 8, 2015). "How to use Google Now cards: 7 tips for managing what they show you, when and why," PC World. Retrieved August 11, 2015, from http://www.pcworld .com/article/2925716/how-to-use-google-now-cards-7-tips-for-managing-what-they-show-you-when-and-why.html

40. (n.d.). "Using location services on mobile devices," Twitter. Retrieved August 11, 2015, from https://support.twitter.com/articles/118492#

41. (n.d.). "The Beacons are Coming! The Beacons are Coming!," mjdInteractive. Retrieved August 13, 2015, from http://www.mjdinteractive.com/retail-beacons/

42. Laney, Brian (May 19, 2015). "5 Things You Need to Know About Beacons Technology," Alerttech. Retrieved August 13, 2015, from http://alerttech.net/retail-technology/

43. Martin, Chuck (April 17, 2015). "37% of Large Retailers to Deploy Beacons This Year," mCommerceDaily. Retrieved August 13, 2015, from http://www.mediapost.com/publications/article/247920/37-of-large-retailers-to-deploy-beacons-this-year.html

44. Smith, Cooper (July 28, 2015). "How beacons—small, low-cost gadgets—will influence billions in US retail sales," Business Insider. Retrieved August 13, 2015, from http://www.businessinsider.com/beacons-will-impact-billions-in-retail-sales-2015-2

45. (n.d.). "PowaTag & Tesco Meal Deal 30 Second Challenge," Powatag. Retrieved August 13, 2015, from http://www.powa.com/powatag/casestudies.html

46. Barraclough, Geoffrey (October 13, 2014). "How I failed the PowaTag Tesco meal deal 30 second challenge. Twice.," Barraclough & Co., Retrieved on August 13, 2015, from http://barracloughandco.com/2014/10/13/how-i-failed-the-powatag-tesco-meal-deal-30-second-challenge-twice/

47. Martin, Chuck (August 12, 2015). "75% Would Skip Stores that Use Facial Recognition for Marketing," MediaPost. Retrieved on August 13, 2015, from http://www.mediapost.com/publications/article/256061/75-would-skip-stores-that-use-facial-recognition.html?utm_source=newsletter&utm_medium=email&utm_content=readmore&utm_campaign=85232

48. Roberts, Mary Lou and Debra Zahay (November 2014). "Designing Satisfying Mobile Customer Experience," LinkedIn. Retrieved August 13, 2015, from https://www.linkedin.com/pulse/20141121175155-6394760-the-importance-of-mobile-customer-experience?trk=mp-author-card

49. (November 15 2012). "Calculating the Economics of Loyalty," Forbes. Retrieved August 13, 2015, from http://www.forbes.com/sites/baininsights/2012/11/15/calculating-the-economics-of-loyalty/

50. (n.d.). "How Micro-Moments are Changing the Rules," Google. Retrieved August 13, 2015, from https://www.thinkwithgoogle.com/articles/how-micromoments-are-changing-rules.html

51. (n.d.). "I-Want-to-Go Moments: From Search to Store," Google. Retrieved August 13, 2015, from https://www.thinkwithgoogle.com/articles/i-want-to-go-micro-moments.html

52. (n.d.). "I-Want-to-Buy Moments: How Mobile Has Reshaped the Purchase Journey," Google. Retrieved August 14, 2015, from https://www.thinkwithgoogle.com/articles/i-want-to-buy-moments.html

53. (July 2015). "A Mobile Moments Mind-Set: New Research Details the Benefits for Brands," Google. Retrieved July 2015, from https://www.thinkwithgoogle.com/research-studies/mobile-moments-mind-set-new-research-details-benefits-for-brands.html

54. Morgan, Jason (May 1, 2015). "Mobile Madness: Mobile Marketing & PR Best Practices," Cision. Retrieved August 16, 2015, from http://www.cision.com/us/2015/05/mobile-madness-mobile-marketing-pr-best-practices/

55. (n.d.). "The Modern Marketer's Guide To Mobile: Orchestrating Mobile Marketing." Chief Marketer. Retrieved August 16, 2015, from http://www.chiefmarketer.com/gated/new-school-marketers-guide-mobile-orchestration/

Social Media Monitoring

Marketers need the right metrics to demonstrate the ROI of their SMM campaigns. That will happen only if marketers map their metrics to their objectives. This allows them to make decisions between quantitative and qualitative metrics and to choose the metrics they need from the vast number available.

Today, many organizations recognize that without social media monitoring, they are like ships at sea without navigation or radar, lacking the capacity to seek out opportunities and circumvent threats. This chapter draws upon the best practices in social media monitoring to help marketers find the elusive treasures and skirt the dangerous shoals of social media and to identify the right approach to monitoring without drowning in the sea of options.

There seem to be as many definitions for the term *social media monitoring* as there are purposes for its use, ranging from simply listening to the social web to performing complex and sophisticated analyses of SMM activities. For current purposes social media monitoring is defined as *the process of tracking, measuring, and evaluating an organization's SMM initiatives.*

Our consideration of social media monitoring actually began in Chapter 2 with a discussion of listening and observing the brand's social media platforms as the initial step in developing a marketing plan. Monitoring is one of the final steps in the planning cycle (Figure 2.1). As you will see in this chapter, the steps of listening and of setting objectives are a necessary precursor to monitoring, especially to the selection of the metrics to monitor.

LEARNING OBJECTIVES

After completing this chapter, students will be able to:

- Explain the nature and importance of social media monitoring
- Discuss the role of listening in tracking social media activities
- Explain the Valid Metrics Framework and how it can be useful to the social media marketer
- Identify some of the issues in choosing the right social media

(Continued)

metrics, both quantitative and qualitative

- Discuss the importance of business objectives and ROI as part of the monitoring process
- Define Key Performance Indicators
- Identify some of the ways in which Google Analytics can shed light on SMM effectiveness
- Explain ways in which platform-specific analytics can be useful to social media marketers and to brand managers

The Importance of Social Media Monitoring

A key question for any business is "What is the ROI (Return on Investment) of _____?" When you fill in the blank with "social media marketing" the question becomes particularly vexing. From the beginning of the social media era CMOs and CEOs have wondered whether social media budgets are well spent. Some find that the answer to that question has been slow in coming.

Figure 13.1a demonstrates the issue. A study published in August 2014[1] shows that only 15% of marketers stated that they could measure the ROI on their SMM. Nevertheless, another question in the survey indicated that SMM spending was expected to increase sharply between 2014 and 2019 (Figure 13.1b). Professor Christine Moorman, the director of the study, observed that, "Getting that all-important quantitative proof, which only 15% have, is essential to justifying this spending."[2]

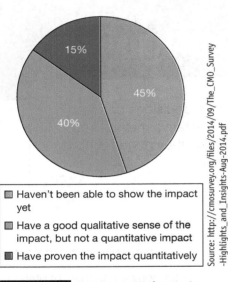

Source: http://cmosurvey.org/files/2014/09/The_CMO_Survey-Highlights_and_Insights-Aug-2014.pdf

Haven't been able to show the impact yet

Have a good qualitative sense of the impact, but not a quantitative impact

Have proven the impact quantitatively

Figure 13.1a How Many Marketers Are Able to Measure Their Social Media ROI

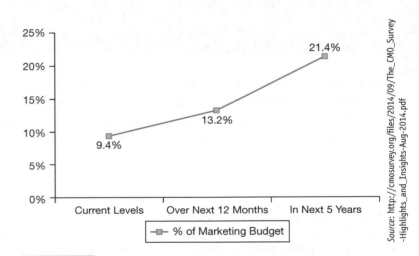

Source: http://cmosurvey.org/files/2014/09/The_CMO_Survey-Highlights_and_Insights-Aug-2014.pdf

Figure 13.1b How Much Will SMM Budgets Increase (Current = 2014)

Listening and Tracking

Social media tracking is the process of finding and listening to content on the social web. Given its size and continued growth, finding specific content on the social web can sound like a daunting task. There are many powerful tools that can help in the actual tracking process, which will be discussed in Chapter 14. In order to use platforms and tools wisely, marketers must understand which metrics have a direct impact on their business results. There is, for instance, no befit to having a Facebook page for a tequila brand that has many followers if most of the followers turn out to be beer drinkers!

Source: http://californiatortilla.com/2015/01/hotsauceface/

Source: http://californiatortilla.com/2015/01/hotsauceface /Posted January 13, 2015

Figure 13.2a California Tortilla Facebook Post

Figure 13.2b Contest Instructions from Facebook Picture Gallery

One way to track brand mentions is to identify the keywords that will retrieve relevant data. Keywords can be tracked using tools like Google Analytics, which will be discussed later in the chapter. Ill-defined search terms not only waste resources but can produce misleading results that will do more harm than good. Worse, incorrect keywords miss the important conversations and trends that are occurring.

Instead of tracking keywords, marketers find it easier to track relevant hashtags. #WorldCup was a standout on the world social media stage while the games were being played. The World Cup was generally acknowledged to be the most tweeted event of 2014 with Twitter saying 672 million tweets were sent during the 32-day period.[3] #WorldCup2014 was also widely used. #WorldCupFinal was popular as the day approached. The second most popular hashtag was #Brasil, but there was also a popular hashtag with the alternate spelling #Brazil.[4] Marketers can track hashtags of interest to them, but this example suggests the care that must be taken in data collection and interpretation.

The most direct way to track is to set up a hashtag and promote it. The hashtag in Figure 13.2a[5] #HotSauceFace is unique to the event and easy to follow. California Tortilla encourages the use of the hashtag by offering an incentive, a common approach. Contest participants are instructed to upload their hot face photos to Instagram, using the hashtag, and the tag @Caltort. That makes it easy to follow the activity while it is happening and to accumulate the traffic results after the contest is over. Tracking takes effort—worthwhile effort as we will soon see. Smart planning of the campaign makes tracking easier and likely to be more accurate.

Measuring

Jim Sterne, author of *Social Media Metrics*, writes that "measurement is no longer optional" for a company's SMM activities: "Whether money is tight or times are good, everybody is bent on improving their business performance based on metrics. You cannot continue to fly by the seat of your pants. Automated systems and navigational

Exposure	Engagement	Influence	Impact	Advocacy
• Opportunity to attend to content	• Interaction with content	• Ability to change opinion or behavior	• Effect on the target audience	• Suggest action to another user
• **Page View**	• **Time Spent**	• Klout Score	• **Purchase**	• **Recommendation**

Figure 13.3 Valid Metrics Framework with Metrics Categories, Definitions, and Sample Metrics

instrumentation are required on passenger planes, and your business deserves no less."[6] That's another way of stressing the importance of measuring ROI, as Figure 13.1 demonstrated.

The need to measure social media remains of paramount concern for businesses because it enables marketers to assess progress toward achieving marketing goals, determine how strategies are performing, and make necessary adjustments to achieve overall business goals.

Many marketers have proposed models for social media measurement. For instance, well-known metrics evangelist Avinash Kaushik has a model that recommends major categories Conversation > Amplification > Applause > Economic Value, and others have similar frameworks.[7] The similarity of the many frameworks, which is often masked by different terminology, has contributed to the confusion surrounding social media metrics. The effort to standardize models and terminology produced the Valid Metrics Framework introduced in Chapter 2. Here we show the model originally presented in Figure 2.4 with the addition of one sample metric at each stage (see Figure 13.3).

Having a framework is an important first step in choosing metrics that really matter. However, before we go further, we should agree on some definitions.

SOME IMPORTANT DEFINITIONS

These definitions are taken from the work of various business writers to take advantage of plain, direct speaking. Most are not textbook definitions and therefore are unlikely to be the exact definitions you have seen in strategy and finance courses. They are, however, useful to demystify the often-confusing subject of social media metrics.

METRIC "A metric is a number," says Avinash Kaushik. He goes on to say that the metric can be either a count (e.g., page visit) or a ratio (e.g., sales lead conversion rate).[8]

A metric can also be either quantitative (objective measures like pageviews or number of followers) or qualitative (an attempt to measure how people feel about something; "I love this product," "This event made me sad").[9] Qualitative metrics are often grouped under the heading of "sentiment analysis." Both are important and have clear uses in evaluating SMM campaigns.

GOAL "A goal is a broad primary outcome."[10] For example, in Chapter 2, Cisco stated that one goal of its social listening program was to become a thought leader in its industry.

STRATEGY "A strategy is the approach you take to achieve a goal."[11] For instance, Cisco described listing as the foundation of its social media strategy and identified social listening tools it used to carry out the strategy.

BUSINESS OBJECTIVE "An objective is a measurable step you take to achieve a strategy."[12] For example, Cisco might set objectives leading to its thought leadership goal as "Achieve x# of IT professionals as followers of its Data Center and Cloud blog" and/or "Achieve x# of guest post invitations to the participating authors in the set of Technology blogs." These are straightforward numeric objectives that can be measured without equivocation.

KPIs "A key performance indicator (KPI) is a metric that helps you understand how you are doing against your objectives," says Kaushik[13]. He gives as examples a retailer who uses a sales target as her primary objective and uses average order size as one KPI. He also uses a newspaper that has a revenue goal to meet and uses number of clicks on display ads as a KPI.

In short, a KPI is a metric that *directly measures impact on achievement of a business objective*. KPIs are important, but establishing them is beyond the scope of this chapter. We will limit ourselves to some examples, bearing in mind that, because KPIs are directly related to business objectives, each brand or business may have a different set of KPIs.

ROI There are many discussions of measuring ROI of social media activities, but many do not contain a usable calculation approach for marketers. An approach to calculation needs to start with a definition of ROI that is acceptable to accountants—or to CEOs, for that matter. Take this one from BusinessDictionary.com: "The earning power of assets measured as the ratio of the net income (profit less depreciation) to the average capital employed (or equity capital) in a company or project."[14] You will recognize a formula that looks like

$$\frac{\text{INCOME FROM OPERATIONS}}{\text{OPERATING ASSETS}} \times 100$$

While that sounds like a definition or a formula that an accountant might offer, brief consideration suggests that some of the terms are difficult to define in a marketing context. This is the essence of the difficulty of calculating the ROI of SMM campaigns. It's not that marketers don't know the formula. Instead, it is how to define terms like depreciation and capital employed in marketing operations.

Angela Jeffrey, writing about the application of the Valid Metrics Framework, recommends the following formula:[15]

$$\text{ROI} = \frac{(\text{Total \$ Earned, Saved or Avoided}) \text{ MINUS } (\text{Total \$ Invested})}{(\text{Total \$ Invested})} \times 100\%$$

An examination of this formula shows expenditures for which marketers are responsible:

- The numerator of the ratio is the profitability of the activity (income − cost)

- The numerator is the cost of the activity.

In the real world of social media campaigns, it may be hard to judge the sales that result from the social media activity. Some financial experts will object to the inclusion of amounts saved or expenditures avoided. Even the total spent on the campaign is not entirely straightforward. Do you include employee time or just out-of-pocket costs? Even though there are difficulties in operationally defining some of the terms, this is an approach that can be used by marketers.

Measuring

Chapter 2 discussed in detail the development of marketing objectives, especially the importance of basing marketing objectives on overall business goals and objectives. Choosing the appropriate metrics is, in turn, based on marketing objectives. *Marketers cannot create measures with business value unless they first have measurable objectives and then map their metrics to the objectives.*

The first step is to turn to the Valid Metrics Framework and determine where the objectives fit into the framework. This task is easier if the SMM campaign is short and focused on a single type of objective. It may be more difficult if the objective is longer term like "become a thought leader."

Looking back at Figure 13.2, what do you think the objective of this campaign is? Looking at the ads, it's obvious that California Tortilla is trying to generate buzz by encouraging activity on its social platforms. This kind of campaign can be useful in a new product introduction. In this case, they had recently introduced new hot sauces, so there could have been product awareness objectives. However, wouldn't a new product promotion have been more specific? It turns out that California Tortilla had just publicly added Instagram to its platforms,[16] although examination shows that content was being posted on the Instagram page for several months prior to the campaign. Facebook was an established platform that was used to promote the contest, as shown in Figure 13.2a. Other social media activity at that time included Twitter @ Caltort, Yelp, Foursquare, and YouTube, all of which may have had some role in the campaign.[17]

The campaign objectives clearly revolved around exposing customers to the Instagram page and engaging them with the brand, perhaps in such a way that their peers were influenced to participate. That requires a purchase, but do you suppose purchase is a primary objective or simply ancillary to the contest? Again, it is likely that they would have approached the subject more directly if purchase had been an objective.

Keeping it simple is good, so let's assume that the primary objective was to make customers aware of the Instagram page and encourage them to participate on it. Metrics chosen might then be:

Number of Likes on each campaign-related Facebook post

Number of Shares on each campaign-related Facebook post

Number of Likes on each campaign-related Instagram post

Number of Shares on each campaign-related Instagram post

Number of customer pictures posted on Instagram

Getting customers to post their #HotSauceFaces on Instagram was the main behavior encouraged in the Facebook posts, so it seems safe to assume that it was the key metric for the campaign. Likes and Shares on Facebook, however, are useful metrics for gauging some level of engagement with the campaign, and Facebook provides them for each post. Facebook provides the page administrators with the reach (number of people the post was served to) of each post, as one of the page Insights for users of business pages. Consequently they have both Exposure and Engagement metrics for Facebook.

The @Caltort tag suggested in Figure 13.2b is their U.S. Twitter handle, so it suggests the campaign includes Twitter. Figure 13.4 confirms that Twitter is being used with the same content but in a way that suits that platform. It shows California Tortilla tweeting the same set of campaign photos used on Facebook one at a time on Twitter. This is efficient use of their content, often called "repurposing." The first tweet in the stream shown is actually a retweet of an article about the campaign that appeared in a trade publication. That is easy content used to keep the Twitter stream active and interesting. You can speculate about how CT found this article—keywords, perhaps?

Source: https://twitter.com/caltort?ref_src=twsrc^google
|twcamp^serp|twgr^author

Figure 13.4 California Tortilla Twitter Page

Twitter also shows retweets and favorites for each post. Finally, if you were able to hover over each image, you would find a Pin It button, encouraging the viewer to post the image on his Pinterest page. You can see how quickly the metrics that need to be tracked can accumulate!

By the end of February when the hot faces campaign concluded, the Instagram element of the California Tortilla seemed to be firmly established. An outsider can't always link activity to precise social media actions, but there were pictures posted and each of the hot faces posts by the company received a few likes. What may be especially significant is that the number of likes on individual posts increased steadily during and immediately after the campaign. Occasionally social media just explodes for a brand as, for example, the Old Spice Guy campaign did. For the most, however, it builds slowly through consistent, systematic attention. The California Tortilla campaign is a good example of a straightforward social media program that, from the outside at least, appeared to have easily measured behavioral objectives.

Let us turn to a brief example of monitoring attitudinal sentiment on the web, provided by a firm that makes one of the tools that can track conversations on the web and provide an assessment of whether the attitudes are positive or negative. uberVU via Hootsuite called this case study The Beyoncé Effect.

The period of time monitored was July 6 to 20, 2014 (Figure 13.5a). During that time the MetLife brand achieved 33,925 mentions. As a comparison, during that time frame the heavily advertised Aflac brand received 4,419 mentions. The reason? A concert by Beyoncé and Jay Z on July 12. On that day the number of mentions spiked to 6,289 and stayed high for a second day as people continued to talk about the concert on social media.

Notice that the stadium itself brought in a high number of mentions—34% of the total when you combine terms. However, everything else on the conversation map reflects the concert in one way or another.

Two marketing insights can be gleaned from this snapshot of social web activity. The first is that the naming of the stadium has led to high brand awareness; it is the MetLife Stadium, not the stadium. Second is the degree to which this newsworthy event increased the buzz around the MetLife Stadium. One assumes the stadium was rented for revenue, not PR. However, what brand wouldn't be happy with the mentions, especially given the data in Figure 13.5b? Only 3% of the sentiment expressed by these mentions was negative, while 56% was neutral.[18] The old PR chestnut, "I don't care what you say about me, just be sure you spell my name right," seems to apply here! MetLife got a huge amount of visibility from the concert and little of that visibility was negative.

MetLife Stadium 34% | Beyoncé 11% | stadium 10% | August 5% | tour 4% | Jay 3%

tickets 8% | at MetLife Stadium 5% | concert 4% | tonight 2% | 2014 2%

REVIEW 4% | Bey 2%

Source: http://blog.hootsuite.com/beyonce-effect-metlife-star-caused-social-surge-financial-services-industry/

Figure 13.5a Conversation Map for MetLife

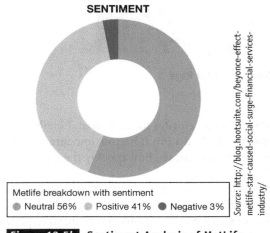

SENTIMENT

Metlife breakdown with sentiment
● Neutral 56%   ● Positive 41%   ● Negative 3%

Source: http://blog.hootsuite.com/beyonce-effect-metlife-star-caused-social-surge-financial-services-industry/

Figure 13.5b Sentiment Analysis of MetLife Conversation

Did that visibility directly result in sales of insurance? The correct answer is that the data does not tell us. The practical answer is probably not. Does, however, a high level of favorable brand awareness impact sales in the long term? What do you think?

So there you have examples of metrics for two different social media situations. First you have a set of quantitative metrics for a carefully planned and executed brand promotion. The impact on the California Tortilla Instagram site is measured with relative ease. The impact on sales is less clear, but the chain certainly looked at sales during the run of the campaign to see whether it could ascertain any lift. The second example was both qualitative and in one sense an unintended consequence of a positive event. However, it would be hard to argue that MetLife paid for the naming rights to a major athletic stadium without expecting to get halo effects from whatever took place there.

These are examples using metrics that are appropriate to the objectives or to the fortuitous situation. However, they only give a glimpse of the richness of social media metrics that are available to the marketer. Table 13.1 provides a more comprehensive listing organized by the categories of the Valid Metrics Framework and classified as either qualitative or quantitative.

Fortunately, the nature of most of the metrics is obvious from their names. In addition, some like Reach and CPM are familiar as traditional advertising metrics. A few seem to need further explanation.

Source of Visitors to a social media platform is essentially the same as the commonly used Number of Referrals to a website used in other contexts. There are perhaps more options in SMM. There are literally hundreds of social media platforms (channels) as well as traditional online (banner advertisement) and offline (print advertisement) channels. Most social media marketers will need to follow only the relatively few channels that their audience frequents. They do, however, need to watch for shifts—from Facebook to Snapchat, for example.

We discussed the audience reached by social media marketers in Chapter 3. Part of audience development is persuading your own audience to share with their audiences

Exposure	Engagement	Influence	Impact	Advocacy
Quantitative	**Quantitative**	**Quantitative**	**Quantitative**	**Quantitative**
Page Visits	Repeat Visits	Links	New Subscribers	Online Ratings
Visitors, Unique Visitors	Time Spent on Site	Association with Brand Attributes	Number of Referrals to website	Ratio Mentions To Recommendations
Visits per Channel (Source)	Total Interactions on Post/Page	Purchase Consideration	Number of Content Downloads	Number of Brand Fans/Advocates
Reach Total Follower (Audience Count)	Likes, Shares Comments, +1s	Likelihood to Recommend	Number of App Downloads	**Qualitative**
Opportunity-to-See	Click-Throughs Number of Followers, Friends	**Qualitative** Sentiment (Positive, Neutral, Negative)	Abandoned Shopping Carts (−)	Content of Ratings/Reviews
CPM (cost per thousand exposures)	Total Audience of All Shares	Net Promoter Score	Number of Sales Leads	Organic Posts by Advocates
	Interaction with Profile	Klout Score	Conversion Rate Sales	Employee Ambassadors
	Use of Hashtags		Repeat Sales	
	Qualitative		Purchase Frequency	
	Mentions		Cost Savings	
	People Talking About Brand		**Qualitative**	
			Satisfaction	
			Loyalty	

Table 13.1 List of Metrics by Valid Metrics Framework Category

(followers). In order to understand the Total Audience a piece of content is reaching, the audiences of the initial audience must be determined.

Interactions with Profile is a simple count (quantitative) of the number of people who have engaged in a platform behavior—chatting about the brand, for example. That behavior becomes qualitative when the marketer engages in sentiment analysis of the content of the conversation to see whether it is positive, neutral, or negative. The terminology used by various platforms differs but the concept is the same.

There are other ways of looking at metrics. By type of channel (paid, earned, owned) and by business purpose are two of the ways used by the Valid Metrics Framework. By now, though, you are getting the idea. *There are a lot of metrics; the challenge is to choose the ones that correctly measure marketing objectives.*

MAPPING METRICS TO MARKETING OBJECTIVES

It's worth repeating: *marketers cannot create measures with business value unless they first have measurable objectives and then map their metrics to the objectives.*

In order to illustrate this point—which is at the heart of good social media measurement—we will use the SMM objectives and the campaign- and platform-specific objectives shown in Figure 2.6. Table 13.2 shows those objectives and pairs each with one or more metrics that could be used to measure achievement (or lack thereof). Looking at the metrics suggests that their choice is relatively straightforward. Sometime it is straightforward; sometimes it is less so.

For instance, for the campaign-specific objective of achieving 60% registration from click-throughs on a program announcement on the brand blog, selecting click-throughs as the only metric required seems like a no-brainer. The objective was written using a standard

Objective	Possible Metrics

Improve Customer Satisfaction Score by 10%	Customer Satisfaction Score
	  Metrics Service
	  Tool
	Proprietary Model
	Net Promoter Score

Make 20% of Customers Aware of New Rewards Program	Page Visits Likes
Achieve 7% Click-Through on Rewards Program Announcement on Blog	Click-Throughs
Achieve 60% Program Registration from Click-Throughs	New Subscribers to Rewards Program
Increase Sharing of Blog Content by 10%	Total Number of Shares Shares to Each Channel
Increase Sharing of Blog Content on Twitter by 25%	Number of Retweets Number of Replies Number of Mentions

Table 13.2 SMM Objectives and Corresponding Metrics

metric, so the choice is obvious. The same is true for using the new subscriber metric to measure new program registrations. They are simply different words for the same concept.

Although customer satisfaction is an often-used objective across all types of marketing, measuring customer satisfaction can be controversial. Does the marketer want to use a specialized satisfaction metrics service or a traditional marketing research firm that has a satisfaction product? Does she want to use an online tool that asks visitors or purchasers to rate the satisfaction with their experience or their purchase? Does the brand prefer to develop its own proprietary model for calculating customer satisfaction? Any of these options can be satisfactory. What is virtually certain, however, is that they will not give the same scores. In fact, the scores may be wildly divergent. Following multiple metrics that purport to measure the same thing but produce different scores is confusing to both marketers and to the executives who are trying to make sense of SMM. In a case like this marketers must work hard to understand what each model is really measuring and choose the one that best meets their business needs. In fact, the marketer may follow two or more models for a time in order to really understand and make the best choice. In the end, consistency is possible but precision is often not, so choose consistency.

On the other hand, the Net Promoter Score is a transparent measure of what is presumed to be satisfaction. Actually, it is a measure of the loyalty of a company's customer relationships. It was developed by Fred Reichheld, Bain & Company, and Satmetrix and has been used as a replacement for customer satisfaction measurements.

The NPS assumes that every company's customer can be divided into three classes: Promoters, Passives, and Detractors. The score is obtained by asking customers to answer a single question using a 0-to-10 rating scale. The question is "How likely is it that you would recommend [company X] to a friend or colleague?" Customers are categorized as follows:

- Those with a 9-to-10 score are Promoters, loyal enthusiasts who will continue to buy and refer other consumer and fuel further growth.

- Those with a 7-to-8 score are Passives, satisfied but unenthusiastic customers, vulnerable to competitive offerings.

- Those with a 6-to-0 score are Detractors, unhappy customers likely to damage the brand and hinder growth through damaging word of mouth.

- The NPS is calculated by taking the percentage of customers who are Promoters and subtracting the percentage who are Detractors. However, the NPS itself is not a percentage but rather uses a plus "+" or minus "−" to indicate the product. An NPS that is above zero (i.e., has a plus sign) indicates a good customer relation's rating, with a +50 being considered indication of excellent customer relations.[19]

Since the Net Promoter Score is a measure of loyalty, not satisfaction *per se*, the marker may want to use both a satisfaction score and the NPS. They are expressing some different but equally useful perspectives on the satisfaction of customers.

Another situation is illustrated by the issue of whether to measure awareness of the rewards program by Page Visits or by Likes (or a corresponding platform metric like +1). The problem here is a common one. Does the fact that a person has visited a page mean that the visitor has seen all of the content, some of it, or none at all? The Page Visit metric gives no answer to that question. Is it, therefore, a valid measure of awareness? Most marketers would agree that it is not. However, in order to Like a post it seems reasonable to assume that the person has paid some attention to the concept. Yes, the person could have clicked on Like by accident, but it is hoped that does not often occur. So while Like is not exactly aware, it seems to be a good proxy.

Finally there are situations in which more than one metric is required to give a complete picture of achievement. Sharing of blog content is encouraged by using one of the sharing tools and offering choice of channels to the viewer. Metrics are provided by the sharing tool on the platform. Twitter provides metrics on tweet sharing, which we will illustrate in the next section of this chapter.

This discussion suggests that while mapping metrics to marketing objectives is not always entirely straightforward, it uses the knowledge and judgment that good marketers have in abundance. It is, therefore, an achievable goal, one that all brands should strive for.

ARE ALL METRICS HONEST?

Before we leave the metrics section, we need to answer this important question. Sadly, the answer is "no!" There are many ways to manipulate the metrics collection on any website, any platform. Even worse, there are dishonest people that make a business out of selling fake metrics. The example of Facebook is replicated on every other platform and most websites.

Facebook has been trying to wipe out commercial vendors of "fake likes" since at least 2011.[20] In 2015 Facebook announced that, as a result of better technology, it had been able to remove over 200,000 fake likes from the system before they ever reached the intended pages. It indicated that the success of their eradication efforts had driven many vendors of fake likes out of business. In the process, it also reminded business page owners of appropriate ways to encourage authentic likes.

"New advances in our pattern recognition technologies helped us halt many of the major exchanges that promote fake like activity on Facebook originating from click farms, fake accounts and malware,"[21] according to Facebook site security engineer H. Kerem Cevahir.

That is only the Facebook example. All platforms have to maintain security against the efforts of click farms, fake accounts, and malware that can mimic authentic visitors liking posts. If they do not, their metrics will lose all value in the minds of business customers. Likewise, websites have to ensure that activities like customer reviews are honestly submitted by real people. It is a never-ending battle!

With that warning in mind, we will turn to the final step in monitoring, that of evaluation.

Evaluation

In the third and final stage of the monitoring process, the social media marketer demonstrates how well she has achieved social media objectives and how successfully social media activities have contributed to the achievement of business objectives (Figure 13.6). Measuring, as discussed in the previous section, is in fact the first step in evaluation. Choosing the appropriate metrics for social media objectives answers the question as to whether social media objectives have been achieved. Metrics alone, however, do not answer the question about whether *social media has contributed to the achievement of business objectives.* That is the issue of social media ROI, the overriding concern of executives (Figures 13.1a and 13.1b).

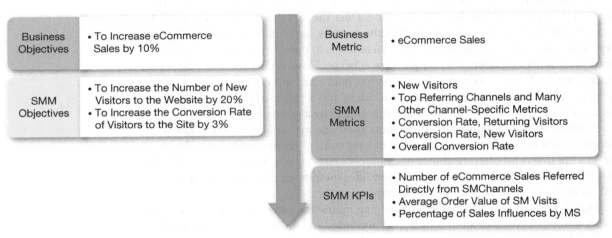

Figure 13.6 The Social Media Measurement and Evaluation Cascade

To address the issue of ROI social media marketers turn to KPIs. Remember our definition from earlier in the chapter: *a KPI is a metric that directly measures impact on achievement of a business objective.* That is a deceptively simple idea. It requires careful thought about business goals and strategies to develop KPIs that can truly guide business decision making.

Nonprofit marketing expert Beth Kanter gives a brief example of how one Internet-based organization is using KPIs to ensure that it is meeting its goal. MomsRising describes itself as "a network of people just like you, united by the goal of building a more family-friendly America."[22] It provides information about and advocacy for issues like maternity and paternity leave, nutritious food for kids, and immigration fairness for all. One direction in which they wish to grow their network is that of multicultural diversity.

With that in mind the network identified three strategic questions, seen in Figure 13.7. The first two business results—increasing the number of new members and decreasing the number of lost members—seem straightforward in terms of the associated KPIs. The number of new members would be tracked as a part of normal business operations. There is no membership fee—just free signup for email and text alerts. That implies that lapsed members are measured by unsubscribes (from email, from text alerts, or from both?), which again is tracked as a normal part of business operations. Diversification of membership seems less obvious. Why don't they use member ethnicity as their measure? Do they ask members for data on ethnic background? If so, it is not obvious on their signup page. Do they want to impute ethnicity from name? There are pieces of software that purport to do that, but experience says the results are fraught

Goal: Grow the Movement   **MomsRising.org**

MomsRising is building a strong multicultural movement of people who care about family economic security and well-being.

Need To Know	KPI
Are we adding new members?	Increased New Members
Are we losing members?	Decreased Lapsed Members
Are we diversifying membership?	Number of Collaborations with multicultural orgs

Top Sources of Member Growth	
Number of New Members	Specific Page Name
#	action page
#	action page
#	action page
#	blog page
#	website sign up
#	tall-a-friend redirect

Source: http://www.bethkanter.org/measurement-bigtv/

Figure 13.7 Mapping KPIs to Business Results

with error. Those are good arguments for using the rather indirect, but easily obtainable, metric of number of collaborations with multicultural groups.

Kanter points out that simply using all the metrics available, for instance, all the metrics in Table 13.1, doesn't answer the question of what to do—what business decisions to make—based on all that data. It takes work and a clear understanding of organizational strategy to sort through all the possible metrics and to identify the ones that best measure goal achievement.[23] When that challenge has been met it will be possible to understand how successful the organization is and to communicate the level of success, and the reasons for it, to CEOs and boards of directors.

Evaluating the Impact of Social Media Activities

The final step in the social media monitoring process is to evaluate the results of campaigns. That requires gathering data about each activity that occurred during the campaign. The process of data gathering is generally referred to as "analytics."

Google Analytics is the largest analytics platform, serving over 30 million websites in 2014 according to one estimate.[24] It provides data about online marketing activities, like websites, social platforms, and email, and offline marketing activities like direct mail. Social media platforms like Facebook and Twitter offer their own analytics. In addition, there are services that provide analytics services for a brand's marketing activity. The way that Google Analytics gathers and presents data forms the basis of most other metrics platforms, so it is a good place to start. Then we will give two brief examples of platform-specific analytics.

USING GOOGLE ANALYTICS

Once a website is connected to Google Analytics data immediately becomes available. Of course, that data becomes more valuable over time as the user begins to see trends, the impact of events or activities, and what is working and what is not. It is important to note that Google Analytics provides the data. It is up to the user to glean marketing insights from the data.

Figures 13.8a and 13.8b show two basic reports.[25] Figure 13.8a shows the Google Analytics Report Profile, which shows the major categories of reports with the Acquisition report content expanded. The Acquisition Overview in Figure 13.8b gives a summary of how customers are being acquired by the site. This is an overview report; social media is only one of the channels by which customers are brought to the site, a relatively small one as shown in the pie diagram. Other overview information is the number of visitor sessions per day and a conversions statistic. "Goal" indicates that the user has defined this metric. In this case it is the number of visitors to the site who have "converted" by signing up for a mailing list.

Under the Acquisitions, Behavior, and Conversions headings, look at only channel 4, Social. You see data like the number of sessions generated by social channels, the bounce rate, and the conversion percentage for three user-defined goals. Bounce rate is defined by Google as "the percentage of single-page sessions (i.e. sessions in which the person left your site from the entrance page without interacting with the page)."[26] This is a good example of a metric that can be defined in different ways by different analytics platforms. It is important to look up the definition of any metric that could be interpreted in more than one way.

Another thing to note about this report is that each of the channels is a live link. Clicking on the link takes the user to more detailed reports. Clicking on the Social link takes the user to the Social Value report (Figure 13.9).

Figure 13.9 shows how effective the social channel is for this site.[27] It shows metrics like the number of conversions to email subscriptions generated directly by social channels. "Contributed social conversions" means that social media was used somewhere in the path to the website while "last interaction social" means that the last recorded interaction was on social media. The Social Sources pane contains data about shared networks. Those include Google+ and other networks that are connected to your website.

Figure 13.8a Google Analytics Report Profile and **Figure 13.8b** Acquisition Overview Report

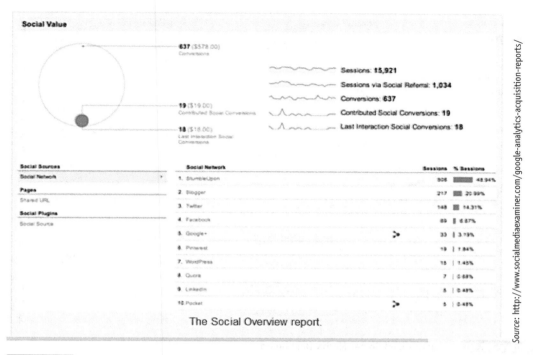

The Social Overview report.

Figure 13.9 Google Analytics Social Overview Report

The Social Networks column shows the important statistics about the networks from which social data is referred to your website. Looking at the figures you can see that StumbleUpon is most important for this site, while Facebook is in fourth spot with less than 7% of the social referrals. The earlier data was interesting, but this is beginning to be the type of data on which business decisions can be made.

Notice that we arrived at this report by clicking through from the Acquisitions Overview Report. This Social Overview Report also has many live links. Each of those links could have one or more click-throughs or it could end there. Look back at Figure 13.8 the analytics profile and note that there are other major sections; only the Acquisitions section is expanded. Now you are beginning to get an idea of how many reports there are in Google Analytics. That is a powerful argument for being clear about your metrics and KPIs. You can look for that important data, not drown in the sea of Google Analytics reports.

Understanding all the metrics and KPIs is likely to require a number of reports, however. Are you going to go back and forth between them? That is time consuming and confusing. Enter the dashboard!

A dashboard is a web page where various graphic reports can be displayed, usually in real time. As you can see from the reports profile in Figure 13.8a Google Analytics offers its own dashboards to users.[28] Many agencies offer custom dashboards to the users of their analytics services. That allows clients to see exactly the reports they want in exactly the way they want to see them. This is especially useful to executives who want to understand the top-line impact of social (and other) media without pouring through page after page of reports.

There is a great deal of data on this single dashboard, which is the intention. You see some of the same metrics that you saw on the Google Analytics reports, "Overall Site Visits," for example. You also see some data like "Most Socially Shared Content" that is specific to this website (Figure 13.10). Various reports in Google Analytics could be customized to produce the site-specific data. The custom dashboards make it easier.

Now that we have a sense of what Google Analytics can do, let's look at examples that come from social media platforms themselves.

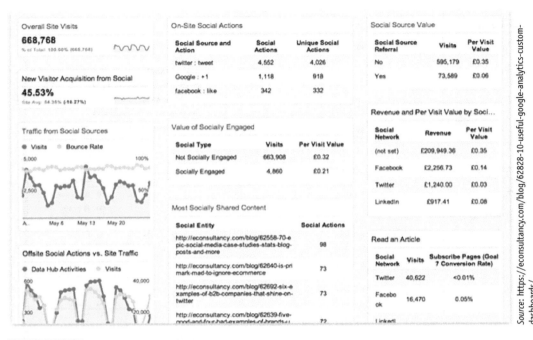

Figure 13.10 A Customized Social Media Dashboard

USING METRICS REPORTS FROM BLOGGER

Figure 13.11 is from Blogger. Blogger, a Google property, lists all blogs for a particular account, whether active or not, on a summary dashboard. Prof. Zahay and her students often create a blog for a digital marketing class. This one, from a few years ago, was called New Interactive Marketing Updates.[29] The owner of the blog has access to a variety of reports, shown in the left column.

The page shown in Figure 13.11 is the Overview report from the Stats section. It shows a number of metrics of great interest to a serious blogger including Pageviews, daily and for specified periods of time. It shows the posts where viewers entered and the online sites from which the viewers entered. The map is a graphic representation of viewer origins. There are other Stats reports, listed on the left panel.

Figure 13.12 gives more detail on sources of traffic to this blog.[30] The first section shows traffic from other URLs including websites and other blogs. Each blog post generates a URL, so each is shown separately. The second section shows sites, not URLs. It includes Google, the university's website, and LinkedIn. The third section contains the top keywords that attracted traffic to the blog. Keywords like "interactive marketing" and "interactive marketing definition" are not unexpected but they do point to the importance of good titles, content, and tagging.

As you can see, the reports feature the metrics that the owner of a blog should follow in order to see how successful it is in attracting an audience of the quality and quantity that is desired. The metrics are not merely "interesting." They represent ways to evaluate blog success and to improve it.

Finally, let's turn first to Facebook and then to Pinterest for brief examples of metrics reports on two platforms that are important to many marketers.

USING METRICS REPORTS FROM FACEBOOK

Facebook Insights are available to business users of Facebook Pages but not to individual users who have Personal Profiles. In early 2015 Facebook revised the Insights page to make it easier to understand what is working on a page, who is engaging with it, and what can be done to improve page results.

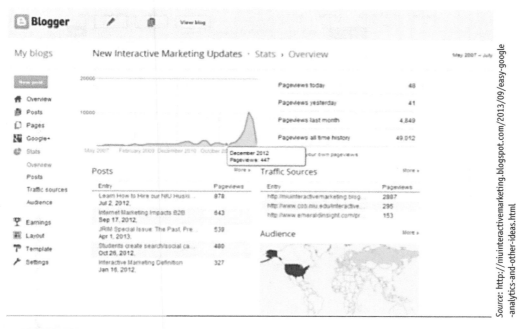

Figure 13.11 A Blogger Statistics Overview Report

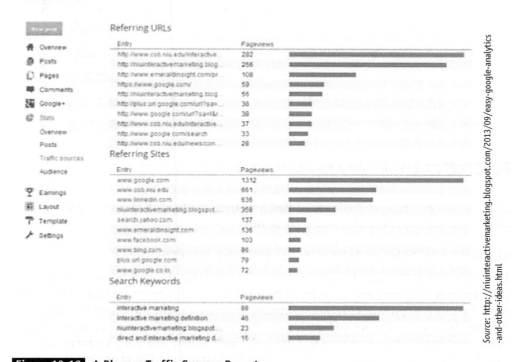

Figure 13.12 A Blogger Traffic Sources Report

Figure 13.13 shows an overview report from a general interest page maintained by Profs. Zahay and Roberts that is targeted to both professors and students who use their Internet Marketing text.[31] It shows weekly data, which is decidedly underwhelming. There were only two posts made during that week and posting activity is needed to stimulate interest and engagement. The most popular post during this week was actually made the week before. The relative popularity of the post on SEO supports previous observation that the most popular posts on this page have been Prof. Zahay's posts on SEM.

This overview pane is only one of six available to the business user. There are also reports with more detail on Likes, Reach, Visits, Posts, and People (audience

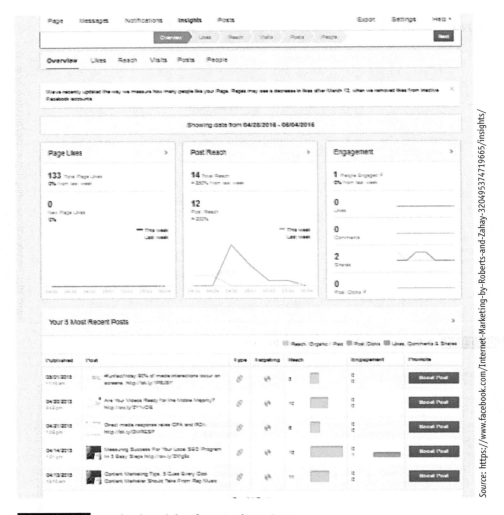

Figure 13.13 Facebook Insights for a Business Page

characteristics). These are basic social media metrics, made available to the marketer in an easy-to-use form for each brand page he has.

USING METRICS REPORTS FROM PINTEREST

Prof. Roberts has Pinterest Boards, organized by topic, that she established when the platform was fairly new and she shares a board with Prof. Zahay. The primary objective of the boards is to provide current information of interest to the professors who use their textbooks, so currency and quality are important in selecting content to pin. She has pinned consistently over time and gradually built a small following for boards like Internet Marketing Infographics and Social Media Marketing without any promotion beyond regular Pinning. The posts are connected to her Twitter account, so she writes careful Twitter-length descriptions for each Pin.

In late 2014 she became aware of unusual activity on the Infographics board. It centered around a single infographic called "The Shift to Visual Social Media,"[32] which received an inordinate number of Repins and Likes in a short period of time. A few weeks later the red Pin It button at the top of the post showed 44 Repins, far exceeding engagement on any of her other posts and boards. Clicking through on the number on the button shows who repinned the post, not why. The assumption is that some site, probably Pinterest itself, promoted this particular post.

The impressions numbers for a selected date range[33] shows an unusual spike in activity on January 10—1,518 impressions and 1,110 viewers (Figure 13.14). The exact numbers are obtained by hovering over the date. The 30-day period shows a pattern that is often seen on websites and platforms. The unusual activity, fueled by an outside source or promotion by the owner, lasts only briefly. It settles back, however, to a new and higher normal level.

Pinterest defines impressions and viewers as follows: "This is the number of times a Pin linked to your website has appeared on Pinterest homefeeds, category feeds, and search. A viewer is anyone who sees a Pin from your website on their feeds."[34] Notice that Pinterest assumes that Pins represent content on the user's website, an attempt to draw traffic for the site. Think of a food manufacturer who posts photos of luscious dishes, offering ingredients and recipes on its website. Many of us, however, post content from other sites in order to fulfill an objective of our own.

The owner is able to change the date range for the graphic, but not for the 30-day summary in the bottom panel. The visual post is still somewhat active, but attention is now entered on an infographic listing the biggest data breaches of 2014. It is by paying attention to these analytics that the owner learns what appeals to the audience she has attracted. Note the availability of audience data in another tab. Pinterest Analytics are found in the settings icon at the top of the owner's home page, for business accounts only.

Pinterest was paying attention to a set of boards that was generating substantial traffic. Imagine Prof. Roberts's surprise when she received a valentine email from Pinterest[35] (Figure 13.15). It informed her of the number of "admirers," the number of people who had liked or repinned her posts since the first of the year. The email made

Source: https://analytics.pinterest.com/

Figure 13.14 A Pinterest Impressions Screen

Source: pinterest.com

Figure 13.15 User Email from Pinterest

it easy to send a Pinterest valentine, so she found and Pinned an infographic about ecommerce on Valentine's Day then sent it to her admirers via the icon that appears at the top of each post. That infographic only received 66 impressions, not making it to the top five shown in Figure 13.14. However, it is by activities like this that an owner gradually builds traffic for her boards.

Notice two other things about the analytics from both Blogger and Pinterest. First, they use many of the same metrics that you originally saw in the section on Google Analytics. They may not all define the metrics in exactly the same way, however, so be careful to understand the meaning of something like "impressions" for each platform. Second, they are all visually similar. That means you don't have to learn to read metrics reports all over again each time you move to a new platform. By the same token, it means that all social media marketers should become intimately familiar with Google Analytics.

Metrics and Analytics Best Practices

Important best practices for choosing the most useful Internet metrics include:

1. Apply Avinash Kaushik's "so what" test. Assume a result for a metric like Bounce Rate; for instance, say the bounce rate for your site is 50% for a time period. "So what?" Does it suggest doing anything that would improve the business results for your site? If so, then select it as a metric. If it doesn't lead to a recommendation that could improve business results, then don't select it.[36]

2. Be sure that the metrics choices are acceptable to the brand managers who will use them. Ensure that the metrics are in line with the business objectives of those users.[37]

3. Identify the metrics that drive business results and make them your KPIs.

Best practices for analytics include:

1. Create dashboards that show real-time data for KPIs in ways managers find easy to grasp.[38]

2. Send an analytics report by email each month to draw managers' attention to their dashboards.[39]

3. Meet with managers on a regular basis to discuss the insights to be drawn from the analytics.[40]

Many marketers, even social media marketers, express confusion over various aspects of metrics and the way they are reported. We do not argue that Internet monitoring is a simple or straightforward subject. Its complexity is compounded by new platforms and changes in reporting on existing platforms. We do argue, however, that monitoring is an understandable topic, especially if you apply the Valid Metrics Framework and other concepts that are presented in this chapter.

What is not in doubt is the importance of metrics KPIs and analytics reports that impact business results. They are important to the business itself, to the SMM effort, and to the social media marketers who participate in it.

Notes

1. McKinsey & Company (August 2014), "The CMO Survey: Highlights and Insights," CMOsurvey.org. Retrieved January 13, 2015, from http://cmosurvey.org/files/2014/09/The_CMO_Survey-Highlights_and_Insights-Aug-2014.pdf

2. (September 3, 2015). "Tweet This: Social Media Important to Company Performance but Difficult to Prove." Retrieved January 13, 2015, from http://cmosurvey.org/blog/tweet-this-social-media-important-to-company-performance-but-difficult-to-prove/

3. Rogers, Simon (July 14, 2014), "Insights into the #WorldCup Conversation on Twitter." Retrieved on January 13, 2015, from https://blog.twitter.com/2014/insights-into-the-worldcup-conversation-on-twitter

4. Barnes, Robert (June 12, 2014), "The Most Popular Hashtags for the 2014 World Cup." Retrieved on January 14, 2015, from http://blog.trendsmap.com/2014/06/top-hashtags-world-cup

5. (January 9, 2015). "california tortilla." Retrieved on January 13, 2015, from https://www.facebook.com/caltort/photos/a.10150738942617195.464409.43773552194/10153643446347195/?type=1&theater

6. Sterne, Jim (2010), *Social Media Metrics: How to Measure and Optimize Your Marketing Investment* (Hoboken, NJ: John Wiley), p. 2.

7. Bartholomew, Don (n.d.), "Unlocking Business Performance." Retrieved December 4, 2014, from http://amecorg.com/wp-content/uploads/2013/06/Social-Media-Valid-Framework2013.pdf

8. Kaushik, Avinash (April 19, 2010), "Web Analytics 101: Definitions: Goals, Metrics, KPIs, Dimensions, Targets." Retrieved November 3, 2014, from http://www.kaushik.net/avinash/web-analytics-101-definitions-goals-metrics-kpis-dimensions-targets/

9. Badshah, Aseem (May15, 2014), "Measuring Social ROI – Quantitative or Qualitative?" Retrieved January 15, 2015, from http://blog.socedo.com/measuring-social-roi-quantitative-or-qualitative/

10. Belicove, Mikal E. (September 27, 2013), "Understanding Goals, Strategy, Objectives and Tactics in the Age of Social." Retrieved January 15, 2015, from http://www.forbes.com/sites/mikalbelicove/2013/09/27/understanding-goals-strategies-objectives-and-tactics-in-the-age-of-social/

11. Ibid.

12. Ibid.

13. Kaushik, Avinash (April 19, 2010), "Web Analytics 101: Definitions: Goals, Metrics, KPIs, Dimensions, Targets." Retrieved November 3, 2014, from http://www.kaushik.net/avinash/web-analytics-101-definitions-goals-metrics-kpis-dimensions-targets/

14. (n.d.). "Return on Investment (ROI)." Retrieved on January 15, 2015, from http://www .businessdictionary.com/definition/return-on-investment-ROI.html

15. Jeffrey, Angela (June 2013), "Social Media Measurement: A Step-By-Step Approach." Retrieved January 22, 2015, from http://www.instituteforpr.org/wp-content/uploads/Social -Media-Measurement-Paper-Jeffrey-6-4-13.pdf, p. 15.

16. (January 15, 2015). "California Tortilla Heating Up Instagram with First-Ever Campaign." Retrieved January 17, 2015, from http://www.fastcasual.com/news/california-tortilla-heating -up-instagram-with-first-ever-campaign/

17. "Social News." Retrieved January 17, 2015, from http://californiatortilla.com/social/

18. Dunham, Kate (August 2014), "The Beyoncé Effect & MetLife: How the Star Caused a Social Surge for the Financial Services Industry." Retrieved January 17, 2015, from http://blog .ubervu.com/beyonce-effect-metlife-star-caused-social-surge-financial-services-industry.html

19. "Net Promoter Score" (2010), REX: Process Excellent Network. Retrieved July 28, 2011, from http://www.processexcellencenetwork.com/glossary/net-promoter-score/

20. (n.d.). "Scam Alert." Retrieved May 10, 2015, from https://www.facebook.com/Caution .FakeFans.BadVendors/info

21. (April 18, 2015). "Facebook Strips 200,000 Pages of Fake 'Likes' in Latest Authenticity Drive." Retrieved May 10, 2015, from http://rt.com/news/250877-facebook-fake-likes-vendors/

22. (n.d.). "MomsRising.org" Retrieved January 18, 2015, from http://www.momsrising.org/

23. Kanter, Beth (February 26, 2013), "Linking Results to Key Performance Indicators Is Like Hooking Up a Big TV." Retrieved January 18, 2015, from http://www.bethkanter.org/measurement-bigtv/

24. "Estimates Say over 30 Million Websites Use Google Analytics. How Did It Get So Big?" (September 2014). Retrieved February 22, 2015, from http://www.quora.com/Estimates-say -over-30-million-websites-use-Google-Analytics-How-did-it-get-so-big

25. Hines, Kristi (August 12, 2014), "How to Use Google Analytics Acquisition Reports to Know Where People Are Coming From." Retrieved December 3, 2014, from http://www .socialmediaexaminer.com/google-analytics-acquisition-reports/

26. (n.d.). "Bounce Rate." Retrieved February 21, 2015, from https://support.google.com /analytics/answer/1009409?hl=eng

27. Hines, Kristi (August 12, 2014), "How to Use Google Analytics Acquisition Reports to Know Where People Are Coming From." Retrieved December 3, 2014, from http://www .socialmediaexaminer.com/google-analytics-acquisition-reports/

28. Charlton, Graham (May 30, 2013), "10 Useful Google Analytics Custom Dashboards." Retrieved December 3, 2015, from https://econsultancy.com/blog/62828-10-useful-google -analytics-custom-dashboards/

29. (September 23, 2013). "Easy Google Analytics and Other Ideas That Work for Teaching Social Media in the Classroom." Retrieved December 7, 2014, from http://niuinteractivemarketing .blogspot.com/2013/09/easy-google-analytics-and-other-ideas.html

30. Ibid.

31. (n.d.). Administrator page. Retrieved May 4, 2015, from https://www.facebook.com/Internet -Marketing-by-Roberts-and-Zahay-320495374719665/insights/

32. Retrieved January 25, 2015, from https://www.pinterest.com/pin/342273640400000446/

33. Retrieved January 25, 2015, from https://analytics.pinterest.com/

34. (n.d.). "Activity from Your Website." Retrieved January 25, 2015, from https://help.pinterest .com/en/articles/activity-your-website

35. Email, February 13, 2015.

36. Kaushik, Avinash (March 8, 2010), "Kill Useless Web Metrics: Apply The 'Three Layers Of So What' Test." Retrieved January 20, 2015, from http://www.kaushik.net/avinash/kill-useless -web-metrics-apply-so-what-test/

37. (n.d.). "Archive for 'Best Practices.'" Retrieved January 20, 2015, from http://michele .webanalyticsdemystified.com/category/best-practices

38. Robbins, Jenna Rose (n.d.), "5 Best Practices for Google Analytics." Retrieved January 20, 2015, from http://www.siteseeingmedia.com/seo/google-analytics-best-practices/

39. Ibid.

40. Yoakum, David (March 17, 2014), "Top 10 Practices of Successful Web Analytics Organizations." Retrieved on January 20, 2015, from http://blogs.adobe.com/digitalmarketing /analytics/top-10-practices-successful-web-analytics-organizations/

Tools for Managing the Social Media Marketing Effort

The right tools can help social media marketers maximize the value of the brand's various social media platforms while making the most efficient use of their own time. Choosing tool for an individual or for a team requires an understanding of marketing tasks and the many tools available to help perform them.

By the time you have reached this point in the text you have been exposed to various social media strategies and to a somewhat bewildering array of social media platforms on which strategies can be executed. In the process, two important points have been emphasized in a variety of ways. They are:

1. Not all social media platforms are equally appropriate for identified target markets at any given time, for any specific campaign

2. Time and skilled personnel are the resources in shortest supply in SMM operations.

Both these issues compel marketers to prioritize their activities and to operate with the greatest possible efficiency. To help achieve that efficiency, an industry has grown up to provide SMM tools and assist marketers in their use.

This chapter will discuss tools that are within the reach of an individual marketer or marketing department and provide a brief introduction to suites of tools that are offered by services providers. We will also provide insight into tools that can be used by the individual in creating and monitoring a personal brand.

As a first step we need a clear understanding of what *SMM tools* means.

LEARNING OBJECTIVES

After completing this chapter students will be able to:

- Describe what SMM tools are and how they can be used
- Identify types of SMM tools
- Discuss how to go about choosing SMM tools for different types of marketing activities
- Give examples of different types of SMM tools and explain how their use can improve the marketing effort
- Discuss the difference between tools and apps
- Give an example of an app for consumer use

What Are Social Media Marketing Tools?

The term *SMM tools* is used often with the assumption that the readers or listeners understand what the term signifies. Before we begin to look at tools themselves, let's stop briefly to examine just what the phrase means and why it is important to the practice of SMM.

The concept of "tools" is not unique to SMM; the idea has been part of marketing from its inception. Consider the following definitions:

> Tool: An item or implement used for a specific purpose. A tool can be a physical object such as mechanical tools including saws and hammers or a technical object such as a web authoring tool or software program. Furthermore, a concept can also be considered a tool. "Creativity is the tool which allows a child's mind to grow."[1]

> Marketing tool: The techniques and materials used by those who are involved in the promotion of goods and services. Most business that need to sell their goods or services to the public will make extensive use of various marketing tools, such as market research and advertising to help further their success.[2]

> Social Media: A new marketing tool that allows you to get to know your customers and prospects in ways that were previously not possible. This information and knowledge must be paid for with output of respect, trustworthiness, and honesty. Social Media is not a fad, but I also think it's just the beginning of the marketing revolution – not the end. Marjorie Clayman – Clayman Advertising, Inc[3]

To find a definition that describes SMM tools, it is necessary to look for "social media management software."

> Social media management software: software designed for marketing departments and organizations to publish to social media platforms. Users can post to many social media platforms at once, respond to customer inquiries quickly, and work in teams without creating any duplication of efforts. Social media management tools have grown in recent years from purely offering publishing features to including social media monitoring and analytics integrations bundled into their products, though there are many standalone social media monitoring products on the market.[4]

The series of definitions gives some sense of the number of ways the term *tools* is used (and not used) in various discussions of performing marketing tasks effectively as well as efficiently. The final definition captures the spirit, but is not presented as a definition of SMM tools. Let's develop our own:

> Social Media Marketing Tools: software designed to support or to automate common SMM activities that include content generation, publishing, scheduling publication and republication, testing, monitoring, analysis, and many more.

There are many ways in which that definition could be elaborated, but that definition captures the essence of the term. This chapter is about the elaboration; what kinds of tools, who needs to use them, why, for what purposes. There are endless examples of tools, but no accepted way to categorize them in order to study them easily. Here are some ways tools have been categorized:

Social Listening Software (aka Social Media Monitoring Software)

Social Conversation Software (aka Social Media Engagement Software, Social Media Management Software)

Social Marketing Software (aka Social Media Management Software and a bunch of gibberish labels)

Social Analytics Software

Social Influencer Software[5]

Social Advertising

Social Commerce

Social Media Developer Apps

Content Curation[6]

Figure 14.1 Types of Tools Available to Social Media Marketers

This is a formidable list of types of tools. To provide structure to our discussion we have categorized tools as shown in Figure 14.1.

Tools perform many functions, as the preceding list makes clear. However, it is reasonable to think of them as tools that support a single marketing task or purpose, tools that support activities on a single platform, tools that allow marketers to work efficiently across multiple platforms and purchased services that offer clients a myriad of options for listening, creating and publishing content, and tracking the results of social media activities and campaigns.

Before we look at each category of tools we should take a moment to consider basic issues in the selection of tools.

Choosing the Right Tool for the Job

The purpose of using social media tools is to make SMM more efficient and to lessen the chance of errors. There are many tools and there is a learning curve for each new tool that is adopted. How does the marketer choose?

If you research the subject, you will find many articles on tools and their uses. You will find many list of the "best" tools. The best of those lists explain how and why the author uses the tools and how effective they have been. But no one really tells the reader how to choose tools for his or her own situation. From the recommendations and the reasons why that are given, however, it is possible to make some inferences. Here are some pointers to get started.

RULE #1 – INVESTIGATE THE TOOLS OFFERED BY A PLATFORM

If you are looking for a platform-specific tool, start by investigating what the platform itself offers. Platforms change frequently, from minor tweaks to major revisions. Tools offered by the platform should be the most reliably up to date. For all tools, be sure to check when it was last updated. On the web, there is little chance that old tools will be good tools.

RULE #2 – THINK ABOUT WHAT YOU NEED TO ACCOMPLISH

This is, after all, the reason for using tools—to do what needs to be done in the most efficient way possible. One suggestion is to come up with the most persistent and aggravating "pain points" in the social media effort. For instance is a lot of time spent repurposing one basic piece of content for several platforms being used in the campaign? If the answer is yes and a tool can be found that reliably configures content for a variety of platforms, the tool may be worth a try. Reliability is an important criterion. So is ease of use, and only a trial can actually demonstrate that.

RULE #3 – BE SURE THE TOOL SERVICES THE PLATFORMS YOU USE

There are many tools and many platforms. As you will see in examples to follow, some tools are limited in terms of the number of platforms they can link to. Other tools allow the user to pick from a large list of the most popular platforms for business use. Be sure the tool links to all the strategically-significant platforms used in your campaigns as well as being sure it can execute the functions you most often employ on them.

RULE #4 – CONSIDER HOW MANY PEOPLE NEED TO USE THE TOOL AND WHAT THEIR ROLES ARE

Some tools have been developed for the primary purpose of helping social media teams collaborate and others can be used by multiple team members. Who needs to collaborate, how often, and perhaps even from what locations should be considered in choosing between tools. Most tools do not require a high level of technological expertise, but technological requirements should also be a consideration.

The questions are basically common sense. The point is not to choose indiscriminately from a "best tools" list but to think carefully about personal and organizational requirements before making a huge investment in learning to use tools that do not meet needs.

RULE #5 – CONSIDER WHETHER A FREE TOOL WILL SUFFICE OR WHETHER A PAID ONE IS NEEDED

There are many good free tools for virtually every SMM purpose. Starting with a free tool and learning to use it before migrating to more complex services is usually good practice.

Blogger Christian Karasiewicz has good advice for a beginner in the tools arena. He recommends that a user first use a tool to help create content. In the next section we will discuss using an editorial calendar to organize content creation and posting. The second step is to use a tool to monitor your activity. We will discuss several tools for monitoring activity on various platforms. Third, use a tool to help you analyze how your social media activity is growing and achieving goals. We will discuss tools analyzing brand activity and for monitoring and analyzing the progress of your personal branding activities.[7]

With these rules in mind, let's consider examples of tools in each of the categories in Figure 14.1. As we do so, remember that these are only examples of perhaps dozens of tools that do the same or a very similar job. They are examples only, not recommendations.

Single-Purpose Tools

Many tools have been developed for a single specific marketing task. Content marketing involves traditional marketing as well as all of digital marketing including social media. It is such an important part of marketing (we could have said "marketing tool") at present that a host of tools specific to content marketing have grown up.

An important one is the editorial calendar. From the simple to the complex, editorial calendars have been used by publishers for years to ensure that writers, photographers, graphic artists, and other specialists involved in content creation meet deadlines for moving work to the next stage in the process so that the newspaper or magazine gets out on time. The same sort of communication and coordination is essential in the fast-paced world of digital marketing where the various specialists often work from different locations.

However, in SMM you will find that many individual publishers, who have a variety of projects and media channels active at one time use an editorial calendar to ensure that they don't neglect anything they need to be doing. For example a small business owner who uses social media as her major promotional channel may use an editorial calendar to schedule her blog posts or to create a schedule for the employee who is assigned to make regular posts to Pinterest. Two people working on different aspects of social media is reason enough to have an editorial calendar such as that shown in Figure 14.2. If one image from each blog post is Pinned with a comment that includes a link back to the blog, then the calendar becomes essential to see that both the blog posts and the Pins are spaced for greatest effectiveness.

The Content Marketing Institute, not surprisingly, produces a great deal of content—posts on their own blog as well as content for a variety of other communications channels. They have written a number of posts on ways to manage the communications flow and one of them includes a template for regulating blog publishing.[8]

In addition to the row dates the spreadsheet includes columns for information about each post. This is the Scheduled Blog posts tab. There are also tabs for posts in progress and for post ideas. This calendar is set up to organize the work of multiple authors.

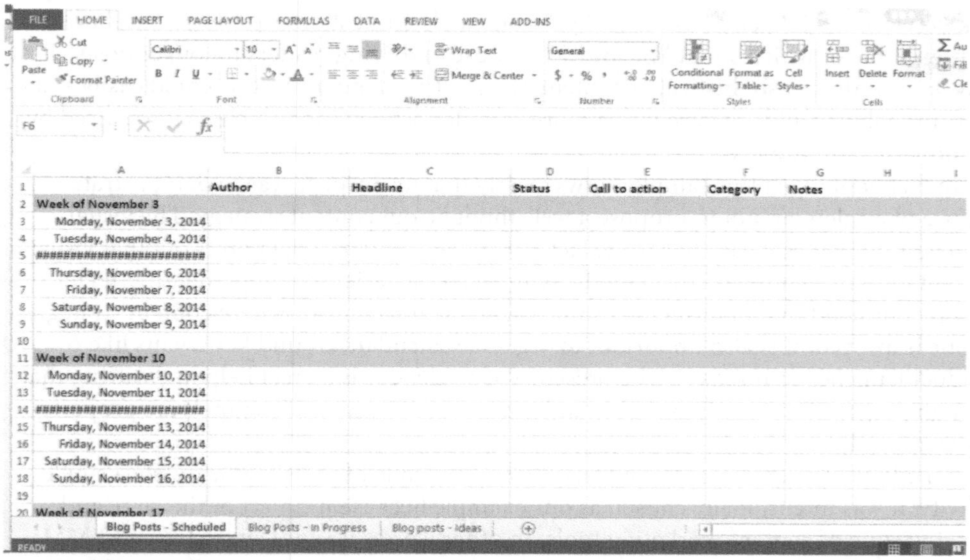

Source: http://contentmarketinginstitute.com/2014/11/content-marketers-checklist-editorial-calendar-essentials/

Figure 14.2 **Spreadsheet Template for Blog Editorial Calendar**

Social Media Editorial Calendar for MONTH ____________________

Facebook Linked In Twitter Blog

Monday	Tuesday	Wednesday	Thursday	Friday
1 Personnel Topic Personnel Topic	2 Personnel Topic Personnel Topic	3 Personnel Topic Personnel Topic	4 Personnel Topic Personnel Topic	5 Personnel Topic Personnel Topic
6 Personnel Topic Personnel Topic	7 Personnel Topic Personnel Topic	8 Personnel Topic Personnel Topic	9 Personnel Topic Personnel Topic	10 Personnel Topic Personnel Topic
11 Personnel Topic Personnel Topic	12 Personnel Topic Personnel Topic	13 Personnel Topic Personnel Topic	14 Personnel Topic Personnel Topic	15 Personnel Topic Personnel Topic
16 Personnel Topic Personnel Topic	17 Personnel Topic Personnel Topic	18 Personnel Topic Personnel Topic	19 Personnel Topic Personnel Topic	20 Personnel Topic Personnel Topic
21 Personnel Topic Personnel Topic	22 Personnel Topic Personnel Topic	23 Personnel Topic Personnel Topic	24 Personnel Topic Personnel Topic	25 Personnel Topic Personnel Topic

Source: http://bigredprintingspotlight.blogspot.com/2012/04/editorial-calendar-will-save-your.html

Figure 14.3 **Editorial Calendar for Posting in Multiple Channels**

An individual blogger can use it to keep track of his own posts by simply eliminating the Author column, but that is pretty simplistic. Most people who blog today promote their blog posts in multiple channels. Content has to be repurposed for various channels and posting times may be different for each to achieve the optimum response. That is a situation where a calendar would be of use to even an individual publisher.

The editorial calendar shown in Figure 14.3 supports work between Facebook, LinkedIn, Twitter, and a blog. It also supports multiple content creators, but the personnel item could be eliminated and it would work for a single publisher.[9] This content group publishes in LinkedIn on Tuesday and their blog on Thursday. They post on Facebook every day and Tweet most days. However, there is no obvious scheduling link between the longer posts on LinkedIn and a blog and shorter posts on Facebook and Twitter, some of which should be for the purpose of driving readers to longer posts. That makes it a rather unsophisticated content plan, but a calendar like this could easily—and most probably would—evolve into a more complex scheduling vehicle as it was used by an individual or by a team.

In fact, looking at this sample shows clearly that its purpose was to demonstrate the use of a calendar, not to propose a well-thought-out content strategy. The visual presentation makes it easy to see the lack of strategy. BufferSocial points out that visual presentation of a complex social media issue makes it easier to comprehend.[10] In fact, they recommend that publishers examine their calendars to see where content strategies can be improved. It is also important to organize calendars around key events like product launches or holidays. The presence of a calendar is a great help in ensuring that enough preparation time is available and that content items and channels are properly synchronized.

An editorial calendar is, of course, only one example of tools that facilitate a single activity. It was intentionally chosen as our example because it is part of the large and growing suite of content marketing tools. In other words, it is not an exclusively SMM task like posting to Facebook, pinning to Pinterest, or creating a visual for your blog. Whatever your SMM activity, consider searching for a tool to make it easier.

Tools to Develop and Monitor Your Personal Brand

Throughout the book we have emphasized the importance of your personal brand and the role various SMM platforms and techniques can play in the personal branding process. We have encouraged you to establish your brand while still a student, to intensify that process as you begin the search for your first or next professional position, and to maintain your brand in a strategic way as you progress in your career.

Admittedly that is one more task to add to an already busy life. Are there tools that can make the task easier? Yes, there are tools specially designed for or especially appropriate for personal branding. We can discuss only a few of them; you are encouraged to continue to follow online resources that keep you updated on the subject.

Here are some examples, organized by the elements of Dan Schwabel's personal branding model:

DISCOVER In the discovery process you conduct a self-assessment of your goals and personal characteristics. As you continue personal brand development, it is useful to discover what others are saying about you in a professional context. Many of us use one or more alert tools by setting up alerts for our name. Google Alerts is probably the best known for content alerts as well as the names of individuals. It is free and easy to set up and has a number of options for the scope of the monitoring and methods of reporting.

In addition to Google Alerts Prof. Roberts uses both Mention and Talkwalker because they tend to report different items. She does not have social platforms connected as you can see from this example.[1] Only uses of her name on the Internet are reported, as shown here in the web listing. The information was initially received by email.

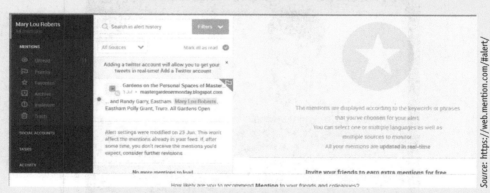

If you want to monitor mentions of your name in social media, consider Social Mention. Prof. Zahay and her classes use it to monitor mentions of their content in social media. Social Mention monitors over 100 social media channels and offers real time and other reporting options.

CREATE Chapters 5 through 12 have discussed platforms on which you can create content and each includes a discussion of personal branding applications. There are tools for each of the platforms, some of which are covered in this chapter. It is important to investigate the tools offered by each platform you are using as a first step.

You may want to use Google Trends to see what others in your geographical region or your industry are publishing. Many publishers use it to generate ideas about what to write. You can simply search when you are in need of inspiration or you can subscribe to reports on topics of special interest.

Additional content creation tools that are useful in personal branding applications include:

- Evernote offers a variety of support options for writers
- Headline Analyzer rates the quality of your headline
- Canva offers easy-to-use graphic design tools

There are literally thousands of others, depending on which aspect of content creation you need assistance with.

As you think about creating original content that supports your personal brand, remember that what you do—what you create—in marketing classes and on the job is a key part of your personal content.

COMMUNICATE There are also numerous tools that can ease the task of communicating across your chosen platforms:

- Hootsuite, discussed in the chapter, offers scheduling options.
- Buffer facilitates scheduling posts across various platforms.
  - Both of these tools also offer monitoring data.
- IfThisThenThat (IFTTT) offers more complex scheduling options called recipes.

An especially important aspect of communicating your personal brand is how to include it in the job search process. Forbes offers a slideshow that offers useful tips on how to present your personal brand in a job interview.[2]

Source: http://www.forbes.com/pictures/fmlm45klkm/how-to-showcase-your-per/

MAINTAIN Part of maintaining your personal brand is to continue to create and post relevant content to your chosen platforms. Another part of maintenance is to monitor the growth of your reach and effectiveness on the various platforms that you use. Broadly-based analytics tools like Google Analytics can be used for this purpose.

Many SMM tools that are used for other tasks also offer analytics. Hootsuite and Buffer were given as examples in the previous section. Others include:

- Sendible, which integrates email and lead generation activities into its platform.
- Cyfe, which is a comprehensive business analytics platform that can include data from all aspects of the business including SMM.

In a different category is Klout, a tool for measuring an individual's influence across all the social media channels in which he participates.

Wishing you well on your personal branding journey

The advice given in the chapter holds true for the personal branding context; start small and simple—and probably free—and add to the number and complexity of your tools as you learn and as you identify a genuine need.

Developing a personal brand that presents you authentically and positively as a person and as a professional is a rewarding process. Good luck in your journey!

Sources:

1. "Mary Lou Roberts," Mention (July 3, 2015). Retrieved July 22, 2015, from https://web.mention.com/#alert/267119

2. (n.d.), "How to Showcase Your Personal Brand in an Interview," Forbes. Retrieved July 22, 2015, from http://www.forbes.com/pictures/efld45fmgi/how-to-showcase-your-per/

Single Platform Tools

Since Facebook is such a dominant force in the social media world it's easy to assume that it has also generated the most tools. There are many tools for using Facebook, but perhaps not as many as for other platforms. It may be that Facebook is so central to the social strategies of so many marketers that they use fewer tools to automate their dealings with it. There are, however, many useful tools to assist marketers in Facebook tasks.

Some basic tools for tracking brand activity and brand mentions on Facebook and other platforms include:

- Facebook Insights. We discussed Facebook Insights in Chapter 13 as a source of Facebook metrics (see Figure 13.13). Is it a tool? Yes, although it is not a standalone tool; it is a tool that Facebook furnishes to business users. It allows them to see a variety of metrics about the use and popularity of posts and is accessed directly from the brand page.

- Mention. Mention allows the user to create alerts (an alert for your own name, for example) and to be notified when it appears virtually anywhere on the web. The user can connect the alert to social media accounts, to Facebook for example, and react as soon as the notification is received. It also provides a variety of metrics and can be shared with other members of the brand team. Like many tools, it has a free version with limited functionality and offers a variety of premium plans.[11]

- NutshellMail. This is a free tool from email firm Constant Contact that monitors activity on Facebook, Twitter, and LinkedIn and consolidates it into an email for analysis and response. It also covers Yelp, FourSquare, and Citysearch, allowing the marketer to stay abreast of ratings on those sites.[12]

Each of these tools (and many others) does similar things, but no two are exactly alike. One is provided by the platform, one is free, and one charges for premium services. There are many other tools that offer these services, but these three were chosen because they have straightforward, limited functionality. Other tools to be discussed in sections that follow offer similar monitoring services but combine them with many other types of services. That may make them more useful, but it also makes them more difficult to learn to use. Starting with some simple tools makes the learning curve easier to climb.

Platforms provide various tools to help marketers make use of various platform features and services. The purpose of these tools is not only to make the services easier to use but also to improve the effectiveness of the marketing activities. Facebook made enhancements to targeting services offered to marketers in late 2014 and quickly announced a set of tools to help marketers take advantage of them. Tools in this set include:

- Interest targeting. Instead of targeting posts to all people who Like their page, marketers can now choose a subset based on their interests. This interest targeting includes the ability to target people who have recently read stories on the subject, not just people who Like the marketer's page. This allows more precise targeting of messages and it also expands the marketer's reach.

- Post end date. Publishers can specify the date a post will no longer appear on the news feeds of followers, although the post continues to be shown on the marketer's page. This may sound trivial, but it is in the best interest of the marketer to show content users are interested in, not the starting quarterbacks for last week's football game.

- Smart publishing. This tool was initially available only to a few large publishers. It allows them to see which of their stories are being posted on Facebook by readers. If enough readers post a link to a story on Mashable, for instance, Facebook will send the content out to everyone who has liked Facebook but will not post the story on Mashable's page. Facebook has developed a dashboard to allow the publisher to monitor this activity, however.[13, 14, 15]

This brief summary barely scratches the surface of tools intended to make use of Facebook more efficient and more productive. Multiply the large number of tools for Facebook by the number of platforms marketers can use and you begin to see the magnitude of the job of choosing productivity tools. You also begin to see the desirability of tools that work across multiple platforms.

Multiple Platform Tools

Multiple platform tools are complex and few are free beyond a typical trial period. That makes the line between multiple platform tools and purchased services a little blurry. We will use as examples two that are accessible to an individual or to a small business. They are tools that are used by a person, not a suite of services that is executed by a supplier and reported to the client.

One such tool used by many of us is Hootsuite. Its basic functions are to allow users to:

- Publish on various platforms and to monitor activity there.

- Schedule their posts.

- Create reports for each of the platforms connected to their accounts.

- Connect apps in order to be able to access other platforms.

- Monitor content from selected blogs and websites.

There is more, including sharing between the entire SMM team, but these are the functions that are available, although limited in number of activities or platforms, to the Pro user of the platform. There is a free plan that allows the beginner to experiment with the tool.[16]

Zahay and Roberts both use Hootsuite to manage their social media efforts. Figure 14.4a shows Prof. Roberts home page, a dashboard she has created from among the social media channels and pages she maintains. It shows her real-time Twitter feed, a record of her own Tweets, one of her Google+ pages, and a tool (app) called Tailwind for scheduling and posting Pins. Tailwind provides analytics that track Pinterest activity over time and allows the user to connect his website to monitor conversions (sales, information requests, and more) from Pinterest activity.

Figure 14.4b shows how Hootsuite is used to post to multiple platforms. Prof. Roberts' various accounts (profiles) on major platforms are listed in the message box. From those she can choose the desired accounts, write a message, and include a link that

Source: Hootsuite Media Inc.

Figure 14.4a A Hootsuite User's Dashboard

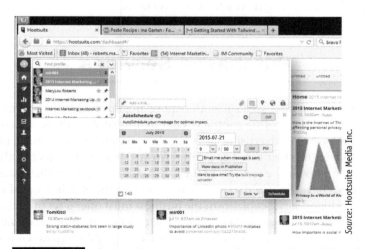

Source: Hootsuite Media Inc.

Figure 14.4b The User's Message Box on the Hootsuite Dashboard

Figure 14.5 A Calendar-Style Dashboard from SocialDraft

is automatically shortened. The Send Now button is not covered in this shot. Instead it shows a calendar that allows the user to select the day and time of the post with an option for notification when the post is made. Among the other options are the ability to include an image in the message or to select a particular group for message targeting.

Optional plans in Hootsuite allow the creation of teams for collaborative work and management of the social media effort. This is typical with the addition of more people and more social media accounts requiring more costly usage plans.

Another approach to multiple platforms is the SocialDraft social calendar such as the one in Figure 14.5.[17] It services Facebook, Twitter, LinkedIn, and Instagram with a drag and drop scheduling calendar. It accommodates social media teams who create content in comma-separated values (CSV), a format that stores numbers and text in plain text format. Users can add images to their CSV file and upload them to the scheduling calendar.

This tool, as is typical for comprehensive tools, includes other tools. Link shortener Bitly allows creation of custom links. Users can monitor social feeds or receive alerts about selected topics. SmartDraft also has a feature that allows users to identify influencers and engage with them about relevant content.

SocialDraft offers the usual free trial and several feature packages, but tools with this level of complexity do not commonly have free versions.[18]

Purchased Services

The tools that have been discussed so far all require ongoing hands-on activity on the part of the user. Purchased services are contracted out to third-party suppliers. In some ways these suppliers behave like advertising agencies; they contract with clients to provide a set of services and advice on their use. The clients are often brands. Clients can also be digital agencies who then provide the services to their own clients as part of their package.

Earlier sections have discussed tools that are somewhat limited in scope. In order to offer a viable purchased services platform the business must offer a set of social media services that meet a wide range of client needs. The exact nature of some of the services differs, but most are organized around basic categories of SMM services reminiscent of the stages in the Social Media Planning Cycle (Figure 2.1). Because of the range of services they offer and because the services supplier furnishes most of the personnel for the effort, you are unlikely to find even entry-level that is free. All, however, offer a free trial period during which they are, of course, going to try to convert the user to a paid account. Even a free trial requires a substantial investment in terms of the time of brand personnel, so one should be undertaken only after careful due diligence research has been completed.

Sprout Social is only one of many complex toolboxes available to the social media marketer.[19] Figure 14.6 shows a main dashboard page for Twitter, in this case a Trends report. Like the analytics packages discussed in Chapter 13 it allows the user to select a date range and then presents several important trends that are aggregated from the Tweets identified by the brand's Twitter profile. They are:

- Shown in Figure 14.6
  - Frequently mentioned topics
  - Frequently mentioned hashtags

- Not shown in Figure 14.6
  - The six top topics and hashtags each day for the user-selected time period
  - The people and brands who frequently mention the brand
  - People and brands frequently mentioned in discussions of the brand

That is just the Trends report!

Move on to a Twitter Profiles report. The one in Figure 14.7 is for a presumably hypothetical brand of Sprout Coffee.[20] This time the user has selected a monthly report.

The figure shows a number of data points for the brand's connections including number and growth of followers and various contacts with them, measures of engagement and influence, demographics including gender and age. Additional data points in the profile not shown in Figure 14.7 are number of mentions, number of

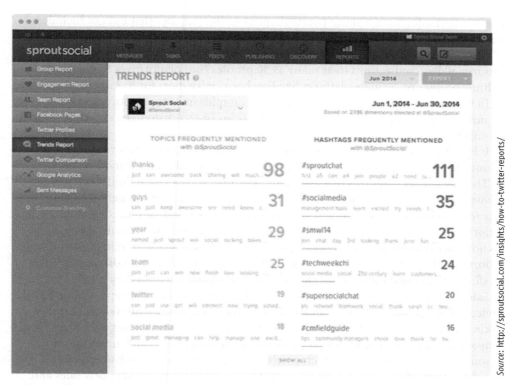

Source: http://sproutsocial.com/insights/how-to-twitter-reports/

Figure 14.6 A Twitter Trends Report

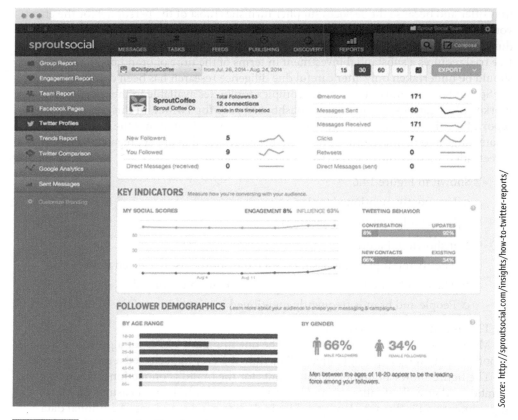

Source: http://sproutsocial.com/insights/how-to-twitter-reports/

Figure 14.7 A Twitter Profiles Report

retweets, and information about tweets themselves like number that did not include visuals and number that included bitly or pic.twitter.com links.

These figures represent two of nine reports about the brand's use of Twitter. The platform allows connections to as many as 30 profiles (not platforms; a brand can have multiple profiles on a single platform like Facebook or Twitter) for its largest customers.

In this section we have only looked at two examples from the Reports section. We did not look at tools for publishing, messaging from and to customers, and collaborating among the social media team.

It is a dizzying array of features and one that must itself be carefully managed to permit the brand to carry out its social media strategies and monitor their success.

The many other platforms that offer comprehensive services have similar features and all have some services that attempt to differentiate them from their competitors. One of the early services suppliers was Radian6. It was founded in 2006 and purchased in 2011 by CRM platform Salesforce.[21] Radian6 became known for its capabilities as a listening platform.[22] It is now part of a comprehensive SMM platform in the Salesforce Marketing Cloud. That platform combines Radian6's monitoring with SMM solution Buddy Media, acquired by Salesforce in 2012 and the data storage and computing power of the Salesforce cloud.[23]

Salesforce itself was formed in 1999 on the basis of a popular concept, modular CRM services. It is a classic Internet example of growth and expansion into related services, making it a powerful supplier to many of the largest Internet marketing and advertising companies. It allows clients to collect data about their customers and automate and personalize contacts with them in channels ranging from email to websites while providing detailed data on all these marketing activities. Because it supports sales and customer service as well as marketing departments its products are complex.

Radian6 is part of the social offering of Salesforce and continues to specialize in the monitoring services for which it initially became popular. It allows clients to understand what customers and prospects are saying about their brand, products, and competitors. Sentiment analysis is included as is the ability for marketing, sales, and customer service personnel to communicate directly with individual customers on social channels. It integrates SMM data into a comprehensive marketing database that supports strong customer relationships.[24]

Two examples provide insight into the services Radian6 provides. Figure 14.8 shows the summary dashboard for a brand.[25] The major data categories are the volume of mentions, positive or negative sentiment, demographics of the people talking about the brand, top influencers in various social channels, and trending topics related to the brand. The first graphic on the screen shows the day's mention volume for the brand and its industry. There are more summary graphics on this page that is reporting on a single day's activity.

Figure 14.9 showns a similar dashboard. This one covers a 7-day time period and is specific to the brand-related topic "beachbodies."[26] It shows the same data as the previous brand summary screen for social mentions that include the term beachbodies.

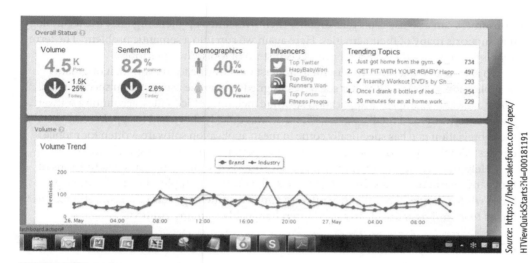

Source: https://help.salesforce.com/apex/HTViewQuickStarts?id=000181191

Figure 14.8 The Radian6 Summary Dashboard

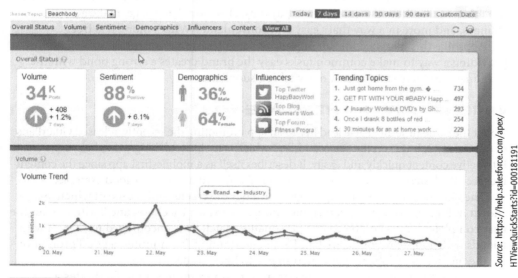

Source: https://help.salesforce.com/apex/HTViewQuickStarts?id=000181191

Figure 14.9 Summary Radian6 Dashboard for a Selected Topic

As the user delves more deeply into the data, she can select any of the data icons on either of these screens—and many others—for detailed data on issues like the demographics of the people who have created the mentions. Radian6 also offers a gargantuan amount of data to the social media marketer who must carefully choose the reports that are relevant to marketing objectives in order to be effective.

Thus far the chapter has discussed tools from the standpoint of a business user or a brand. The initial use of marketing tools seems to have been to support business activities and the chapter emphasizes their importance to the social media marketer. Consumers can also use tools to make their daily lives easier, and we end the chapter with brief examples of consumer tools.

Consumer Tools for Productivity and Engagement

Consumers can also use tools that simplify their lives and help them organize the technology that supports many of their activities. Here again we run into a semantic problem. The term *apps* is generally used in consumer markets instead of tools. Are apps tools?

To answer that question, it is useful to understand how the term evolved. It originated as application software, computer software designed to help the user perform specific tasks. There are many examples of application software including office suites, accounting software, graphics software, and media players. The term was quickly shortened to *app*. In recent years, the abbreviation *app* has specifically come to mean application software written for mobile devices. Mobile apps allow the cell phone user to perform one or more specific tasks.

"Help the user to perform specific tasks" sounds a lot like our earlier definitions of tools and marketing tools. In case you are still wondering Apple calls its site the App Store while Google Play calls the software apps on some pages and tools on others. The terms *tools* and *apps* are clearly used interchangeably in many contexts.

AT&T WANTS TO MAKE CUSTOMERS' LIVES EASIER

Not long ago Prof. Roberts received an email from her mobile carrier, AT&T. The subject line assured the recipient that AT&T had all her needs covered. The theme of Making Your Life Easier is always attractive to the harried professional. The app shown in Figure 14.10 allows the customer to pay bills, check on data usage, make account changes, and more in a way that's easy and convenient.[27] What's more, it is free.

Apps like this have become an important part of customer retention strategies. By providing a way to make common tasks easy the brand creates a strong bond with the customer and increases the cost of switching suppliers.

WHICH GUARDIAN HERO ARE YOU?

About the same time an article lead her to an app promoting the recently-released Guardians of the Galaxy 2. It was on the site of Riddle,[28] which is itself a tool designed to help users create interactive content quickly and easily. It describes itself as a mobile-first app since the content is especially designed for mobile consumption. The Guardians app is a good example.

The Guardians personality quiz has a number of screens, only some of which are shown in Figure 14.11. Each screen has share buttons for Facebook and Twitter. After the user completes a quiz and receives a personality match he is encouraged to share it with friends with a more robust share bar. It's an entertaining few minutes, a good promotion for the movie, and probably generated shares to like-minded friends.

These are two of many possible consumer app examples. One facilitates a serious task. The other is light entertainment. Both seem to do the job for which

Source: http://ebm.e.att-mail.com/c/tag/hBViWZoB8a3L2B9CynuABGFZnxg/doc.html?t_params=I_CNTCTUS%3D1%26I_DOWNLOAD%3D1%26I_ LANDINGPAGE%3D1%26I_PROMO%3D1%26I_PRVCY%3D1%26I_STARTED%3D1%26I_UNSUB%3D1%26BN_FRST_NM%3DMary%26EMAIL%3Droberts. marylou001%2540gmail.com

Figure 14.10 AT&T Customer Service App Email

they were designed. The scope of consumer apps is limited only by marketer objectives and creativity.

The choice and use of SMM tools is a huge subject, much too large to be completely covered in a single chapter. However, we have given you an overview of types of tools and their uses. Experimentation and experience will allow the marketer to choose the right tools for her organizational and marketing requirements.

We can, however, leave you with some best practice recommendations for dealing with this important marketing task.

BEST PRACTICES FOR SOCIAL MEDIA MARKETING TOOLS

1. Don't fondle the tool. Consultant Jeremiah Owyang gave this advice several years ago with a hammer as his illustration.[29] At the time he was talking about technology in general. It is just as applicable to SMM tools. It is not the tool—it is not the technology— that is important (Figure 14.12). It is what the marketer needs to accomplish that determines appropriate choice and use of tools.

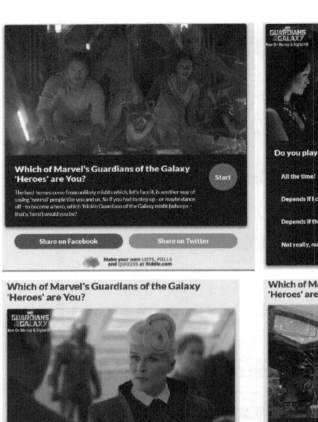

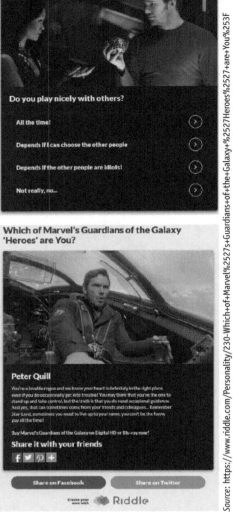

Figure 14.11 Selected Screens from a Movie Promotion App

Figure 14.12 The Tool Is Not the Primary Concern

2. **Focus on the strategy, not the tools.** The blog Wired Advisor counsels its financial services audience that even the best tools cannot rescue a poor strategy or substitute for lack of a strategy. The strategy comes first, then tools can be chosen to help execute it.[30]

3. **Next think about the marketing tasks that must be accomplished and the person(s) who will have the task assignments.** What marketers must do, in some order of priority, is the first consideration. It is also important to think about who and how many people will be using the tools for task execution and who will be accessing the monitoring data and the reports.

4. **Start small, with simple tools that can be mastered quickly.** We have stressed this point throughout the chapter. It will save money to use free or inexpensive tools in the beginning. Mastering the tools quickly will provide a quick return on the investment in time and dollars, if any.

5. **Use dashboards to put tasks and monitoring data in easy-to-comprehend visual formats.** A key reason for using tools is efficient accomplishment of tasks. Efficiency will not be achieved if users must search many sites to find monitoring data. Bringing the key strategic issues together in a single place not only saves time, it also promotes use of the data for decision making.

Operating efficiency, better decisions, and strategy improvement can all be achieved with best practices use of appropriate tools and the monitoring data they provide.

Notes

1. (n.d.) "Tool," Business Dictionary. Retrieved May 22, 2015, from http://www.business dictionary.com/definition/tool.html
2. (n.d.) "Marketing Tools," Business Dictionary. Retrieved May 22, 2015, from http://www .businessdictionary.com/definition/marketing-tools.html
3. Cohen, Heidi (May 9, 2011), Actionable Marketing Guide. "Social Media Definitions," Retrieved May 13, 2015 from http://heidicohen.com/social-media-definition/
4. (n.d.) "Social Media Management Software Definition," G2Crowd. Retrieved May 22, 2015, from https://www.g2crowd.com/categories/social-media-mgmt
5. Baer, Jay (n.d.), "Clearing Clouds of Confusion—the 5 Categories of Social Media Software," Convince & Convert. Retrieved May 22, 2015, from http://www.convinceandconvert.com/ social-media-tools/clearing-clouds-of-confusion-the-5-categories-of-social-media-software/
6. Cleary, Ian (March 23, 2015), "The Definitive List of Social Media Marketing Tool Categories for Businesses." Razor Social. Retrieved May 22, 2015, from http://www.razorsocial.com/ social-media-marketing-tools-for-businesses/
7. Karasiewicz, Christian (April 23, 2012), "My Current Social Media Tools," Christian K. Retrieved June 23, 2015, from http://www.christiankonline.com/my-current-social-media-tools/
8. Harris, Jodi (November 18, 2014), "A Content Marketer's Checklist: Editorial Calendar Essentials," Content Marketing Institute. Retrieved June 21, 2015 from http://content marketinginstitute.com/2014/11/content-marketers-checklist-editorial-calendar-essentials/
9. "An Editorial Calendar Will Save Your Sanity!," Big Red Printing Spotlight (April 4, 2012). Retrieved June 21, 2015, from http://bigredprintingspotlight.blogspot.com/2012/04/editorial-calendar-will-save-your.html
10. Lee, Kevan (May 13, 2014), "The Complete Guide to Choosing a Content Calendar and More," Buffer Social. Retrieved June 21, 2015 from https://blog.bufferapp.com/all-about-content-calendar
11. (n.d.), "Discover our Features," Mention. Retrieved June 23, 2015 from https://en.mention .com/features
12. (n.d.), "Save Time Monitoring and Managing Facebook. Twitter & More," NutshellMail. Retrieved June 22, 2015 from https://nutshellmail.com/

13. Ormseth, Holly (December 10, 2014), "New Tools and Insights for Publishers," Facebook. Retrieved June 21, 2015 from http://media.fb.com/2014/12/10/new-tools-and-insights-for-publishers-2/

14. Abbruzzese, Jason (December 10, 2014), "Facebook Cozies Up to Publishers With New Tools," Mashable. Retrieved June 21, 2015 from http://mashable.com/2014/12/10/facebook-cozies-up-to-publishers-with-new-tools/

15. "Upgraded Tools for Creating and Managing Facebook Ads," Facebook for Business (June 18, 2015). Retrieved June 21, 2015 from https://www.facebook.com/business/news/upgraded-ad-tools

16. (n.d.), "Schedule. Manage. Measure." Hootsuite. Retrieved June 23, 2015 from https://hootsuite.com/plans

17. "The Socialdraft Drag & Drop Scheduling Calendar." SocialDraft (January 20, 2015). Retrieved June 24, 2015 from https://www.youtube.com/watch?v=TtXAgNDVWvs

18. (n.d.), "Features," SocialDraft. Retrieved June 24, 2015 from http://socialdraft.com/tour/

19. Cuttica, Patrick, (March 11, 2014), "How to Create Twitter Reports With Sprout Social," SproutSocial. Retrieved June 26, 2015 from http://sproutsocial.com/insights/how-to-twitter-reports/

20. Cuttica, Patrick, (March 11, 2014), "How to Create Twitter Reports With Sprout Social," Sprout Social. Retrieved June 28, 2015 from http://sproutsocial.com/insights/how-to-twitter-reports/

21. (n.d.),"Salesforce Radian6." Retrieved June 28 2015 from https ://www.crunchbase.com/organization/radian6

22. Barker, Melissa S., Donald I. Barker, Nickolas F. Bormann, and Krista E. Neher, (2008), *Media Marketing: A Strategic Approach.* (Cengage Learning), pp, 303–304.

23. (n.d.), "Salesforce.com Signs Definitive Agreement to Acquire Buddy Media," salesforce. Retrieved June 28, 2015 from http://www.salesforce.com/company/news-press/press-releases/2012/06/120604.jsp

24. (n.d.), "Salesforce Marketing Cloud Overview," Salesforce. Retrieved July 25, 2015 from https://www.salesforce.com/form/conf/demo-marketing-social-sem.jsp

25. (n.d.), "Radian6 Summary Dashboard," Salesforce. Retrieved July 25, 2015 from https://help.salesforce.com/apex/HTViewQuickStarts?id=000181191

26. Ibid.

27. (n.d.), "From paying bills to tracking data, the my AT&T app has got you covered," AT&T. Retrieved June 8, 2015 from http://ebm.e.att-mail.com/c/tag/hBViWZoB8a3L2B9CynuABGFZnxg/doc.html?t_params=I_CNTCTUS%3D1%26I_DOWNLOAD%3D1%26I_LANDINGPAGE%3D1%26I_PROMO%3D1%26I_PRVCY%3D1%26I_STARTED%3D1%26I_UNSUB%3D1%26BN_FRST_NM%3DMary%26EMAIL%3Droberts.marylou001%2540gmail.com

28. (n.d.), "Which of Marvel's Guardians of the Galaxy 'Heroes' Are You?" Riddle. Retrieved June 10 2015 from https://www.riddle.com/Personality/230-Which+of+Marvel%2527s+Guardians+of+the+Galaxy+%2527Heroes%2527+are+You%253F

29. Qwyang, Jeremiah (January 21, 2010), "Social Media Trends for 2010," Altimeter Group. Retrieved June 27, 2015 from http://www.slideshare.net/jeremiah_owyang/social-media-trends-for-2010

30. Sammons, Stephanie (n.d.), "How to Choose the Right Online Marketing Tools for Your Practice," WiredAdvisor. Retrieved June 27, 2015 from http://blog.wiredadvisor.com/digital-marketing-tools-selection/

Social Media Marketing Plan

The single most important action a marketer can take to improve an organization's chances of success in executing SMM activities is to develop a solid plan. Indeed, one of the major reasons SMM efforts fail is poor planning.[1] This chapter draws on everything that has come before in the textbook in order to demonstrate how to craft the elements of an effective SMM plan.

Introduced in Chapter 2, the SMM Planning Cycle provides an eight-step model for developing a SMM plan, as originally shown in Figure 2.1 and displayed here as Figure 15.1. In this chapter, a fictitious XYZ Coffee Company (envision a nationwide chain of well-known coffee shops) will serve to illustrate how to effectively apply each of these steps in constructing the plan.

In addition to these steps, no SMM plan would be complete without a budget listing its costs and a return on investment analysis. These two additional elements will be covered in detail at the end of the chapter.

When combined, these ten steps provide the core components for building a winning SMM plan. A few finishing touches will make the plan presentable for dissemination and consumption. They include a title page, table of contents, and executive summary.

LEARNING OBJECTIVES

After completing this chapter, students will be able to:

- Define the key elements of a SMM plan
- Create a title page, table of contents, and executive summary
- Compose a brief plan overview
- Observe the social media presence of an organization
- Conduct a SWOT analysis
- Identify the target market
- Set social media goals
- Determine social media strategies

(Continued)

- Describe how to implement the plan
- Explain how to monitor progress
- Create a budget
- Estimate return on investment
- Explain how to get C-Suite backing

Figure 15.1 SMM Planning Cycle

Each of these elements will be explained in sequence, using sections from the imaginary XYZ Coffee Company's current plan and results as points of reference. The appendix that follows contains the entire example plan and provides an overview of how these pieces fit together. It is worthwhile to frequently refer to this appendix while reading the chapter in order to avoid losing sight of the forest for the trees.

Creating an Informative and Eye-Catching Title Page

Figure 15.2 Sample Title (Cover) Page

A sharp title page makes a SMM plan not only stand out; it instantly provides the reader with the information necessary to identify the purpose and authors of the document as well as the release date. Using eye-catching graphics and tasteful fonts helps to accent important information on the title page.

A title page of the plan should begin with a descriptive name for the document, followed by the company name, address, contact information, and the authors who prepared it. Do not forget to include the publication date of the document. (A word of caution: avoid using lengthy or elaborate descriptions of the plan on the title page—they only serve to distract the reader from the key information on the page.)

Figure 15.2 shows the title page from the XYZ Coffee Company's SMM plan. Note the clean layout, snappy graphic, and the use of fonts to enhance the other relevant information on the page. In addition, observe the effective use of background colors to clearly differentiate the types of information on the page. The net effect is to attract attention and provide a tantalizing hint of what lies within the document.

Automatically Generating a Table of Contents

A table of contents is essential for a lengthy document such as a SMM plan. If manually prepared, a table of contents should not be assembled until the plan is finished. This approach requires going through the entire manuscript to find and record all the section headings, subheadings, and page numbers. This task is laborious, monotonous, and error-prone.

Fortunately, modern word processors, such as Microsoft Word, provide the ability to automatically generate a table of contents from formatted section headings in the document.[2]

Formatting the sections of a SMM plan can be done either during or after the preparatory phrase. The most efficient and safest method is to designate the section heading levels during composition, thus minimizing the chances of missing important items and simultaneously creating the initial organization of the document. Further, this technique makes it easy and quick to modify the structure of the plan during its preparation by demoting sections (indenting them in the table of contents), promoting sections (reducing their level of indentation), and changing the sequence of sections (simply dragging and dropping heading names in the panel on the left side of the document moves the heading name and accompanying section to the new location).

Once the document is written, with the section headings properly formatted and arranged, the table of contents can be automatically generated, showing the heading levels and associated page numbers, as seen in Figure 15.3. This process provides a fast, flexible, and reliable way to structure and automatically generate a table of contents for a SMM plan.

Writing a Compelling Executive Summary

A persuasive executive summary highlights the main benefits and components of a SMM plan.[3] It provides the first impression of the plan. Research shows that it can take just "17 seconds to make a lasting impression."[4] Therefore, an executive summary is one of the most important parts of the plan because decision makers will use it to quickly determine whether the plan's ideas are worth pursuing.[5] This momentary glimpse will either inspire them to learn more or to lose interest.[6]

Given the importance of the executive summary, it is worthwhile to put in the time and effort to write a great one. The following tips offer direction in preparing an executive summary that makes the best possible first impression. They have been used in preparing the executive summary in Figure 15.4.

- **Lead with Why the Plan Should Be Adopted**: The executive summary should begin with a justification for management to make the investment necessary to take the actions proposed by the plan.[7] The reasons provided should resonate and be ones that decision makers consider important. In business this importance typically means a short-term monetary return, although long-term considerations, such as brand building and improved customer relationships, may also play a critical role in the decision to proceed.

Table of Contents

Figure 15.3 Sample Table of Contents

Executive Summary

XYZ Coffee Company has a wide range of market segments, ranging from luxury coffee drinkers to professionals. However, younger people are not typically coffee drinkers, and they represent a lucrative, massive, untapped market segment, especially the more affluent youths.

The primary focus of this SMM plan is to use the social web as a means to find, engage, attract, and retain this upscale youth market as XYZ Coffee Company patrons. It is based on comprehensive research of the company's current social media presence, competitive intelligence, and target market analysis. This thorough examination and appraisal has resulted in a set of specific actionable social media goals and in optimal strategies for reaching those goals as well as the best social media tools for successfully executing and monitoring the plan.

Social media goals for the XYZ Coffee Company include:
- Strengthening the brand, primarily among the more affluent youth market segment
- Driving word-of-mouth recommendations
- Improving customer satisfaction
- Generating and implementing new product ideas
- Promoting advocacy
- Increasing foot traffic in the stores
- Search engine optimization (SEO) to increase traffic and conversions

A set of comprehensive social media strategies will be employed to achieve the above goals. These strategies include listening, interacting, engaging, influencing, and contributing to the social web.
In addition, this plan describes how the progress of social media efforts will be tracked, measured, and evaluated. These actions will enable the plan's execution to be tuned to obtain optimal results.

A detailed budget shows the cost of implementing the plan. The plan concludes with a return on investment analysis. The team leaders responsible for preparing, overseeing, and executing the plan include the VP of marketing, Lisa Shea; the director of communications, Mark Jones; and the SMM manager, Susan Monroe.

Figure 15.4 Sample Executive Summary

- **Keep the Audience in Mind**: Use the language appropriate for the readership. How you word the executive summary will differ depending on what the intended audience cares most about. In other words, the wording must satisfy the audience's needs.[8] For example, top executives will expect business terminology that helps them determine the value of the proposal.

- **Organize the Summary to Reflect the Structure of the Plan**: Readers will expect to see a summary that mirrors the organization of the components in the SMM plan. Consequently, the executive summary should be written in the same sequence as that plan's components were introduced.[9]

- **Provide a General Overview of the Main Components**: The executive summary should provide a synopsis of the primary elements in the plan, such as a brief overview, the organization's current social media presence, a competitive analysis, goals, strategies, target market, tools, implementation, monitoring, tuning, and budget.[10]

- **Limit the Length**: People reading executive summaries are habitually short on time. So keep the executive summary to a page, two at the most.[11] A careful balance must be struck between being too brief, which could indicate a lack of thoroughness, and too lengthy, which might be seen as unfocused and rambling.

- **Include the Names of the Plan's Authors**: This list should include the team leaders who prepared the plan, along with their respective titles.[12]

- **Compose the Executive Summary Last**: This maxim is well-known but often ignored in the haste to complete a plan. In reality, writing the executive summary before finishing the plan will actually lengthen the process. Once the plan is done, a comprehensive overview of the most significant components is available, making it not only simpler but faster to summarize the highlights in the executive summary. In addition, during the development of the plan, portions are typically in constant flux that will introduce inaccuracies in a prewritten executive summary and require that it be rewritten repeatedly.[13]

Figure 15.4 provides an example of an executive summary that makes use of all these tips.

Composing a Brief Overview

To maximize the chances that decision makers reading the SMM plan will fully appreciate its value, it is important to lay down a contextual foundation for readers to understand the information in the plan. This overview should not only lay the groundwork for reading the plan but should also stress the benefits of enacting it. The following tips provide suggestions for constructing an effective overview section:

- Describe the industry and company in order to set the stage for the decision makers by providing a quick look at the past, present, and likely future of the industry and the company's track record within that industry.[14]

- Explain the competitive advantage in order to show how the company can realize significant gains by using SMM. This explanation will help decision makers understand the importance of the plan.

- Describe how SMM can contribute by concisely listing the social media actions that will be required to secure the competitive advantage. It is dangerous to assume readers of the plan will readily grasp the value of SMM, let alone how it can deliver results.

Figure 15.5 demonstrates how to implement these recommendations in order to create an effective overview.

Brief Overview

Over the last two decades, coffeehouses have become part of the American landscape. Millions of people purchase an espresso-based coffee drink daily. The willingness to spend $3 to $5 for a cappuccino, mocha latte, or chocolate-ice-blended drink occurred within just the last decade, largely due to Starbucks. The specialty-coffeehouse industry continues to grow at a strong pace.

Affluent youth, not normally heavy consumers of coffee, represent a niche market that has yet to be tapped. As explained below in detail, social media can be used to observe, interact, engage, and influence this market segment. These actions will help attract and retain this youth market as XYZ Coffee Company patrons, in combination with XYZ Coffee Company's high-volume, upscale, inviting atmosphere, and high-quality products. Moreover, most of the XYZ Coffee Company's locations are near university or college campuses, locations that provide easy access for this target market.

Figure 15.5 Overview Section from the XYZ Coffee Company SMM Plan

Observing Social Media Presence

The first step in the SMM Planning Cycle is to listen to what people are saying about a company, thereby enabling the organization to determine its current social media presence. There are two primary ways to assess the social media presence of an organization: *holistically* and *granularly*. The holistic approach looks at brand health, a collective measure of a company's social media presence from many different sources.[15]

A useful analogy is to compare brand health with the general assessment a medical doctor might give a patient at the end of an examination. Rather than going through each test result separately, the physician might simply say that the patient has a clean bill of health. Likewise, brand health is "a high-level assessment that tells a company everything's alright or, conversely, there are problems that need to be addressed."[16]

If the sweeping pronouncement of social media brand health is good, then marketers have an overall indication that their SMM initiatives are working. On the other hand, if the news is bad, then, like the doctor, it is necessary to zero in on specific social media platforms and look at each platform's metrics and key performance indicators (KPIs) to identify the sources, nature, and extent of the problem. See the definitions of metrics and KPIs in Chapter 13.

Measuring social media brand health can be done in a number of ways. The most frequently used method is sentiment analysis of the entire social web (or at least as much of the social web as any given monitoring tool is capable of assessing). By listening to the conversations that are taking place about a particular company on the social web, marketers can determine if the general consensus about a brand are mostly positive, neutral, or negative.

In addition to measuring the sheer volume of positive, neutral, and negative brand mentions, the velocity at which these brand mentions are changing, for better or worse, can provide clues about the future of brand health.[17] Brand health measurements should also include visibility—the number of people aware of the brand, who they are, and what they are saying about it.[18] Finally, the volatility of brand sentiment can expose rapid changes caused by ill-advised changes in product quality, licensing terms, customer support policies, and so on.[19] For example, when Starbucks changed its long-established logo, a spike in negative comments on social communities alerted the company to the problem, which they addressed in an expeditious and forthright manner, averting a PR disaster.

Finally, it is worth noting that analyzing a company's sentiment score in isolation only reveals how happy people are with the company, not how it compares with competitors or even with the entire industry. By comparing the company's sentiment score with the competition's scores, marketers can determine the company's brand health relative to its rivals.[20]

Even when the overall news about the social media health of a brand is good, it is still useful to look at the metrics for individual social media platforms as a means of determining where SMM efforts are performing well and where there is room for improvement. This practice also establishes benchmarks with which to measure progress in implementing platform-specific tactics and achieving social media goals (a topic that is discussed more fully in the implementing and monitoring sections below).

The following are five key metrics for auditing a company's social media presence on individual social media platforms:

- **Sentiment Analysis**: Shows the number of positive, neutral, or negative mentions on each social media platform where the company has a sizable presence[21]

- **Reach**: Indicates the number of Twitter followers, Facebook fans, LinkedIn group members, Instagram view count, and so on[22]

- **Company Posts:** Measure how often the company posts on each social media platform[23]

- **Feedback:** Shows the number of comments, likes, or replies to company-generated content[24]

- **Average Response Time:** Assesses response time to user comments on the company's social media properties

Table 15.1 shows key metrics for the platforms currently being utilized.

Metric	Sentiment	Reach	Company Posts	Feedback	Average Response Time to Feedback
Facebook Page	Positive 58% Neutral 31% Negative 11%	1,200,000 fans	2 daily	10 comments and 20 likes daily	2 hours
Twitter Account	Positive 60% Neutral 28% Negative 12%	350,000 followers	3 or more daily	50 @tweets 200 retweets daily	1 hour or less for customer service issues
YouTube Channel	Positive 45% Neutral 27% Negative 28%	5,000 subscribers	2 per month	5 comments per video monthly	2 days
Instagram	Positive 45% Neutral 50% Negative 5%	3,000 monthly views	1 or 2 daily	2 comments per photo	1 week
Mobile	Strategy to be developed and tested during current operating year Strategy to be ready for deployment chain-wide by beginning of next operating year				

Table 15.1 Platform-Specific Measurements of the Social Media Presence of the XYZ Coffee Company

Conducting a Competitive Analysis

As mentioned before, the *first* step in the SMM Planning Cycle is to listen to the social web. In addition to determining an organization's social media presence, these observations can provide valuable competitive intelligence. For example, a careful examination of what people are saying online about competitors on relevant platforms can expose potential threats from competitors as well as possible lucrative opportunities.[25]

One useful way to conduct a competitive analysis of the social web is with a SWOT Analysis. SWOT is an acronym, which stands for Strengths, Weaknesses, Opportunities, and Threats.[26] It was developed in the 1960s at Stanford Research Institute (SRI) by grants from Fortune 500 companies who wanted to improve the success of strategic planning.[27] A Social Media SWOT Analysis identifies a company's strengths and weaknesses on social media platforms as well as the opportunities and threats on the social web.[28] It is a useful decision-making technique to identify attractive social media opportunities for an organization.

In a Social Media SWOT Analysis, the internal factors within an organization that affect its performance on various platforms are classified as strengths and weaknesses, while the external factors on the social web that impact the performance of the organization on social media platforms are categorized as opportunities and threats. This form of SWOT Analysis provides the means to match the organization's social media platform strengths and weaknesses with opportunities and threats in the social media environment in order to find areas of competitive advantage.

The first step in a Social Media SWOT Analysis is to find and list an organization's strengths and weaknesses on social media platforms, along with the relevant opportunities and threats in the social media realm.[29] This step can be accomplished by answering the questions in Table 15.2.

Strengths	Weaknesses
• Does the organization have a strong brand presence on multiple social media platforms? • Has the company a proven track record on social media platforms? • Are most of the company's actions successful on social media platforms? • Does the organization have experienced staff adept at various social media platforms? • Is the staff enthusiastic about working with social media platforms? • Are all the company's SMM efforts monitored to assess progress in achieving marketing goals? • Are top executives supportive of social media efforts? • Are ample resources available for participating on social media platforms? • Does the company currently have a variety of vibrant social media properties? • Does the company have unique products or services that satisfy the needs of social media users?	• Does the organization have a weak brand presence on multiple social media platforms? • Is the company's track record on social media platforms spotty? • Do the majority of the company's actions on social media platforms fall short in expected outcomes? • Does the organization lack sufficient expertise to work effectively on social media platforms? • Is the staff apathetic or apprehensive about working with platforms? • Does the company lack the ability to fully monitor its SMM efforts in order to measure progress in achieving marketing goals? • Are top executives reluctant to fully commit to SMM? • Are resources insufficient for building and maintaining a presence on social media platforms? • Does the company lack a variety of vibrant social media properties? • Does the company lack distinctive products or services or do the current offerings fail to satisfy the needs of social media users?
Opportunities	**Threats**
• Which social media platforms have the greatest concentration of the company's target audience? • What does the target market do on these sites? • Do they have any unfulfilled needs on the platforms that the company can satisfy? • Are there emerging target markets on these platforms with needs the company can satisfy? • What social media technologies provide opportunities for the company? • Are there ways the company and its competitors can benefit by working together on the platforms? • Are there opportunities for collaborating with customers to build brand presence on platforms? • Are suppliers present on these platforms? • What do customers value about the company? • Is market demand increasing?	• Who are the company's direct competitors on the major social media platforms? • Are there emerging competitors on these major platforms? • What are the social media strategies and tactics that competitors pursue on these platforms? • How successful are these strategies and tactics in building brand presence on the company's key social media platforms? • In what ways are competitors' products or services superior to the company's offerings? • How are competitors likely to respond to any changes in the way the company markets on the platforms? • Is the company behind in adopting new technologies? • Are international competitors taking away market share? • What do customers dislike about the company? • Is market demand decreasing?

Table 15.2 Profiling an Organization's Social Media Platform Strengths, Weaknesses, Opportunities, and Threats

Once all the factors for a company have been profiled using Table 15.2, it is possible to determine the appropriate strategy in the SWOT Matrix, shown in Table 15.3.[30] For example, if a company has many social media platform strengths and considerable opportunities on the social web, as depicted in Table 15.4, then the SWOT Matrix recommends the pursuit of an S-O (strength-opportunity) strategy, which encourages the company to follow opportunities on the social web that are a good fit for the organization's social media platform strengths. On the other hand, if the profile indicates substantial weaknesses in an organization's platform performance and many external threats exist on the social web, then a W-T (weakness-threat) strategy might prove helpful in preventing the company's weaknesses from making it highly susceptible to external threats.

SWOT Matrix	Strengths (S)	Weaknesses
Opportunities (O)	S-O strategy	W-O strategy
Threats (T)	S-T strategy	W-T strategy

Table 15.3 SWOT Matrix

Strengths	Weaknesses
• XYZ has a strong brand presence on the majority of the major social media platforms.	• XYZ has less than desirable brand presence on YouTube, LinkedIn, and Instagram. It has no presence on Swarm by Foursquare, an important platform for location marketing.
• The company has a proven track on social media platforms, such as Facebook and Twitter.	• The company's track record on YouTube, LinkedIn, and Instagram is spotty.
• Most of the company's actions result in the desired outcomes on social media platforms.	• The company's actions on YouTube, LinkedIn, and Instagram have fallen short of expected outcomes.
• XYZ has an experienced staff adept at effectively using Facebook and Twitter to market the company.	• XYZ currently lacks the expertise to effectively market on YouTube and LinkedIn.
• The staff is enthusiastic about working with Facebook and Twitter.	• The staff is apprehensive about working with platforms such as YouTube and LinkedIn.
• XYZ's quantitative SMM efforts are monitored to assess progress in achieving marketing goals.	• The company presently lacks a comprehensive monitoring tool to track and measure progress across the social web and on specific platforms.
• Most of XYZ's management is supportive of XYZ's social media efforts, especially on Facebook and Twitter because they have proven their usefulness in improving the company's bottom line.	• There has been an understandable reluctance by management to fully commit to an aggressive SMM campaign because of the inherent risks and costs in undertaking such an endeavor.
• Resources are adequate for participating on some social media platforms, such as Facebook and Twitter.	• Resources are insufficient for building and maintaining a substantial presence on YouTube, LinkedIn, Instagram, and Swarm.
• XYZ's Facebook and Twitter are lively social media properties.	• XYZ currently lacks a robust mobile marketing strategy, which provides for corporate promotions and local events and promotions.
• The company's high-quality beans, distinctive coffee blends, and coffee shop atmosphere satisfy the needs of the current social media target market.	• The present social media presence does not satisfy the needs of the affluent youth market.

Table 15.4 XYZ Coffee Company SWOT Profile

Opportunities	**Threats**
• Facebook, Twitter, and YouTube have the largest concentration of the company's current target audience. • The target audiences on these sites tend to be spectators and joiners. • Significant portions of the affluent youth target audience are content creators and critics with needs that are not currently being met. • The affluent youth market is a strong emerging target market on all the major social media platforms, with need to observe, join, converse, create content, and criticize content. • The emergence of social location services, ubiquitous smartphone usage, and mobile apps for checking in from locations to earn awards make these technologies a significant opportunity for XYZ. • Starbucks, McDonald's, and XYZ could cooperate in sponsoring social media events that support major charities. They could also work together to develop an open source wiki with information about coffee. • XYZ can collaborate with customers to build brand presence on social media platforms by engaging in activities such as inviting contributions from customers (e.g., YouTube videos). • Suppliers are present in large numbers on LinkedIn. • XYZ customers value the high-quality, unique coffee drink blends and the warm, friendly atmosphere of the company's coffee shops. • Market demand is currently slowly increasing.	• Starbucks is the closest direct competitor on the major social media platforms. • McDonald's low prices and widespread locations are making it an emerging competitor, especially on key social media platforms like Facebook and Twitter. • Starbucks pursues aggressive social media strategies across the social web, including its own brand community and location-marketing initiatives. • Starbucks has been extremely successful in building brand presence on the company's key current social media platforms, such as Facebook, Twitter, YouTube and, recently, on mobile. • Starbucks has more locations and a wider selection of coffee drinks and foods than XYZ. • Starbucks and McDonald's already have robust mobile marketing strategies that include loyalty programs. • XYZ has yet to use social location services like Swarm from Foursquare to participate in location check-in marketing. • International competitors have yet to make inroads in competing with XYZ, but their market penetration should be tracked carefully in case this situation changes. • The customers dislike the wait to get support and lack of opportunity for input about XYZ products. • Market demand for coffee drinks dropped off during the height of the recession.

Table 15.4 **XYZ Coffee Company SWOT Profile** *(Continued)*

The SWOT options are:

- **S-O Strategy**: Follow social media platform opportunities that match the organization's strengths on the social web.

- **W-O Strategy**: Overcome weaknesses in social media platform performance to follow opportunities on the social web.

- **S-T Strategy**: Identify ways the organization can use its platform strengths to reduce its vulnerability to external threats from competitors or new technologies on the social web.

- **W-T Strategy**: Create a protective strategy that reduces the chances the organization's social media weaknesses will make it vulnerable to external threats. This strategy would likely take the form of monitoring the social web to detect customer complaints and handling them before they become a PR disaster.

In conclusion, a SWOT Analysis of social media should always be part of a SMM plan because of its substantial contributions to crafting effective strategies for achieving marketing goals.[31]

Setting Goals

With the above reconnaissance and analysis complete, it is possible to determine the social media goals that stand the best chance of achieving a competitive advantage for the organization. Chapter 2 introduced a set of general social media goals, which provide a good starting point for crafting organization-specific goals. They include brand building, increasing customer satisfaction, driving word-of-mouth recommendations, producing new product ideas, generating leads, crisis reputation management, integrating social media with PR and advertising, and search engine optimization (SEO).

The process of adapting these overall goals to take advantage of a particular organization's unique opportunities will no doubt involve revising, integrating, or dropping a few of them. Figure 15.6 illustrates how this set of general social media goals has been modified to fit the situation and needs of the hypothetical XYZ Coffee Company.

Goals

In consideration of the above reconnaissance and analysis, it is apparent that a significant opportunity exists for the XYZ Coffee Company to attract and retain a new, younger generation of coffee drinkers with a comprehensive SMM campaign.

The following social media goals are designed to achieve this undertaking:
- Strengthening the brand, primarily among the upscale-income youth market segment
- Driving word-of-mouth recommendations
- Improving customer satisfaction
- Generating new product ideas
- Promoting advocacy
- Increasing foot traffic in the stores
- Search engine optimization (SEO) to increase traffic and conversions

Figure 15.6 Goal Section from the XYZ Coffee Company SMM Plan

---

Determining Strategies

Once the social media goals have been set, the next step is to identify the strategies best suited for helping the organization reach them. Chapter 2 also introduced the Eight C's of Strategy Development (see the sidebar), which are guidelines for constructing SMM strategies for a particular organization.

However, like the general social media goals discussed above, these strategic guideposts only provide broad brushstrokes in the strategy design process. They must be fitted to fulfill a particular organization's social media goals. Figure 15.7 demonstrates how these overall strategies have been customized for the imaginary XYZ Coffee Company.

Strategies

XYZ Coffee Company will pursue a highly aggressive set of strategies for its SMM campaign. Such a comprehensive approach is obviously not without risks, because it represents a sizable investment in personnel and is time consuming and expensive. In addition, since no one controls the social web and since blunders do harm to a brand, in-depth engagement standards will be established for company employees interacting on the social web.

XYZ Coffee Company's comprehensive social media strategies include:

- **Listening** to the social web to determine where the company brand is being mentioned, who is talking about it, and what attracts consumers to the brand, as well as what is being said about competitors' brands.
- **Interacting** with consumers on Facebook and Twitter, where high concentrations of the target audience reside. Always acting as a contributor, not an overt promoter, to strengthen the brand by improving brand awareness, recognition, and perception. In addition, connecting with suppliers on LinkedIn to improve provider relationships.
- **Engaging** customers to drive word-of-mouth recommendations with YouTube viral brand videos and Flickr pictures showing the warm, friendly atmosphere of the coffee shops, where people hang out looking trendy.
- **Influencing** the target market with YouTube videos that feature interviews with the thought leaders in the coffee industry (mass influencers), enlisting them to help shape opinions about the company's products and services to promote brand advocacy on the social web.
- **Connecting** with customers by starting a location marketing program that rewards consumers for regular mobile check-ins at store locations using Foursquare.

Figure 15.7 Strategy Section from the XYZ Coffee Company SMM Plan

Identifying the Target Market

A company may already have an accurate understanding of the profile of its target audience; however, the behavior, interests, and tastes of that target market might be slightly or even radically different on the social web. As Chapter 3 describes in detail, personas provide an effective means for a company to categorize target audiences on the social web. A variety of characteristics can be used to group a target audience into personas, including *demographics* (such as age range, gender, income range, occupations, and education); *needs, interests, and tastes* (such as a desire for a friendly atmosphere, enjoying coffee drinking, an interest in sports, or the preference for exotic blends of coffee); and *behavior* (such as spending habits). Essentially, a persona is a detailed profile of a particular subset of people within the broad target audience.

One popular way to define personas is with Forrester Research's Social Technographics Profile, which enables marketers to use age, location, and gender to identify the type of activities that characterize people engaged on the social web: creators, critics, conversationalists, collectors, and spectators, among others.

For example, Figure 15.8 profiles the personas for the hypothetical XYZ Coffee Company. Depending on the behavior of the target market, it is possible to determine

Target Market

XYZ Coffee Company has a wide range of market segments, ranging from luxury coffee drinkers to professionals. However, the members of the current generation of young adults are not typically coffee drinkers, and hence they represent a lucrative, massive, untapped market segment, especially the slightly upscale higher-income youths.

Forrester's Social Technographics Profile Tool indicates that 93% of U.S. males in the age range 18 to 24 are spectators on the social web. Eighty-four percent of this market segment exhibits the persona of joiners, with 53% acting as social media critics and only 44% creating content. U.S. females in the same age range are slightly less inclined to engage in the social web as spectators (85%), and more likely to be joiners (86%) and creators (48%), but less inclined to be critics (47%).

Forrester Research surveys have determined that Generation Y online users constitute the largest group of creators, consisting of 37% of consumers ranging between ages 18 and 29. In other words, young urban social media users are the most active of the personas in producing videos, blog posts, articles, discussion forum text, and so on. In addition, these studies have found young women to be far more active on the social web as conversationalists than young men.

Figure 15.8 Target Market Section from the XYZ Company SMM Plan

which social media platforms these personas are most likely to frequent. As an example, spectators are not likely to participate in such social networks as Facebook or LinkedIn, but they might watch YouTube videos and read blogs, but not comment on the posts. The technographics profiles can be enriched with the company's own data, demographic and especially behavioral, collected by monitoring its social media accounts.

Selecting Platforms

Once the demographic and behavioral characteristics of the personas have been used to define a company's target market, the social media platforms with the highest concentration of the target audience should be chosen. For instance, if the personas for the target market primarily include conversationalists and content creators, then marketers will want to divide their attention between social networks and other online communities where people frequently converse and on social media platforms where people contribute content, such as video and photo sharing sites as well as article directories.

Implementing

Implementation is the process whereby the goals, strategies, target market, and tools are taken into consideration in creating actionable social media platform-specific tactics. In addition, implementation includes the generation and distribution of content as well as the assignment of staff to be responsible for preparing and carrying out platform-specific tactics and the development and dissemination of content on the various platforms.

SELECTING PLATFORM-SPECIFIC TACTICS

Each social media platform requires unique and customized tactics to successfully execute the company's overall strategies for reaching its marketing goals. The following sections summarize the marketing tactics for key social media platforms as discussed in earlier chapters. Chapter 5 discusses Facebook and LinkedIn. Chapter 6 discusses marketing strategies for Twitter. Chapter 8 discusses YouTube, while Chapter 9 covers Instagram. Mobile marketing strategies and examples are the subject of Chapter 12.

FACEBOOK Facebook is the most popular social network, having grown from 750 million users in 2011[32] to 900 million in 2015 (see Table 15.1). It is especially well suited for interacting with end consumers. Although not exhaustive, the following list of Facebook tactics can strengthen a brand by improving brand awareness, recognition, and perception as discussed in Chapter 5.

Facebook tactics:

- If not already done, create an officially branded company Facebook page (not profile) that represents the business and allows users to follow or become fans of a company.

- Customize the page to reflect the company's style and values, but provide some content distinct from the firm's primary website.

- Frequently update the company page with content that is relevant and engaging for Facebook users—no more than three updates per day. Be persistent, consistent, and genuine.

- Focus on content:
  o Create share-worthy content that encourages further discussions among the target market to advance a brand's position by making the brand more memorable or personable.
  o Content needs to be light, engaging, and informative.
  o Offer a special deal or value.
  o Give away free products to encourage likes so that the company's brand will spread rapidly through Facebook friend networks.
  o Run contests or offer discounts to Facebook members to convince people to follow a Facebook profile. Contests should be tailored to the product being offered.
  o Give useful tips, or ask open-ended questions that will interest the audience.
  o Not every content item must be original; sharing links to interesting items can also be valuable.

- Facebook is about personal connections, so letting some personality through in updates and giving a human voice to a brand are some of the most powerful advantages of this social networking platform. Engage with users to create an emotional connection; this engagement will build brand loyalty. Used correctly, Facebook is an excellent tool for business-to-consumer marketing.

- Facebook users are often picky about which items they will like. To get an idea of what sort of content to post, look at other Facebook pages—particularly those of businesses offering a similar product or service to the one being marketed—and see which statuses or comments are being liked the most. This investigation will give some insight into what potential fans want to see. Often less serious posts will be liked more, so keep content funny, personable, and entertaining.

- To gain viewers for a page, put links on other websites, email signatures, business cards, and outgoing communications.

- To make the URL for the Facebook page easy to write and remember, use a shorter vanity URL. A customized URL makes the page more memorable, increasing the chance Facebook users will visit and become fans.

- Use Facebook ads to generate traffic to the company website.

- Use the Facebook ad tool to specify race, gender, interests, and location; the Estimated Reach section can give an idea of how many users fit the target market. Facebook ad costs can be set very low (well under $100 per month) depending on the budget.

Figure 15.9 shows how some of these Facebook tactics can be customized for a specific company.

TWITTER Twitter is currently the second most popular social media platform, with over 200 million unique monthly visitors in 2011,[33] growing to 310 million in 2015 (see Table 15.1). With Twitter it is possible to instantly reach a large (often mobile) audience with brief but focused messages, making it a great marketing platform for interacting with users on the go. These features make Twitter especially useful for customer service. Marketing on Twitter is discussed in Chapter 6.

Twitter tactics:

- Customize the company's profile page, starting with a good avatar picture and customized background, text color, and company description.

- The profile's description should complement the avatar by providing context and important details. Writing space is limited, so the description will have to be concise.

- A custom-made background image can display personality, a longer explanation of the product or services, and past accomplishments. The background is also a place to put URLs for other social networking profiles, websites, or blogs.

- Use Twitter to start a discussion or to participate in an ongoing conversation.

Facebook

Facebook is the most popular social network, with more than 900 million monthly users. It is especially well suited for interacting with existing and potential consumers. Hence XYZ Coffee Company will use its Facebook presence to strengthen the brand by improving brand awareness, recognition, and perception, especially with the affluent youth target market.

Following are the key tactics that will be implemented on Facebook to help build the company brand:
- Post content that is of interest to the youth target market such as popular coffee drinks, music, teenage icons, and fashion, funny YouTube videos, community events, etc.
- Post content three times each day
- Light or funny ads to direct traffic to company website
- Promote offers, coupons, promotions, and events
- Participate in industry pages
- Include links to company Facebook page on all outbound communications such as promotional materials, brochures, and email signatures, as well as on the company website

Figure 15.9 Facebook Tactics for the XYZ Coffee Company

- Twitter can operate as a "global human search engine" in almost any field of expertise. It is possible to find someone on Twitter with relevant information to share.

- Use *targeted follow* strategy—search for and follow target markets and always follow back. Use the phrase "You should follow me on Twitter."

- Putting out updates when people are online to see them is essential to make an impact; research shows that midday and midweek tend to produce the best results.

- Promptly respond to questions and comments.

- Providing useful information can build a brand's reputation and thought leadership.

- Ask for opinions or product reviews to seek feedback and engage the followers.

- Being kind, polite, and appreciative helps to grease the apparatus and keep it running smoothly.

- Tweet things that are of interest to your target market. Be sure to use appropriate hashtags.

- Twitter profile must answer the question "Why follow and listen to the messages being offered?"

- Offer special deals on Twitter including coupons, promotional discounts, special products, and free shipping.

- Use Twitter to increase brand awareness, connect with customers, provide support, and distribute information.

- Use Twitter to identify influential people and those who have common interests in order to create potentially valuable relationships.

- Provide content that is fun, interesting, and valuable, and people will come looking for more.

- Be creative in persuasively conveying much larger ideas.

- Use link-shortening services such as bit.ly to track real-time interest in posts.

Figure 15.10 depicts how several of these Twitter tactics can be tailored for a particular company.

Twitter

Twitter is currently the second most popular social media platform, with over 310 million unique monthly visitors. With Twitter, it is possible to instantly reach a large (often mobile) audience with brief but focused messages, making the site a great marketing platform for interacting with users on the go, especially the upscale-income youth market that XYZ is targeting. These features make Twitter especially useful for customer service.

The following tactics will be pursued to take the utmost advantage of this platform for strengthening the brand among the target audience:
- Respond to questions and comments promptly
- Average of 10 to 15 tweets daily and use hashtags frequently
- Use shortened links to share interesting articles, videos, breaking news, etc.
- Use Twellow to search for targeted users to follow 20 new people daily to generate more followers
- Retweet to increase sharing of our content in return
- Cross promote Facebook offers, coupons, promotions and events
- Include links to company Twitter on all outbound communications such as promotional materials, brochures, and email signatures, as well as on the company website

Figure 15.10 Twitter Tactics for the XYZ Coffee Company

LINKEDIN LinkedIn is one of the most popular social media platforms, with over 200 million unique monthly visitors in August 2011,[34] growing to 255 million in 2015 (see Table 15.1). With the great majority of business-to-business marketers using LinkedIn, it is the dominant B2B social network, making it ideal for a company to connect with suppliers in order to improve provider relationships. LinkedIn as a B2B marketing platform is discussed in Chapter 5.

LinkedIn tactics:

- Create a company page, and use it to showcase job openings, new positions, or similar information in order to develop a large company following and to raise awareness of a brand because more people will see that company as a suggestion based on their contacts' interests.

- All employees should strive to complete 100% of their profiles and optimize with appropriate keywords. In addition, employees should include links to the company website, Facebook, Twitter, and blog, among others. Also include such applications as SlideShare to add relevant content and link to third-party articles in order to appear less self-promotional.

- Employees should ask contacts, past customers, industry analysts, and employees to join the group and/or follow the brand.

- Each employee should request recommendations from past employers, customers, supervisors, and so on to showcase expertise.

- Key employees should be assigned the responsibility of regularly participating in industry groups.

- Groups should be launched with descriptive names in order to address a common issue or problem.

- Content should be formatted so that it follows the group's theme, using a regular series of tips and showcasing the company's product's subtlety.

- Employees should post regularly in the group with contents of interest to the group members such as the latest industry information or thoughtful questions.

- Join associated group, first taking the time to learn what the group deems relevant before posting. Be courteous and show respect for other users' time by posting only relevant, well-considered, and valuable thoughts to group discussion boards.

- LinkedIn Answers should be used by employees to contribute valuable and well-considered answers in order to draw in business leads by highlighting personal expertise.

- Company representatives should focus on fostering relationships before asking for assistance and personalizing communications in order to demonstrate sincere interest in getting to know a person.

- Posted titles and summaries should use catchy, keyword-rich titles.

- Use InMail to ask to be connected. Send a personalized message, and explain why you would like to be connected.

Figure 15.11 shows how several of these LinkedIn tactics can be adapted for a particular company.

YOUTUBE YouTube is the largest video platform (see Table 8.1). According to YouTube Statistics it has over a billion users worldwide and gets over half its views from mobile.[35] As more people choose to consume information visually, YouTube's vast (and growing)

Figure 15.11 LinkedIn Tactics for the XYZ Coffee Company

reach and compelling content make it the perfect platform for engaging consumers to drive word-of-mouth recommendations.

YouTube tactics:

- Create authentic videos with real people in actual locations to make the videos more persuasive in order to engage viewers. Offbeat and unusual videos tend to get more attention.

- Include links to videos on all other social media properties (Facebook, Twitter, etc.).

- Actively comment on videos that relate to your industry in order to make connections. The more influential you can appear in the community, the more credibility your business will have.

- Choose keywords for videos carefully. Tag videos with various keywords to rank higher in the YouTube search engine. Make them relevant to the subject matter or niche. Think about what customers will be searching for, and target those keywords.

- Produce videos that are informative and entertaining. Use videos to educate the audience about issues its members face in your industry. Be sure to provide helpful hints.

- Get to the point quickly, and make the video 2 minutes or less to encourage viewers to watch the video to completion.

- Email the video links to customers.

- Cross-marketing: be sure to include links to your website or other social media properties in your videos, and promote the video on your company website and social media properties.

- Ask friends and associates to share the videos on their social media properties.

- Identify YouTube opinion leaders, and ask them to rate the videos.

- Create contests or feature user-submitted videos on the corporate website or blog. The result can be a series of testimonials, how-to tutorials, or other indirect promotions, which cost nothing for a social media campaign that achieves substantial results.

- Start a video channel, and update contents regularly.

YouTube

YouTube, owned by Google, is the largest video platform with over 1 billion users worldwide. As more people choose to consume information visually, YouTube's vast (and growing) reach and compelling content make it the perfect platform for engaging consumers to drive word-of-mouth recommendations.

The following YouTube tactical actions will be taken on behalf of the company:
- Creative, entertaining, light-hearted videos focused on the youth market
- Tag videos with relevant keywords to rank higher in the YouTube search engine
- Videos should be 2 minutes or less in length
- Embed company logo/image in all videos
- Post one video per month
- Reply to comments daily
- Cross-marketing by using Facebook and Twitter to promote videos

Figure 15.12 YouTube Tactics for the XYZ Coffee Company

Figure 15.12 illustrates how several of these YouTube tactics can be adapted for implementing a particular company's overall strategies and marketing goals.

INSTAGRAM Instagram has experienced explosive growth since its founding in 2009 and had over 100 million unique monthly visitors in 2015 (see Table 15.1). It is well suited for engaging customers with photos of the business, thereby personalizing the company in ways no other social media platform can match. For example, sharing photos of a coffee shop with a warm, friendly atmosphere humanizes the business. When a business creates a buzz on the social web by sharing photos, people start sharing and talking about it, causing others to become interested in knowing more about the company. This level of engagement with customers can help drive word-of-mouth recommendations and traffic to the website.

Instagram tactics:

- Use the company's Instagram page to share pictures with customers, thus keeping them up to date with current events at the business.

- Use Instagram to personalize the company by showing what is going on behind the scenes, featuring interesting and informative pictures of product preparation, customer service, festive holiday parties, or employees just enjoying doing their jobs.

- Use photo sharing on the company's Instagram page as a teaser for more information elsewhere, such as the company's website and Facebook page.

- Share photos of employees at a philanthropic event, and provide a linking to the corporate blog for followers to learn more about the event.

- Ask customers to share photos of the business that capture distinctive aspects of it, such as a storefront's appearance during a beautiful sunset. Recognize the best submissions with some form of award.

- Create a positive buzz about the company by sponsoring a photo contest in which the person sharing the most innovative picture of the business wins a discount or other prize.

- Upload images of a product with detailed specifications and technical details. Include customer reactions. Place a link to the company website in the description that will bring traffic to the company website.

- Company pictures can be highly persuasive for potential buyers, even when they are not directly about the product. Posting photos online can give "a strong sense of culture and provide a human face to the company."[36]

- Use photo sharing to help draw traditional press attention. In addition, with appropriate keywords, a photo result often shows up on the first page of results, bringing many to view the content.

- Use multiple photo sharing sites to upload images in order to expand the company's reach to different audiences.

- Be diligent about using titles, descriptions, photo sets, and tags to secure top Google Search results. Hashtags, headlines including hashtags and emojis are important Instagram tools.

- The most popular shared images tend to be humorous, unplanned, or spontaneous in appearance. Detailed, up-close photographs with a simple background draw more interest than landscapes.

- Post a link to images using Facebook, Twitter, and a company website to generate traffic.

Figure 15.13 illustrates how several of these Instagram tactics can be adapted for implementing a particular company's overall strategies and marketing goals.

SWARM Swarm is Foursquare's replacement for its popular Foursquare app, in partnership with Twitter. Like Foursquare, Swarm provides the ability for people to share their location with friends and to win prizes for visiting businesses and checking in. Since its launch in May 2014 the Swarm app has experienced some technical difficulties but managed to acquire about 2 million unique mobile users.

Foursquare provides merchant data and other services to Swarm, so brands must use the two in conjunction with one another, although consumers will use Swarm for its check-in and other social functions.[37]

Instagram

Instagram is the most popular photo sharing site with over 300 million monthly users. It is well suited for engaging customers with photos of the business, which can personalize the company in ways no other social media platform can match. For example, sharing photos of a coffee shop, with a warm, friendly atmosphere, humanizes the business. When a business creates a buzz on the social web by sharing photos, people start talking about it and cause others to become interested in knowing more about the company. This level of engagement with customers can help drive word-of-mouth recommendations. The best use of Instagram is to encourage customers to post their own photos of enjoyable and satisfying brand experience.

The following Instagram tactical actions will be taken:
- Upload photos featuring funny pictures, interesting events, product preparation, customers enjoying coffee, festive holiday parties, or employees just enjoying doing their jobs
- Be diligent about using titles, descriptions, photo sets, and tags to secure top Google Search results
  - Use hashtags, headlines with hashtags and emojis to generate attention and engagement
- Upload high-quality pictures weekly or more frequently to highlight promotions and events
  - Run a contest and in other ways encourage customers to upload photos to Instagram
- Reply to comments daily
- Cross-marketing by posting the most interesting pictures on Facebook and links on Twitter to photos, etc.

Figure 15.13 Instagram Tactics for the XYZ Coffee Company

Swarm and Foursquare tactics:

- Verify or create a Foursquare business listing.

- Update all account information.

- Create special offers for customers on Foursquare.

- Add customer tips.

- Advertise on Foursquare.

- Encourage customers to download and use the Swarm mobile app.

  o Customers still enjoy game-like features including becoming mayors and earning stickers (originally called badges on Foursquare).

  o Any updated information to Foursquare shows on Swarm.

  o Customer photos uploaded to Swarm appear on Foursquare as well.

  o Customers can view special offer on Foursquare as well as Swarm.

- Brands can still see who has checked in to your place of business via a Foursquare profile.

Figure 15.14 demonstrates how several of these social location marketing tactics can be modified for a particular company.

CREATING CONTENT

Although each social media platform will require specific types of content, it is possible to provide some general guidelines for generating and using content across most platforms:

- **Developing or Acquiring Content**: A thorough analysis of the content needs for each social media platform should be conducted, identifying the specific needs of each community, finding the gaps in content, and either creating or acquiring the content. A careful inventory of existing content within an organization may uncover material that can be repurposed for use on social media platforms. In addition, third parties, such as freelance writers, can be contracted to prepare platform-specific content.

- **Managing Content**: Regardless of whether platform content is prepared in-house or outsourced, it will still require editing. Moreover, user content on

Swarm by Foursquare

Swarm is a popular check-in service, providing the ability for people to share their location with friends and win prizes for visiting businesses and checking in.

The following Foursquare tactical actions will be taken:
- Create or verify a Foursquare business and ensure that the profile is complete and correct
- Upload photos to your Tips and check-ins
- Offer coupons and special discounts
- Offer free product after a certain number of check-ins
- Offer stickers or special status to loyal customers after a certain number of check-ins
- Create special deals to encourage customers to bring their friends
- Place a QR code on coupons and special offers in order to provide instant links to the company's social media properties such as Twitter, LinkedIn, Facebook, blog, corporate website, etc.

Figure 15.14 Swarm and Foursquare Tactics for the XYZ Coffee Company

private social networks, brand communities, and company-run discussion boards should be moderated, with careful grafting and pruning of discussion threads to keep them on-topic and generating productive conversations.

- **Cross-Utilizing Content:** A great way to leverage content across platforms is to restructure it for cross-platform utilization. Be careful not to overutilize this procedure because it may trigger unwanted attention from search engines, which might deem too much similar content as spam and lower its search ranking. In some cases, search engines may even exclude the content from their primary search index. Either situation would certainly reduce traffic to the company's sites via search engines.

- **Breaking Apart Content:** Making content into smaller chunks and reformatting it will stretch the utilization of the material, allowing it to appear in various forms on multiple platforms, such as article directories, blogs, microblogs, podcasts, webinars, and discussion boards.[38]

Figure 15.15 displays the content tactics for the imaginary XYZ Coffee Company.

ASSIGNING ROLES

In order to execute platform-specific tactics and generate content, specific roles and responsibilities must be assigned based on expertise and availability of staff. Some traditional approaches to making these assignments include giving the job to the marketing, public relations, or advertising department or entirely outsourcing the undertaking to an agency. Unfortunately, these approaches have not met with a great deal of success because existing department personnel typically lack the skill and expertise to engage effectively in SMM and outside agencies lack the intimate knowledge of a company's products, customer support, and culture.[39]

The most successful SMM efforts result from having nontraditional roles lead the conversation. For example, Home Depot has its associates respond to questions on Twitter, Ford has its mechanics tweet about their automobiles, and Starbucks has its baristas lead the conversation.[40]

In short, roles for executing the SMM plan should be assigned to those with the knowledge, expertise, and training to effectively engage with consumers on the

---

Content Development

Although each social media platform will feature specific types of content, the following tactics will maximize the generation of quality content that can be repurposed multiple times, saving time and money and creating the greatest possible impact:

- **Developing Content:** A thorough analysis of the content needs for each social media platform will be conducted, identifying the specific needs for each community, finding the gaps in content, and filling them with content that satisfies consumer needs. A careful inventory of existing content within an organization will be undertaken to find material that can be repurposed for use on social media platforms.
- **Managing Content:** Social media content will be carefully edited before posting and consumer contributions will be moderated to ensure the brand community conversation stays on topic.
- **Cross-Utilizing Content:** To leverage existing content, it will be adapted to each type of platform for proper cross-utilization. Care will be taken not to overutilize this procedure because it may trigger unwanted attention from search engines.
- **Breaking Apart Content:** Breaking content into smaller chunks and reformatting it will stretch the utilization of the material, allowing it to appear in various forms on multiple platforms, such as article directories, blogs, microblogs, podcasts, webinars, discussion boards, and so on.

Figure 15.15 Content Creation Tactics for XYZ Coffee Company

Figure 15.16 Role Assignments for XYZ Coffee Company

social web. These individuals can be employees with the proper social media training or SMM specialists and community managers hired by the company and then thoroughly trained in the use of its products and services, as well as indoctrinated with the organization's culture and values, as depicted in Figure 15.16.

Monitoring

As defined in Chapter 13, social media monitoring is the process of tracking, measuring, and evaluating an organization's SMM activities. Each of these activities presents unique challenges and opportunities for marketers.

TRACKING

Tracking is the process of finding and following content on the social web. One of the biggest challenges marketers face in setting up a tracking plan is to identify the right keywords and phrases for finding and following relevant data. A tracking plan should choose optimal topics of focus, select platforms with the greatest concentration of the target audience, identify optimal keywords and phrases by studying how people actually describe brands or other topics, use Boolean operators to zero in the desired data, and adjust searches when they do not produce the desired results. Tracking in order to listen to conversations on the web was discussed in Chapter 2.

MEASURING

The process of measuring SMM endeavors is an incredibly fast moving field. The intense pressure to demonstrate the value of expenditures on SMM is driving the rapid development of new measurement techniques, metrics, methodologies, technologies, and tools. Both quantitative and qualitative metrics were discussed in Chapter 13 along with their contributions to calculating ROI and developing KPIs for the brand.

Despite the obstacles, no SMM plan would be complete without well-defined quantitative and qualitative metrics and KPIs to assess the headway being made in reaching the organization's marketing goals. Table 15.5 shows the quantitative metrics for the XYZ Coffee Company. Note these performance metrics are granular, designed to measure progress on individual social media platforms being used in the implementation of the current plan.

Social Media Platform	Suggested Quantitative Metrics for the Next Year
Facebook	• 40% growth in the number of likes • 20% growth in the number of fans • 20% increase in the number of comments and likes on admin post • 5% growth in the number of wall response time • 40% increase in the number of Facebook Places check-ins • 30% increase in visits to company website from Facebook ads
Twitter	• 30% growth in the number of followers • 30% growth in the number of retweets (message amplification) • 30% growth in the number of mentions • 10% increase in click-through rate (CTR) of the links posted in tweets (Note: Observing which types of links garner the highest CTRs can help in tuning tweets to provide consumers with links they are interested in and hence further improve the CTRs.) • 20% increase in visits to website from tweet links • 5% increase in website conversions (i.e., sales) from tweet links
LinkedIn	• 20% growth in the number of connections • 10% increase in the number of recommendations • 20% growth in the number of posts and comments in discussion groups • 20% increase in the number of group members • 15% growth in the number of questions answered or asked
YouTube	• 30% growth in the number of videos viewed • 20% growth in the number of unique visitors • 10% increase in the number of subscribers to company channel • 10% increase in positive comments • 15% growth in visits to company website from YouTube • 10% increase in average rankings of videos by viewers
Instagram	• 20% growth in the number of views of video/photo • 30% growth in the number of replies • 20% growth in the number of page views • 30% growth in the number of comments • 30% growth in the number of subscribers • 15% growth in visits to company website from Flickr
Swarm	• 30% growth in the number of impressions • 40% growth in the number of check-ins • 40% growth in the number of redemptions (comes from point-of-sale systems) • 30% growth in the number of visitors to business after viewing venue/special on foursquare (foot traffic)

Table 15.5 Quantitative Metrics for XYZ Coffee Company

A number of KPIs are available for measuring the qualitative performance of SMM activities. As discussed in Chapter 13, KPIs should be developed based on the specific marketing goals of a business.

Table 15.6 depicts the qualitative KPIs for the XYZ Coffee Company. These metrics are arranged by the qualitative social media goals, indicating the name of the KPI, its formula, and its performance target.

Social Media Goals	Key Performance Indicators	KPI Formula	KPI (One-year) Performance Targets
Brand Strengthening	Sentiment Ratio (SR)	$SR = \dfrac{\text{Positive: Neutral: Negative Brand Mentions}}{\text{Expenses}}$	10% increase
Word of Mouth	Share of Voice (SV)	$SV = \dfrac{\text{Brand Mentions}}{\text{Total Mentions}}$	15% increase
Word of Mouth	Audience Engagement (AE)	$AE = \dfrac{\text{Comments + Shares + Trackbacks}}{\text{Total Views}}$	20% increase
Word of Mouth	Conversation Reach (CR)	$CR = \dfrac{\text{Total People Participating}}{\text{Total Audience Exposure}}$	10% increase
Customer Satisfaction	Issue Resolution Rate (IRR)	$IRR = \dfrac{\text{Total \# Issues Resolved Satisfactorily}}{\text{Total \# Service Issues}}$	10% increase
Customer Satisfaction	Resolution Time (RT)	$RT = \dfrac{\text{Total Inquiry Response Time}}{\text{Total \# Service Inquiries}}$	20% increase
Customer Satisfaction	Satisfaction Score (SC)	$SC = \dfrac{\text{Customer Feedback}}{\text{Total Customer Feedback}}$	25% increase
Generating New Product Ideas	Topic Trend (TT)	$TT = \dfrac{\text{\# of Specific Topic Mentions}}{\text{All Topic Mentions}}$	20% increase
Generating New Product Ideas	Idea Impact (II)	$II = \dfrac{\text{\# of Positive Conversations, Shares, Mentions}}{\text{Total Idea Conversations, Shares, Mentions}}$	15% increase
Promoting Advocacy	Active Advocates (AA)	$AA = \dfrac{\text{Total \# of Active Advocates within 30 days}}{\text{Total Advocates}}$	20% increase
Promoting Advocacy	Advocate Influence (AIN)	$AIN = \dfrac{\text{Unique Advocate's Influence}}{\text{Advocate Influence}}$	15% increase
Promoting Advocacy	Advocacy Impact (AIM)	$AIM = \dfrac{\text{Number of Advocacy Driven Conversations}}{\text{Total Volume of Advocacy Traffic}}$	20% increase

Table 15.6 Qualitative KPIs for XYZ Coffee Company

EVALUATING

As defined in Chapter 13, evaluation is the process of interpreting data once it has been measured with the intention to derive insights and understanding from it. Just measuring the impact of social media activity is insufficient—measurement only gains meaning through analysis. Such analysis enables management to determine whether social media strategies are achieving the organization's goals.

The aim of an appropriately focused evaluation is to produce a thorough description of the progress of SMM activities over time to reveal where strategies have succeeded or nose-dived, along with how things went right or wrong and why. Accordingly, "[such analysis] allows the program team to see where it must focus its efforts and resources next. It identifies success and failure, opportunities and risks, potential improvements, and new courses of action."[41]

SELECTING MONITORING TOOLS

As discussed in Chapter 2 and explained in the measurement section above, well-defined marketing goals should drive the decision regarding which social media metrics to measure and, consequently, the selection of the most appropriate monitoring tools. Free monitoring tools work well for listening to social media (i.e., observing what people are saying about a brand). Google Alerts, Google Trends, Google Reader, and SocialMention are popular free tools for tracking quantitative metrics. Google Analytics is useful for assessing the effectiveness of social media efforts directed at driving traffic to the company website and the consequent conversions (e.g., sales). Paid monitoring tools, such as Radian6, provide all-in-one solutions for tracking, measuring, and aiding in the analysis of qualitative metrics. Pricing of these tools should also be a key consideration in the selection process. Chapter 14 discusses popular free and paid tools along with which tasks each is best suited to accomplish.

Tuning

As defined in Chapter 2, tuning is the constant and continuous process of adjusting and improving the elements of the plan to maximize the chances of success. This process involves assessing a company's progress in implementing its social media strategies and then adjusting the SMM plan based on this feedback to optimize goal achievement.

Reevaluating the goals, strategies, and execution of the plan is necessary because of the ever-changing nature of consumer tastes, countermoves by competitors, and the continual introduction of new social media technologies. For example, if the number of views of the company's YouTube channel begins to decline, marketers must react quickly to adjust the content to match the target market's evolving interests.

If comments on the YouTube Channel are falling off as well, marketers need to reexamine and modify platform-specific tactics, possibly creating more humorous or how-to videos, which better fit the target market's shifting tastes. If this does not work, then additional adjustments in content should be made until the number of audience comments pick up again. In short, planning and executing SMM activities is a never-ending cycle. Marketers must constantly monitor and tune the plan to attain the maximize results.[42]

Budgeting

Although there are no hard and fast rules about how much a company should invest in SMM, a survey of 140 global corporations provides some valuable budgetary guidelines (the following material was adapted and excerpted from the report, *How Corporations Should Prioritize Social Business Budgets*, courtesy of the Altimeter Group).* This 2010 study found that these corporations had spent between $66,000 and $1,364,000 on SMM, largely dependent upon the maturity level of the company, as depicted in Table 15.7.

---

*From Owyang, Jeremiah, and Charlene Li (2011, February 11), *Report: How Corporations Should Prioritize Social Business Budgets*, Altimeter. Retrieved August 12, 2011, from http://www.altimetergroup.com/2011/02/report-how-corporations-should-prioritize-social-business-budgets.html

	Novice	Intermediate	Advanced
Average Budget	$66,000	$1,002,000	$1,364,000
Average Team Size	3.1	8.2	20.8
Most Common Organizational Models	Centralized (37%)	Hub and Spoke (49%)	Hub and Spoke (44%)
	Decentralized (23%)	Centralized (25%)	Centralized (28%)
	Hub and Spoke (23%)	Multiple Hub and Spoke (18%)	Multiple Hub and Spoke (19%)

© The Altimeter Group

Table 15.7 Maturity Drives Average Budget, Team Size, and How Corporations Organized for Social Business in 2010

These 140 companies were categorized into *novice*, *intermediate*, and *advanced* groups using the questionnaire shown in Figure 15.17. The questionnaire assessed the social business maturity level of the company based on six general areas: Program, Leadership and Organization Model, Processes and Policies, Education, Measurement, and Technology. Companies with a score of below 6 are classified as Novice, a score of 7–12 are Intermediate, and a score above 12 are Advanced.

According to Table 15.8, spending in social media was growing dramatically in 2011 in the following three categories and the growth appears to be continuing:

- **Internal Soft Costs in Three Areas**: Staff to manage social media, training and education, and research and development

- **Customer-Facing Initiatives in Four Areas**: Boutique agencies specializing in social media, spending on advertising and marketing, traditional agencies deploying social media campaign, and influencer/blogger program

- **Technology Investments in Five Areas**: Custom technology development, community platforms, brand monitoring, social customer relation management (SCRM), and social media management systems (SMMS)

Since this study was conducted mobile apps have become an important part of SMM budgets. Costs for an enterprise mobile app with advanced features such as payment systems can be as high as $1million and simple content apps can be as little as $100,000. Cost is also affected by whether the app development is done in-house, by a large agency, by a small agency, or by a freelancer.[43,44]

So how should a company prioritize its social media spending? It depends on a company's maturity level. When a company is just experimenting with social media, without much presence on any social media platform and, hence, is in the novice stage, a dedicated core team should start with monitoring the social web to create a social media plan and develop a training program for the core team before deploying a SMM campaign.

During the intermediate stage, with management buy-in and the core social media team garnering addition funding, the company is in a position to utilize social media management

Assess Your Social Business Maturity Level

For each section, choose the statement that best describes your social business program. Give yourself 1 point if you choose "1," 2 points if you choose "2," and 3 points if you choose "3." Add up your total score below to determine your social business maturity level.

A. Program
____ **1.** We are mostly experimenting with social media.
____ **2.** We've launched long-term initiatives that are part of an overall social strategy.
____ **3.** Social business permeates the enterprise — it's transcended the Marketing department, and impacts Product, Support, R&D, etc.

B. Leadership and Organizational Model
____ **1.** We do not have a formalized Social Strategist role or organizational model.
____ **2.** We've organized into a Hub and Spoke model with a formal Social Strategist role at the helm.
____ **3.** We've evolved to a Multiple Hub and Spoke or Holistic model, and business units can deploy on their own with little guidance from the Hub.

C. Processes and Policies
____ **1.** We have not conducted internal audits or established processes or policies for governance.
____ **2.** We've conducted internal audits and established processes and policies across the enterprise.
____ **3.** We've created clear processes and workflow across cross-functional teams.

D. Education
____ **1.** There is no formal education program to train internal associates.
____ **2.** We've launched an education program but it's not rolled out to the entire company.
____ **3.** We've formalized an ongoing education program that serves as a resource for all employees.

E. Measurement
____ **1.** We've tied our social media efforts back to engagement metrics, like number of clicks, fans, followers, RTs, check-ins, etc.
____ **2.** We've tied our social media efforts back to social media analytics, like share of voice, resonation, word of mouth, etc.
____ **3.** We've tied our social media efforts back to business metrics, like revenue, reputation, CSAT, etc.

F. Technology
____ **1.** We've invested in brand monitoring to listen to and develop understanding of our customers.
____ **2.** We've invested in scalable technologies such as community platforms or social media management systems (SMMS).
____ **3.** We've invested in social integration with other digital touchpoints like the corporate website, kiosks, mobile devices, etc., across the entire customer lifecycle.

Total score _____

If you scored between **0 and 6** points, your program is at the **Novice** level.
If you scored between **7 and 12** points, your program is at the **Intermediate** level.
If you scored between **13–18** points, your program is at the **Advanced** level.

Your Social Business Maturity Level _____

Figure 15.17   SMM Budget Questionnaire

	Novice		Intermediate		Advanced	
	Adoption	Spending	Adoption	Spending	Adoption	Spending
Internal Soft Costs						
Staff to Manage	68%	$133,000	76%	$303,000	88%	$406,000
Training and Education	85%	$9,000	76%	$15,000	76%	$66,000
Research and Development	55%	$8,000	75%	$59,000	74%	$56,000
Customer-Facing Initiatives						
Boutique Agencies (specializing in SM)	32%	$31,000	55%	$96,000	59%	$233,000
Ad/Marketing Spend	63%	$36,000	78%	$204,000	76%	$195,000
Traditional Agencies (deploying SM)	52%	$51,000	49%	$162,000	35%	$87,000
Influencer/Blogger Programs	37%	$12,000	66%	$60,000	85%	$50,000
Technology Investments						
Custom Technology Development	28%	$11,000	58%	$55,000	66%	$272,000
Community Platforms	42%	$78,000	58%	$126,000	78%	$196,000
Brand Monitoring	60%	$42,000	87%	$108,000	89%	$150,000
Social CRM	6%	$1,000	42%	$27,000	44%	$116,000
Social Media Management Systems	39%	$4,000	60%	$28,000	72%	$23,000

Base: 140 Global Corporate Social Strategists; for spending, those who have adopted each social business category.

© The Altimeter Group

Table 15.8 Average Adoption and Spending on 12 Social Business Categories by Corporations in 2011 by Program Maturity Level

systems (SMMS) to create "highly engaged communities across the social web."[45] The growing importance of mobile marketing makes it necessary to consider mobile as an important platform for developing an engaged community leading to increased brand loyalty.

As the company graduates into the advanced stage, the focus will shift into integrating social media throughout the entire business. Instead of having a core team of social media strategists, the company is ready to develop a set of clearly defined social media guidelines to educate all employees, and unleash them onto the social web.

To allow employees to be brand ambassadors, it is crucial to develop "a social media policy that [goes] so far as to show employees the best way to be interesting, add value and build their own networks online."[46] Investment in a scalable social customer relations management (SCRM) is also required "to gather and analyze the increasing amount of data from social profiles and interactions, then connect this information to core customer data . . . to deepen relationships and anticipate customer needs."[47]

Figure 15.18 displays the budget for the XYZ Coffee Company.

Budget

The following are the estimated expenses to implement this plan and achieve the stated goals within the next year:

A Mobile Manager	$80,000
A Multimedia Content Specialist	$50,000
Content Creation and Copyediting	$50,000
Two Social Media Specialists	$100,000

Figure 15.18 Budget for the XYZ Coffee Company

Mobile App Development and Maintenance	$100,000
Content Management and Platform Monitoring Services	$50,000
Total expenses for the year	$430,000

Figure 15.18 Budget for the XYZ Coffee Company *(Continued)*

Calculating Return on Investment

In finance, return on investment (ROI) is calculated by subtracting expenses from sales and then dividing the result by the expenses. If the subsequent ratio is positive, then the investment shows a return (the larger the ratio, the higher the return). Unfortunately, it is often difficult, if not impossible, to calculate a financial ROI for many SMM investments, especially those with qualitative goals, such as improving brand awareness, brand engagement, and word of mouth.[48] A workable process for computing ROI for SMM programs is laid out in Chapter 13.

In some cases, marketers have been forced to develop reasonable proxies for financial measures of success.[49] A Proxy ROI is an estimate of the long-term impact of SMM investments on customer response.[50] Common Proxy ROIs include brand awareness, customer satisfaction, sentiment analysis, share of voice, Net Promoter scores, and so on.

The majority of SMM initiatives are aimed at impacting these qualitative goals metrics, such as using Facebook and Twitter to strengthen a brand or using a brand community to improve customer relationships. Debates about the validity of Proxy ROIs are heated and ongoing, with some critics challenging whether they can actually measure ROI.[51] However, some studies have found direct linkages between Proxy ROIs and financial performance over the long run.[52] If a linkage can be shown, KPIs should be developed.

Whenever it becomes unrealistic or infeasible to calculate financial ROIs for a SMM plan, estimates of proxy ROIs should be considered as a means to explain the expected rewards for investing in the plan, as illustrated in Figure 15.19.

Return on Investment

The mobile marketing strategy is designed to increase website traffic and hence sales, so it will be possible to calculate its financial ROIs using the method presented in Chapter 13. However, the majority of the social media goals for the XYZ Coffee Company are not directly connected to sales, and consequently, standard ROI analysis will not be feasible. Fortunately, there are viable alternatives for estimating the return on investment for these social media goals.

Proxy ROIs measure the long-term impact of SMM investments on customer response. They include both quantitative and qualitative measurements, such as the number of views of the company's social media properties, the company's posting activity, and the customer responses rates, as well as sentiment analysis, share of voice, satisfaction scores, and advocacy impact. These proxy ROIs provide a meaningful way to judge the expected rewards for investing in this plan.

Figure 15.19 ROI for XYZ Coffee Company

Getting C-Suite Buy-In

With the SMM plan complete, the time has come to convince the "C-Suite" that the investment in social media will payoff for the company. The *C-Suite* is a term widely used for a corporation's top executives, who have titles that often start with the letter *C*, for *chief*, such as in chief executive officer, chief information officer, chief financial officer, and chief operating officer.[53] The following are a few tips to help gain the buy-in of these top level decision makers:

- **Identify with the Mindset of These Executives**: These are busy big-picture people who want to hear the broad brushstrokes of the plan, not the minute details of how the company will gain followers on Facebook.

- **Show Them the Payoff**: In asking for a sizeable investment, the first question these top executives will want answered is "What is the return on investment?" With SMM efforts, the ROI may likely have to be couched as proxy results, such as improved sentiment analysis scores showing brand strengthening or improved customer relationship metrics. Stress that it takes time to realize returns from social media efforts, but emphasize that payoff can be big—and have at least a process for calculating ROI for specific campaigns handy to back up this assertion.

- **Present a Detailed Budget Request**: These executives will also want to know how the company's money is being spent. Be as specific as possible as to what social media initiative will cost, and link the expenditures to desired outcomes.

- **Show Them the Timetable for Reaching Milestones**: Although SMM should be an ongoing activity for a company, progress in achieving marketing goals should have milestones. These milestones are often best given in conjunction with the metrics or KPIs so that executives can quickly see the projected time it will take to reach each milestone (such as 6 months to increase the company's share of voice; a 4 month-long national campaign will increase the number of Facebook followers by 10%, half of the year's objective).

- **Close the Deal**: Summarize the key benefits of the implementing of the plan while being transparent about potential downsides and the preparations that will be taken to mitigate them if they occur. Underscore that having a plan and executing it efficiently enables the company to act proactively rather than retroactively on the social web[54] and better able to measure results.

Notes

1. Ballenthin, Andrew (October 5, 2009), "5 Reasons Why 90% of Social Media Efforts Fail," *Community Marketing Blog*. Retrieved August 6, 2011, from http://communitymarketing .typepad.com/my_weblog/2009/10/5-reasons-why-90-of-social-media-efforts-fail.html
2. "Create a Table of Contents or Update a Table of Contents" (n.d.), Microsoft. Retrieved August 7, 2011, from http://office.microsoft.com/en-us/word-help/create-a-table-of-contents-or-update-a-table-of-contents-HP010368778.aspx
3. "Writing Guide: Executive Summaries" (n.d.), Colorado State University. Retrieved August 7, 2011, from http://writing.colostate.edu/guides/documents/execsum/index.cfm
4. Clay (February 9, 2011), "Getting It Right: How to Write a Winning Executive Summary," Towson University. Retrieved August 5, 2011, from http://tuoutreach.com/2011/02/09 /getting-it-right-how-to-write-a-winning-executive-summary/

5. Menzies, M. Dusty, M. Edward Rister, Saudah Sinaga, Victoria Salin, Eluned Jones, and Jenny Bialek (August 31, 2009), *Agricultural Economics Undergraduate Writing Handbook—2009* (College Station: Texas A&M University). Retrieved August 8, 2011, from http://agecon2 .tamu.edu/people/faculty/williams-gary/429/Complete%20Writing%20Guidelines.pdf

6. "How to Write an Executive Summary" (January 10, 2011), Succeed as Your Own Boss. Retrieved August 5, 2011, from http://succeedasyourownboss.com/01/2011/how-to-write-an-executive-summary/

7. "Writing Executive Summaries: Justification" (n.d.), Colorado State University. Retrieved August 7, 2011, from http://writing.colostate.edu/guides/documents/execsum/pop2h.cfm

8. Foster, Lorne (June 2005), "Writing the Executive Summary," York University, Toronto. Retrieved August 7, 2011, from http://www.yorku.ca/lfoster/2005-06/soci4440b/lectures /PolicyPaperWriting_TheExecutiveSummary.html

9. Greenhall, Margaret (n.d.), "Writing an Executive Summary, with Examples," UoLearn. Retrieved August 7, 2011, from http://www.uolearn.com/reportwriting /writingexecutivesummaries.html

10. "How to Write Executive Summary" (January 24, 2011), Invest Engine. Retrieved August 5, 2011, from http://investengine.com/blog/how-to-write-executive-summary

11. "Executive Summary" (n.d.), Howe Writing Initiative, Miami School of Business, Farmer School of Business. Retrieved August 7, 2011, from http://www.fsb.muohio.edu/fsb/content /programs/howe-writing-initiative/student-resources/Writing%20an%20Executive%20 Summary.doc

12. "Suggestions for Improvement—Executive Summary Example" (January 23, 2011), Executive Plan. Retrieved August 5, 2011, from http://www.businessplanexecutivesummary .com/2011/01/suggestions-for-improvement-executive-summary-example.html

13. "How to Write Executive Summary" (January 24, 2011), Invest Engine. Retrieved August 5, 2011, from http://investengine.com/blog/how-to-write-executive-summary

14. "How to Write an Effective Business Plan" (May 16, 2011), BigHospitality. Retrieved August 8, 2011, from http://www.bighospitality.co.uk/Business/How-to-write-an-effective-business-plan

15. Evans, Mark (July 20, 2011), "Brand Health and Social Media," *Sysomos Blog*. Retrieved August 9, 2011, from http://blog.sysomos.com/2011/07/20/brand-health-and-social-media/

16. Ibid.

17. Engler, Glenn (March 5, 2011), "Social Media—The Future of Your Brand Health," Random Patterns of Thoughts. Retrieved August 9, 2011, from http://www.glennengler.com/brands /social-media-the-future-of-your-brand-health/

18. Rahman, Faria (May 24, 2011), "Factors to Consider When Determining Brand Health," Retrieved August 9, 2011, from http://blog.openviewpartners.com/factors-to-consider-when-determining-brand-health-2/

19. Ibid.

20. Ogneva, Maria (April 10, 2010), "How Companies Can Use Sentiment Analysis to Improve Their Business," Mashable. Retrieved August 9, 2011, from http://mashable.com/2010/04/19 /sentiment-analysis/

21. Qian, Albert (May 22, 2011), "Is There a Standard Format for Preparing Social Media Audit?" Quora. Retrieved August 9, 2011, from http://www.quora.com/Is-there-a-standard-format-for-preparing-social-media-audit

22. Seiple, Pamela (July 1, 2011), "Top 5 Metrics for Auditing Your SMM ROI," *HubSpot Blog*. Retrieved August 14, 2011, from http://blog.hubspot.com/blog/tabid/6307/bid/18643/Top-5-Metrics-for-Auditing-Your-Social-Media-Marketing-ROI.aspx and "Social Media Metrics" (August 11, 2009), *Emerging Technologies Librarian Blog*. Retrieved August 14, 2011, from http://etechlib.wordpress.com/2009/08/11/social-media-plan-metrics/

23. Stephan, Nikki (May 5, 2011), "How to Conduct a Comprehensive Social Media Audit," *Arik Hanson Communications Conversations Blog*. Retrieved August 14, 2011, from http://www .arikhanson.com/2011/05/05/how-to-conduct-a-comprehensive-social-media-audit/

24. Ibid.

25. Hoult, Kevin (n.d.), "Strategic Planning for SMM: Strategic Planning Worksheet" [SWOT and Target Marketing template], Social Media Conference NW. Retrieved October 7, 2011, from http://www.socialmediaconferencenw.com/speakers/presentations/Strategic%20Planning%20 for%20Social%20Media%20Workbook.pdf

26. Kokemuller, Neil (n.d.), "Purpose of a SWOT Analysis," Chron, Small Business. Retrieved August 10, 2011, from http://smallbusiness.chron.com/purpose-swot-analysis-15364.html

27. Rothwell, Phil (May 25, 2010), "What Is a SWOT Analysis?" FreshBusinessThinking. Retrieved August 10, 2011, from http://www.freshbusinessthinking.com/business_advice.php?AID=5743&Title=What+Is+A+SWOT+Analysis?

28. "Social Media SWOT Analysis" (n.d.), Entrepreneurship in Box. Retrieved August 8, 2011, from http://www.entrepreneurshipinabox.com/1484/social-media-swot-analysis/

29. "Social Media SWOT Analysis" (n.d.), Entrepreneurship in Box. Retrieved August 8, 2011, from http://www.entrepreneurshipinabox.com/1484/social-media-swot-analysis/

30. "SWOT Analysis" (n.d.), QuickMBA. Retrieved September 1, 2011, from http://www.quickmba.com/strategy/swot/

31. "Social Media SWOT Analysis" (n.d.), SEO Wizardry. Retrieved August 8, 2011, from http://www.seowizardry.ca/social-media-swot-analysis

32. Kincaid, Jason (June 23, 2011), "Facebook Now Has 750 Million Users," Tech Crunch. Retrieved August 11, 2011, from http://techcrunch.com/2011/06/23/facebook-750-million-users/

33. "Top 15 Most Popular Social Networking Sites" (August 8, 2011), eBizMBA. Retrieved August 11, 2011, from http://www.ebizmba.com/articles/social-networking-websites; and "Top 15 Most Popular Web 2.0 Websites" (August 8, 2011), eBizMBA. Retrieved August 11, 2011, from http://www.ebizmba.com/articles/web-2.0-websites

34. "Top 15 Most Popular Web 2.0 Websites" (August 8, 2011), eBizMBA. Retrieved August 11, 2011, from http://www.ebizmba.com/articles/web-2.0-websites

35. (n.d.). "Statistics," YouTube. Retrieved October 31, 2015, from https://www.youtube.com/yt/press/statistics.html

36. Borges, Bernie (2009), *Marketing 2.0* (Tucson, AZ: Wheatmark), p. 85.

37. Shontell, Aylson (October 8, 2014), "How Foursquare Made the Bold Decision to Split Its Product in Two, and How Both Apps Have Been Doing Since," Business Insider. Retrieved October 21, 2015, from http://www.businessinsider.com/the-swarm-and-foursquare-backstory-and-progress-2014-10

38. Murthey, Steve (October 13, 2010), "Eight Components for Social Media Success: #3 Content Plan/Programming Schedule," Social Media Considerations. Retrieved August 5, 2011, from http://stevemurthey.com/2010/10/13/eight-components-for-social-media-success-3-content-plan-programming-schedule/

39. Martin, Erroin A. (June 7, 2010), "7 Components of a Winning Social Media Plan," Von Gehr Consulting. Retrieved August 5, 2011, from http://vongehrconsulting.com/Finding-Answers-Blog/2010/06/7-components-of-a-winning-social-media-plan/

40. Ibid.

41. Blanchard, Olivier (2011), *Social Media ROI: Managing and Measuring Social Media Efforts in Your Organization* (Boston, MA: Pearson Education), p. 196.

42. Barker, Melissa S. (April 14, 2011), "5 Steps to a Winning SMM Plan," *New SMM Blog*. Retrieved August 12, 2011, from http://www.new-social-media-marketing.com/blog/5-steps-to-a-winning-social-media-marketing-plan/

43. (n.d.). Savvy Apps, "How Much Does an App Cost: A Massive Review of Pricing and other Budget Considerations." Retrieved October 31, 2015, from http://savvyapps.com/blog/how-much-does-app-cost-massive-review-pricing-budget-considerations

44. Hurd, Mary (September 29, 2015), User Manual, "What Does it Cost to Develop an App?" Retrieved October 21, 2015, from https://fueled.com/blog/how-much-does-it-cost-to-develop-an-app/

45. Swallow, Erica (February 10, 2011), "HOW TO: Optimize Your Social Medial Budget," Mashable. Retrieved August 12, 2011, from http://mashable.com/2011/02/10/optimize-social-media-budget/

46. O'Dell, Jolie (July 28, 2011), "HOW TO: Help Employees Talk about Your Brand Online," Mashable. Retrieved August 12, 2011, from http://mashable.com/2010/07/28/internal-brand-management-online/

47. Owyang, Jeremiah, and Charlene Li (February 11, 2011), *Report: How Corporations Should Prioritize Social Business Budgets*, Altimeter. Retrieved August 12, 2011, from http://www.altimetergroup.com/2011/02/report-how-corporations-should-prioritize-social-business-budgets.html

48. Hoffman, Donna L., and Marek Fodor (Fall 2010), "Can You Measure the ROI of Your SMM?" *MIT Sloan Management Review*, vol. 52, no. 1, SlideShare. Retrieved August 12, 2011, from http://www.slideshare.net/MichaelGaspar/mit-5769540

49. Briody, Kevin (April 22, 2011), "Social Media ROI Revisited: 4 Ways to Measure," Ignite. Retrieved August 12, 2011, from http://www.ignitesocialmedia.com/social-media-measurement/social-media-roi-revisited-4-ways-to-measure/

50. Briody, Kevin (April 22, 2011), "Social Media ROI Revisited: 4 Ways to Measure," Ignite. Retrieved August 12, 2011, from http://www.ignitesocialmedia.com/social-media-measurement/social-media-roi-revisited-4-ways-to-measure/; and Hoffman, Donna L., and Marek Fodor (Fall 2010), "Can You Measure the ROI of Your SMM?" *MIT Sloan Management Review*, vol. 52, no. 1, SlideShare. Retrieved August 12, 2011, from http://www.slideshare.net/MichaelGaspar/mit-5769540

51. Briody, Kevin (April 22, 2011), "Social Media ROI Revisited: 4 Ways to Measure," Ignite. Retrieved August 12, 2011, from http://www.ignitesocialmedia.com/social-media-measurement/social-media-roi-revisited-4-ways-to-measure/

52. "New Study: Deep Brand Engagement Correlates with Financial Performance" (July 20, 2009), Altimeter. Retrieved August 12, 2011, from http://www.altimetergroup.com/2009/07/engagementdb.html

53. "C-Suite" (n.d.), *Investopedia*. Retrieved August 7, 2011, from http://www.investopedia.com/terms/c/c-suite.asp

54. Kelly, Nichole (April 11, 2011), "7 Tips for Selling Executives on Social Media," Social Media Examiner. Retrieved August 8, 2011, from http://www.socialmediaexaminer.com/7-tips-for-selling-executives-on-social-media/

XYZ Coffee Company

Social Media Marketing Plan

Prepared by:

Lisa Shea | Mark Irick | Susan Monroe

6/1/2012

XYZ Coffee Company

Headquarters: Spokane, WA

Voice: 000-000-0000 | Fax: 000-000-0000

Appendix

XYZ Coffee Company Social Media Marketing Plan

Table of Contents

Issues to consider as you read this plan. In Chapter 15 we presented a comprehensive overview of the development process and elements of a SMM plan. In this appendix we present a sample marketing plan. Remember that this is a hypothetical company and many things are not known about it. Reasonable assumptions are required in order to develop a plan. The chapter was also constructed to showcase many social media platforms. The number of platforms that are part of the SMM effort—especially of a small business or one that is not flush with resources—requires careful consideration. Objectives, platforms chosen, and evaluation metrics must all be chosen with the nature of the business and its resources in mind. This will require adapting elements discussed in Chapter 15 to the specific situation of the business.

Keep asking yourself, "How well does this strategy recommendation fit the needs of the business and the resources the business is willing to commit to SMM?" If the fit is good, you have a plan that has a fighting chance of successful implementation.

Executive Summary

XYZ Coffee Company has a wide range of market segments, ranging from luxury coffee drinkers to professionals. However, younger people are not typically coffee drinkers, and they represent a lucrative, massive, untapped market segment, especially the more affluent youths.

The primary focus of this SMM plan is to use the social web as a means to find, engage, attract, and retain this upscale youth market as XYZ Coffee Company patrons. It is based on comprehensive research of the company's current social media presence, competitive intelligence, and target market analysis (see Chapter 15). This thorough examination and appraisal has resulted in a set of specific actionable social media goals and strategies for reaching those goals as well as the best social media tools for successfully executing and monitoring the plan.

Social media goals for the XYZ Coffee Company include:

- Strengthening the brand, primarily among the more affluent youth market segment

- Driving word-of-mouth recommendations

- Improving customer satisfaction

- Generating and implementing new product ideas

- Promoting advocacy

- Increasing foot traffic in the stores

- Search engine optimization (SEO) to increase traffic and conversions

A set of comprehensive social media strategies will be employed to achieve the above goals. These strategies include listening, interacting, engaging, influencing, and contributing to the social web. In addition, this plan describes how the progress of social media efforts will be tracked, measured, and evaluated. These actions will enable the plan's execution to be tuned to obtain optimal results.

A detailed budget shows the cost of implementing the plan. The plan concludes with a discussion of how to determine return on investment. The team leaders responsible for preparing, overseeing, and executing the plan include the VP of marketing, Lisa Shea; the director of communications, Mark Jones; and the SMM manager, Susan Monroe.

Brief Overview

Over the last two decades, coffeehouses have become part of the American landscape. Millions of people purchase an espresso-based coffee drink daily. The willingness to spend $3 to $5 for a cappuccino, mocha latte, or chocolate-ice-blended drink occurred within just the last decade, largely due to Starbucks. The specialty-coffeehouse industry continues to grow at a strong pace.

Affluent youth, not normally heavy consumers of coffee, represent a niche market that has yet to be tapped. As explained below in detail, social media can be used to observe, interact, engage, and influence this market segment. These actions will help attract and retain this youth market as XYZ Coffee Company patrons, in combination with XYZ Coffee Company's high-volume, upscale, inviting atmosphere and high-quality products. Moreover, most of the XYZ Coffee Company's locations are near university or college campuses, locations that provide easy access for this target market.

Social Media Presence

XYZ Coffee Company began utilizing social media in 2009. Today, the social media health of the brand is good. Analysis of sentiment (opinion) across the social web shows that 55% of customer mentions of the company are positive. However, this sentiment analysis also reveals that 30% of company mentions are neutral, with a troubling 15% negative.

This last figure is less disturbing when compared with the negative sentiment analysis scores for the company's two closest competitors, also hypothetical, ABC Coffee and Dolt Coffee Shops. Forty three percent of social mentions about ABC are negative, with a staggering 57% of social mentions of Dolt being negative. In this context, XYZ's lower negatives indicate the company is doing a better job than the competition.

In addition to this holistic assessment of the social media presence of the company, it is useful to examine how the company is performing on individual social media platforms. The following are five key metrics for auditing a company's social media presence on individual social media platforms:

- **Sentiment Analysis**: Shows the number of positive, neutral, or negative mentions on each social media platform where the company has a sizable presence

- **Reach**: Indicates the number of Twitter followers, Facebook fans, LinkedIn group members, Instagram view count, and so on

- **Company Posts**: Measure how often the company posts on each social media platform

- **Feedback**: Shows the number of comments, likes, or replies to company-generated content

- **Average Response Time**: Measures response time to user comments on the company's social media properties

Table A.1 shows key metrics for the platforms currently being utilized.

Metric	Sentiment	Reach	Company Posts	Feedback	Average Response Time to Feedback
Facebook Page	Positive 58% Neutral 31% Negative 11%	1,200,000 fans	2 daily	10 comments and 20 likes daily	2 hours
Twitter Account	Positive 60% Neutral 28% Negative 12%	350,000 followers	3 or more daily	50 @tweets 200 retweets daily	1 hour or less for customer service issues
YouTube Channel	Positive 45% Neutral 27% Negative 28%	5,000 subscribers	2 per month	5 comments per video monthly	2 days
Instagram	Positive 45% Neutral 50% Negative 5%	3,000 monthly views	1 or 2 daily	2 comments per photo	1 week
Mobile	Strategy to be developed and tested during current operating year Strategy to be ready for deployment chain-wide by beginning of next operating year				

Table A.1 Platform-specific Measurements of a Company's Social Media Presence

Notice that the table indicates a strong and active social media presence on Facebook and Twitter, with respectable figures for YouTube. The company's Instagram metrics are low, but this is not surprising because the platform is relatively new to XYZ. The company is developing a strategy for mobile marketing but does not have any baseline metrics since this has not been implemented.

Competitive Analysis

By carefully listening to the social web and thoroughly assessing the company's social media resources, the following **Social Media SWOT Analysis** identifies the company's strengths and weaknesses on popular social media platforms, as well as the potential opportunities and threats posed by competitors and technological advancements on the social web, as shown in Table A.2.

Strengths	Weaknesses
• XYZ has a strong brand presence on the majority of the major social media platforms. • The company has a proven track on social media platforms, such as Facebook and Twitter. • Most of the company's actions result in the desired outcomes on social media platforms. • XYZ has an experienced staff adept at effectively using Facebook and Twitter to market the company. • The staff is enthusiastic about working with Facebook and Twitter. • XYZ's quantitative SMM efforts are monitored to assess progress in achieving marketing goals.	• XYZ has less than desirable brand presence on YouTube, LinkedIn, and Instagram. It has no presence on Swarm, an important platform for location marketing. • The company's track record on YouTube, LinkedIn, and Instagram is spotty. • The company's actions on YouTube, LinkedIn, and Instagram have fallen short of expected outcomes. • XYZ currently lacks the expertise to effectively market on YouTube, LinkedIn, and Instagram. • The staff is apprehensive about working with platforms such as YouTube, LinkedIn, and Instagram.

Table A.2 Social Media SWOT Analysis for the XYZ Coffee Company

- Most of XYZ's management is supportive of XYZ's social media efforts, especially on Facebook and Twitter because they have proven their usefulness in improving the company's bottom line.
- Resources are adequate for participating on some social media platforms, such as Facebook and Twitter.
- XYZ's Facebook and Twitter are lively social media properties.
- The company's high-quality beans, distinctive coffee blends, and coffee shop atmosphere satisfy the needs of the current social media target market.

- The company presently lacks a comprehensive monitoring tool to track and measure qualitative progress across the social web and on specific platforms.
- There has been an understandable reluctance by management to fully commit to an aggressive SMM campaign because of the inherent risks and costs in undertaking such an endeavor.
- Resources are insufficient for building and maintaining a substantial presence on YouTube, LinkedIn, Instagram, and Swarm.
- XYZ currently lacks a robust mobile marketing strategy, which provides for corporate promotions and local events and promotions.
- The present social media presence does not satisfy the needs of the affluent youth market.

Opportunities

- Facebook, Twitter, and YouTube have the largest concentration of the company's current target audience.
- The target audiences on these sites tend to be spectators and joiners.
- Significant portions of the affluent youth target audience are content creators and critics with needs that are not currently being met.
- The affluent youth market is a strong emerging target market on all the major social media platforms, with need to observe, join, converse, create content, and criticize content.
- The emergence of social location services, ubiquitous smartphone usage, and mobile apps for checking in from locations to earn awards make these technologies a significant opportunity for XYZ.
- Starbucks, McDonald's, and XYZ could cooperate in sponsoring social media events that support major charities. They could also work together to develop an open source wiki with information about coffee.
- XYZ can collaborate with customers to build brand presence on social media platforms by engaging in activities such as inviting contributions from customers (e.g., YouTube videos, Instagram photos and videos).
- Suppliers are present in large numbers on LinkedIn.
- XYZ customers value the high-quality, unique coffee drink blends and the warm, friendly atmosphere of the company's coffee shops.
- Market demand is currently slowly increasing.

Threats

- Starbucks is the closest direct competitor on the major social media platforms.
- McDonald's low prices and widespread locations are making it an emerging competitor, especially on key social media platforms like Facebook and Twitter.
- Starbucks pursues aggressive social media strategies across the social web, including its own brand community and location-marketing initiatives.
- Starbucks has been extremely successful in building brand presence on the company's key current social media platforms, such as Facebook, Twitter, and YouTube and is a leader in mobile marketing.
- Starbucks has more locations and a wider selection of coffee drinks and foods than XYZ.
- Starbucks and McDonald's already have robust mobile marketing strategies that include loyalty programs.
- XYZ has yet to use social location services like Swarm from Foursquare to participate in location marketing.
- International competitors have yet to make inroads in competing with XYZ, but their market penetration should be tracked carefully in case this situation changes.
- The customers dislike the wait to get support and lack of opportunity for input about XYZ products.
- Market demand for coffee drinks dropped off during the height of the recession.

Table A.2 Social Media SWOT Analysis for the XYZ Coffee Company (Continued)

SWOT Matrix	Strengths (S)	Weaknesses
Opportunities (O)	S-O strategy	W-O strategy
Threats (T)	S-T strategy	W-T strategy

Table A.3 SWOT Matrix

Given the factors profiled in Table A.2, it is possible to determine a general strategy using the SWOT Matrix shown in Table A.3. Since XYZ Coffee Company's social media platform strengths and external opportunities are substantial, the SWOT Matrix recommends the pursuit of an S-O (Strength-Opportunity) strategy, which (according to the bulleted recommendations below) advises XYZ to pursue opportunities on the social web that are a good fit for the organization's social media platform strengths. As a consequence of this SWOT profile, the company should focus resources on the social media platforms: Facebook, LinkedIn, YouTube, Instagram, and a mobile strategy. These platforms represent the best opportunities for the company and are a good fit for the organization's strengths.

- **S-O Strategy**: Follow social media platform opportunities that match the organization's strengths on the social web.

- **W-O Strategy**: Overcome weaknesses in social media platform performance in order to follow opportunities on the social web.

- **S-T Strategy**: Identify ways the organization can use its platform strengths to reduce its vulnerability to external threats from competitors or new technologies on the social web.

- **W-T Strategy**: Create a protective strategy that reduces the chances the organization's social media weaknesses will make it vulnerable to external threats. This strategy would likely take the form of monitoring the social web to detect customer complaints and handling them before they become a PR disaster.

Goals

In consideration of the above reconnaissance and analysis, it is apparent that a significant opportunity exists for the XYZ Coffee Company to attract and retain a new, younger generation of coffee drinkers with a comprehensive SMM campaign.

The following social media goals are designed to achieve this undertaking:

- Strengthening the brand, primarily among the upscale-income youth market segment

- Driving word-of-mouth recommendations

- Improving customer satisfaction

- Generating new product ideas

- Promoting advocacy

- Increasing foot traffic in the stores

- Search engine optimization (SEO) to increase traffic and conversions

Strategies

XYZ Coffee Company will pursue a highly aggressive set of strategies for its SMM campaign. Such a comprehensive approach is obviously not without risks because it represents a sizable investment in personnel, and is time consuming and expensive. In addition, since no one controls the social web and since blunders do harm to a brand, in-depth engagement standards will be established for company employees interacting on the social web.

XYZ Coffee Company's comprehensive social media strategies include:

- **Listening** to the social web to determine where the company brand is being mentioned, who is talking about it, and what attracts consumers to the brand, as well as what is being said about competitors' brands.

- **Interacting** with consumers on Facebook and Twitter, where high concentrations of the target audience reside. Always acting as a contributor, not an overt promoter, to strengthen the brand by improving brand awareness, recognition, and perception. In addition, connecting with suppliers on LinkedIn to improve provider relationships.

- **Engaging** customers to drive word-of-mouth recommendations with YouTube viral brand videos and Instagram pictures showing the warm, friendly atmosphere of the coffee shops, where people hang out looking trendy.

- **Influencing** the target market with YouTube videos that feature interviews with the thought leaders in the coffee industry (mass influencers), enlisting them to help shape opinions about the company's products and services to promote brand advocacy on the social web.

- **Connecting** with customers by starting a mobile marketing program that rewards consumers for regular mobile check-ins at stores.

Target Market

XYZ Coffee Company has a wide range of market segments, ranging from luxury coffee drinkers to professionals. However, the members of the current generation of young adults are not typically coffee drinkers, and hence they represent a lucrative, massive, untapped market segment, especially the slightly upscale higher-income youths.

Forrester's Social Technographics Profile Tool indicates that 93% of U.S. males in the age range 18 to 24 are spectators on the social web (see Chapter 15). Eighty-four percent of this market segment exhibits the persona of joiners, with 53% acting as social media critics and only 44% creating content. U.S. females in the same age range are slightly less inclined to engage in the social web as spectators (85%), and more likely to be joiners (86%) and creators (48%), but less inclined to be critics (47%).

Forrester Research surveys have determined that Generation Y online users constitute the largest group of creators, consisting of 37% of consumers ranging between ages 18 and 29. In other words, young urban social media users are the most active of the personas in producing videos, blog posts, articles, discussion forum text, and so on. In addition, these studies have found young women to be more active on the social web as conversationalists than young men.

Platforms

With the demographic and behavioral characteristics of the personas defined for the company's target market, the social media platforms with the highest concentration of the target audience have been chosen. The types of personas within the target market played a key role in the selection of each social media platform. For example, since the personas for both male and female demonstrate a high propensity to be joiners, the company's Facebook page was chosen to interact with them as a means of strengthening the brand.

Furthermore, females within the youth target audience are strong conversationalists, making the company's Twitter account an ideal social media platform for interacting with them, further strengthening the brand among this important target market. Using Twitter to provide customer service will also make it attractive to affluent young males. Moreover, given that many of the company's suppliers participate in LinkedIn, it was decided to also focus on this social network as a means to improve the quality of supplier relationships.

Given that Generation Y social media users constitute the largest group of creators, consisting of 37% of consumers ranging between ages 18 and 29, YouTube and Instagram were chosen in order to engage with this group by offering how-to videos about coffee drink selection and behind-the-scenes footage of how XYZ takes painstaking care preparing its own distinctive coffee blends. Additionally, there is an opportunity to use YouTube and Instagram to show the company's above-and-beyond customer service with videos featuring employees helping customers in humorous nontraditional ways, such as running around and around a car in front of the store in order to help retrieve the customer's runaway pet. XYZ will develop contests and promotional campaigns to encourage customers to post their own content on the company's YouTube channel and Instagram page.

Over the coming fiscal period, XYZ will develop a mobile marketing strategy. It must be both strategically sound and attainable within the resources XYZ is willing to devote. The first step will be to conduct consumer research among the primary target market, affluent young people, especially college students. One key output of the research will be to understand their expectations for a satisfactory coffee house experience and how well XYZ meets these expectations. It will be helpful to learn if mobile is an important part of the experience at other food establishments and, if so, what they like and dislike about current mobile programs and what expectations are not being met by them.

The second step will be to use the research to design the specifications for an affordable mobile program. Most beverage and food chains have their own branded app, but other solutions should be investigated. Assuming that XYZ's IT department does not have resources to develop the necessary mobile technology, suppliers must be identified, requests for proposals developed, and a winning supplier chosen.

The third step will be to test at least one mobile program throughout the chain and at least two local programs that can serve as models for other locations. Since the primary target market for this plan is affluent young people no initiative on the B2B platform LinkedIn will be undertaken.

Implementation

The above goals, strategies, target market, and platforms have been taken into consideration in creating the following actionable social media platform-specific tactics. In addition, this section of the plan indicates how content will be generated efficiently and effectively for each social media platform, as well as assigning staff to be responsible for carrying out these tactics and preparing content for dissemination on the various platforms.

PLATFORM-SPECIFIC TACTICS AND TOOLS

The social media platforms and tactics below where chosen as the optimal means for implementing the company's overall strategies and reaching its social media goals. Table A.1 includes benchmarks for the important questions of how often to post on each platform and how quickly to respond to comments and queries.

FACEBOOK Facebook is the most popular social network, with more than 900 million users. It is especially well suited for interacting with existing and potential consumers. Hence XYZ Coffee Company will use its Facebook presence to strengthen the brand by improving brand awareness, recognition, and perception, especially with the affluent youth target market.

Following are the key tactics that will be implemented on Facebook to help build the company brand:

- Post content that is of interest to the youth target market such as popular coffee drinks, music, teenage icons, and fashion, funny YouTube videos, community events, etc.

- Post contents two times each day[1]

- Light or funny ads to direct traffic to company website

- Promotions to increase the number of Facebook fans

- Coupons or giveaways once every month to increase the number of likes

- Campaigns to encourage Facebook fans to post their own content

- Include links to company Facebook page on all outbound communications such as promotional materials, brochures, and email signatures, as well as on the company website

TWITTER Twitter is currently the second most popular social media platform with 310 million monthly unique users in 2015. With Twitter it is possible to instantly reach a large (often mobile) audience with brief but focused messages, making it a great marketing platform for interacting with users on the go. These features make Twitter especially useful for customer service.

The following tactics will be pursued to take the utmost advantage of this platform for strengthening the brand among the target audience:

- Respond to questions and comments promptly

- Make an average of three tweets daily

- Research relevant and trending hashtags; develop and promote one or more brand-related hashtags

- Use shortened links to share interesting articles, videos, breaking news, etc. relevant to XYZ

- Develop a campaign to increase the number of Twitter followers

- Cross promote all coupons, giveaways, and promotions with Facebook

- Encourage customers to tweet to the XYZ account

- Answer all customer service related tweets within a time frame established by the social media team; 1 hour is desirable[2]

- Include links to company Twitter on all outbound communications such as promotional materials, brochures, and email signatures, as well as on the company website

LINKEDIN LinkedIn is the third most popular social media platforms, with over 255 million unique monthly visitors in April 2015. With 83% of business-to-business marketers using LinkedIn, it is the dominant B2B social network, making it an ideal platform to connect with business professionals including suppliers. The primary target for this plan is affluent young people, especially college students. LinkedIn will not be effective in reaching them in their consumer role, so it will not be a platform for the current plan, although it could be used in succeeding time periods.

YOUTUBE YouTube is the second most popular website according to Alexa, with more than 1 billion unique monthly visitors in October 2015.[3] As more people choose to consume information visually, YouTube's vast (and growing) reach and compelling content make it the perfect platform for engaging consumers to drive word-of-mouth recommendations.

The following YouTube tactical actions will be taken on behalf of the company:

- Creative, entertaining, light-hearted videos focused on the consumption of coffee beverages by youth market

- Tag videos with relevant keywords to rank higher in the YouTube search engine

- Videos should be 2 minutes or less in length

- Embed company logo/image in all videos

- Post one video per month

- Reply to comments daily

- Cross post on Instagram

- Cross-marketing by using Facebook and Twitter to promote videos

INSTAGRAM Instagram had over 100 million unique monthly visitors in 2015. It is well suited for engaging customers with photos of the business, thereby personalizing the company in ways no other social media platform can match. For example, sharing photos of a coffee shop with a warm, friendly atmosphere humanizes the business. When a business creates a buzz on the social web by sharing photos, people start talking about it, causing others to become interested in knowing more about the company. This level of engagement with customers can help drive word-of-mouth recommendations.

The following Instagram tactical actions will be taken:

- Upload photos featuring engaging pictures, interesting events, product preparation, customers enjoying coffee, festive holiday parties, or employees just enjoying doing their jobs

- Be diligent about using titles, descriptions, photo sets, and tags to secure top Google Image Search results

- Use hashtags, headlines with hashtags and emojis to convey liveliness and sentiment and encourage customers to do the same

- Upload high-quality pictures once or twice each day or more frequently, especially during promotions[4]

- Reply to comments daily

- Cross-market by posting the most interesting pictures on Facebook and Twitter

CONTENT DEVELOPMENT

Although each social media platform will feature specific types of content, the following tactics will maximize the generation of quality content that can be repurposed multiple times, saving time and money and creating the greatest possible impact:

- **Developing Content**: A thorough analysis of the content needs for each social media platform will be conducted, identifying the specific needs for the primary target market of young adults. A careful inventory of existing content within an organization will be undertaken to find material that can be repurposed for use on social media platforms.

- **Managing Content**: Social media content will be carefully edited before posting and consumer contributions will be monitored to ensure they are appropriate.

- **Cross-Utilizing Content**: To leverage existing content, it will be adapted to each type of platform for proper cross-utilization. Care will be taken not to over-utilize this procedure because it may trigger unwanted attention from search engines.

- **Breaking Apart Content**: Breaking content into smaller chunks and reformatting it will stretch the utilization of the material, allowing it to appear in various forms on multiple platforms.

ASSIGNMENTS

In order to execute platform-specific tactics and generate content, specific roles and responsibilities will be assigned based on expertise and availability of staff. Assignments for executing the SMM plan will be carried out by those with the knowledge, experience, and training to effectively engage with consumers on the social web. The following personnel will be involved in the implementation of the social media plan:

- VP of marketing, Lisa Shea

- Director of communications, Mark Jones

- SMM manager, Susan Monroe

- Hire the following positions:
  o A mobile manager
  o A multimedia content specialist
  o A professional writer
  o Two SMM specialists

Monitoring

Social media monitoring is the process of tracking, measuring, and evaluating an organization's SMM activities. The following sections explain how each of these activities will be executed to determine if the plan is achieving the desired social media goals laid out above.

TRACKING

The company will implement a sustainable and actionable tracking plan that identifies the right keywords to find and follow the relevant data on the social web. The tracking plan will choose optimal topics of focus, select platforms with the greatest concentration of the target audience, identify optimal keywords and phrases by studying how people actually describe brands or other topics, use Boolean operators to zero in the desired data, and adjust searches when they do not produce the desired results. It will also identify hashtags that are relevant and follow them. It will develop brand hashtags for appropriate campaigns to help track campaign results.

MEASURING

QUANTITATIVE METRICS With the above considerations in mind, Table A.4 lists the quantitative metrics that have been chosen to measure progress in achieving the company's marketing goals on the social media platforms chosen for implementation in this plan.

QUALITATIVE KPIs Table A.5 shows the qualitative KPIs designed to measure the social media goals for the XYZ Coffee Company (naturally, benchmarks will be established for each of these metrics so that progress can be assessed).

Social Media Platform	Quantitative Metrics for the Next Year
Facebook	• 40% growth in the number of likes • 20% growth in the number of fans • 20% increase in the number of comments and likes on admin post • 5% growth in the number of wall response time • 40% increase in the number of Facebook Places check-ins • 30% increase in visits to company website from Facebook ads
Twitter	• 30% growth in the number of followers • 30% growth in the number of retweets (message amplification) • 30% growth in the number of mentions • 10% increase in click-through rate (CTR) of the links posted in tweets (Note: Observing which types of links garner the highest CTRs can help in tuning tweets to provide consumers with links they are interested in and hence further improve the CTRs.) • 20% increase in visits to website from tweet links • 5% increase in website conversions (i.e., sales) from tweet links
YouTube	• 30% growth in the number of videos viewed • 20% growth in the number of unique visitors • 10% increase in the number of subscribers to company channel • 10% increase in positive comments • 15% growth in visits to company website from YouTube • 10% increase in average rankings of videos by viewers
Instagram	• 20% growth in the number of views of video/photo • 30% growth in the number of replies • 20% growth in the number of page views • 30% growth in the number of comments • 30% growth in the number of subscribers • 15% growth in visits to company website from Instagram

Table A.4 Quantitative Metrics for the XYZ Coffee Company

Social Media Goals	Key Performance Indicators	KPI Formula	KPI (One-year) Performance Targets
Brand Strengthening	Sentiment Ratio (SR)	$SR = \dfrac{\text{Positive: Neutral: Negative Brand Mentions}}{\text{Expenses}}$	10% increase
Word of Mouth	Share of Voice (SV)	$SV = \dfrac{\text{Brand Mentions}}{\text{Total Mentions}}$	15% increase
	Audience Engagement (AE)	$AE = \dfrac{\text{Comments + Shares + Trackbacks}}{\text{Total Views}}$	20% increase
	Conversation Reach (CR)	$CR = \dfrac{\text{Total People Participating}}{\text{Total Audience Exposure}}$	10% increase
Customer Satisfaction	Issue Resolution Rate (IRR)	$IRR = \dfrac{\text{Total \# Issues Resolved Satisfactorily}}{\text{Total \# Service Issues}}$	10% increase
	Resolution Time (RT)	$RT = \dfrac{\text{Total Inquiry Response Time}}{\text{Total \# Service Inquiries}}$	20% increase
	Satisfaction Score (SC)	$SC = \dfrac{\text{Customer Feedback}}{\text{Total Customer Feedback}}$	25% increase
Generating New Product Ideas	Topic Trend (TT)	$TT = \dfrac{\text{\# of Specific Topic Mentions}}{\text{All Topic Mentions}}$	20% increase
	Idea Impact (II)	$II = \dfrac{\text{\# of Positive Conversations, Shares, Mentions}}{\text{Total Idea Conversations, Shares, Mentions}}$	15% increase
Promoting Advocacy	Active Advocates (AA)	$AA = \dfrac{\text{Total \# of Active Advocates within 30 days}}{\text{Total Advocates}}$	20% increase
	Advocate Influence (AIN)	$AIN = \dfrac{\text{Unique Advocate's Influence}}{\text{Advocate Influence}}$	15% increase
	Advocacy Impact (AIM)	$AIM = \dfrac{\text{Number of Advocacy Driven Conversations}}{\text{Total Volume of Advocacy Traffic}}$	20% increase

Table A.5   Qualitative KPIs for the XYZ Coffee Company

The social media team will develop an internal process that matches metrics to business goals and objectives and specifies the metrics to be monitored for each. It will specify how and when metrics are to be recorded. It will establish a reporting format, reporting time frames and the executives to whom reports are to be sent.

EVALUATING

Once the social media data have been gathered and measured, they will be carefully evaluated. Only through establishing the relationship between social media metrics and business goals can the marketing team properly analyze the impact and value of SMM activities and then present the results to management.

The end game is to produce a thorough description of the progress of the company's SMM activities over time in order to reveal when strategies have succeeded or when they require adjustment. This evaluation process will uncover opportunities and threats, potential areas for improvement, and possible new courses of action. Such analysis will enable the marketing team to see where it must next focus its efforts and resources.

SOCIAL MEDIA MONITORING TOOLS

Platform-specific metrics will be used to monitor all active platforms. Google Analytics will also be used wherever possible. Google Analytics will be especially important in identifying social media platforms as the source of traffic to the XYZ website and in tracking their activities on the site. At present there are no funds in the budget for paid monitoring tools.

Tuning

The SMM team will constantly monitor and adjust the elements of the plan to maximize the chances of success. The company's progress in implementing its social media strategies will be continually assessed, and then, based on this assessment, strategies and tactics will be adjusted to optimize goal achievement.

Reevaluating the goals, strategies, and execution of the plan is necessary because of the ever-changing nature of consumer tastes, countermoves by competitors, and the continual introduction of new social media technologies. In short, planning and executing SMM activities is a never-ending process. Hence the marketing team will constantly monitor and fine-tune the plan to maximize results.

Budget

Table A.6 presents the estimated expenses for implementing this plan and for achieving the stated goals within the next year.

Budget

The following are the estimated expenses to implement this plan and achieve the stated goals within the next year:

A Mobile Manager	$80,000
A Multimedia Content Specialist	$50,000
Content Creation and Copyediting	$50,000
Two Social Media Specialists	$100,000
Mobile App Development and Maintenance	$100,000
Content Management and Platform Monitoring Services	$150,000
Total expenses for the year	$430,000

Table A.6 Budget for the XYZ Coffee Company

Return on Investment

The mobile marketing strategy is designed to increase website traffic and hence sales, so it will be possible to calculate their respective financial ROIs. However, the majority of the social media goals for the XYZ Coffee Company are not directly connected to sales, and consequently, standard ROI analysis will not be feasible. Fortunately, there are viable alternatives for estimating the return on investment for these social media goals.

Proxy ROIs measure the long-term impact of SMM investments on customer response. They include both quantitative and qualitative measurements, such as the number of views of the company's social media properties, the company's posting activity, and the customer responses rates, as well as sentiment analysis, share of voice, satisfaction scores, and advocacy impact. These proxy ROIs provide a meaningful way to judge the expected rewards for investing in this plan.

SMM PLANNING EXERCISES

1. The plan includes goals for the SMM effort but has no quantified marketing objectives. In Chapter 2 we discussed in some detail the importance of SMART marketing objectives. Develop what you consider a reasonable number of SMART objectives based on the goals presented. The objectives should present a challenge to the SMM team but they should not be out of the reach of the human and financial resources devoted to the SMM effort.

2. The plan describes the target market only in terms of Technographics. Do secondary research to add demographic and behavioral descriptors to the personas described in the Target Market Section of the plan.

3. Many of the XYZ coffee shops are located near college campuses. Assume college students are an important target market, especially for mobile initiatives. Conduct primary research to determine what college students expect from a local coffee house experience. How could a mobile app help to improve the experience and strengthen the relationship with the local coffee house and the chain of which it is a part?

4. Make recommendations for one mobile campaign that is national in scope and another that could be used by any local coffee shop. Make whatever assumptions you need to about the nature of the mobile app that will be required to execute the campaign. Remember that SMM campaigns can, and often do, run for shorter periods of time than the customary one year planning cycle. Other campaigns, however, run for long periods of time with performance reviews at specified intervals.

5. The Tracking section identifies tools to be used for tracking and monitoring the SMM effort. It does not discuss productivity tools. Research and recommend one or more productivity tools that could be used by the SMM team described in the plan to make the SMM effort smoother and less time-consuming.

6. Make a specific recommendation, based on the content of Chapter 13, about how ROI should be calculated for this plan.

Notes

1. Lee, Kevin (February 25, 2015), "Infographic: How Often Should You Post on Social Media?" BufferSocial. Retrieved November 2, 2015, from https://blog.bufferapp.com/how-often-post-social-media
2. Fredrick, Kevin (March 4, 2015). "4 Ways to Provide Great Customer Service on Twitter," Desk.com Blog," Salesforce Desk. Retrieved November 2, 2015, from http://www.desk.com/blog/4-ways-to-provide-great-customer-service-on-twitter/
3. (n.d.). "youtube.com," Alexa. Retrieved October 31, 2015, from http://www.alexa.com/siteinfo/youtube.com
4. Lee, Kevin (February 25, 2015), "Infographic: How Often Should You Post on Social Media?" BufferSocial. Retrieved November 2, 2015, from https://blog.bufferapp.com/how-often-post-social-media

Index

Note: Page numbers in *italic* type indicate figures, illustrations or tables.

Q

QQ, 81, *82*
Qualitative metrics, 230
Quantitative metrics, 230
Question-and-answer (Q&A) sites
    future of, 186–188
    marketing with, 185–186
Question tweets, 102
Quora, 186
Qzone, 81, *82*

R

Radian6, 30, 262–264
RadiumOne, 188
Ravelry, 90
Reach, social media presence, 274, 275
RealityDigital, 90
Red Bull, 150
Reddit, 178–179, 187
    "Digg moment," 179
    as popular social news site, *178*
    Upvoted, 179
Reichheld, Fred, 236
Reputation effect, 61
Resourceful, 66
Respect, 69
Responding, 108
Responsibility, 69
Return on investment (ROI)
    calculating, 298
    defined, 231
    social media, 7
    for XYZ Coffee Company, *298, 317–318*
Role assignments for XYZ Coffee Company, *291*
Rowley, Jennifer, 115
RSS (Really Simple Syndication), 125
Ryze.com, 80

S

Salesforce, 262–263
Satmetrix, 236
Schawbel, Dan, 16, 126
    Octopus Model Of Relevancy, *17*
Schick, 62–63
Schmidt, Eric, 89, 218
Schwabel, Dan, 255
Scoble, Robert, 119–120
Scobleizer, 119–120
Scott, David Meerman, 13, 197, 203
Search Engine Journal, 188
SearchEngineLand, 48
Search engine optimization (SEO), 24, 48
Search engine visibility, 48

SearchMetrics study, 32
Search ranking, 32
S-ecommerce
    defined, 182
    marketing with, 182–185
Secondary sharing, 152–153
Second Life, 13
Selecting platforms and channels, 24
Self-promotion, 37–38, 108
Sendible, 257
Sentiment analysis, 274, 275
SEO. *See* Search engine optimization
Shareacoke.com, 8
Sherman, Richard, 14
Sims, Andrew, 129
Single platform tools, 257–258
    Facebook Insights, 257
    interest targeting, 258
    Mention, 257
    NutshellMail, 258
    post end date, 258
    smart publishing, 258
Single-purpose tools, 253–254
Situational triggers, 45
SixDegrees.com, 79–80
Skype
    mobile apps, used as, *213*
    number of active users, 4–*5, 209*
Slashdot, 177
    as popular social news site, *178*
Slick, Shirley, 195
Sloan Management Review, 26
SmartArt, 160
Smartphones, 11
Smart publishing, 258
Smith, Ben, 181
Snapchat, 149, 157
Snapfish, 159
Social Blog, 30
Social blogs, 117
Social bookmarking
    future of, 186–188
    marketing with, 182–185
Social commerce. *See* S-ecommerce
SocialDraft social calendar, 260
Social media
    age of user base, *6,* 6–7
    best practices for, 91–92
    defined, 250
    as fad, 4–6
    global perspective, 71–72
    goals, 305
    is free, 11
    listening centers, 28–31
    platforms list, 77–79
    return on investment (ROI), 7
    strategies, best practices for developing, 39
    as time consuming, 10–11

Z